Communicating Faith

Communicating Faith

EDITED BY JOHN SULLIVAN

The Catholic University of America Press
Washington, D.C.

Copyright © 2011
The Catholic University of America Press
The paper used in this publication meets the minimum
requirements of American National Standards for Information
Science—Permanence of Paper for Printed Library Materials,
ANSI Z39.48-1984.
∞
Library of Congress Cataloging-in-Publication Data
Communicating faith / edited by John Sullivan.
p. cm.
Includes bibliographical references and index.
ISBN 978-0-8132-1796-3 (pbk. : alk. paper)   1. Communication—
Religious aspects—Christianity.   2. Evangelistic work.   I. Sullivan,
John, 1949–   II. Title.
BV4597.53.C64C66 2011
248′.5—dc22   2010019406

To Jean, who was with me at the genesis of this book,
through to its completion, as with so many other fruitful
experiences in our married life

Contents

Contents   ix

Acknowledgments

Several individuals and groups deserve my thanks for their diverse but crucial contributions to this work. First, there is my colleague at Liverpool Hope University, Associate Professor David Torevell. David has helped me over the last few years through some deep conversations as we supported each other in articulating what we mean by education for wisdom, an emphasis that never loses sight of the elusive, but more important, aims of our theology teaching. Second, there is the Reverend Professor Jeff Astley, from Durham, UK. Jeff models for me what effective Christian communication can be. He displays a lightness of touch, sense of humor, and clarity of exposition, and combines these qualities with a deeply informed scholarly awareness, a self-effacing style and a warmly invitational manner. Third, I am indebted to the many students who have taken my third-year undergraduate course, Educating Faith, in the period between 2006 and 2009. Their insights, questions, and perplexities and the challenges they posed as they explored different dimensions of the task of educating people in matters of faith in many contrasting contexts have assisted me in developing my understanding of some of the issues that surface in this book. They will recognize themes that sometimes first came into focus through our class discussions. They tested out—and thereby improved—earlier versions of some of the chapters here. Fourth, a dozen or so doctoral students who, over the past decade, I have had the privilege of supervising, have sharpened up my appreciation of the elements and techniques in writing that facilitate the effective communication of ideas. Fifth, Colin Brown in the Arts and Humanities office worked hard, efficiently, and without complaint on the demanding and complex task of developing the final bibliography, drawing from earlier end-of-chapter lists of references. Along the way he carefully identified a range of issues to be addressed, thereby significantly reducing the number of errors there might have been. Sixth, I would like to use this opportunity to put on record my gratitude to Professor Gerald Pillay, vice chancellor of Liverpool Hope University. His steadfast vision of what higher education in the twenty-first century can be when inspired by Christian principles and deep commitment, his leadership, which never allowed the mechanisms of management to obscure our *raison d'être*, and the frequent signals of personal support and affirmation for my own contribution—all these reinforced my faltering attempts to integrate teaching, the life of scholarship, and the call of discipleship.

Important debts elsewhere need to be acknowledged. My youngest son, Paul, was always ready to help me in practical ways when I (frequently) got stuck because of my inadequate knowledge of and confidence with computers. A huge thank you to Jean, my wife, best friend, and dancing partner (see chapter 22), for her love, understanding, sacrifices, and constant support throughout our (so far) 39 years of married life. I am grateful to all the contributors to this book. Despite being often submerged under many other pressing duties, they responded promptly and uncomplainingly to the various requests for chapters, modifications, and information. Finally, to Jim Kruggel, Theresa Walker, and the staff at the Catholic University of America Press I give thanks for their patience, encouragement, advice, and guidance in the lengthy process of bringing this book to publication; thanks, too, are owed to their referees, who made helpful suggestions for improvements, not all of which I was able to take on board. A special word of thanks is due to Aldene Fredenburg, one of CUAP's freelance copy editors; she has been impressively prompt positive, professional, and sensitive in her meticulous checking of issues of presentation, consistency, and style.

Much more might have been touched upon with regard to communicating faith, and much might have been better said. With regard to such an endless subject, beyond the capacity of any single person or team to cover adequately, I am very conscious of my deficiencies and shortcomings. Without the help of all the above, the book's faults would have been all the more obvious and any virtues it may have would have been even less evident.

Introduction

John Sullivan

As the Benedictus for January 26, the day that I write this, the morning prayer of the church offers the following words: "Proclaim the Gospel, insist on it in season and out of season, convince, rebuke, and exhort, do all with patience and in a manner that will teach men." In order to carry out this demanding instruction, Christians need knowledge and understanding of holy scripture and of their faith, as well as commitment, dedication, and perseverance to the twin (and integrally linked) tasks of living it out and communicating it to others. They also need to be constantly nourished by their particular faith community and to dwell in its living tradition, affirmed in their efforts, forgiven and lifted up when they fall short, and encouraged to try again. If they are wise, they will ensure that the foundation for any attempt to communicate faith is built, not upon their personal competencies, but upon prayer—private and constant, yet also communal worship in the setting of the liturgical cycle that conveys salvation history and the ever-new invitation to humanity to share God's life. If they are to have any chance of convincing others, they will need to exercise intelligence, paying attention to the use of reason. If they are to rebuke without alienating their hearers, it will be important to temper this with humility and respect. If they are to exhort effectively, they must be in tune with the strengths and weaknesses of those they address, balancing challenge and support. If they are to reach out in cogent communication, this depends on a sensitive awareness of the specific contexts of their conversation partners, responding to their diverse assumptions and questions, hopes and fears, temptations and opportunities.

St. Paul describes his approach to flexibility and sensitivity in a famous speech, where he refers to himself as becoming "everything in turn to people of very sort, so that he may save some."[1] As Margaret Krych puts it, "Without adaptation to our hearers' lives, experiences, and categories of understanding, we lose people."[2] However, readiness to adapt our presentation needs to be qualified by concern for the truth, for "if we adapt the message in the wrong way, we may be in danger of losing the gospel."[3] Flexibility and responsiveness to people's lives and the issues arising for them and fidelity to the Gospel have to be combined and held together. There has to be a match, or harmony, between the *logos* or meaning of the message to be communicated, the *pathos* or real state of the audience or target group one hopes will receive it, and the *ethos* or character and style of the person doing the communicating. Traditionally, this is what rhetoric has entailed. Those engaged in the task of communicating faith should monitor how confluent or disparate this *logos, pathos,* and *ethos* are. The gift, the giver, and the receiver are, however, not easy to separate; at different times roles become interchangeable. God is the source of the message but we all play a part in mediating his word. Each of us can be both a giver and receiver of this word, often in the same act of communication. Communicating faith, at its best, is a process of generous giving and grateful reception. Yet we know, too, that it can slip into an impositional instead of an invitational mode, and that, even when offered appropriately, it can be resented and resisted.

Communicating faith is an integral part of discipleship. David Attfield offers a general theory of religious communication, covering evangelism, interfaith dialogue, nurture of adults and children, religious education, the academic study of religion, and ministerial formation.[4] This book will touch upon many, though not all, of the seven types of religious communication

1. Cor 9:19–23 (New English Bible, slightly modified).

2. Margaret Krych, "What Are the Theological Foundations of Education and Evangelism?" in *Christian Education as Evangelism,* ed. Norma Cook Everist (Minneapolis: Fortress Press, 2007), 30.

3. Krych, 30.

4. David Attfield, *Proclaiming the Gospel in a Secular Age* (Aldershot, UK: Ashgate, 2001).

analyzed by Attfield. One volume cannot begin to do justice to the subtle yet important differences in context, purpose, and methodology required in these various forms of religious communication, but it can bring out key features of the processes involved.

In each setting disciples have to learn how to read the Gospel, their culture, their own and other people's lives, the opportunities and limitations presented by particular contexts, and the grace of God present in all of these. The call to all communicators of faith is to be person-centered, allowing God, already always present and at work, to be our teacher. Thus we should be attentive to each other and to God's work in the other (as well as in ourselves). The educator has to be bifocal in the sense that she is able to see both where learners are now, and thus rooted in reality, and also where these learners could be but are not yet, and thus holding onto a vision or ideal of what is possible for them with human help, personal commitment, and the grace of God. Those who seek to communicate faith also need to be bifocal in the following ways. They need to be rooted in culture and local needs in order to be relevant. They need to be able to transcend culture in order to be free to be adequately Christian. They need to engage the specific and particular with sympathy in order to connect. They need to see and hold before people the bigger picture in order to help them move on from local and immediate concerns.

St. Paul addressed one of his audiences: "You yourselves are our letter of recommendation, written on your hearts, to be known and read by all men."[5] Thereby he emphasized personhood or humanity as the principal medium of communicating faith. If we take this point seriously, then a range of verbs can be identified that jointly describe (in no particular order) what is entailed by evangelization. These include the following expressions of personhood: be present, pay attention, listen, wait, welcome, invite, be hospitable, share, bless, give, forgive, reconcile, heal, celebrate, encourage, be vulnerable, pray. This list, while incomplete, is indicative of the range of ways the good news can be conveyed. This book illustrates some of the diverse ways these verbs have been carriers of and catalysts for faith. The centrality of the human person as the agent and medium for transmitting the Gospel has been reiterated recently by Pope Benedict XVI. In his recent address on the lessons of monasticism for contemporary Europe given at the

5. 2 Cor. 3:2.

Collège des Bernardins, Paris, he said, "God only speaks to us through the humanity of human agents."[6]

This book seeks to enrich our appreciation of the huge diversity of ways that Christian faith is communicated and to cast light on the sensitivities, skills, and qualities that must be brought into play for an effective communication of faith, one where justice is done both to the "seed" to be sown and to the "soil" being cultivated. What is conveyed, who is reached, how this is achieved—all rely heavily on the type of relationships that are at the heart of the processes involved in communicating faith.

Contributors were asked to draw upon their substantial academic or pastoral experience to highlight key features of the contexts where faith is communicated. These include the home, parish life, schools, universities, adult education, literature, the arts, and new communications media. Taken as a whole, the collection of essays combines careful treatment of specific contextual issues with an exposition and analysis of the general principles that should govern all efforts to communicate faith. The book is Catholic but also ecumenical. It offers perspectives from clergy, religious, and lay people and has strong representation of both academics and practitioners. It offers new theoretical reflection and conceptual tools for analyzing and evaluating central features of the tasks inherent in communicating faith, supported by reports "from the front line," with a more "hands-on" orientation. With a substantial set of essays from the United Kingdom and Ireland as its basis, the book also provides complementary insights from scholars working across three continents.

I hope that these essays have something worthwhile to say for the wider communities to which the contributing academics and practitioners belong. Among the academic readers the contributors hope to engage would be not only those teaching and researching in theology and religious education, but also Christian scholars from other disciplines interested in or committed to relating faith to their academic work and institutional context. Among the practitioners we hope to interest would be parents, schoolteachers, catechists, clergy, youth ministers, university campus ministers, and diocesan officers responsible for faith development.

Very often, specialists with an interest in one sector or context for com-

6. Benedict XVI, quoted by Daniel McCarthy, "Maturing towards God," *The Tablet* (October 18, 2008).

municating faith do not look "over the fence" at other sectors or contexts. They speak to those in the same field as themselves and read works addressed to their particular context, but do not see the bigger picture. A major goal for *Communicating Faith* is that it facilitates dialogue and mutual learning among people working in different sectors and contexts for faith formation, development, education, and renewal. Despite the differences in the diverse settings for communicating faith that must be taken into account, it becomes clear that there is a reassuring level of commonality to be identified within the complex and sensitive dynamics of this endeavor: common challenges to be faced, common lessons to be learned, and common styles of approaching and relating to people that are called for.

The book is in six parts. Part 1 lays down some basic principles that should govern any attempt to communicate Christian faith. Part 2 opens up some of the starting points for communicating faith, for children and adults, in the home and in church life. Part 3 explores the school context for communicating faith, drawing upon spiritual, leadership, curriculum, and pedagogical perspectives. The focus of Part 4 is on communicating faith in the university context. Part 5 considers key issues for communicating faith in diverse national settings, including the U.S., Africa, and Europe. Part 6 examines key features of the processes involved in communicating faith, highlighting philosophical, pedagogical, and aesthetic dimensions of this endeavor, taking into account the wider culture and contemporary media for communication.

Part 1. The Grammar of Faith

Two chapters address the basic grammar of faith and what should be communicated. In Chapter 1, "From Formation to the Frontiers: The Dialectic of Christian Education," John Sullivan focuses on two essential elements within the task of communicating faith: formation and work "at the frontiers," showing how both of these features are necessary and how they are interrelated. The chapter provides a foundation for the book as a whole, bringing out key aspects of the basic grammar of communicating faith.

Jeff Astley, to support the initial task of providing an overview of the ground to be covered in the book, explores in Chapter 2, "Forms of Faith and Forms of Communication," what might be meant by "communicating Christian faith." He is particularly concerned with bringing out the breadth of coverage of what should be communicated, going beyond (but including) the cognitive, and embracing the affective and attitudinal dimension. Beliefs must be buttressed by trust, commitment, and approval if they are to lead to relationship with the object of faith. Astley distinguishes formative from critical education and argues that both are needed. Finally, he offers five models for understanding the nature of education within the church.

Part 2: Baselines

Four chapters consider family and church life as loci for communicating faith. The first chapter in this part of the book addresses our starting place in life and the initial location for our faith life, the domestic church. In Chapter 3, "Communicating Faith in the Home," Clare Watkins combines theological penetration and parental insight. She brings into the light the pedagogical vocation of the Christian household, acutely aware of the challenges this presents, yet also ultimately positive and full of hope about the opportunities that emerge from daily life in this context. Watkins bridges the gap between, on the one hand, church teaching and the theological tradition, and, on the other, the realities of family life in contemporary culture as she demonstrates both the theological nature of the household and the potential of domestic pedagogy in matters of faith.

From the home we move to the parish. Atli Jónsson, in Chapter 4, "Communicating Faith in the Parish: Maintaining a Presence, Care, and Mission," brings out how the community experienced in a parish shapes how people envisage the church. The parish they participate in both defines for its people what they understand faith to entail, in terms of welcome, witness, worship, and service, and simultaneously opens them up to and links them with the universal church. Jónsson offers a pastorally informed theological reflection on the workings of the parish and its role in communicating faith in our contemporary culture. He deploys the image of the parish as *sanctuary* and shows how this sanctuary may be animated in order to promote the Gospel in a full and rounded way.

The final two chapters in Part 2 focus on different elements or expressions of parish and ecclesial life as contexts for communicating faith: sacramental preparation and liturgy and adult religious education. In Chapter 5, "Sacramental Preparation: Uneasy Partnership," Peter McGrail provides insights into school-age sacramental initiation in England and Wales. The twentieth-century background to current school and parish practices is sketched in and an outline offered of recent developments in the partnership between home, school, and parish with regard to preparing children to receive the sacraments, especially Holy Communion. Here, the contribution of leading figures and key texts is analyzed. Then flesh is put on the theory when McGrail draws upon his recent significant (both interesting and disturbing) ethnographic study of how different parishes manage sacramental preparation. Catechesis in the Catholic community is shown to be vulnerable to deeply rooted disparities in the perspectives of participants and subject to conflicting priorities.

In order to examine how faith is communicated through adult education, Stephen McKinney, in Chapter 6, "Burning Hearts: Scripture and Adult Faith Formation," provides a case study of how a particular parish group in the archdiocese of Glasgow in Scotland devoted much time to exploring scripture. He shows how the group operated, how they interacted, and the diverse starting points, motivations, and types of impact the study group had for its members. Wider lessons about communicating faith are drawn out, for example, in relation to informality, attention to the real needs of participants, perseverance, flexibility in how scripture is approached, and the building of a sense of community, collegiality, and commitment.

Part 3: The School Context

The five essays in Part 3 all hold in view the school context. In Chapter 7, "Text and Context: Mediating the Mission in Catholic Schools," Sullivan spells out key features of the multidimensional "text" to be communicated in Catholic schools and comments on the theology underpinning this text, showing both continuity and change in how this has been understood. Then he examines how the context in which such schools work makes a significant difference to how the text is interpreted and received. A range of factors that mediate between the mission and its reception are identified and the task of communicating faith in Catholic schools is shown to be one that requires the development of an intermediate discourse by teachers and leaders.

Ralph Gower, in Chapter 8, "The Challenges of Postmodernity," takes into account the very real challenges posed by the wider postmodern culture for the communication about matters of faith within schools. He exposes how emphases in postmodern culture influence our thinking in ways that sometimes threaten to unravel faith or which undermine the conditions for its healthy flourishing. Those wishing to communicate about matters of faith effectively in schools should note carefully Gower's analysis of the bearing of contemporary culture on the thinking of children and young people. He provides an "on the ground" report of his engagement with groups of pupils, leading to proposals for how churches might respond to the challenges clarified by his engagement and analysis.

In a second contribution to this volume, McKinney in Chapter 9, "Communicating Faith through Religious Education," shifts his attention from adult faith formation through scripture to curriculum and classroom religious education in Catholic schools in Scotland. He offers a historical perspective for this endeavor as it has developed since Vatican II and, through the medium of an interview with a leading and influential practitioner, brings out key features of how religious education has changed over the past forty years and some of the challenges that have been faced by religious educators. A nuanced and positive vision emerges of how, despite constraints and inevitable criticisms from some quarters, religious education in Catholic schools has much to celebrate and much that is worthwhile still to offer.

If classroom and curriculum religious education in faith schools is to flourish, then school leaders need to ensure that the overall ethos and the working practices of the school are conducive to its mission. In Chapter 10, "Leadership and Transmission: Empowering Witnesses," Michael Edwards addresses how school leaders and school staff more generally might be equipped, motivated, supported, and encouraged to live out the mission through their work. This chapter shows how the priority of integrating spiritual development for staff as a key element in their professional growth might be tackled. Drawing upon his substantial experience of leading staff in-service activities in and for Catholic schools, and after exploring general principles for spirituality for underpinning the work of such schools, Edwards deploys an Ignatian model for articulating how a school's mission and vision has at its heart the communication of faith.

In Chapter 11, "Questioning for Faith Commitment," Topley brings out the important role of questioning—by teacher and student—within the broader process of faith communication. His analysis of the nature, scope, and function of questions in Christian religious education is undergirded by Lonergan's theory of knowledge and learning. Topley shows how levels of learning are linked to types of questions posed, holding in view the long-term aspiration of eliciting commitment. He is well aware that such commitment can be neither compelled nor guaranteed, since there must be room for both grace and free will. He also addresses positively any doubts that may arise about either the viability or the appropriateness of emphasizing the important part that questioning can play in religious education.

Part 4: Higher Education

Three chapters on higher education comprise Part 4. In Chapter 12, "Plasticity, Piety, and Polemics," John Sullivan examines three qualities for teachers that should be integral to the task of communicating a faith tradition in higher education: first, adapting to the needs of students, here called "plasticity"; second, displaying and encouraging the virtues required, epistemologically as well as morally, by the religious tradition, here called "piety"; and third, "polemics," which entails questioning and critiquing the tradition in an intellectually serious manner as a contribution to its ongoing development. The mutually correcting interaction among these three qualities is stressed.

In Chapter 13, "Thick and Thin: Personal and Communal Dimensions of Communicating Faith," Frederick Aquino also concentrates our attention on the qualities and dynamics central to the teaching of religion in any university setting. If that teaching is to be effective there must be a route that connects intellectual development and formation in faith. Aquino, drawing deeply on his own experience as a teacher, provides a series of meditations that help us to construct that path. He explains how the crisis of authority affects the quest for certainty and often leads to a divide between public (secular) and private (religious) modes of discourse. Then he shows the importance of the intellectual virtues for guiding the educational process and for demonstrating that autonomy and authority can be held in a creative tension. Finally, providing an echo of Topley's advocacy of the centrality of judgment in religious education in schools, Aquino calls for the development in university students of the capacity to reach informed judgments, ones that allow them to move back and forth smoothly between particular (tradition-specific) ways of thinking and broader (but thinner) styles of discourse that deliberately seek to omit reference to particular affiliations and traditions. Here theology, philosophy, and pedagogy find a rarely encountered harmonious rapprochement.

Drawing from his experience as head of Theology and Religious Studies in a secular university, but offering an explicitly Roman Catholic theological position, in Chapter 14, "Windows into Faith: Theology and Religious Studies at the University," Gavin D'Costa examines some of the differences between these two disciplines, which have come to be yoked together in many universities. He brings out the tensions that arise from the contrasting expectations and accountabilities of the academy and the church. He traces the origins and development of theology and of religious studies as university disciplines and asks: "whose faith will be communicated in the university?" After analyzing and showing the relevance of key Roman Catholic documents on the university and on faith and reason, he advocates (what is likely to be a contested case for) a central role for theology as a "servant queen of the sciences" in a Christian university, but also he argues for a more theologically informed religious studies in all universities.

Part 5: International Perspectives

Five chapters offer international perspectives on the task of communicating faith. Based in Rome, in the role of vicar general working with her order's schools and Sisters across the world, Frances Orchard, CJ, in Chapter 15, "Charism and Context," draws upon this experience to review the hugely important work of religious congregations in giving witness to faith. Such congregations have frequently been in the forefront on missionary activity and on new initiatives in communicating faith. Sister Frances explores the nature and meaning of charism and shows how this has been expressed, lived out, and developed further in different international contexts. Finally, she indicates strategies that are being employed for sharing the charism with the laity.

Victorine Mansanga, SND, turns our attention to a very different context. In Chapter 16, "Communicating Faith in Africa: Yesterday and Today," she illustrates important aspects of what is entailed by inculturation, the mutual interaction between faith and culture in particular settings, and the enduring task of incarnating the Gospel in specific cultures. She outlines key features of the context for receiving the Gospel in Africa and indicates some of the ways that the church has sought to convey the good news of God's kingdom to the people of her continent. A positive but discerning engagement with local ways of speaking, thinking, and living is required for effective evangelization, combining boldness and creativity with caution and the capacity to identify and resist what is not in harmony with the Gospel. The profound links between evangelization and human development and liberation are brought into clear relief in this chapter.

One country where there have been massive shifts in the relationship between religious faith and the wider culture is Ireland. In Chapter 17, "Communicating Faith in Ireland: From Commitment through Questioning to New Beginnings," Gareth Byrne traces some of the new developments: the crisis of confidence, increased questioning and uncertainty, and the need for renewed vitality, realism, and sensitivity in how faith is communicated. He faces constructively key questions about communicating faith in his country. These relate to clarifying the faith context, considering the kind of communication being considered, the content of what is to be conveyed, the different strategies required for addressing young people and adults, the imperative to be inclusive or hospitable to all, and the best ways to structure and source the processes of communicating faith.

Mimi Schuttloffel, in Chapter 18, "Communicating the Catholic Faith in the United States," considers the task of religious education (broadly interpreted) through the prism of the contemplative principle, a concept that allows her to integrate reflection on faith, leadership, and communication. Schuttloffel examines Catholic identity within the American context today and its inevitable impact upon religious education. Then she explains the contemplative principle and the centrality of communication in leadership. She analyses various models of religious education, in a variety of contexts, bringing out some leadership features and dimensions, before offering some reflections, reservations, and recommendations for the future.

From his vantage point as a professor at the ancient and famous Catholic university of Leuven and as president of the European Society for Catholic Theology, Lieven Boeve, in Chapter 19, "Communicating Faith in Contemporary Europe: Dealing with Language Problems In and Outside the Church," confronts some of the difficulties in communicating faith stemming from issues of language. Boeve sheds light on the sociocultural processes that are influencing the role and health of religion in Europe. The challenges that arise for communicating Christian faith, inside and outside church communities, are brought into focus, in the light of the unraveling of tradition, increasing individualization, pluralization of religion, and the dissolving of a distinctive Christian identity. Boeve distinguishes carefully the task of communicating the faith in the public forum (*ad extra*) and faith communication in the church (*ad intra*) and argues that it is a mistake to ignore the differences between these two tasks; conflating them undermines effective communication in both cases. He indicates how to guard the border between these two communicative tasks and how understanding of both is required.

Part 6: Aspects of Communication

In the final part of the book the first two chapters open up further contexts for communicating faith—aesthetic communication and virtual learning technologies—while the two concluding chapters highlight the dynamics and relationships at the heart of all forms of communicating faith. David Torevell, in Chapter 20, "'The Attempt Was All': The Endeavor of Aesthetics in the Communication of Faith," takes us from a consideration of the novel and film *Atonement* into a deeper reflection on the ways that aesthetic communication works on us, unpacking some of the power, while acknowledging at the same time the limits, of artistic effort. An attempt to express, in various aesthetic forms and genres, the things that matter most to us is central to art bringing it about that how we experience the world can be changed in significant ways. Human depths and hopes are brought to light by art that has the potential to encourage feelings of transcendence and to provoke revelatory insight into religious understandings of the world. Torevell relates the embodied dimension of artistic expression to a theology of the incarnation.

From looking back to cultural expression in the past, Ros Stuart-Buttle, in Chapter 21, "Communicating Faith and Online Learning," turns our attention to cutting-edge and contemporary forms of communication that are rapidly transforming the learning environment for people at all stages of life, within and beyond formal educational settings. Deeply rooted in a Catholic theological perspective, Stuart-Buttle shows how this perspective can be maintained and promoted while embracing the challenges and opportunities afforded by new learning technologies. She provides an overview of recent changes in communications technologies, indicating some of the cultural impact this is having, and draws on her own pioneering experience in developing online learning as a way into religious education for adult learners in order to highlight implications, possibilities, and pitfalls about which to be alert. Two issues concerning online learning and adult faith education come under scrutiny: first, how individuality relates to community; and second, how collaborative learning relates to authority. The discourse of the church is hereby brought into dialogue with the discourse emerging from online learning. This reflection on the pedagogical implications of online learning for faith educators, through its opening to "new wineskins," illustrates another arena of inculturation for the church.

To round off this series of explorations into the richly complex endeavor of communicating faith, John Sullivan offers two syntheses of his reflections on what is at the very heart of the task of sharing faith. In Chapter 22, "Education and Religious Faith as a Dance," he compares two contrasting and equally unsatisfactory ways of relating education and religious faith before exploring the potential of the metaphor of dance as casting light on some of the principal qualities required by faith educators and showing some of the delicate balancing acts they need to sustain if their efforts are to benefit those they seek to reach. In Chapter 23, "Communicating Faith and Relating in Love," Sullivan steps outside educational settings in order to consider acts of communication more generally. He argues that what is central in all settings for communication (and via whatever media are employed) is relationship. Building from scriptural insights, he shows the crucial importance of attending to the presence of God in our work and simultaneously attending to the particularity of those with whom we communicate. These two kinds of attention are shown to be intimately and necessarily interlinked, even though they are not identical. Similarly, listening carefully and speaking in the right voice are closely connected; there can be no right speaking that is not guided and qualified by real listening.

Bernard Lonergan placed communication as one of the eight functional specialties in theology, seeing communication and community as mutually implicating.[7] A major focus of this book is on what is happening in acts of communication, rather than the content of what is communicated, though content, exchange, and application cannot easily be separated in practice. It has recently been suggested that

---

7. Bernard Lonergan, *Method in Theology* (London: Darton, Longman, and Todd, 1972), 363.

Theology is not "some thing" that then is communicated; rather communication is the central content of theology. So communication is neither a thing added or applied to theology nor a substitute for what theology should really be. Theology is itself a communicative event, and when it no longer is this it stops being theology.[8]

This book gives a high profile to the dynamics at work and the relationships at play in the communication of faith. In communicating faith we are sharing a world and a way of life, not just information. In communication the content is inseparable from the methods and media employed. All communication is also inexorably linked to the immediate situation and wider context where it takes place, as well as intimately connected to the sense of identity of communicators and recipients and the quality of relationships pertaining to those on both sides of the exchange. If the insights contained here enable readers to appreciate better these dynamics, to promote more intentionally the loving relationships that are essential in the process, and to engage more effectively and with enhanced confidence in the communication of faith, this work will have served its purpose.

8. Matthias Scharer and Bernd Jochen Hilberath, *The Practice of Communicative Theology* (New York: Crossroad, 2008), 13.

PART 1

The Grammar of Faith

These two chapters bring out the breadth of the task of communicating Christian faith. They imply that a multidimensional approach is required to do justice to the nature of human beings. They also provide typologies or templates against which other, more specific accounts of communicating faith in particular settings, described in later chapters in this book, might be considered, lest such approaches lean toward one-sidedness or incompleteness in emphasis. In each case, we find that communicating faith has cognitive, affective, and behavioral components, all of which require attention. In both of the chapters in Part 1, communicating faith is envisaged as an activity that combines a concern for distinctiveness (that what is communicated is *Christian*) with a striving toward inclusivity (of people, subject matter, situations). In the process of passing on and receiving, of mutual exchange and reciprocal learning, there will be both conservation and innovation. The treasures of the past will be engaged and mediated in such a way as to facilitate a readiness to welcome the graces available in all times and places.

Sullivan stresses the twofold and unending movement in Christian education—of building up and equipping persons to be disciples and providing testing applications of their formation in ever-more-inclusive contexts. One might describe this chapter as a call for balance between the *ad intra* dimension of communicating faith (it must be constitutive and transformative of the disciple) and the *ad extra* dimension (it must reach out beyond the familiar borders of the church and seek to be all-embracing). The formative imperative aims for solidarity with and embeddedness within the Christian tradition and community, while the "frontier work" advocated here opens up disciples to what is beyond. Both formation and frontier work can be carried out without adequate reference to the other pole, in each case with accompanying dangers and imbalances. The task is to keep open an appropriate balance between these two aspects of communicating faith, living with a creative tension between them.

Astley shows how, if the whole person is to be addressed, communication in faith should include the cognitive, the affective and attitudinal, and the behavioral aspects of our being. He too wants justice to be done to both the formative and the critical: people should be offered both a sound and comprehensive induction into faith, but also be helped to develop the capacity to question what they receive, so that in due course this faith can be personally owned and appropriated with integrity. We shall see, in later chapters, how what Astley implies, rather than spells out explicitly, comes into play in diverse contexts for communicating faith: learners (and thus disciples) need both a degree of affiliation with the faith community and a degree of distancing from it (to see it clearly). They need to develop both the capacity for constancy and the capacity for change (for only thus will their fidelity provide a foundation for continuing openness). He allows for a plurality of emphases within Christian faith while ensuring that an underlying commonality is preserved. He analyses the notions of faith, of communication, and the relations between learners and the Christian tradition that are implied in his typology of five models for Christian education. These are (1) the faith community approach, which entails socialization in the church, (2) critical Christian education, where learners are encouraged to assess truth claims for themselves, (3) Christian development, enabling personal maturity in faith, (4) Christian liberation, where learners are aided in perceiving and resisting social realities that hold back human flourishing, and (5) faith translation, which treats religious learning as analogous to learning a new language. No one model is adequate on its own; all play a part in promoting the fullness of development called for in discipleship.

1 From Formation to the Frontiers

The Dialectic of Christian Education

John Sullivan

Christian education requires two major movements, if it is to develop health-ily, if it is to remain Christian, and if it is to be really educational. The first of these movements is formation. The second is what I shall call "work at the frontiers." There is an order of precedence, both logically and chronological-ly. Formation has priority, but work at the margins is also necessary. Further-more, formation does not have to be completed before work at the margins begins; indeed, the first cannot be completed without attention being given to the second.

My claim is that both movements are necessary. Formation without work at the frontiers is inadequate to the Gospel imperative to be inclusive, while work at the frontiers without sufficient attention to formation lacks the dis-tinctiveness, specificity, or "salt" of Christian faith. Those who emphasize formation at the expense of work at the frontiers run the risk of producing

An earlier version of this chapter was published as "From Formation to the Frontiers," Jour-nal of Education and Christian Belief 7, no. 1 (Spring 2003): 7–24. The material appears here with permission of the journal's editor.

people who are inward-looking, isolationist, elitist, and, ultimately, idolatrous. They care more about the church than the world; they believe that they possess the faith, rather than are possessed by it; they mistake the signposts about God's presence and work for the destination of God's kingdom. They disconnect worship and doctrine from earthly concerns. They point us so strongly toward the transcendence of God that they lose sight of God's immanence. They spend so much energy in preserving the past and inducting people into tradition that there is little energy left for creativity, not much will to display openness, and scarcely any opportunity to practice improvisation in response to new needs and changing circumstances.

On the other hand, those who disregard formation in favor of working at the frontiers run the risk of "running on empty," with insufficient motivational fuel to drive ahead or even to sustain what they are currently doing. They neglect the resources of tradition, slip into a worthy but probably sterile activism, and ignore hard-earned insights by rushing to embrace the new with insufficient discrimination. They attend so sensitively to the immanence of God that they lose sight of God's transcendence. In engaging so positively with the world, they fail to restore and to replenish the church and thereby leave it derelict; in this way its spiritual capital is exhausted and its capacity to heal is diminished. In heeding so faithfully the call to inclusiveness, they run the risk of downgrading distinctiveness. In privileging praxis and in sitting lightly with regard to orthodoxy, they become vulnerable to the accusation that they end up eroding respect for the truth. By focusing too quickly on the fruits of faith, they tend to neglect its roots and the development of Christian character. In the first section of this chapter I bring out some of the features of the first of the two movements essential to Christian education—that is, formation. In the second section, attention is given to the second movement: work at the frontiers. In the third section, "The Dialectic Between Formation and Frontiers," I comment on the relationship between these two movements, formation and frontier work.

Formation

Formation is a long-term, deliberate, and multi-faceted process that seeks to produce a character of substance, one who is thoroughly inducted into the way of life of a particular community and tradition. There will be a way of thinking to internalize, with key concepts and a coherent story to tell. In this case, we might claim, there is a Christian way of thinking. There will also be a way of behaving, a pattern of actions and practices, that we might say operationalizes, implements, or expresses the set of beliefs. Thus, Christians need to engage in a set of actions, not just assent to a set of beliefs. Then there is a way of worshipping, for at the heart of faith is an acknowledgment of and a response to almighty God, our Creator, Redeemer, and Sustainer. Although some of this worship happens in private, much of it occurs in the context of a community, for we are brothers and sisters in God's family; we need each other, not only in coming to belief, not only in learning about and then in maintaining Christian conduct, but also in worship. Finally, there is a way of belonging; there are disciplines and forms of celebration, sharing and common work that bind us together in the church, that gradually transform us into a Christian community. It will be obvious that my fourfold description of the elements of formation—a way of thinking, behaving, worshipping, and belonging—reflects quite closely O'Connell's analysis of discipleship in terms of relationship, understanding, commitment, behavior, and affiliation.[1]

One of the reasons I feel that emphasis on formation is necessary is that we live in a society that has relied heavily on procedural, or what might be called "spacemaking," morality. This is in contrast to substantial morality. In centuries gone by, and partly in response to the malign effects of a one-sided formation and of a blinkered and constricting orthodoxy, forms of liberalism have developed that emphasize autonomy, tolerance, freedom of choice, and a willingness to question everything and all authorities. Thus, we relegate religion to the realm of the private option because we cannot agree about it. In public life we assume the minimum level of agreement compatible with getting things done and with providing for our safety and material needs. In avoiding imposing "our" truth on others in any unwarranted way, we withdraw religious truth claims from the public domain. However, with the failure of liberalism to deliver the hoped-for peace, harmony, sense of purpose, and common good, in recent years, especially in the communitarian movement, there has been a recognition of the limits of relying on procedural rules that make no reference to more substantial forms of life or the constituent concepts and practices. The pluralist society probably requires a cultural bilingualism among us all, that is, the capacity

---

1. Timothy O'Connell, *Making Disciples* (New York: Crossroad, 1997).

to belong to and to "speak" the language of commonly accepted principles and organizations that allow us to cooperate despite our deep-seated differences, at the same time as belonging to and "speaking" the language of a specific group with a coherent worldview. Put differently, I believe that we need to be both universalists and particularists. I believe that our universalism is enriched by, receives motivational fuel from, and is grounded in our particularism. At the same time, our particularism is enriched, enlivened, and challenged by our universalism.

All forms of faith-based education—and institutions founded to promote such faith-based education—depend upon a "thick" rather than a "thin" conception of the good. What I have to say here about Christian education applies also, I believe, to other forms of faith-based education. By a "thin" description of the good I have in mind four features. First, it relies on procedural principles that command a very wide level of acceptance within society, partly because they are envisaged as not being founded on any one particular, more substantive view of life. Second, these principles are not necessarily so interrelated that they constitute any coherent system. Third, even taken together, these principles do not attempt to cover all the major dimensions of life, since they concentrate on what is needed for peaceful cooperation. Fourth, they are held to be normative for instrumental rather than for intrinsic reasons.

In contrast, a "thick" description of the good is one where its several interlocking parts jointly constitute a system (rather than a loose collection of disconnected elements). Second, it is far-reaching in its scope and explanatory power. Third, it is highly developed over a substantial period of time. Fourth, it is embedded in a particular community. Fifth, it is transmitted in the context of traditions, narratives, and prescribed actions. Finally, it possesses normative status for its adherents.

Christian education is based on such a thick description of the good. A thick description of the good, if it is to be sustained, requires a form of induction that is itself thicker than training, more intelligent than indoctrination, and more coherent than the national curriculum. It will have permeating through it a worldview, a set of concepts and beliefs, a pattern of behavior, a way of worship, and a fostering of substantial affiliation. In short, it will be education into and for discipleship. Such education, to use the language of information technology, will develop the "hardware" of character and Christian personhood, rather than the "software" of readily transferable skills that remain external to the learner. Christian education, I will argue, of the kind that builds hardware, necessarily entails induction into a set of practices and an associated way of reading. Let me say something more about these practices.

Too often intellectual interrogation of beliefs is treated quite separately from an examination of the practices that underpin or, alternatively, undermine them. When this happens, beliefs become anemic, merely a matter of theory, and disconnected from life, while practices become blind, imprisoned by custom and power structures, and distorted from their original rationale. Such separation also leads to too much distance and too little dialogue between doctrinal, moral, and liturgical theology, whereas, in fact, the interactions between these should be readily apparent. Academic judgment, spiritual discernment, moral wisdom, and practical efficacy all should feed into each other, qualifying excesses, correcting imbalances, and making up for partial or incomplete perspectives. In this way, the Christian life has more chance of displaying greater wholeness, consistency, and efficacy—and therefore credibility—in the eyes of other believers and of nonbelievers. To focus on practices rather than just on beliefs allows us to bring together thinking and acting, to emphasize the social and historical nature of Christian discipleship, and to allow for the fact that important insights into this discipleship can be achieved by people who are not specialists in theology.

Practices play a crucial part in the Christian life, which is not to say, of course, that they are determinative of salvation, nor that they render beliefs true. Practices combine elements of skills, commitments, attitudes, and stories, and they are deployed according to the availability of gifts and resources and in response to context and needs. A practice can refer to almost any meaningful action, to specific ascetical and spiritual disciplines, to descriptions of cultural patterns of behavior, and to pursuing certain social goods. The term "a practice" is used by social scientists, moral philosophers, religious writers, church ministers, and community leaders, as well as in common parlance. I borrow from Dorothy Bass in viewing them as "patterns of co-operative human activity in and through which life together takes shape over time in response to and in the light of God as known in Jesus Christ."[2]

2. Dorothy Bass, "Introduction," in *Practicing Theology*, ed. Miroslav Volf and Dorothy Bass, 1–9, at 3 (Grand Rapids, Mich.: Eerdmans, 2002).

Put otherwise, the focus on practices ensures that theological reflection is not unduly cerebral, that it is incarnated, that it displays concreteness, rather than abstractness, and that it deliberately draws from and contributes to living tradition. It also ensures that the Christian life is conceived as one that is essentially communal, rather than in an individualistic manner, for, as one commentator puts it, "it is in communities of conversation as much as in solitude and silence that we discern the Gospel message. Our individual readings of sacred texts were never meant to stand on their own. They must be abetted, amplified, corrected, and amended by the insights and inspirations of others."[3] Here the company we keep in participating in practices becomes an important element in formation. We need "the companionship of friends who care about what we care about and care about us caring for it."[4]

Among such practices Christians have included at different times and places, for example, fasting, almsgiving, Sabbath keeping, service to the needy, care of the sick, attendance at liturgy, scripture reading, private prayer, prophetic witness against the powers of evil, acts of generosity and selfless giving, and hospitality. Cumulatively, such practices "create distinctive ways of seeing, understanding and being," as Craig Dykstra puts it.[5] They "enhance our powers to achieve the good and extend our very conceptions of what the good is."[6] Sarah Coakley describes this steady modification of our powers brought about by such practices as "the effects of a life of multiple forms of faithfulness, forging the participants by degrees into 'the image of [God's] Son.'"[7] By participating in practices, we find not so much that we are agents, but that something is done to us and in us; we are being drawn ever more deeply into the life of God and being radically changed in the process.

Desires and dispositions play an important role in connecting beliefs and practices. If Christian faith is to reach deep down into our real, multidimensional selves, and if it is to reach out to embrace others in the diversity of their situations and needs, then a full-bodied appreciation and appropriation of Christian practices will be essential. Practices will equip us to com-

---

3. Bonnie Miller-McLemore, "Contemplation in the Midst of Chaos: Contesting the Maceration of the Theological Teacher," in The Scope of Our Art, ed. L. Gregory Jones and Stephanie Paulsell, 48–74, at 66 (Grand Rapids, Mich.: Eerdmans, 2001).

4. Paul Wadell, "Teaching as a Ministry of Hope," in The Scope of Our Art, 120–34, at 134.

5. Craig Dykstra, Growing in the Life of Faith (Louisville, Ky.: Geneva Press, 1999), 7.

6. Ibid., 69.

7. Sarah Coakley, "Deepening Practices: Perspectives from Ascetical and Mystical Theology," in Practicing Theology, 78–93, at 79.

bine conformity and fidelity to the mind of Christ with spontaneity and innovation in the face of a changing world. If the grip of sin on us is "shaped by corrupt habits of activity, confused and even wrong convictions, and distorted desires," as Gregory Jones says,[8] then unlearning this will require attention to our desires, habits, and actions, as well as to our beliefs. Croatian theologian Miroslav Volf claims that "'right communal doing' seems . . . a precondition for right understanding. The obverse is also true: 'wrong doing'—especially if deeply patterned and long lived—leads to twisted understanding."[9]

The practices that comprise the Christian life are interdependent. They support and sustain each other, prevent distortions, offer healthy motivational force, help to reduce excess, and minimize blinkered pursuit of one value at the expense of other values. Christine Pohl expresses this interdependence in the following way: "Faithful attention to many practices is crucial to keeping a single practice from deformation and failure. But it is also the case that faithfulness in one practice helps persons to recognize deformations in other practices. Faithfulness in one practice requires and elicits increasing competence in other practices, and tensions internal to a single practice press persons to learn other practices."[10]

Another kind of interdependence is that by participating in congregations, academies, and social engagements. While the different requirements of these contexts must be kept in mind, the way we worship, the way we think, and the way we act in the world must be brought continually together to encourage congruence, to deepen understanding, and to enhance commitment. It is not just theology that will benefit from close contact with and reflection on practice; the converse is also true. The critical questioning, rigorous examination, and sustained thought offered by theology can help to prevent situations from arising where, as David Cunningham says, "the practices that sustain belief can become hollow, insignificant, and ultimately unpersuasive."[11]

8. L. Gregory Jones, "Beliefs, Desires, Practices, and the Ends of Theological Education," ibid., 185–205, at 189.

9. Miroslav Volf, "Theology for a Way of Life," ibid., 245–63, at 257.

10. Christine Pohl, "A Community's Practice of Hospitality: The Interdependence of Practices and of Communities," ibid., 121–36, at 132–33.

11. David Cunningham, quoted by Amy Plantinga Pauw, "Attending to the Gaps between Beliefs and Practices," ibid., 41.

The Frontiers

There are many aspects to work at the frontiers. Part of the very nature of such work is that it cannot be adequately defined or comprehensively described. Nor can it be predicted, because it is constantly in a state of flux, open to new developments, and essentially liable to controversy and dispute. All I can do is give a few indications, sample features of what I mean by working at the frontiers, and say why I think such work is an integral part of the dialectic of Christian education.

The very word "frontiers" is suggestive of notions such as borders, boundaries, margins, edges, and crossover points. We can associate frontiers with mechanisms for defense, such as walls, and mechanisms for communication and access, such as bridges. A frontier is where something stops being that thing and becomes another thing, where a nation's territory stops belonging to that country and where we enter another country's land. We stop being native and become foreign; we stop being "at home" and risk being an alien, or at least, we enter into a situation where we do not fully belong. At the frontiers we can choose to emphasize either security or continuity, depending on the relationship that exists between those on either side of the frontier. Borders can be too tightly policed, thereby restricting travel, communication on many fronts, and reciprocal learning; this would prevent mutual enrichment. Borders can also be too loosely managed, thereby making us vulnerable to those who might invade or enter intrusively, or undermine our currency, or erode our culture, risk our security, or threaten our sense of identity. At different times in history we have emphasized either high walls or low walls at the frontiers in regard to matters of currency, culture, language, movement of goods and people, education, and religion.

If my suggestion that there is a basic or essential dialectic between formation and work at the frontiers has any cogency, then it is possible for Christian education to focus too strongly on formation, establishing borders that are too firm and leading to attitudes that are too inward-looking. This is stultifying. However, it also means that insufficient attention can be paid to formation, and this leads to work at the frontiers ultimately dissolving identity, trading on past cultural, religious, and educational capital but investing nothing for the future, developing "software" in terms of new perspectives and skills that cannot be accommodated or consistently and coherently deployed because there is no appropriate "hardware" available. My concern here is with the lack of attention to work at the frontiers, its potential value for and, indeed, essential contribution to Christian education.

Let me focus on three broad categories of frontier work. First, work at the frontiers might be about listening for the voices of those who have not been adequately heard by the established authorities within a religious tradition. These might include, most obviously, women, whose experience is still marginalized in many parts of the Christian church. The recasting of various parts of Christian theology is already under way as a result of the feminist movement. It is not yet clear that the enterprise of Christian education is being sufficiently reconstructed to take into account insights from women's perspectives on, for example, the connections between experience, narrative, and learning, or on the connections between relationships, motivation, negotiation, and styles of leadership. Such listening, with regard to gender issues, must also take into account the views of those who perpetuate paternalism, patriarchy, and sexism, for they won't be converted merely by being preached at or resisted.

In schools, we are beginning to seek to include the bully as well as the victim in efforts to restore right relationships. So, too, in the church we need to engage constructively with those we consider are deaf to the full humanity and real insights of those considered "beyond the pale," unqualified, on the receiving end of our teaching, leadership, or service. This will require attention to the views of those who reject others as well as the "others" themselves. These include prisoners and prostitutes, the addicted and delinquent, the awkward and the trouble-makers, failures and spongers, heretics and doubters. I use loaded language here to bring out the threat posed by those at the margins to those in control of society's orthodoxy and purse strings. As one theologian recently comments, "people living on the margins of social and economic prosperity, women in male-dominated societies, victims of ecological exploitation and warfare have a very different interpretation of human existence and Christian faith from that of their counterparts (people at the centre, men, the exploiters) in those same situations."[12] Somehow, we need in Christian education to become better at integrating a love of learning with a desire for justice, as a collection of essays with that title suggests.[13]

12. Robert Kinast, *What Are They Saying about Theological Reflection?* (New York: Paulist Press, 2000), 55–56.
13. William Reiser, *Love of Learning, Desire for Justice* (Scranton: University of Scranton Press, 1995).

Second, a rather different aspect of what I mean by frontier work is the area of interdisciplinary and multidisciplinary inquiry. Here we seek to explore the ramifications of one area of investigation and learning for another. We seek connections between different modes of discourse, conceptual schemes, and methodologies. We attempt to integrate separate disciplinary findings, to correlate them, to bring them into dialogue, even possibly to build a more ambitious, a more all-embracing intellectual perspective. Of course, it is important not to conflate one form of inquiry into another; we must avoid reductionism in our effort to broaden our understanding and to seek connections between one area of study and another. We should also avoid any form of theological imperialism, where religious concerns or presuppositions dictate to or distort what is studied (and how) across the curriculum.

Ultimately, however, from a Christian perspective, the curriculum should not be fragmented, a mere collection of disparate and separate "subjects" that have no connections with each other. Surely any religiously based education inducts us, via the various curriculum areas, into a deeper understanding and appreciation of God's world, God's people, and God's purposes. The multiple forms of intelligence, as outlined, for example, by Howard Gardner, collectively cast light on life as a rich whole, showing up different facets of human life when it is flourishing.[14] The traditional or easily recognizable academic subjects, for example, history, geography, science, technology, language, and literature, have their special characteristics that give them an identity. They each have their key concepts and governing principles, their own procedures for investigation, and their special modes of evaluation. They each have their particular canons, touchstones, or guardians of tradition, which might be individuals, artifacts, writings, or institutions. These subjects and approaches, although valid, should serve not to cut the world up into separate pieces for us, but to allow us temporarily to analyze its parts in order to get a better sense, not only of its complexity, but also of its wholeness. Frontier work in Christian education will question the mutual bearing on each other of religion and science, of morality and technology. It will seek to minimize any sense of disciplinary isolation. It will aim to situate our understanding of the human person in the context of insights gained

14. Howard Gardner, *The Unschooled Mind* (London: Fontana, 1993).

from all the different subjects and to relate these to our ultimate environment, which is God as made to known to us in Christ Jesus.

Third, another aspect of frontier work is simply being open in education to questions, to doubt, to new perspectives, to leaps of imagination, to playing with alternatives. Formation can be too strong, even imprisoning. Teaching is not a form of kidnapping; it should instead be a liberating experience. It should facilitate the capacity to see things afresh, to take risks, to innovate, as well as to conserve, to improvise from and not simply to repeat the "script" of tradition. Many of the breakthroughs, the new concepts, the new paradigms, the recasting of old thought in new clothes—in various forms of learning—seem to come from those at the margins or frontiers of society, or at the edge of respectability in academic or religious terms. In a book called *Living in the Margins* the Australian theologian Terry Veling speaks of the space of the margins as "a site of vital creativity."[15] Coming up against the other, the person who is different, the outsider, can only cause us to reflect more carefully about our own identity, the things we hold onto, our customary ways of proceeding, and the validity of our traditions and practices. In Christian education we need "genuine conversation with a diversity of perspectives and worldviews, . . . to see the world through someone else's eyes, . . . to critique ourselves from another's point of view."[16] Otherwise we slip into idolatry, freeze our traditions, and develop mentalities that are confined. In this way we end up unable to respond positively to pluralism, to promote tolerance, to tackle elitism, to face uncomfortable questions. In short, we refuse God's own call to us to grow. The Christian religious tradition itself has such a depth and breadth that, if we engage with it properly, both in education and in life, it will inevitably present to us an otherness, a strangeness, even alien features that force us to revise and enlarge our earlier conceptions.

The Dialectic between Formation and Frontiers

I have argued that in Christian education both formation and frontier work are necessary. Each needs the other and each affects the other. We

15. Terry Veling, *Living in the Margins* (New York: Crossroad, 1996), 2.
16. Richard Hughes, *How Christian Faith Can Sustain the Life of the Mind* (Grand Rapids, Mich.: Eerdmans, 2001), 3.

move back and forth between them. Surely it is part of our nature to want to belong, but also to go beyond any particular limitations. Christian education should help us to develop an authentic religious identity, one that is true to the living tradition of the church which seeks to respond ever less inadequately to the Spirit's call to us to follow Christ, to share in God's life. It should also equip us for responsive work at the frontiers. Together, and properly related, formation and frontier work facilitate a critical appreciation and a creative appropriation of what discipleship entails in any context. Frontier work prevents formation from becoming static, and therefore stultifying, while formation prevents the fluidity and flexibility of frontier work from lacking direction, continuity, or balance.

In an essay with the subtitle "Educating for Religious Particularity and Pluralism," American theologian and religious educator Fayette Veverka suggests felicitously that "border crossings and boundary building need to feed into one another," and she poses the challenge: "is it possible to foster commitment to our particular faith traditions without demonizing, absorbing, or relativizing the other?"[17] I take her question to be asking, can we promote particularity without slipping into parochialism? Can we encourage openness without leading to emptiness? Put differently, can we combine distinctiveness with inclusiveness? I believe that our global society currently suffers from both undercommitment and overcommitment. That is, aimlessness, anomie, and angst stem at least partly from a certain lack—of roots, identity, and purpose—all these being both causes of and features in undercommitment. One European commentator on youth culture and spirituality refers to "Meanderthal man" in order to bring out the temporary and shifting nature of contemporary commitments.[18] In contrast, the danger of overcommitment is shown when premature, stunted, narrow, blind, self-centered, and inward-looking commitments threaten social harmony. Keeping in mind both the need for formation and for work at the frontiers helps us to avoid either undercommitment or false forms of commitment. The process of formation gives us identity, stability, rootedness in tradition, a sense of belonging and confidence, and a plausibility structure. Work at

17. Fayette Breaux Veverka, "Boundaries and Border Crossings: Educating for Religious Particularity and Pluralism," paper presented at the Education and Ethos Network Symposium "Identity: A Contested Concept," Nijmegen, The Netherlands (February 2001): 6, 4.

18. Jacques Janssen, "Youth Culture and Spirituality in Europe," Networking 3, no. 3 (2002): 11.

the frontiers, in contrast, unsettles us, opens us up to the new, to the unexpected, and the uncomfortable, and shows us that God is at work outside of us and ahead of us, not merely within the confines of our tradition.

The dialectic between formation, which gives us a center, a base from which to operate, and frontier work, which simultaneously connects with and widens the circumference of our experience, is shown by the endless processes of differentiation and integration. A sign of effective growth is our capacity to exercise our independence, to leave home, to take the road out, to be open to new ideas and experiences, to respond to new needs, to widen our horizons. But, if this outgoing is not to lead to dissipation of energies, loss of focus, and insufficient concentration of effort, to uncoordinated and incoherent projects, we also need to come back, to return things to our center, to bring them together, into order and harmony, to integrate them insofar as we can. This is as true for religious traditions as it is for individuals. The relationship between formation and frontier work resembles closely the relationship between tradition and the pastoral perspective as described by theologian Robert Kinast: "Sometimes the pastoral perspective *confirms* the tradition, sometimes it *clarifies* aspects of it, sometimes it *challenges* it and calls for change. Conversely, the tradition can confirm the meaning of an experience, clarify overlooked or hidden aspects of it, challenge people's attitudes and actions and call for change."[19]

If the starting point for ordering Christian education is Christ and discipleship, then let me reiterate that, in the process of such discipleship, and as equally essential components of Christian education, there are two moves, two polarities, that have a dialectical and mutually implicating relationship. We learn to look *at* and to live *in* Christ, within the body of the church, as participants within the stream of living tradition. This is the goal of formation. This task is incomplete until we learn to see and respond to other people and creation *as* Christ, to be his eyes and ears, his hands and voice. The understanding gained through formation is thus applied through work at the frontiers, which consolidates, tests, extends, and revises the principles and personhood we develop in that earlier phase.

19. Kinast, *What Are They Saying*, 12.

2 Forms of Faith and Forms of Communication

Jeff Astley

A piece of advice to examinees that may still circulate in those places where people sit written, unseen examinations, is to begin by questioning the question. If this focuses the student's mind on what it is that he or she is really being asked to do, the advice is obviously sound. But I have read scripts where it has been taken to its illogical—and imprudent—conclusion, resulting in a lengthy analysis of the range of possible meanings of the question, and the intentions of its author, that leaves the frustrated examiner shouting, "Get on with it."

I hope this does not happen here. But it is a danger inherent in the procedure I have adopted in this essay, which is to attempt to answer the question, "What is meant by 'communicating faith'?"

It is a question I have tried to wrestle with for many years, ever since I took up the post of director of the North of England Institute for Christian Education, an independent ecumenical research center located in Durham, UK, and allied to its university, which was founded in order to forge links between the subject area of Christian theology, on the one hand, and the theory and practice of education, on the other. Admittedly, the form the above question has usually taken on the lips of people who first learned the name of my institute is "What is Christian education, then?" But perhaps that is preferable to the assumption that some make that they know quite well what is meant by such a phrase, without noticing that others routinely use the same words rather differently. The problems this can cause are as widespread in the U.S. and other English-speaking countries as they are in Britain.

But by now you are probably reflecting that, as I must have had long enough to think of an answer, it is high time that I gave you one. So here goes . . . .

Naming of Parts: Faith, Religion, and Christianity

Defining religion and specifying a particular religion is not as easy a task as many seem to think. The word "religion" derives from the Latin *religio*, meaning a bond, obligation, or reverence; it is sometimes said to reflect the idea of being bound (Latin *religo*) by rules, observances, or objects of veneration. But beyond this minimal agreement there has been much debate about the defining characteristics of a religion. Certain beliefs are often said to mark out the phenomenon, but nontheistic (Theravada) Buddhism is usually taken to be a religion, although in its purest form it is agnostic about the existence of any god or of a life after death, which are the top two entries on most lists of religious beliefs.

The most convincing analyses of the nature of religion recognize that it is multidimensional. Sociologists and psychologists of religion identify a range of factors that can be mapped onto Newman's more conceptual analysis of three aspects: the dogmatic or philosophical, the devotional or properly religious, and the practical or political.[1] Ninian Smart's dimensions of doctrines, myths, ethical teachings, social institutions and practices, and rituals and religious experiences, to which he later added religious artifacts, unpacks the phenomenon of religion further. Interestingly, Smart implies that what makes these dimensions of a religion "religious" is their relationship to "'ultimate' value-questions related to the meaning of human life."[2]

1. John Henry Newman, *The Via Media of the Anglican Church I* (1877), in *A Newman Synthesis*, ed. Erich Przywara (London: Sheed and Ward, 1930), 164–65.
2. Ninian Smart, *The Phenomenon of Religion* (London: Macmillan, 1973), chap. 1; Smart,

Others have made a similar point, even defining religion as "an institutionalized way of valuing most comprehensively and intensively"—comprehensively, in that what is valued is relevant to the whole of life, and intensively, in
that it is valued above all things.[3]

Two implications of these analyses are relevant to our reflections on religious communication. The first is that a religion comprises much more
than its belief component, and that in order for a religion to be "passed on"
the whole person must be addressed, involving changes in her attitudes and
emotions, and her dispositions and motivations toward experience and behavior, in addition to cognitive changes. "Christians are called . . . to live and
not just to think obediently, . . . worshipfully and appreciatively. . . . I simply
don't think that we can say that the essence of Christian education lies in the
imparting of a view."[4] The second implication is that if the heart of religion
lies in its focus on issues of (affective) value, and therefore of meaning (for
our valuing is both an ascription and a recognition of something's meaningfulness to us), then teaching the proper religious attitudes of worshipping ("worth-shipping") God and celebrating the "things of God" must be
central to any full religious communication. In which case, even "imparting
a view" cannot be merely a cognitive matter. As one philosopher has put it:

[W]e entirely fail to capture what is involved in someone's adoption or rejection of
a religious worldview if we suppose we can extract a pure cognitive juice from the
mush of emotional or figurative coloration, and then establish whether or not the
subject is prepared to swallow it.[5]

For those of us who are concerned with Christianity or "the Christian
religion," the task of definition must involve a further specification. Hans
Küng was content to allow that "everything can be called Christian which
in theory and practice has an explicit, positive reference to Jesus Christ."[6]

Dimensions of the Sacred: An Anatomy of the World's Beliefs (London: HarperCollins, 1996); Smart,
"What Is Religion?" in *New Movements in Religious Education*, ed. Ninian Smart and Donald
Horder (London: Temple Smith, 1975), 20.

3. Frederick Ferré, *Basic Modern Philosophy of Religion* (London: Allen and Unwin; New
York: Charles Scribner's Sons, 1967), 73.

4. Nicholas P. Wolterstorff, *Educating for Life: Reflections on Christian Teaching and Learning*
(Grand Rapids, Mich.: Baker Book House, 2002), 108.

5. John Cottingham, *The Spiritual Dimension: Religion, Philosophy and Human Vocation* (Cambridge: Cambridge University Press, 2005), 80.

6. Hans Küng, *On Being a Christian*, trans. Edward Quinn (Glasgow: Collins, 1977), 125; see
also Ninian Smart, *The Phenomenon of Christianity* (London: Collins, 1979), 7, 11, 128; Stephen

The "reference" here is hardly precise, but perhaps that makes this more honest than some other definitions, by allowing for the plurality that has always existed across and within the Christian churches. "If there is such a thing as Christianity, it will necessarily be in the form of a containment of diversity within bounds."[7] The confessions of faith in the ancient Roman baptismal "Apostles' Creed" and the more theologically reflective, conciliar "Nicene Creed" are much more detailed. However, many who confess and call themselves Christians would prefer to be defined by particular practices of worship (baptism or the Eucharist) or life (active Christian compassion or forgiveness), or by the spiritual and moral attitudes that undergird such behavior (including the "theological virtues" of faith, hope and love).

There is an issue here concerning the difference between what we may call exclusive, definitive and distinctive, as opposed to merely characteristic, features of Christianity. The former category marks those things that are unique to the religion, distinguishing it from others; while the latter includes features such as love, fellowship, or prayer, which—although they are typical of and integral to Christianity—are shared by adherents of other religions, and often by humankind more generally.[8]

It would appear from these reflections that a religion, even the Christian religion, is essentially a human phenomenon: a function of human attitudes, beliefs, and practices. This seems to fly in the face of Karl Barth's notorious critique of religion and his insistence on "the revelation of God as the abolition of religion."[9] But even Barth allows for the possibility of "true religion," as opposed to "religion as unbelief," where and when the Christian religion is justified, sanctified, and exalted by God's revelation and grace.

What should we now make of the notion of faith? In the rather loose phrase "the Christian Faith," the noun seems to be synonymous with "religion." In this usage it labels something which is the *object of faith*, where faith is now understood in a different sense—that is, as the *human faculty or activity of faith*. Here we meet again the inner aspect of the religions, located in the individual's spiritual experience and grounded in his or her percep-

Sykes, The Identity of Christianity: Theologians and the Essence of Christianity from Schleiermacher to Barth (London: SPCK, 1984), 255–61.

7. Sykes, Identity, 240.

8. Cf. John Sullivan, Catholic Education: Distinctive and Inclusive (Dordrecht: Kluwer Academic Publishers, 2001), 63.

9. Karl Barth, Church Dogmatics, vol. I, part 2, trans. G. T. Thomson and Harold Knight (Edinburgh: T. and T. Clark, 1956), 303, 314, 325–61.

tion of what is of ultimate value and meaning. In this context, faith may be thought of as comprising our orientation, evaluation, and commitment toward something or someone, processes that are well captured by the term "believing-in."

The distinction between belief-in and mere belief-that (or belief-about), where the latter is understood as a propositional or cognitive belief concerning the existence and nature of something, is clear enough. Nevertheless, it is often ignored, not least by the designers of questionnaires. Simply to believe that God exists, however, is compatible with having no trust in God, no sense that God is supremely valuable, and no commitment to fulfill God's will. Believing in God, by contrast, involves these additional elements. (The same distinction applies to other objects of faith. "Do I believe in baptism?" asks the grumpy interviewee, missing the point; "Dammit, I've seen it done.") According to St. James, "even the demons believe" that there is one God (James 2:19), but this is not enough to make them believers in God. They do not deny God's existence, but they will not go so far as to worship him nor to engage in the works of faith.

Much theological ink has been spilled in debates between (1) those Christians who follow St. Thomas Aquinas in construing the notion of religious faith essentially as a belief-that—that is, as the intellectual conviction of believing what God has revealed; and (2) those who share Martin Luther's concern that true faith must show the personal commitment, trust, and approval that mark out the Christian's relationship with God. Yet this latter, more Protestant concept of faith in God itself involves a belief that God exists; and Catholic theology, for its part, also recognizes the importance of submitting one's will as well as one's intellect to the revealing God. For both traditions, faith is understood as "saying 'amen' to what God speaks"—and to whom God is.[10]

The distinction between faith as content and faith as faculty is interestingly developed by the practical theologian and religious psychologist James Fowler. Fowler asserts that religious faith is faith in (directed to) specifically religious objects, understood as religious centers of value and power and re-

10. F. Gerrit Immink, Faith: A Practical Theological Reconstruction (Grand Rapids, Mich.: Eerdmans, 2005), 245. See the essay by James L. Price, "The Biblical View of Faith: A Protestant Perspective," chap. 6, and the essay by Avery Dulles, "The Systematic Theology of Faith: A Catholic Perspective," chap. 7, in Handbook of Faith, ed. James Michael Lee (Birmingham, Ala.: Religious Education Press, 1990); and Richard Swinburne, Faith and Reason (Oxford: Clarendon Press, 2005), chap. 4.

ligious "master stories." But Fowler insists that everyone—at least everyone who is not about to commit suicide—possesses generic *human faith*; everyone, after all, believes in something or someone. This "faithing" is "an integral, centering process, underlying the formation of [the] beliefs, values and meanings" that all humans embrace, and which gives coherence and direction to their existence and helps them face up to their lives and their deaths. In this more inclusive sense, faith is our activity (or state) of knowing, understanding, and valuing whatever we take to be of ultimate significance in our lives: a complex "in which *cognition* (the 'rational') is inextricably intertwined with *affectivity* or *valuing* (the 'passional')." It is also our "way-of-being-in-relation" to what we take to be our "ultimate environment," and therefore plays a central role "in shaping the responses a person will make in and against the force-field of his or her life."[11]

There are other understandings of faith-as-a-process. Some radical accounts of religion advocate forms of faith in which beliefs-that play no part. For those who interpret religion noncognitively (that is, as not asserting, for example, that God or an afterlife exists), faith takes the place of God, since God is no more than a symbolic representation of religious faith. Here "God is the role God plays in developing our self-understanding, focusing our aspirations, and shaping the course of our lives."[12] This overlaps with the idea of faith as a profound hope, in which one acts *as if* God exists without believing that he does, while acknowledging—unlike some noncognitivists—that God's existence is possible.[13] John Hick prefers a rather different understanding of faith, construing it as the interpretative element within religious experience, by which we experience the world *as* God's world, "life as divinely created and ourselves as living in the unseen presence of God."[14]

In all these analyses of the concept of faith, the link with the notion of evidence is significant. The activity of faith seems to involve our believing, trusting, or acting in ways that "go beyond"—or even run in the face of—

11. James W. Fowler, *Faithful Change: The Personal and Public Challenges of Postmodern Life* (Nashville, Tenn.: Abingdon, 1996), 56; Fowler, "Foreword," in Jeff Astley and Leslie J. Francis, eds., *Christian Perspectives on Faith Development: A Reader* (Leominster, UK: Gracewing Fowler Wright; Grand Rapids, Mich.: Eerdmans, 1992), 5; Fowler and Sam Keen, *Life Maps: Conversations on the Journey of Faith* (Waco, Tex.: Word Books, 1978), 25.

12. Don Cupitt, *Life Lines* (London: SCM Press, 1986), 103.

13. Louis P. Pojman, *Religious Belief and the Will* (London: Routledge and Kegan Paul, 1986), 228.

14. John Hick, *The Second Christianity* (London: SCM Press, 1983), 47; Hick, *Who or What Is God?* (London: SCM Press, 2008), chap. 2.

the available evidence. In this sense, faith is "the assurance of things hoped for, the conviction of things not seen" (Heb 11:1). For Richard Dawkins and others, the fact that faith is not based on evidence in the way that the sciences are is enough to condemn it. But the rationality or reasonableness of faith, which is inherent in the claim that the faithful have good reasons or grounds for their faith (it is "justifiable"), has been convincingly defended by many philosophers of religion. Their work includes positive reconstructions of the arguments for the existence of God, analyses of religious belief as "properly basic," and claims for the veridicality of religious experience.[15] Certainly, it is by no means obvious that it is necessarily irrational to continue to trust in someone or something, despite the existence of evidence that appears to undermine that trust. Rather, it is almost a defining characteristic of being human.

More extreme accounts of the relationship between faith and reason have been offered by religious believers. For St. Thomas, faith was a necessary prerequisite for reasoning; and other philosophers (e.g., John Locke) have held that faith may be reached through reason. But Protestantism has often drawn a sharp line between the two, as the earlier reference to Barth illustrates, treating faith as a direct gift of God's grace that must destroy our fallen reason, because unaided human thought can only delude us concerning the saving truths of God. Many have therefore argued that a "leap of faith" is required and that, in terms of human reasoning, true faith is focused on what in worldly terms will always seem to be absurd. Richard Dawkins would at least half agree!

Naming of Parts: Communication and Education

"Christian education," like St. Paul (1 Cor 9:19–23), often comes dangerously close to becoming all things to all people. The same may be said, *mutatis mutandis*, of "communicating faith."

The term "communication" may be traced back to the same linguis-

---

15. See, for example, William P. Alston, *Perceiving God: The Epistemology of Religious Experience* (Ithaca, N.Y.: Cornell University Press, 1991); Caroline Franks Davis, *The Evidential Force of Religious Experience* (Oxford: Clarendon Press, 1989); Hick, *Faith and Knowledge* (Glasgow: Collins, 1974); Basil Mitchell, *The Justification of Religious Belief* (London: Macmillan, 1973); Mitchell, *Faith and Criticism* (Oxford: Clarendon Press, 1994); Alvin Plantinga and Nicholas Wolterstorff, eds., *Faith and Rationality: Reason and Belief in God* (Notre Dame, Ind.: University of Notre Dame Press, 1983); Richard Swinburne, *The Existence of God* (Oxford: Clarendon Press, 2004).

tic root as "common" (Latin, *communis*), presumably because communication makes things common or general by imparting, transmitting, or sharing them. The word is used primarily of information, but it also has a wider sense of sharing or bestowing less purely cognitive elements. The latter connotation is employed in metaphorical discourse about "communicating rooms" and in describing the giving and receiving of holy communion ("communicating"), as well as in more direct references to communicating hopes, fears, and enthusiasms to others. In this broader usage, communication may be taken to be synonymous with a wide sense of *teaching* as the (usually) intentional facilitation of *learning*. Learning may itself be taken in the widest sense as including any persistent change in human disposition or capability that comes from some outer experience or self-discovery ("a learning experience"), rather than from inner processes of growth or maturation. On this view, we may be said to learn (change in) attitudes and skills, as well as knowledge. These broad definitions chime in with the broadest interpretation of *education* as a simple label for the processes whereby learning takes place.[16]

Many philosophers of education, however, understand some or all of these terms more narrowly, arguing that they imply certain cognitive norms of knowledge and understanding.[17] They therefore distinguish their normative concept of "real education" from the more inclusive usage of common parlance, as well as from the psychologists' employment of the concept of learning to refer to *any* long-term change brought about by experience. Some have adopted an even more restrictive notion of education, limiting it to those situations where the learner learns to engage in an open questioning of a variety of options, rather than being initiated into one set of ("radically disputable") beliefs. As a result, Christian education has sometimes been dismissed as a contradiction in terms, although the author of that notorious critique (Paul Hirst) later came to stress the priority in education of induction into certain social practices that constitute a flourishing life, rather than (while not neglecting) the learners' critical reflection on those practices; and consequently acknowledged that religious education crucially

16. See Jeff Astley, *The Philosophy of Christian Religious Education* (Birmingham, Ala.: Religious Education Press, 1994), chap. 1, 3; Gabriel Moran, *Showing How: The Act of Teaching* (Valley Forge, Pa.: Trinity Press International, 1997).

17. Thus Paul H. Hirst and Richard S. Peters, *The Logic of Education* (London: Routledge and Kegan Paul, 1971); David Carr, *Making Sense of Education* (London: Routledge Falmer, 2003).

involves "directly introducing pupils to the kinds of practices" that are involved in religion, as well as getting them to reflect critically on them.[18] This element of "formation" or "nurture" is now generally regarded as an important component of all education and an essential preliminary to the development of reflective evaluative attitudes and self-critical thinking skills.[19] In *formative education* the learner receives and is formed in a tradition of values, beliefs, and dispositions, whereas *critical education* teaches her how to reflect on and evaluate that tradition (and other traditions). Both are needed, at least for a fully adult Christian education that allows Christians to reflect on the Gospel they embrace.

With Christian communication of this nature, the standard indoctrination critique misses the mark, since neither the aim nor the outcomes of this process may properly be described as "cementing in" fixed beliefs so that these cannot be changed, despite the learner later discovering that there is good evidence against them. In any case, this account of rational believing is itself rather suspect in that it cannot easily be applied to a whole range of common beliefs, as well as to all metaphysical and many moral beliefs, because they are not open to conflicting evidence in the same way as our beliefs about tables, chairs, and leprechauns.[20]

A wide concept of communication allows us to explore a very broad range of ways in which faith is communicated from one person or group to another. While we may be (negatively) critical of some of these ways and prefer others (perhaps because they are more "critically open" or more consonant with the values implicit in Christianity), it is useful at the outset to employ the widest possible survey of Christian communicative acts before we begin to pick and choose among them. Otherwise, we may overlook some of the most potent forms of Christian communication.

---

18. Hirst, "Education, Knowledge and Practices," in *Beyond Liberal Education*, ed. Robin Barrow and Patricia White, chap. 9 (London: Routledge, 1993).

19. Elmer John Thiessen, *Teaching for Commitment: Liberal Education, Indoctrination, and Christian Nurture* (Leominster, UK: Gracewing; Montreal and Kingston: McGill-Queen's University Press, 1993); Astley, *Philosophy*, chap. 5.

20. Astley, *Philosophy*, chap. 4; Michael L. Peterson, *With All Your Mind: A Christian Philosophy of Education* (Notre Dame, Ind.: University of Notre Dame Press, 2001), 196.

Putting the Parts Together: Approaches to Communicating Faith

Communicating faith, however, may be understood in two significantly different ways. As with the term "Christian education," it may be taken to label *either* (1) passing on religious content (the "Faith") and/or processes ("faith" as "faithing") with the aim and/or outcome of the other person's *adopting* these elements, *or* (2) communicating *information about* the religious beliefs, attitudes, values, dispositions, and activities of the religiously faithful. The first form is an induction into faith or the Faith; the second is communication about these things.[21]

Some aspects of the debates outlined above, as well as these different understandings of communicating faith, connect with the different contexts in which people claim to be engaged in this activity. The debate about the proper form that "religious teaching" should take *in schools*, where such teaching is permitted by law, is discussed elsewhere in this volume. All I wish to do here is to point out the danger of making too hard and fast a distinction between an education about religion ("teaching about religion"), and those educational processes that lead to the adoption of a religious faith or further growth within it ("teaching religion").[22]

There are a number of reasons for blurring this distinction. Not only does an empathetic understanding of the feeling-states of religion demand that the student possess such states, or something very similar, but properly studying the transforming narratives, concepts, values, and practices of religion also lays the learner open to being transformed by them (even converted to them). Further, in religious education ("RE") in schools in Britain and a number of other states, the nonconfessional "religious studies" aim,

---

21. See Astley and David Day, eds., *The Contours of Christian Education* (Great Wakering, UK: McCrimmons, 1992), chap. 1.

22. See Astley, "The Place of Understanding in Christian Education and Education about Christianity," *British Journal of Religious Education* 16, no. 2 (1994): 90–101, reprinted in Astley and Leslie J. Francis, eds, *Critical Perspectives on Christian Education: A Reader on the Aims, Principles and Philosophy of Christian Education*, 105–17 (Leominster, UK: Gracewing Fowler Wright, 1994); Astley, "Crossing the Divide," in *Inspiring Faith in Schools: Studies in Religious Education*, ed. Marius Felderhof, Penny Thompson, and David Torevell, 175–86 (Aldershot, UK and Burlington, Vt.: Ashgate, 2007). Cf. Gabriel Moran, *Religious Education as a Second Language* (Birmingham, Ala.: Religious Education Press, 1989); Kieran Scott, "To Teach Religion or Not to Teach Religion: Is That the Dilemma?" in *Religious Education as Practical Theology*, ed. Bert Roebben and Michael Warren, 145–73 (Leuven: Peeters, 2001).

which is focused on understanding a variety of world faiths without advocating conversion, is frequently complemented by a concern to develop the learners' own spiritual sensitivities (loosely interpreted) and to encourage them in a quest for personal meaning and truth.[23] The subject area is thus interpreted as a combination of a phenomenological study (through which the pupil *learns about* religion) and an attempt to use religious insights to stimulate personal insights about the pupil's "understanding of self" with respect to her own identity, values, and commitments (sometimes described as *learning from* religion about oneself).[24]

Being able to interpret another's worldview is not the only basic aim of religious education. . . . The interpretive process starts from the insider's language and experience, moves to that of the student, and then oscillates between the two. Thus the activity of grasping another's way of life is inseparable in practice from that of pondering on the issues and questions raised by it. Such reflective activity is personal to the student.[25]

In these respects, school RE is said to contribute to the students' personal development, which in reality may well include their spiritual/religious development. Plainly, this second dimension of RE overlaps conceptually with the hermeneutical dialogue that is such an important element in confessional Christian education.[26]

This is the thinking behind the practice of religious education in many "common," "community," or "state" schools. Other nations, of course, including the U.S., forbid the teaching of religion in public education. Most Western countries, however, including the U.S., permit religious schooling of one sort or another. While some Christian *faith schools* or *church schools* are committed to a type of religious education that is identical to church Christian education understood in its transmission-and-adoption form, others endorse something of a mixed-economy of both confessional and noncon-

23. See John M. Hull, *Studies in Religion and Education* (Lewes, UK: Falmer, 1984), 54; Peter R. Hobson and John S. Edwards, *Religious Education in a Pluralist Society* (London: Woburn Press, 1999), chap. 1; 162.

24. See Michael Grimmitt, *Religious Education and Human Development* (Great Wakering, UK: McCrimmons, 1987), 165.

25. Robert Jackson, *Religious Education: An Interpretive Approach* (London: Hodder and Stoughton, 1997), 130.

26. See Andrew Wright's account, "The Spiritual Education Project," in *Pedagogies of Religious Education: Case Studies in the Research and Development of Good Pedagogic Practice in RE*, ed. Michael Grimmitt (Great Wakering, UK: McCrimmon, 2000), chap. 9.

fessional educational aims for school RE. This is particularly appropriate where these schools are "halfway houses" financially maintained or grant-aided by a secular state. In these schools more emphasis tends to be placed on learning about the Christian faith by giving the students a fuller experience of its worship and other practices, and this can merge into the more formative type of religious communication. But many wish to retain a stronger distinction between religious education in church schools and that which is appropriate in the local church congregation or Christian family.[27]

On my definition, Christian communication *within the church* is something that occurs in a wide variety of contexts. In particular, Christians may be said to learn to be Christian not only—indeed not mainly—in explicitly "educational" contexts, or through systematic, sustained, structured, and long-term processes. They also learn Christianity in and through the worship, spirituality, ministry, and fellowship of the church, and in other contexts and in response to other situations that carry no particular Christian designation. Wherever, whenever, and however people become more Christian as a result of their experiences, they are learning Christianity (and not just learning about it).

We may distinguish a number of different models for this type of Christian education.[28] The typology that I find most useful identifies five different approaches that show somewhat different aims and objectives, with varied understandings of the role of the teacher and the learner; as well as emphasizing diverse contexts for and styles of Christian teaching and learning.

For the *faith community* approach, Christian communication is something that best takes place in the context of the church's communal worship and fellowship, and the church itself may be said to be the main agent of this form of socialization or enculturation into Christianity. Sometimes its life

27. Church Schools Review Group, *The Way Ahead: Church of England Schools in the New Millennium* (London: Church House Publishing, 2001), 12.

28. See Astley, ed., *Learning in the Way: Research and Reflection on Adult Christian Education* (Leominster, UK: Gracewing, 2000), chap. 1; John L. Elias, *A History of Christian Education: Protestant, Catholic and Orthodox Perspectives* (Malabar, Fla.: Krieger, 2002), chap. 6–8; Jack L. Seymour and Donald E. Miller, eds., *Contemporary Approaches to Christian Education* (Nashville, Tenn.: Abingdon, 1982); Seymour and Miller, eds., *Theological Approaches to Christian Education* (Nashville, Tenn.: Abingdon, 1990); Seymour, ed., *Mapping Christian Education: Approaches to Congregational Learning* (Nashville, Tenn.: Abingdon, 1997); Richard R. Osmer and Friedrich Schweitzer, *Religious Education between Modernization and Globalization: New Perspectives on the United States and Germany* (Grand Rapids, Mich.: Eerdmans, 2003), chap. 5; Hans-Georg Ziebertz, *Religious Education in a Plural Western Society: Problems and Challenges* (Munster, Hamburg, and London: Lit Verlag, 2003), chap. 5.

and worship are deliberately structured so that people are helped to learn to be Christian, but often the church exercises this role without knowing it. The learner, too, may be unaware that she is engaged in learning the faith that comes to her through the church's "hidden curriculum": a set of learning experiences that do not explicitly advertise themselves as educational.

On the faith community approach, Christian communication is understood very much in its formative mode, as "a process which aims to aid persons to internalize and adopt the community's faith as their own and to apply that faith to life in the world."[29] The content conveyed is the whole gamut of Christian identity, without any particular focus on its beliefs. It may need to be supplemented by a cooler form of education, perhaps best done outside the context of worship, in which the learner can distance himself from the belief system he is embracing and celebrating within the community. While the faith community approach treats Christian communication as a dimension of all aspects of the church's life and work, this second approach understands it as a much more distinctly organized and separate affair in which the emphasis is primarily on the cognitive aspects of Christianity and the learner's reflection on them. "Understanding" and "evaluation" are key terms here, and "critical" is not a dirty word. *Critical Christian education* is my phrase for this "process of exploring the church's tradition and self-understanding in such a way that persons can understand, assess, and therefore respond to the truth of the gospel for themselves."[30]

The development of people's structures of moral and religious thinking and the way they hold their faith is driven largely "from within"; and many interpret the primary task of the Christian educator as assisting this internal change, by supporting and encouraging the faithful in their *Christian development*. On this approach, the Christian educator acts rather like a counselor or spiritual friend, although he or she may also provide learning experiences to help the child, young person, or adult complete any developmental transition on which she has already embarked. Fowler views this educational ministry in part as one of "sponsorship," set within a faith community that has an expectation of such faith development. "By sponsorship in this context I mean the way a person or community provides affirmation, encouragement,

29. John Westerhoff, "Christian Education as a Theological Discipline," *Saint Luke's Journal of Theology* 21, no. 4 (1978): 287.

30. Sara Little, "Religious Instruction," in *Contemporary Approaches*, ed. Seymour and Miller, 41.

guidance and models for a person's ongoing growth and development."[31]

Many who embrace the approach of *Christian liberation* argue that the faith community approach is too conservative, the developmental approach too individualistic, and the critical Christian education approach too intellectual. For liberation educators, *all* education should be critical, but in a moral, social, and political manner—rather than merely as a rational critique of the truth-claims of religion. Education, after all, is about opening people's eyes to reality, especially to the social reality that confines, determines, and oppresses their lives. Liberation Christian educators may applaud when children rebel against received views, for education is not a matter of inheriting, ingesting, and absorbing the past, but of changing the present and moving on to a new, revised future.

> By what we reclaim from our past heritage or propose for our future, by what we ignore from our past and refuse for our future, Christian religious educators are being political. We have no choice about whether or not Christian education will have political implications. It is inevitably political and our choice is about the direction in which we should shape the future of society by our present engagement as Christians within it.[32]

Although one or two of the approaches to Christian education already listed tend to conflict like this, many overlap with or supplement one another. The approach of *faith translation* identifies a feature that is common to all the others. It treats the relationship between the Christian tradition (with its culture, beliefs, values, stories, texts, and rituals) and the Christian learner (with her present and past experiences, concerns, actions, beliefs, reasoning, and spirituality) as parallel to what happens whenever people try to relate to someone who speaks another language. All translation is interpretation: putting one set of ideas into a form that another language-culture can recognize and understand. (As we saw above, RE in schools shares this interpretative approach; but in confessional Christian education the outcome is more likely to be conversion and conviction.)

As the meeting between tradition and learner proceeds, the two enter into an exchange or (metaphorical) conversation, with the tradition ("the

---

31. Fowler, *Stages of Faith: The Psychology of Human Development and the Quest for Meaning* (San Francisco: Harper and Row, 1981), 287.

32. Thomas H. Groome, *Christian Religious Education: Sharing Our Story and Vision* (San Francisco: Harper and Row, 1980), 26.

text") speaking and the learners responding out of their own experience and situation. In this dialogue of interpretation, the learner's "horizon"—the limits of her field of vision and understanding—touches and fuses with the horizon of the tradition. Only then can the learner truly learn what the tradition has to teach her; and she can only learn that in and from her own perspective, as she comes to articulate what is contained in neither, but represents her "new creation of understanding."[33]

To encourage this, the Christian communicator must take on the role of a translator, standing in between the Gospel tradition and the learner, interpreting the one to the other and promoting a dialogue between the "Christian story and vision" and the learner's own biography, life experience, beliefs, and hopes. This dialogue has the potential to change both sides, which helps to explain the development of Christian faith down the centuries as it interacts with the faithing of those who respond to it.[34]

This is perhaps the most dynamic and the most significant element in "communicating faith," and one that in some manner or another is present in every event that we might label with this rich and multifaceted expression.

33. Hans-Georg Gadamer, *Truth and Method*, trans. Joel Weinsheimer and Donald G. Marshall (London: Sheed and Ward; New York: Crossroad, 1993), 462, 473.
34. Astley and Francis, *Critical Perspectives*, 215–50.

PART 2

Baselines

In the chapters of Part 2 there is scope for greater flexibility, intimacy, and attention to individuality in communicating faith than in some of the other settings explored later on in this book. In the home and in the parish the quality of the way of life shared and the tone of voice adopted will be much more important than the content of what is conveyed, although this is a matter of degree rather than a radical difference, because these things will also exert a great deal of influence in other settings, too.

Watkins reminds us that parenthood and family life transcends all timetables; a family is a family for twenty-four hours, seven days a week, open for three hundred and sixty five days a year. The family is an enduring place of formation, where communication of faith is pervasive, part and parcel of all we do, taking place, even if unrecognized, in the midst of eating, arguing, embracing, and organizing. As a mother of four children, Watkins is well aware of the challenging pedagogical vocation of homes. She shows how in the fabric of family life there is an intersection between the sacraments of the church and domestic sacramentality. As elsewhere in this book, her specific focus on the home still holds in view the connections between this context and the wider ecclesial and social networks from which any particular home receives guidance, illumination, and challenge. No setting for communicating faith should be seen in isolation, despite the need to be discerning about its special features. As she says, "the home is not a school, nor the kitchen a classroom, nor the bedroom a chapel."

Watkins comments on the task (and privilege) of communicating faith in the home in a way that combines being theologically informed, culturally sensitive, and practically based. She is aware of the potential of the home to communicate faith, but she is not blind to the countervailing pressures exerted by the patterns and norms of behavior prevalent in the cultural context surrounding all homes. Conscious of the importance for faith development of the quality of our conversation, she steers a way that avoids abdicating responsibility for witnessing discipleship, on the one hand, and, on the other, imposing an inappropriate vocabulary and grammar in the informal setting of a home: "We are called to craft a language of traditional faith in the contemporary ordinariness in our home life."

Jónsson too is aware that the parish cannot be limited to its explicit "curriculum" and planned events, conscious that equally influential will be what is implicit in its life and the way things are done and experienced; indeed, what is omitted also plays a part. A parish priest can ask, "What isn't being done? Whose voices are not being heard? Which experiences are not being named?" As with Watkins' treatment of the home, Jónsson shows that while the parish is a reality in its own right, it is only to be understood in communion with the life and mission of the wider church. Tradition, welcome, liturgy, formation, and service are shown to be cornerstones for communicating faith. By his subtle interweaving of attention to his own pastoral realities and insights drawn from theological literature, he emphasizes that a proper perspective is both enriched and limited by closeness to the people one serves. Fed by the church and facing the people of his parish, he displays how to operate with confidence and trust in the midst of flux and uncertainty.

Too often there is a wide gap between the official "story" of the faith and how this is received "on the ground." Fine-sounding principles and ideals espoused by the church can seem far removed from their implementation at the parish and school levels. While it is to be expected, in this dispensation, that there will always be such gaps, it behooves those charged with communicating faith to stay as closely in touch with reality as they can, without losing sight of the ideals toward which they are striving. McGrail offers a useful overview of developments in sacramental preparation for children in the Catholic Church in England and Wales. Changes in the self-understanding and mode of being of families, schools, and parishes all impinge on their mutual interaction. In his chapter McGrail helps us to appreciate some of the operating factors at the local level that influence how the sacraments are approached and how parents, clergy, parish catechists, and teachers in Catholic schools work in varying degrees of partnership. If inculturation is to be effective and if pastoral strategies are to be effective, then close attention should be paid not only to McGrail's findings about the (sometimes uncomfortable) realities of home-school-church relationships, but also to the need for further ethnographic investigations into the diverse ways the church is experienced in practice. Only in the light of such "reality checks" will there be opportunities for more effective communicative strategies within the church.

The study of scripture as a primary source of nurture is, of course, an enduring baseline for any communication of Christian faith. McKinney uses an example of such scripture study to bring out the kind of factors at work in mediating the relational knowledge required by faith. The approaches used by faith educators must be congruent with the knowledge made possible through revelation. This requires attention to the nature and personalities of participants, care about how they are brought together and engaged, and the building of a mutually supportive learning community. The concrete and experiential basis of McKinney's account opens up features of faith communication that have wide application, transferable to many other settings. This kind of Bible study feeds into the development of discipleship and the empowering of lay ministry. Even the brief portraits of participants in the scripture study group given by McKinney remind us of the unique preciousness and perspective that each person brings to the word of God. His account suggests that we ignore motivation at our peril. Why people attend any study group or function is closely linked to what they get out of their engagement (though what they learn often goes beyond their expectations and cannot be predicted with any accuracy). We do well to seek feedback along the lines shown by McKinney if our efforts to communicate faith are to have a chance of staying in touch with reality and of bearing fruit in the long term.

3   Communicating Faith in the Home

The Pedagogical Vocation of the Christian Household in Late Modern Society

Clare Watkins

> In a certain sense nothing replaces family catechesis, especially for its positive and receptive environment, for the example of adults, and for its first explicit experience and practice of the faith.
>
> <div align="right"><i>General Directory for Catechesis,</i> 178</div>

There is, for many a parent, something rather chilling about being reminded of the ways in which our post-Freudian culture recognizes the complex manner in which we are formed by childhood. The Catholic psychiatrist Jack Dominian has developed a whole scheme for understanding marriage and adult relationship, based on what we know of childhood development; we need, he suggests, to be ever mindful of those first intimacies of childhood, if we are to work well with relationships of the "second intimacy."[1] Such wis-

---

1. See Jack Dominian, *Living Love: Restoring Hope in the Church* (London: Darton, Longman, and Todd, 2004), esp. chap. 10–13.

dom makes me uneasily aware of how my own actions, inactions, and just plain temperament as a mother shape my children's notions and practices of love and intimacy. Together, my husband and I, through our own relationship, and through our ways of living as parents of four children, are forming the relationship capacities and strategies of these new, individual people who have been gifted to us.

This is an intractable reality. As parents we *never stop* shaping our children's emotions and thoughts. Even our occasional choice to be absent speaks to our children. Parenting is not, in any ordinary sense, a skill, an exercise of expertise—though those things may come into it. Rather, the family in which we are parents develops continuously as a place of personal formation, with enormous complexity, as we live, love, and fail in loving, across a variety of interwoven relationships. "Everyone in the family plays a part by sustaining a network of reciprocity that not only forms us but is also formed by us."[2] The family is the most remarkably powerful and enduring formative fact of our lives—for good and, we must also recognize, for ill.

This socio-psychological reality provides the context for our Christian account of communicating *faith* in the home. This context makes clear that, unlike other, formal places of education and faith transmission, the home practices act as faith formation, which cannot properly be given limits, boundaries, beginnings and ends. Communicating faith is never a discrete act; but, in the context of the home, that pervasive reality of faith takes on a fundamental realism. It is for this reason that, among its objectives, the Education Department of the U.S. Bishops' Conference lists the aim: "To provide leadership for actualizing the vital role of parents, as primary educators, and pastors in the enterprise of Catholic education."[3] The home presents us with *the* primary way of faith communication. However, for all the growth in home schooling among some sectors of the Catholic population, especially in the States, we need to recognize that the transmission of faith in the home cannot really lend itself to any sense of program or course, but rather engages the whole of our living. It is here that the most fundamental living of faith formation takes place (or not). What the insights of psychiatrists like Dominian make clear is that, in many ways, what happens in our

2. David Matzko McCarthy, *Sex and Love in the Home*, new ed. (London: SCM Press, 2004), 159, 152–74.
3. United States Conference of Catholic Bishops, "Mission Statement: Objectives," http://www.usccb.org/education/whoweare.shtml, accessed January 2009.

homes will always be present (positively and negatively) in any communications of faith that occur beyond that first experience of living.

This also means that the subject matter for this chapter is necessarily quite complex and far-reaching, which is not to say that it is not "practical." As a parent and theologian whose pastoral and theological, "housewifely" and parental vocations have grown around and through each other for over twenty years, I have learned that the theological tradition has a real power and resonance within the apparently (and really!) mundane ups and downs of domestic life. Our patterns of daily life, our eating, arguing, embracing, and organizing—all this is not only the stuff of that intractable web of formation described by psychologists, but also the necessarily rich and embodied living and communicating of faith (or not).

This fundamental and complex theme can only be opened up in a preliminary way in so short a space as this. In what follows, an initial account of our immediate context is offered, referring both to recent church teaching[4] and also to those aspects of late modern culture that both challenge and engage us in the vocation of communicating faith in the home. A second section draws on certain features in the Christian theological tradition, with regard both to "teaching faith" and the theological nature of the household. This will give some properly theological substance to the emerging pedagogical vocation of the home. These ideas carry with them suggestions for livable domestic pedagogy. My conclusion is simply an open challenge to all those involved with nurturing and supporting the handing on of faith in the home. Effective response to this challenge could transform the life and mission of the Christian community in unexpected and fruitful ways.

Faith and the Home Today
Reflections on Our Ecclesial Context

For many Christian parents the first explicit and public faith response to the gift of a child is baptism. The desire to have the child baptized is deeply related to the wish to have him or her share in the life of—belong to—the church, with the parent(s). What is also clear in the church's understanding

---

4. This section is written from a specifically Roman Catholic perspective, but relates to the concerns and debates going on in other Christian traditions. I hope that the Roman Catholic focus will not discourage readers from these traditions, but rather encourage us together to recognize our common call to similar missionary/evangelizing activity with regard to the home as a place of faith communication.

of baptism is that this is not simply a discrete ritual or rite of passage. It is, rather, the beginnings of a life of faith—the opening up of a new Christian to the endless possibilities of God's grace in Christ, through the scriptures, the sacraments, and the life of the church, in the Spirit. This ongoing nature of the sacrament needs to be firmly established in our minds, as it has deep consequences for the parents of the baptized infant or child.[5] Something of these consequences is set out in the rite of baptism itself:

You have asked to have your children baptized. In doing so you are accepting the responsibility of training them in the practice of the faith. It will be your duty to bring them up to keep God's commandments as Christ taught us, by loving God and our neighbor. . . .

God is the giver of all life, human and divine. May he bless the fathers of these children. With their wives they will be the first teachers of their children in the ways of faith. May they also be the best of teachers, bearing witness to the faith by what they say and do, in Christ Jesus the Lord. . . . [From the *Rite of Baptism*.]

There are a couple of things we should note here. First, that the very act of having one's child baptized implicates the parents in a commitment of their own—the responsibility of training their children "in the practice of the faith." This is what being a Christian parent means: nurturing and training in, teaching and forming in, faith.

The second part of this quote, from later in the rite, acts as a reminder of that intractable truth of parental transmitting of life and learning to children, to which we referred in the opening paragraphs of this chapter. Parents are seen as "the first teachers of their children in the ways of faith." This is saying more than that parents teach their children before anyone else has a chance to; this is a primacy of that "first relationship of intimacy" Dominian speaks of, which is inevitably and powerfully formative. What this means is that we are teaching our children about the faith even when we don't mean to: when I'm cross with Mrs. B. across the way; when I think my TV program more important than listening to my daughter; when I fail to let prayer, or sacrifice, or thanksgiving, or the language of faith have any place in our domestic conversations, beyond the liturgical events of Sunday church. We teach our children the ways of faith because they can see unerringly the extent of our own faith, and the integrity with which we live it and allow

5. This notion of baptism is developed at length in the present author's book: Clare Watkins, *Living Baptism: Called Out of the Ordinary* (London: Darton, Longman, and Todd, 2006).

it to transform family decisions and practices. Parents are, in this sense of primacy, always the child's first teachers—whether we intend to be, want to be, or make any effort to be, or not.

This deep, baptismally-centered sense of the household as the primary place of faith formation, becomes especially vivid when we consider the late modern church as fundamentally missionary. The growing sense, across the Christian communities, of what John Paul II called "the New Evangelization," is an important context for a renewed wisdom about the household's vocation to communicating faith.

In recent church teaching, parents, and families as a whole, have been increasingly described as evangelists in their key role of communicating faith. So, Christian parents "by word and example, are the first heralds of the faith with regard to their children."[6] For, just as evangelizing is about actions and words, witness of life and proclamation, together,[7] so communicating faith in the home is not simply about "teaching" or "training" in the sometimes limited sense that these terms have been used. Indeed, Christian parenthood might appropriately be seen as a primary place of understanding the integrity of evangelization in today's world. The Christian parent needs continually to reflect on how the very fabric of family life forms the household as a "domestic church."[8] Such reflection draws us to see all aspects of our home life "theologically"—how we eat together, how we touch and speak to one another, what the patterns and routines of our daily and weekly lives are saying about priorities, and shared realities, how we share things in conversation, in play, in common projects.

The understanding of the Christian household as "domestic church" is key in this evangelizing, teaching vision of the home. In modern Catholic thinking this understanding develops out of references at the Second Vatican Council that see the Christian household as having a true "ecclesial identity" that is given particular apostolic importance through its also being the place where "new citizens of the human society are born."[9] By 1975 Paul VI is

6. Second Vatican Council, Lumen Gentium 11 (1964), in Vatican Council II: The Conciliar and Post Conciliar Documents, ed. Austin Flannery (Leominster, UK: Fowler Wright Books, 1981).

7. Paul VI, Evangelii Nuntiandi 21–23 (1975), available online at http://www.vatican.va/holy_father/paul_vi/apost_exhortations/documents/hf_p-vi_exh_19751208_evangelii-nuntiandi_en.html (accessed November 13, 2007).

8. This is a term to which we will return later in this chapter.

9. Lumen Gentium 11; see also Second Vatican Council, the Decree on the Apostolate of Laity Apostolicam Actuositatem 11 (1965), in Vatican Council II, ed. Flannery.

able to give the Christian home a fundamental role in the evangelization of modern society, called in a particular way to the *consecratio mundi*, the consecration of the world to Christ.[10] The Christian home is called to be "a place where the Gospel is transmitted and from which the Gospel radiates."[11]

This theology of the home as characteristically evangelizing becomes more fully developed throughout John Paul II's teaching. In particular, it is repeatedly stressed that it is the family's gift of ordinary humanity, its nature as "the bearer of the heritage of humanity itself,"[12] which makes it such a vital place for the communicating of faith. Here we should note: this is not simply about parents communicating faith to children (though this is central), but also about the home's embodiment of a life of faith which evangelizes all its members, and all those touched by that household's living. Here "communicating faith" embraces both the traditionally pedagogical and the traditionally missionary or evangelizing; for to be a Christian household is also, always, to be a part of a wider network of society, beyond the visible structures of church or Christian community.[13] The home stands at the "edges" or borders of the ecclesial institution and wider culture. It is this that describes its centrality to church life and mission.

This observation about the cultural locating of the Christian household brings us to the point where we need to recognize more explicitly the implications of late modernity for our stress on the home as the primary place of communicating faith.

Reflection on Our Cultural Context

The theme of evangelization refers us to one of the fundamental and perennial ways in which the Christian community has understood itself in relation to the world about it. That evangelization should be so strong a theme

10. *Evangelii Nuntiandi* 70.

11. Ibid., 71

12. John Paul II, *Ecclesia in Asia* (1999), 46, available online at http://www.vatican.va/holy_father/john_paul_ii/apost_exhortations/documents/hf_jp-ii_exh_06111999_ecclesia-in-asia_en.html). This vision is also articulated in *Ecclesia in America* (1999), 76, available onlineathttp://www.vatican.va/holy_father/john_paul_ii/apost_exhortations/documents/hf_jp-ii_exh_22011999_ecclesia-in-america_en.html.) See also *Ecclesia in Africa* (1995), 80–85, available online at http://www.vatican.va/holy_father/john_paul_ii/apost_exhortations/documents/hf_jp-ii_exh_14091995_ecclesia-in-africa_en.html (accessed November 4, 2007).

13. For more on this, see Clare Watkins, "Traditio: The Ordinary Handling of Holy Things—Reflections *de Doctrina Christiana* from an Ecclesiology Ordered to Baptism," *New Blackfriars* 87 (March 2006): 166ff.

in Christian thinking today, as compared to, say, 150 years ago, is, in part, related to the churches' changing relation to a highly secular and "post-Christian" society in the West. We are increasingly and more urgently being called to proclaim the Gospel in fresh ways, which engage with our own culture, as is reflected not only in the teaching of the New Evangelization of John Paul II, but also through local initiatives such as the U.S. Bishops' Catholic Communication Campaign. For the purposes of this chapter it is important to articulate some of the particular aspects of contemporary culture that impact on the communication of faith in the home.[14]

Perhaps the first observation here concerns the shape of home life itself. The reality of the late modern household, where marriage may or may not be a feature, where there may be one present parent, or two of the same gender, or where the structure of the home may be shaped by a series of marriages or parental relationships, and a more complex set of sibling relationships, is clearly significant for Christian understanding. John Paul II's vision of the home as "domestic church" takes for granted a sacramentally married, Christian couple as its center; but the pastoral realities in which we minister are often quite different. Within the Christian community, too, that late modern disintegration of "traditional" family is a clear feature. This reality clearly poses some important challenges for us and our theme; but this essay will not take this as its cultural contextual focus. Rather, by reflecting on the more general aspects of late modernity—many of which are factors in the difficulties surrounding marriage and parenthood today—I want to provide a more basic understanding of cultural context, which, I hope, can serve all Christians living in households, "traditional" or "orthodox" or not; and can help us understand more deeply the universal vocation of communicating faith in the home—however fractured or imperfect our particular home may be.[15]

14. What follows relies on the document commissioned by the Catholic Education Service (Agency of the Bishops' Conference of England and Wales) and authored out of the Heythrop Institute for Religion, Ethics and Public Life, *On the Way to Life: Contemporary Culture and Theological Developments Framework for Catholic Education, Catechesis and Formation* (2005). This clearly reflects the authors' specifically Western European understanding, which nevertheless speaks vividly of a number of cultural features affecting Western, liberal democratic cultures, both of Northern America and of Australia and New Zealand.

15. For thoughtful accounts of Christian approaches to "non-traditional" families, see McCarthy, *Sex and Love in the Home*, 197–226, and his helpful comments on this chapter in the Preface to the new edition; and Florence Caffrey Bourg, *Where Two or Three Are Gathered: Christian families as Domestic Churches* (Notre Dame, Ind.: University of Notre Dame Press, 2004), chap. 7–8.

One of the key cultural factors affecting our domestic life today is *a culture of busyness*: we are all—parents and children—in a more or less permanent state of rushing from one thing to another. This seems to be something affecting all developed countries of the global North, with the U.S. overtaking Japan in 1997 as the industrialized country with the longest working hours.[16] Even our "leisure" has become something we must plan, organize, and make time for, as we become "frenetic longeurs," for whom the idea of time simply passing seems frighteningly dull.[17] This overactivity can be related to a certain dissatisfaction with a life that fails to provide much meaning;[18] it is also a by-product of the modern emphasis on progress, especially of the technological or material kind.

In a way that is unprecedented in human history, we have developed, in late modernity, an expectation for material progress, and an optimism (in the main) regarding what can be achieved technologically. Such an emphasis on progress carries with it socio-psychological shifts, as we are formed into a people always looking for the next big thing, the next advance.[19] We expect to be always and immediately in touch—with world affairs, with grown-up children, with our friend on the other side of the world; and we expect, too, to be constantly entertained, whilst continually seeking new ways of relieving ourselves of domestic chores.

What all this translates to in the home will vary from household to household. It may be that this culture impresses itself in the ways in which one or both parents are finding themselves driven at work, to "get on," to advance, to "fulfill their potential," to the detriment of their home life. Or it may be that the availability of the delights of media technology in the home has drawn family members into "virtual" relationships, or the entertaining worlds provided by Internet, gaming, and TV, whilst leaving them unable to relate to one another, or to share properly in the common life of the home. In all this, something is being communicated about what is most real, most important; we are communicating, or failing to communicate, our faith. It seems clear that the Christian traditions of prayer, stillness, conversation, attentiveness to one another cannot but be undermined by such cultural pressures. Here the Christian household is called to reflect on its own col-

16. Carl Honore, *In Praise of Slow: How a Worldwide Movement Is Challenging the Cult of Speed* (London: Orion Books, 2005), 163f.
17. Heythrop Institute, *On the Way to Life*, 23f.
18. Ibid., 22f, 24f.   19. Ibid., 20f.

lusion with, and need to live critically toward, a late modern culture of the busy, the "successful," and even, perhaps, the technological. We are called to think about our *Christian living in respect of God's gift of time.*

Another striking feature of our culture can be described through attention to the question of *meaning.* In what is now a profoundly secular society, it is more or less taken for granted that "religion" is a private affair.[20] Whilst there is some evidence that individuals may have their own "spirituality," or notions of "the divine," it is also clear that organized religion is experiencing what appears to be an inexorable institutional decline,[21] whilst the language of public discourse is systematically stripped of the language of faith, in the interests of pluralism and rationalism.[22]

One of the effects of such secularization concerns the basic human struggle for meaning. What characterizes this struggle in late modernity is the isolation of the individual in it, as she is left, culturally speaking, to work it out for herself, and then to get on with it in private. Unsurprisingly, the question of meaning in such circumstances becomes the question of "what works for me," as the authority of the subject herself, her experience and tastes, come to the fore.[23]

For the household all this has its implications. Our surrounding environment makes the establishment of a common way of living—even shared meals and ways of behaving—verge on the countercultural. The idea of being held as a unit in a common faith and prayer-life, or public liturgy, does not have an evident authority or recommendation. Further, as the authority of the subjective—"the turn to the subject"—becomes the prevalent voice in coming generations' thinking, the dullness of traditions, the "not-doing-it-for-me" experience of liturgy or family prayer, and the diminishing sense of what is past as in any way authoritative, contribute to enormous challenges in handing on faith. We are called anew, as contemporary Christian households, to think and to envision boldly ways of embodying a common life of faith. Above all, the quality of our conversation, and the way it might enable all those in the formative life of the home to grow in a confident literacy of faith expression, deserve attention. Language is "shared meaning"; and in a culture where meaning is privatized, the language traditions of our faith, and their new expression within a new generation, present themselves as an

---

20. Ibid., 16f.
22. Ibid., 13f.

21. Ibid., 17ff.
23. Ibid., 20, 16f.

important locus for domestic communication of faith. *We are called to craft a language of traditional faith in the contemporary ordinariness in our home life.*

The challenges of our culture are especially felt in the Christian home. By its very nature the household is osmotic in relation to culture; not only our children, but especially they, are formed by these cultural ways of knowing and thinking about life and the world, as well as by the primary formation of the home. Further, the ways in which we pattern our Christian homes will, almost inevitably, bear the marks of this culture. The only alternative is that they become hermetically sealed countercultures—a position certainly not in tune with the Catholic theological tradition concerning the world and grace. In terms of communicating faith in the home the Christian family is thus located at a most potent and painful *place of discernments*, as it is necessarily called to engage, critically and thoughtfully, with a hyperactive culture for which the language of shared faith, of common religion and public proclamation, are inimical. If this is the call of the Christian household today, then the question must be raised as to how it is equipped to respond to such a vocation, or formed for such an office. My suggestion is that we need a strong and accessible theology/spirituality of the Christian household's pedagogical vocation, if those of us entrusted with this mission are to be strengthened for it. In what remains of this essay I will try to outline some features for such a pastoral theological understanding.

The Vocation of the "Domestic Church" in Faith Education: Insights from the Theological Tradition

A Vision of Faith Communication from the Tradition: Integrated, Personal and Conversational

Christians are familiar with the ideas of handing on (traditio), proclaiming, and teaching; it is not for nothing that the followers of Jesus are called "disciples"—those who learn. We naturally have come to see teaching, learning, communication, and preaching as central features of living faith, as we recognize ourselves as the People of God who gather round a creed, a body of "doctrine" or teaching, with whose communication to the world we are charged. What is perhaps more problematic for us—especially in our post-Enlightenment and post-Christendom culture—is an ongoing, critical awareness of how our traditions of teaching and communication might differ from those prevalent in our society.

Since the Enlightenment there has been a growing sense of the primacy of the "rational," with its accompanying splitting up of the rich and various ways in which people come to true and personal knowledge; the patterns of late modernity and hypersecularism are, in many ways, the logical conclusions to this major reorientation of human knowing. In particular, in so highly developed and technologically based a context as our own, it is all too easy to think of the communication of something in terms of *information* or *useful* (i.e., materially helpful) *skills/knowledge*. Whilst it is true that all true communicating of the Gospel must include such types of "education" as these, it is also worth reminding ourselves that such information and training are, in the Christian tradition, held in a very particular context. This is a context conditioned by its goal: that of meeting, and learning to live in love, with Jesus Christ.[24]

With this in mind, it seems especially important for the Christian household not to attempt to mimic too closely many of the patterns of communication and teaching most prevalent in our culture. If we imagine, for example, that communicating faith in the home is *simply* about children's learning the "truths of their faith," and having knowledge of doctrine, then our project is doomed to failure.[25] For the home is not a school, in the normal sense of the word; nor is the kitchen a classroom, nor the bedroom a chapel. Our homes are where we are "at home"—most ourselves, relaxed; and communicating of faith needs to be authentic to the human personal and domestic ways of communicating that are already a part of any one particular household's culture. Anything that jars with this—using a strange formality, unease with an odd vocabulary—will fail to live up to that evangelizing power that is the promise of true domestic faith formation.

This is not simply a pastoral or commonsense observation—though it is both of these. It is also of a piece with an enduring Christian tradition concerning *how we come to knowledge of God*. We need only look at the Roman Catholic tradition of saints named as "doctors," or authorized teachers, of the church to see a vision of teaching that is consistently caught up with the profoundly personal struggle for holiness. Here "teaching" is manifest-

24. See Second Vatican Council, *Dei Verbum*, chapter 2, articles 2–6 (1965): "where all our knowing in scripture and tradition has, as its end, a *personal knowledge* of Jesus as the Word made flesh," trans. in *Vatican Council II*, ed. Flannery, 1981.

25. This would be a concern, or question, for me with much of the more conservative homeschooling literature emerging from the U.S., especially among Catholics. For example, see http://www.keepingitcatholic.org.

ed in integrated ways of communication: personal ways of life and charity; preaching and prayer; the fashioning of a "spirituality"; or, better, a discipline of life that shapes the whole of a person's way of being in and looking at the world.[26] Quite simply, for faith to be authentically (authoritatively) communicated, it needs to be *embodied in persons of prayer*, and shared through personal relationship and ordinary interaction with such persons, in a shared struggle to grow in faith.

This integrated and personal understanding of what it is to communicate faith emphasizes "persons"; and here a ready theme for a spirituality of the Christian household can be seen. However, on its own it is in danger of losing the focus of what any communication of faith must be about in the Christian tradition: that is, the deepening of knowledge and relation, not with each other, but *with God*, the Trinity. Here, too, the Christian tradition has something important to say to us. For our tradition is careful to point out that, on a profound level, it is only God who communicates Himself to people, and that any of our efforts, teachings, ideas are only, at their best, facilitative of the Divine speaking of Himself in His Word, into each unique and mysterious human heart.

So, for Thomas Aquinas, the text of Matthew 23:8—"you are not to be called rabbi, for you have one teacher . . . "—is to be taken with utmost seriousness. For here, he suggests, it becomes clear that *only* God can truly cause a person to learn *anything true* in the interior reality of his person. What the human teacher or preacher does, at best, is to "bring to light" that ongoing communication of our heavenly Father to the pupil. In the end, we are all properly "pupils"; and, from time to time, we may be called into a service of accompanying another pupil as he learns from the Father, privileged to be participants in what is, essentially, a mysterious divine-human encounter, a communion of knowledge.[27]

If this vision of communicating faith is true—and it has clear resonances in both Tertullian[28] and Augustine[29]—then it has some striking consequences for our subject. What it seems to suggest is a way of communicating faith

26. See Bernard McGinn, *The Doctors of the Church: Thirty-three Men and Women Who Shaped Christianity* (New York: Crossroad, 1999).

27. Thomas Aquinas, *De veritate*, Question XI, Article 1, in vol. 2, *Truth*, trans. James V. McGlynn, 77–87 (Indianapolis: Hackett Publishing, 1994).

28. McGinn, *The Doctors of the Church*, 4.

29. See St. Augustine, *De Doctrina Christiana*, trans. Roger P. H. Green (Oxford: Oxford University Press 1997).

which is first and foremost about attentiveness to what the Spirit is already about in the lives of those around me. That is to say, I can trust that God is, himself, working in the lives of those in whose lives I share, to communicate his life to them; my job is (simply!) to learn to see this divine communication at work, and respond in small and serviceable ways to enable this communication better to be heard. In addition, Aquinas' vision of Christian teaching suggests I must always be on the lookout for how my husband and our children are themselves enablers of God's loving communication to me.

These aspects of our Christian tradition offer a strong and rich foundation for a spirituality/theology for the domestic handing on of faith. What emerges is not a pattern of "telling people things" (though that certainly has its place), but rather, a vision of attentiveness, to each other and to God's work in the other, and of a deepening personal appropriation of faith as the living power in our lives, which fashions everything we do and say. Central to this is surely prayer: not just, or even primarily, "family prayers"—which can be uncomfortable and insensitive to the various needs in a diverse household—but, more particularly, personal prayer, to which, perhaps, parents are called in a particular way. That such prayer is necessarily accompanied by an attentive reading of scripture and of the spiritual/theological tradition would also seem necessary, if that personal life of faith, which is the authority behind faith communication, is to be more deeply formed in Christian households. This suggests that we need to focus as much attention on the spiritual formation of parents as we do on that of our ordained ministers.

The Domestic Church: A Sacramental Spirituality for Handing on the Faith

There is a further theme—one we have already mentioned—that can contribute to the spirituality needed for the communication of faith in the home: the emerging theology of "the domestic church." This theology, championed most prolifically by John Paul II, has its roots in the Early Fathers, and has been brought to light in our own time in the teaching of the Second Vatican Council.[30] Here it will be explored as offering a sacramental and ecclesiological spirituality of the home and its mission to communicate faith.

30. *Lumen Gentium* 11; *Apostolicam Actuositatem* 11; *Evangelii Nuntiandi* 70. For more on the history and provenance of this term, see Watkins, "Traditio: The Ordinary Handling of Holy Things"; and Bourg, *Where Two or Three Are Gathered*, 8–22.

The theology of domestic church makes clear the ecclesiological significance of the home as a properly lay expression of church, situating its living of faith in a place where there can be no divisions of faith and life, church and world. The home is both, and at the same time, domestic church and "the primary vital cell of society."[31] As such, it speaks especially of that lay vocation of all the baptized—to live out the Gospel in and for the world about them. That same conciliar text just quoted goes on to describe a true "apostolate" of the Christian home in which it communicates faith through hospitality, works of justice, charity, and the support of families, young people, and the elderly. Here is a formation in faith, through the active living of baptismal vocation.

Such a lay emphasis in an ecclesiology of "domestic church" also calls us to recognize the true place of those ways of communicating faith that are generally carried out by institutional bodies in our churches. The catechesis program, the Sunday school, even preaching—none of these, nor all of them together, can do what the proclamation of the domestic church of the home can do by virtue of its very everyday-ness, its "worldliness." It is its particular basis in the living of baptismal grace in and for the world that makes the domestic church the "primary school of virtue."[32] The living of our baptismal anointing in Christ as priests, prophets, and sovereigns needs to find embodiment within the "ordinary" and "mundane" particularities of domestic life.[33]

Within the Catholic tradition it is not only the sacrament of baptism that might be reflected on for a deeper and more divinely empowered theology/spirituality of "domestic church," but also the sacrament of marriage. Like baptism, marriage is a sacrament to be lived, an ongoing, daily call to conversion of life toward the other(s), spouse and children, in a long learning of selfless love and friendship, which is to be put "at the service of communion" in the church and in the world.[34] According to John Paul II it is specifically the sacrament of marriage that grounds the educational and evangelizing mission of parents in the "ministry" of the church, giving it a special dignity and power.[35]

31. Apostolicam Actuositatem 11.

32. See Florence Caffrey Bourg's working out of this idea, through a use of Aquinas, in Where Two or Three Are Gathered, 122–35.

33. The Second Vatican Council offers a profound spirituality of baptism in its reflections on this participation in Christ's three-fold office; see Lumen Gentium 10–13; 33–36.

34. Catechism of the Catholic Church, 1533–35 (London: Geoffrey Chapman, 1994).

35. John Paul II, Familiaris Consortio 38 (1981), available online at http://www.vatican.va/

Drawing on a sacramental understanding of the relationship and covenant between the parents within a Christian household has its obvious difficulties. Nonetheless, the Christian tradition concerning marriage offers us a strong basis for a spirituality for enriching the possibility of the effective communication of the Gospel in the home. Christian marriage as sacrament proclaims the physical intimacy and care between the "others" of man and woman as a place of grace; it is centered on personal covenanting through the unpredictable ups and downs of life, made possible and blessed by the grace of God, in whose creation the couple is called to cooperate. Marriage has always challenged the Catholic tradition's notions of sacrament, grounded as it is so firmly in *creation* and human society, and expressed in so human, bodily, and mundane ways as family life manifests. Yet it is precisely the unquenchable need to call this thing "sacramental"—to proclaim it with certainty as to do with the life of holiness, a means of grace—that seems to me so important for understanding the home as the place of Christian formation. In marriage, sacramental grace—the grace of Jesus' death and resurrection—is lived out most physically, most personally, and most (extra)ordinarily. Here is a rich spiritual/theological basis for the home as a place of communicating embodied, sacramental faith.

Challenges and Implications

In this chapter we have seen not only the theological and cultural centrality of the home as the place of faith formation and transmission, but also the rich possibilities that exist within the Christian tradition for a theology or spirituality that might better enable this essential work of Christians. In the end, this theology can only be appropriately embodied in ways proper to the variety of contexts in which Christian households, and those who work with them, find themselves. And, when it comes to family life, this variety is, indeed, manifold and complex. At the end of such thinking the challenge goes out to each of us, in our different situations and contexts: how are we better to serve and enable the Christian household as the primary place of faith communication? Unless we can begin to provide a serious and practical response to this question, it is my conviction that all our other attempts at handing on the good news of Jesus Christ will be dangerously undermined.

---

holy_father/john_paul_ii/apost_exhortations/documents/hf_jp-ii_exh_19811122_familiaris-consortio_en.html.

4 Communicating Faith in the Parish

Maintaining a Presence, Care, and Mission

Atli Jónsson

The parish is a privileged location for communicating faith. Busy with keeping long-standing activities alive, it needs to step back and reflect on the limits and opportunities it has for making the faith that sustains us known in this familiar setting.

For the purpose of this chapter, four presuppositions are made about how the parish is perceived and about its nature. First, the experience most people have of the church is in their parish, and the two, church and parish, are virtually synonymous. As they refer to church they intend mostly what they themselves have experienced in the parish, the community they are part of, the people they have met, and the concerns that arise from this experience. The second observation is that, theologically speaking, the parish is a valid expression of church. As the community gathers for the celebration of the Eucharist, the summit and source of the church's life are realized.[1]

---

1. Cf. *Christus Dominus* 30/2, *Presbyterorum Ordnis* 5, Second Vatican Council, *Sacrosanctum Concilium* 2 (1963) and *Lumen Gentium* 11 (1964), in *Vatican Council II: The Conciliar and Post Conciliar Documents*, vol. 1., ed. Austin Flannery (Grand Rapids, Mich.: Eerdmans, 1984).

Third, the parish is a place of communion with the local church, a bond expressed in the person of its own pastor (*pastor proprius*), the representative of the diocesan bishop.[2] Finally, the parish shares in the mission of the church to bear witness to the Christian faith (*martyria*), to offer worship and sanctify (*leiturgia*), and to serve neighbor (*diakonia*). These core activities structure the work that is done in the parish. Consequently the success of parish life can be seen from how these three essential elements of liturgy, formation, and service help the community to live as Christians and indicate how vibrant or otherwise a parish is.

This contribution is based on the particular experience of life in an English parish. I assume that many, even most, of the challenges we face are similar to the rest of the developed world, where many institutions can no longer rely on loyalty or convention for belonging. This situation is particularly evident with younger people, who see meaningful participation in terms of self-identity and evaluate their involvement in terms of how successfully it is attained.[3] The educationally, economically, and socially deprived may not have the same aspiration to *realize themselves*. Reaching those who—for whichever reason—are distant from faith is made more difficult in the UK as public religious discourse is often seen as suspect.[4] The rhetoric in the 2008 U.S. presidential elections, broadcast worldwide, shows a very different situation, where religious references are not only possible but positively encouraged.

The content of this reflection was helped along by three ideas of the late German Jesuit theologian Karl Rahner, whose interest in the situation of the *modern* believer and the future of the church's mission is evident in his numerous publications. Two reports to the Catholic Bishops' Conference of England and Wales on *Collaborative Ministry* and *Evangelisation in England and Wales* have been useful resources, as has the detailed study of Callum G. Brown, *The Death of Christian Britain*.[5]

2. Cf. *Sacrosanctum Concilium* 42; *The Code of Canon Law* (London: Collins, 1983); canons 515 par. 1, 517 par.1–2, 519, 520 par.1 list the various ways in which the appointment of the *pastor proprius* can be made and the categories of persons that can serve in this capacity.

3. Carol E. Lytch, *Choosing Church: What Makes a Difference for Teens* (Louisville, Ky., and London: Westminster John Knox Press, 2004), 84–85.

4. Many examples could be given of how religious discourse does not sit easily in public life in Britain. One famous example may, however, suffice. In an interview for *Vanity Fair Magazine* in 2003, reporter David Margolick asked Prime Minister Tony Blair about his Christian faith. One of Mr. Blair's unelected assistants, Alistair Campbell, interrupted the Prime Minister's reply to say, "I'm sorry, we don't do God"; quoted by Brian Walden on the BBC website, http://news.bbc.co.uk/1/hi/magazine/4903424.stm (accessed February 16, 2009).

5. Catholic Bishops' Conference of England and Wales, *The Sign We Give: A Report of the*

To communicate is an interpersonal process, and for it to be effective the situation of those we would like to reach has to be appreciated. It asks of the communicators to consider their own subjective situation and reflect on how these various dimensions interrelate in order to identify the opportunities that emerge. Looking at where our contemporaries are seems, therefore, to be a good place to start this reflection. I then present the experience of practicing Catholics in their parish and the opening that the spiritual search of modern people potentially offers our communities. The meeting ground of church and those who are on a spiritual search will be reflected on as I deploy to the image or model of the parish as *sanctuary*. Finally, I consider what is needed for animating the life of this sanctuary, where the spirituality of our Christian tradition, liturgy, formation, and service of neighbor are the cornerstones.

When Old Certainties Fail

At the end of the Second Vatican Council, Karl Rahner used the Greek word *diaspora* to describe the situation of the Christian in the modern world. Originally the term referred to the dispersion of the Jews in Roman times after the fall of Jerusalem in A.D. 70, which is still ongoing. Rahner, however, did not see this as a precise historical parallel, but found in it a term that describes the new and emerging situation of future believers who, leaving aside those influenced by a Christian upbringing, "will not be Christians by custom or tradition," but "only because of their own act of faith attained in a difficult struggle and perpetually achieved anew."[6]

This was over fifty years ago, and since then much has happened that shows this prognosis to be well underway, if not already realized, both on the European continent and in Britain. Christian churches have in the last few decades seen a steady decline in membership, many religious orders have not received a single candidate for years, the number of priests in active ministry is disproportionate to the number of parishes, and many dioceses are in the process of adapting their pastoral structures to meet the needs of

Working Party on Collaborative Ministry, 1995; and Philip Knights and Andrea Murray, *Evangelisation in England and Wales*, Catholic Bishops' Conference of England and Wales, 2002; both available online at http://www.catholic-ew.org.uk/ccb/ca_church/publications (accessed June 9, 2007); Callum G. Brown, *The Death of Christian Britain: Understanding Secularisation 1800–2000* (London: Routledge, 2001).

6. Karl Rahner, *The Christian of the Future* (London: Burns and Oates 1969), 79.

a fast-shrinking church community. Although for some this situation has been underway for a long time, others see it as relatively recent.[7] Whichever way one approaches the decline of Christian practice in Britain, it can be argued that the present situation is unlike the more distant and immediate past. This is evident simply by looking at diocesan statistics for sacramental practice and by analyzing the age profile of active parishioners.

According to Callum G. Brown, a change occurred with the Enlightenment as the emphasis in religious discourse shifted from church structures to the personal, from male to female.[8] Again, as the nature of femininity changed and "women cancelled their mass subscription to the discursive domain of Christianity," the collapse set in,[9] not primarily as the decline of institutions, but on the level of the personal and existential as faith ceased to be part of how a person understands him/herself. Brown calls this "discourse change," which happens when religion "as narrative structure, the cement of community, and as motif"[10] disappears and concludes that there is sufficient evidence to demonstrate that Christianity is not articulated or reflected anymore. The result was "a new silence of 'history,' which marks the birth of Britain's dechristianized generations in the 1960s."[11]

Whereas previously the heralds of secularism such as Marx, Freud, and Nietzsche appealed to the educated elite, there now emerged a new situation where the questions of religion in the personal and the social spheres were no longer seen as relevant. In modern-day Britain this situation is evident; one need only look at the objections to the role of the bishops in the House of Lords, the growing demands for the separation of church and state, the status of faith schools, the right of the church to speak on moral issues— and the list could go on. In this debate the demand is made that religion be relegated to the personal or private sphere and denied expression in the public domain.

The evidence of how this change has affected the Catholic Church is well documented in the report on *Evangelisation in England and Wales*. For our purposes it is not necessary to reproduce the entire statistical evidence here; it suffices to mention that in the general population, 66 percent of those aged 18 to 24 say they have no religious adherence. For the other end of the age spectrum, those aged 65 and over, this figure is 24 percent.[12] This finding

7. Cf. Brown, *Death of Christian Britain*, 2–3.
8. Ibid., 195.   9. Ibid., 197.
10. Ibid., 169, 181.   11. Ibid., 169, 186.
12. Cf. Knights and Murray, *Evangelisation in England and Wales*, 70–71.

bears out that the majority of the children of those who were growing up in the 1960s do not regard themselves as members of any church. Those whose family background is only a generation or two removed from the practicing parent or grandparent are not necessarily asking to have their children baptized or getting married in church or show any signs of wanting to be involved. Among the younger generation the number of those who are unbaptized is growing, and each generation is being removed further away from the Christian roots that have inspired and formed the culture and social institutions of Britain. There is no option but to accept these bleak facts and admit that to an ever-growing portion of the population, the message of the Gospel is no news at all.

How the Parishioners Experience the Parish

Evangelisation in England and Wales presents an overall positive evaluation of the parish. Its strengths are the warmth of welcome, degree of care for its members, and the liturgy it offers.[13] The report to the bishops affirms the parish as a very useful location of evangelizing, and the report includes many statistics that confirm how the majority of the parishioners find the liturgy enriching; the celebration of the Eucharist is at the center of their positive experience. They feel they gain help for their daily lives from the sermons they hear, and affirm that the values of the Gospel guide their personal lives.[14] Without analyzing the data further, it can be said that the present-day parishioner relates to his parish in an appreciative and positive way.

The parish, however, according to the experience of the parishioners, is not perfect. There are identifiable weaknesses; the parish can be both "insular and self-serving,"[15] showing "a marked tendency to . . . be inward looking with an apparent reluctance to proclaim the Gospel in the broader community or in an overtly secular environment."[16] It is clear that reaching the unchurched means leaving the comfort zone, and that most traditional church activities engage people who have at least some contact already.[17] A prime example of this kind of contact is the catechetical programs, where those who have at least marginal contact prepare for the reception of the sacraments. Although these occasions for catechesis and liturgical con-

---

13. Cf. Ibid., 95.   14. Cf. Ibid., 98.
15. Ibid., 123.   16. Ibid., 98; see also 123, 132.
17. Cf. *Evangelisation in England and Wales*, 163.

tact fail to produce the ongoing commitment that makes a difference to the life of a parish, they are not the biggest challenge in terms of outreach. The greatest challenge is reaching those who have no contact with church and, correspondingly, "that many are happy to receive the Good News, but less so to communicate it to others!"[18]

This situation directly jars with the church's understanding of itself as a sacrament of unity among all peoples,[19] for missionary activity belongs to the very nature of the church[20] and to every Christian by virtue of her baptism.[21] The mission to live and share the Gospel is "the root identity of the entire church, in all places and the work of all Christians."[22] The origin of the parish as a pastoral structure in the church takes us back to the third century, when it became an instrument for the bishop's mission in the periphery of the city, the surrounding villages, and the countryside. For the parish to continue to be part of this mission of the local church to those who are on its boundaries or outside it, we need to look at where our contemporaries have an experience that can be a meeting place offering the occasion for an ongoing interaction.

The Spiritual Search of Modern People

"Tomorrow's devout person will either be a mystic—someone who has *experienced* something—or else they will no longer be devout at all."[23] These are probably the most quoted words of Rahner. They refer to the experience that makes us believers, an experience which even against all odds brings peace and focus to our lives. The personal act of faith, no longer carried by social conventions or cultural institutions, rests on this experience. It is in the spiritual search of our contemporaries that we find a point of convergence between what they look for and what the church, because of its experience and competence, has to offer.

To understand this phrase attention must be given to the meaning Rahner attaches to the word *mystic*. For him the mystic is the believer, and his expe-

---

18. Ibid., 131.

19. Cf. Second Vatican Council, *Lumen Gentium* 1 (1964).

20. Cf. Second Vatican Council, *Ad Gentes* 2 (1965).

21. Cf. *Lumen Gentium* 32; *Ad Gentes* 35.

22. Knights and Murray, *Evangelisation in England and Wales*, p.58.

23. Karl Rahner, *The Practice of Faith: A Handbook of Contemporary Spirituality* (New York: Crossroad, 1983), 22.

rience is simply the natural experience of the transcendent made thematic.[24] It is a basic or root experience shared by all humans of self-transcendence that is exemplified in every act of knowing, found in the contemplation of what is beautiful and good. This experience points beyond the horizon of our own limited vision.[25] The spiritual is not purely private or personal but is a constitutive dimension of human nature and experience. For many people with a spiritual awareness, this experience translates into an attempt to integrate one's life in terms of self-transcendence to the highest values perceived and pursued.[26] For the Christian the mystical is experienced as God's self-communication, and so concurs with the biblical experience of faith in its most foundational moment. Whichever form the transcendental experience takes it is not elitist, but accessible to all. The Belgian scholar Dupré rightly points out that the Christian faith is more than the individual's subjective experience of "profound insights and wholesome feelings. It requires an active response, a commitment of the whole person."[27] It is this experience, which belongs to the essence of religion, that can be a starting point for faith for many of our contemporaries who seek the spiritual life, and the Christian community draws on its riches as it offers an opportunity to accept faith explicitly to those who seek God and wish to commit themselves to the Gospel as a way of life.

Christianity proposes itself to the fragmented culture of the present moment, where "we live on bits of meaning and lack the overall vision that holds them together in a whole"[28] as the way for reading life and as a language that gives coherency to our experiences. In this way the world, neighbor, and self are seen from a different perspective, as the relationship of God and the believer is the underlying reality that defines and structures other relationships in life.[29] In this sense the parish is challenged to be a place for meeting God, finding meaning, and giving structure to the journey through life.

24. Rahner and Herbert Vorgrimler, *Concise Theological Dictionary* (London: Burns and Oates, 1983), 325.
25. Cf. Rahner: *Foundations of Christian Faith* (New York: Crossroad, 1978), 44–89.
26. Cf. Michael Downey, *Understanding Christian Spirituality* (New York: Paulist Press, 1997), 14–15.
27. Donald Ottenhoff, "Seeking Christian Interiority: An Interview with Louis Dupré," *The Christian Century* (July 1997): 654–60, available online at http://www.religion-online.org/showarticle.asp?title=214 (accessed August 25, 2007).
28. Ottenhoff, "Seeking Christian Interiority."
29. Cf. Col 2:6.

The Parish as Sanctuary

Whatever pastoral structures the future has in store must support the community that has already gathered and help it keep an open door to our contemporaries who seek an encounter with God and the personal commitment that faith requires. As we look for an image or model that will help us organize and animate this kind of parish life, we turn to Rahner again.

In the 1950s Rahner wrote about the nature of the territorial parish. He concluded that, although it exists as an extension of the diocese, which is of divine right, the parish is a human institution in origin. He emphasized that pastoral care has to be given to people where they are, even when these situations do not overlap with the geographical boundaries of the parish. Consequently he argued that the territorial parish may not be the only measure for meeting the need for pastoral care, whether this is for practical reasons or in principle.[30] The point Rahner makes is of interest. We have all become more mobile; people commute to work, to shop, to go to school, for leisure, and also for church. The choices we make are less dependent on where we physically live than on where we want to be. Secondly, flexibility in the organization of pastoral structures will help the local church to adapt to new circumstances. Whatever the changes made entail, they have to be a positive step, removing the debris that prevents us from seeing through to what is essential.[31] Faith that, in the words of Rahner, "clings to forms once effective but are now ineffective and meaningless" is faith that "will involve itself in its destruction."[32]

This is not the place for developing detailed theories about the future provision of pastoral care. In the uncertainty of what we will be able to maintain, and what we have to let go, it will have to suffice to say that what continues must center on the two tables that feed us: the word of God and the Eucharist.[33] These two constitutive elements of the church animate and hold together the life of the local community, and from here the commit-

---

30. Cf. Rahner, "Peaceful Reflections on the Parochial Principle," in *Theological Investigations*, vol. 2, *Man in the Church*, 283ff (London: Darton, Longman, and Todd, 1963); also Simone Giusti, *In Parrocchia Ho Incontrato Cristo* [In the Parish I Have Met Christ] (Rome: Edizione Paoline 2004), 113.

31. Cf. Joseph Cardinal Ratzinger, *Called to Communion* (San Francisco: Ignatius Press, 1996), 140ff.

32. Rahner, *Belief Today* (New York: Sheed and Ward, 1976), 52.

33. Cf. *Sacrosanctum Concilium* 48 and 51.

ment to serving neighbor is given life and focus. The parish will continue to be of service to us as an extension of the diocesan bishop's pastoral care for those who belong to the church. At the same time, the local community has to share in the missionary outreach of the church and become *a place that holds the heavens open* to those who seek God.[34] An image or a model of the parish/church that might help us see how to integrate the two aspects of those in communion and the openness towards those who do not belong is the church as sanctuary—a concept that is more than a private holy place, for it is *nothing less than a house of God and gate of Heaven*,[35] an open space where there is freedom to explore, to dialogue, and to have genuine interpersonal encounters. The Archbishop of Canterbury, Dr. Rowan Williams, talked of the the church as a sanctuary, a place where we find God and a place of refuge or asylum.[36] This model of parish life is valuable both for ecclesiological and pastoral reasons.[37]

The firm biblical roots of this image connect it to the sources of faith. It recalls how God was with his people journeying from captivity in Egypt to the promised land. He was present in the tent of meetings and in the Jerusalem temple, a sanctuary for his chosen people and a place of pilgrimage for the nations. The New Testament saw this prophetic vision of opening to the nations as rooted in the life and ministry of Jesus and an inalienable part of the church's mission. The temple of stone became the temple of Jesus' body, torn down and rebuilt in three days, a symbol of his death and resurrection. Since then every generation of Christians has lived with an awareness of its community being a sanctuary, a place where Christ is present as two or three of his followers gather, not closed in on itself, but open to humankind through the working of the Holy Spirit.

We have already seen that the parish is a valued institution. Belonging to it gives the parishioners a sense of corporate identity; it fosters the values and virtues they aspire to and helps them in their personal lives. But how can the notion of sanctuary enhance their sense of mission? The sanctuary as a shelter for those who seek authentic spirituality and a place of atten-

---

34. Cf. Acts 7:56.

35. Cf. Genesis 28:17.

36. From a sermon preached by the Archbishop of Canterbury, Rowan Williams, in St. Patrick's Cathedral, Armagh, Northern Ireland, February 22, 2005, quoted by Timothy Radcliffe, *What Is the Point of Being a Christian?* (London: Burns and Oates, 2005), 179.

37. Cf. the evaluation of the models of the church according to seven criteria in Avery Dulles, *Models of the Church* (New York: Doubleday 1987), 191–92.

tive listening to the word of God can be the meeting ground needed, where those who are distant from the faith connect with its sources. It would give them the opportunity to learn the language of faith and form the personal relationships that make the commitment needed for living the faith possible. The parish, although not the only occasion for this faith sharing, has an important role in making the Gospel as a way of life accessible where people find themselves, where they live. In this sense it is church at grassroots level, a place where Christians relate successfully in an atmosphere of openness to outsiders, be it in terms of ecumenical or interfaith commitment and dialogue or to the wider community.

This sketch of how the sanctuary meets the criteria for being a genuine expression of church may well be good in theory, but what are the concrete stones that would allow us to build it? It is a parallel program to what the abbot of Worth, Christopher Jamieson, has written for the individual seeking genuine spirituality.[38] We have to ask how the pastoral structures of our local communities can become the sanctuary that offers shelter to the parishioners and at the same time keeps the doors open to those outside it. The first step in making this vision reality is a shared sense of mission.[39]

It is a prerequisite that, as the number of clergy diminishes and as opportunities now make it possible for lay people to be actively involved in the mission of the church, new ways for working together in a common mission are needed. In 1995 a report to the Bishops' Conference on Collaborative Ministry presented how this can be done. The parish of the future is not to be a one-man show; it needs to draw on the gifts and talents of the parishioners as well as those of clergy and religious. It involves shared decision making and ultimately the hard questions of "how we organize parish life with smaller and more disparate communities. . . . Increasingly, we will face choices about which activities we want to maintain, develop or discontinue altogether."[40] Although necessity is the mother of all invention, it is preferable that the impetus for working together come from a shared vision and the good will of those committed to furthering the faith. The Sign We Give, in a short summary, lists the steps for introducing collaborative ministry: introduce a pastoral council, a development plan for parish ministries, and

38. Christopher Jamieson, Finding Sanctuary: Monastic Steps for Everyday Life (London: Phoenix, 2006).
39. Cf. Catholic Bishops' Conference of England and Wales, The Sign We Give, 36ff.
40. Ibid., 15.

mechanisms for decision making; experiment, to involve as many as possible in the process of adapting to changed circumstances; look out for opportunities for continuing the development of the parish and ways to celebrate what has been achieved.[41] Collaborative ministry is at the end of the day a radical change in the way we work. It is not simply demarcation and differentiation of roles and areas of competence among those involved in pastoral work, but a change of vision, whereby what is shared and common is put to the forefront.[42] At its heart is something more than just a response to the shortage of priests—namely the shared priesthood of all the baptized.

Good collaboration depends not only on people's usefulness. The elderly and the housebound, the disabled and those whose many commitments leave them with little time for direct involvement can all be included through their prayer and ideas, the challenges they pose, and the encouragement they offer. It is enhanced and promoted through thanks and affirmation, and is focused through celebration of what is achieved. This is, of course, not a simple self-gratulatory gesture, but the fruit of having evaluated and reflected on what has been done. Just as the planning and implementation of pastoral strategies should be an open process, so too should be the assessment of their results. It is this openness that keeps the sense of shared vision alive and engenders a sense of positive ownership to all who contribute to the life of the sanctuary.

Animating the Life of the Sanctuary by Return to the Sources of Faith

For the parish to work as a sanctuary it has to focus on the dimensions of its life: care for those already committed and active, keeping an open door to the seeker, and serving the wider community—in other words, fostering prayer and liturgy, formation, and service.

Welcome

As the doors to the sanctuary are opened, the community has to be aware of the need to be both welcoming and respectful of those who enter. Some come needing to share, others want, with a degree of anonymity, to simply

---

41. Ibid., 46.
42. Cf. Medard Kehl, *Die Kirche: Eine katholische Ekklesiologie* [The Church: A Catholic Ecclesiology] (Würzburg: Echter Verlag, 1993), 445ff.

be or explore. One of the weaknesses often referred to by newcomers and parishioners is that they do not feel welcome. At times this is not simply a feeling, but verifiable by concrete things that were expressed in the reception they found. A concern is that a significant number of those who join our church do not find a permanent home in it. It leads us "to ask ourselves the uncomfortable questions about how we welcome people and how we invite people to be involved in our parishes—especially when it concerns those we meet on the threshold."[43] A key to improving how we receive newcomers, and support those involved, is to listen to their stories and experience, the concerns of those involved in pastoral work, and maintaining an open space where respectful sharing can take place.

Liturgy

The sanctuary has at its heart the celebration of the Eucharist and other liturgy built around the word of God. In these celebrations there is scope for directly communicating in word, music, silence, and gestures the content of faith. How we handle words, people, objects, and situations shows what we actually believe. It is not just a rite or ritual that is offered, for the liturgy "contains much instruction for the faithful," both in the word of God and in the music, prayers, and gestures of liturgy.[44] This is expressed again in the purpose of the sacraments, which "because they are signs they also instruct."[45] It is in the celebration of the Eucharist that these elements come together in a preeminent way and the whole celebration is a communicative act that constitutes the community through the reenactment of the redemptive mystery of Christ.[46]

The liturgy of the word and the associated ministries are a direct opportunity for explicit proclamation. But this ministry is not just about words of comfort. The church as it shares the word of God cannot omit what challenges, calls for a change of heart and conversion. Placing the Gospel at the center means that the person seeking a firsthand experience of God has to be given the chance to hear the Gospel message in its entirety. The church can help them understand what the Old and New Testament say about God,

43. Susan Kowal, "After That First Elation," *The Tablet* (July 21, 2007).
44. *Sacrosanctum Concilium* 33; cf. also 59.
45. Ibid., 33.
46. Cf. Peter Hünermann, *Ekklesiologie im Präsens, Perspektiven* [Ecclesiology in the Present, Prospects] (Münster: Aschendorff, 1995), 236ff.

who has a life of his own and does not meet all our wishes or preconceptions. Here the homily can be of help as it explains the readings and brings them into contact with the lives of the community, opens up ways of understanding, and actualizes the message. But even more important are people proven in their ability to accompany those who want to approach God and the life he gives.[47]

Recognizing the importance of scripture study does not mean that the most fruitful use of the Bible is in the classroom. The need to open the Bible to all as a form of prayer requires nonexpert- and nonspecialist-led initiatives such as Gospel sharing, lectio divina, and other forms of engaging prayerfully with the scriptures. At the heart of the sanctuary is the word of God; not just as an object for study, but through the community engaged in prayer, it becomes a force of life. For when we

have no more religious words of our own, the ones on which our faith rests remain with us. No advanced Biblical criticism is needed to let these words speak and to give voice to our own feelings of joy or sadness or even despair. They translate for us what otherwise might remain unexpressed or constricted within the all too narrow limits of private needs and feelings.[48]

Scripture, therefore, holds a central place as the community returns to the sources of faith. The words of scripture are the primary source of religious language and imagery that form the basis of the narrative whereby the natural experience of God is articulated.

In the time poverty of many people, a careful celebration of the Eucharist and other liturgies can bring together the worship of God, a deepening of faith, and a communication of its content. In this way they help the faithful to make a connection between faith and their daily lives. In accompanying people on their sacramental journey there are numerous opportunities where the liturgy helps make the content of faith relevant. Among them is the chance to actively involve parents in planning, delivering, and celebrating the various stages of the First Holy Communion preparation. Their involvement shows their wider family and friends that they are participating in the faith journey of their children and their immediate family. Those preparing for marriage and baptism should be made aware of the life of the church

47. Cf. Paul M Zulehner, *Aufbrechen oder Untergehen: So geht Kirchenentwicklung* [To Take Off or Go Under: How the Church Evolves] (Ostfilderns: Schwabenverlag 2003), 46.

48. Ottenhoff, "Seeking Christian Interiority."

and be actively invited to come along and see for themselves. Confirmation candidates need to link their instruction to Christianity as a way of life and as a call to serve neighbor. For many young people this is the missing link: what they learn about the faith and where and how it is put into practice. Finally, in the Rite of Christian Initiation for Adults (RCIA) program, the candidates must, as ordinary participants, share in the life of the community, be it at prayer, at social occasions, or at the service of neighbor. In all of these programs the Sunday Eucharist should be emphasized, not as an optional activity, but as the center of the life of the community to which those preparing for the sacraments, at least implicitly, say they want to belong.

Formation

Formation is necessary for the continuation of many church-based activities and ministries. This need is felt both by laity and clergy who regret that they have not received adequate training for the various ministries they presently exercise. The need for formation is felt especially acutely in youth work, which, together with other outreach, is the most challenging aspect of parish work.[49] A few other needed areas of training and support for ministry are spiritual guidance, children's and adult catechesis, and liturgy, and more can be found. The emphasis is not just on training a few select people for ministry, but on serving the whole community. Christianity is not a program, but a way of life that needs to be nurtured and reflected on.

It is precisely here that the weakness of catechetical programs is seen. They are perceived by many purely as a means to receiving a sacrament or a stage in the initiation into the church. In dealing with the persons wanting to join such a program, we often concentrate on the requirement for obtaining what is the goal of the particular program. In fact, the language used emphasizes it as the goal. In this sense we end up with a product-oriented dialogue, and once the product is received, once the end is achieved, there is no need for participation in the life of the church. Our choice of words should reflect the long-term aim of all catechetical preparation: the life of full participation in the church. As we respect people and their freedom to choose, we also have the obligation of making the full offer of the Christian way of life as lived in our Catholic tradition.

The RCIA and the welcoming of those who return to the practice of faith

---

49. Cf. Knights and Murray, *Evangelisation in England and Wales*, 141.

are two privileged ministries where the renewal from the sources of faith is seen in a particularly relevant way. For many people who return to or join the RCIA, faith is not a mere social convention, a comforting relic from the past, but the center from where they live their lives. Both groups show the wider parish our constant need for conversion and the importance of deepening one's personal faith by personal prayer, celebration of the sacraments, and listening to the word of God. Listening to their stories is a way to find out how those who are distant come to faith and make a commitment to a life in the church.

Service

The church's social doctrine and commitment to justice and peace are not optional extras to the life of a parish. The involvement in serving neighbor, both in the local community and further afield, is a tangible and strong sign of what we believe in. It is highly desirable for projects to be identified that enable as many people as possible to be involved. One can aim for a simple and practical outreach to local people in need and/or an overseas project that is well explained so that the purpose of the action is understood and supported. In this sense a project involving homeless people, the mentally ill, long-term residents in institutions, prisoners, and people in need in other parts of the world can bring about an awareness of belonging to the parish and foster links with the wider community. This work is not done for promoting the church or raising its status. It is an expression of what we believe and should flow naturally from the commitment to God. By serving neighbor the sanctuary is prevented from being self-serving and introverted, inasmuch as it helps the parishioners to *be doers of the word, and not hearers only.*[50]

Conclusion

Communicating the faith in the parish is challenged by the changes that have taken place in British society during the last forty to fifty years. The underlying human experience of the transcendent is a constitutive element of human nature, and people continue to have an experience of God even when the previous underpinning by cultural convention and social institutions ends. This situation is verified, both outside and within the Christian

50. James 1:22.

church, as people are drawn to spirituality and hunger for this experience. In this climate it is important to offer to those who seek a genuine encounter with God the possibility to explore and experience in freedom.

The parish shares in this mission of reaching out to those who have not been evangelized, but its members find they are ill-equipped for this task. At the same time, the territorial parish, as the form for pastoral care, is becoming an institution that cannot be maintained as personnel, resources, and active parishioners become scarce. To meet the present situation, a model of parish ministry is suggested—that of a sanctuary. This model/image offers a context for making an experience of God, the language to express it, and the community needed to sustain a commitment to the Gospel as a way of life. As the local church is restructured it would offer a center of life with fluid boundaries, thus making the riches of the church's patrimony available to those who are interested, be they curious or committed.

5 Sacramental Preparation

Uneasy Partnership

Peter McGrail

Most education goes on quietly and out of the general gaze; while its contours may be fiercely disputed among practitioners, for the main part it occupies a relatively low profile in public discourse at the local level. However, within the Roman Catholic (henceforth, "Catholic") community, there is one dimension of specifically religious education that of its nature annually breaks onto the highly public liturgical stage and has been and continues to be a source of concern, debate, and, at the local level, even of conflict. This dimension is the preparation of children for the sacraments—specifically first confession, First Communion, and confirmation.

While a considerable amount has been written on catechetical theory, and a good many catechetical resources have been produced, there has been relatively little detailed work done on how such catechetical sacramental material plays out in the real world. To fully engage with these realities an ethnographic approach is required. Perhaps surprisingly, contemporary ethnography into the preparation for and celebration of school-age sacraments has been limited. With regard to the major ritual enacted during the primary-school stage, First Communion, only two published full-scale studies are currently available—those of Susan Ridgely-Bales in the United States[1] and my own work from England.[2] There are a few published article-length ethnographic accounts of First Communion[3] and a similarly small number of unpublished Ph.D. theses.[4] This gap is surprising, given the raised profile that the event enjoys. Therefore, while this chapter focuses on my own fieldwork in England and Wales, it is offered as a stimulus to questions that generally are still waiting to be answered elsewhere. For example, the educational framework in England and Wales may differ considerably from that experienced by most American children—but one may ask the extent to which the underlying tensions that I have identified can also be found in some American settings.

I begin by mapping the broad historic contours of school-based sacramental preparation in England and Wales. I then examine in closer detail the educational and theological positions that underpinned the formal embracing of a parish—rather than a school-based catechetical process. Finally I shall examine the degree to which that new formal position is actualized on the ground through my own ethnography of the study of the processes for the preparation and celebration of First Communion in four parishes within the Archdiocese of Liverpool, England.[5]

Twentieth-Century Background

To foreign educationalists visiting England and Wales, the extensive provision at all levels of Catholic schools that attract government funding is remarkable. This network of schools has its roots in the instinctive desire of the nineteenth-century Catholic community for a separate system of Cath-

1. Susan Ridgely Bales, *When I Was a Child: Childrens' Perceptions of First Communion* (Chapel Hill: University of North Carolina Press, 2005).

2. Peter McGrail, *First Communion: Ritual, Church and Popular Religious Identity* (Aldershot, UK: Ashgate, 2007).

3. For example, Michael J. McCallion, David R. Maines, and Steven W. Wolfel, "Policy as Practice: First Holy Communion in a Contested Situation," *Journal of Contemporary Ethnography* 25, no. 3 (1963): 300–26; Anne Lodge, "First Communion in Carnduffy: A Religious and Secular Rite of Passage," *Irish Educational Studies* 18 (Spring 1999): 210–20.

4. E.g., Carlos Alberto Tozzi, *Parent and Family Religious Education: A Case Study Based on an Ecological Theory of Human Development* (Ph.D. diss., Fordham University, 1994); Catherine E. Williamson, "Passing on the Faith: The Importance of Parish-Based Catechesis" (Ph.D. diss., University of Brighton, England, 1999).

5. McGrail, *First Communion*, 87–167.

olic schools to safeguard the integrity of that faith community and to prevent "leakage" in the face of a frequently hostile sectarian society. Within that perspective, schools functioned not only as educational, but also as catechetical, centers, and preparation for the reception of the sacraments traditionally took place within the religious education class. Thus, the Graduated Instruction for Holy Communion approved by the English and Welsh bishops in 1911, in the wake of the 1910 decree *Quam Singulari* on early First Communion, was incorporated into diocesan school syllabuses of religious instruction.[6] The trend continued across the century: the 1943 Syllabus of Religious Instruction authorized for schools in the Archdiocese of Liverpool offers a very detailed list of the material that teachers were expected to deliver to their pupils ahead of first confession and Communion.[7] Well over a century of familiarity with Catholic parish schools instilled into the English and Welsh Catholic consciousness an expectation that the school classroom was the default location of sacramental formation. As a consequence, English and Welsh parishes did not for many years perceive a need to develop a parish-based catechetical framework.

However, in the final quarter of the twentieth century, that comfortable preconception began to be seriously challenged. Increasing pressures on time and energy within schools to deliver the National Curriculum, established in the late 1980s and buttressed by the apparatus of a far-reaching and stringent national system of assessment of pupils and inspection of schools, have squeezed the time available to teachers to perform the detailed preparation once given. More significantly, there has been a reorientation in formal Catholic thinking in the wake of catechetical developments since the Second World War, and especially the liturgical revision and explosion of catechetical material after the Second Vatican Council. This reorientation has led to a reassessment of the relative roles of parish and school in the sacramental preparatory process.

The 1980s saw the importation of two catechetical schemes that continue to have a lasting effect on at least the formal expectations for sacramental preparation in England and Wales. The first was Wim Saris' *Together We Communicate*, which rooted the experience of sacramental preparation with-

6. For example, Archdiocese of Liverpool, *Syllabuses of Religious Instruction* (Liverpool: Rockliff Brothers, 1915), 10–11.

7. Archdiocese of Liverpool, *Syllabus of Religious Instruction for Schools* (Liverpool: Rockliff Brothers, 1943), 4–5.

in the family.[8] The second was Christiane Brusselmans' *We Celebrate the Eucharist*, which was taken up in many parishes.[9] At the heart of Brusselmans' approach was an attempt to translate into a child's experience the previously somewhat abstract notion that the approach to First Communion was a deepening of Christian initiation. This she did by mapping First Communion catechesis onto the structure of adult initiation envisaged by the *Rite of Christian Initiation of Adults*. What rendered her approach appealing to parishes was the wealth of materials produced to support it, and the quality of their production; the "Golden Book" became a mainstay of catechesis in many parishes and schools.[10] The combined impact of these two programs was to introduce to English and Welsh parishes a sense that the preparation for First Communion could encompass a broader process than its traditional classroom setting alone.

The National Project of Catechesis and Religious Education (1985–Present)

The catechetical approach of engagement with the parish and/or family—based in such schemes as those devised by Wim Saris or Christiane Brusselmans—took place in a relatively uncoordinated manner, albeit frequently with the encouragement and support of diocesan religious education departments. A development of the mid-1980s saw the approach being endorsed nationally. This was the launch of a National Project for Catechesis under the aegis of the formal structures of the Catholic Bishops' Conference of England and Wales. The educational rationale for future catechetical programs was mapped out in the first publication issued under the Project, *Our Faith Story: Its Telling and Its Sharing*, by A. Patrick Purnell, then national advisor for religious education.[11] This book established as official policy the notion that religious education was to be approached within the framework of a partnership between a child's family, the parish community, and the Catholic school. In one sense this was nothing new—*Quam Singulari* in 1911 had envisaged an active role for a child's parents in the discernment of

8. Wim Saris, *Together We Communicate* (London: Collins, 1982).

9. Christiane Brusselmans and Brian Haggerty, *We Celebrate the Eucharist* (Morristown, N.J.: Silver Burdett, 1986).

10. For an analysis of this program in action in one English diocese, see Williamson, "Passing on the Faith."

11. A. Patrick Purnell, *Our Faith Story: Its Telling and Its Sharing* (London: Collins, 1985).

the child's readiness for the reception of First Communion. However, Purnell's work reflected a major shift in the perceived balance among the three parties involved, presupposing a radical reduction in the role played by the Catholic school—as is best illustrated by the relatively brief discussion of sacramental preparation in Our Faith Story.

Purnell acknowledges the influence of post-war catechetical developments, and the Brusselmans scheme in particular, in pressing the case for the lead in sacramental preparation to be taken by the worshipping community rather than the parish school:

More and more in recent years we have come to conclude that preparation for first sacraments is best done in a parish setting. In this setting parents come forward freely to present their children and offer themselves to take part in their preparation. The preparation of its nature is essentially catechesis and therefore belongs to the community of believers.[12]

However, the introduction of a clear distinction between the parish school as educational establishment and the parish as catechizing community raises the question of exactly how the Catholic school was now to be understood in its relationship to the parish. For over a century the Catholic school had been perceived as an extension of the parish as faith community—and successive engagement with government inspection and funding regimes over that century had been carried out in a way that safeguarded the distinctive nature of the Catholic school system. Purnell acknowledged that his pressing for a parish-based approach was experienced by some teachers as a "threat" to their traditional role, but stressed that a distinction needed to be drawn between liturgico-spiritual preparation and a broader education in the underlying human religio-anthropological phenomena that underpinned the sacramental system. It was education in this broader field that he understood as complementing parish catechesis, and that was for him the proper responsibility of the Catholic school:

There is a whole world surrounding the sacraments and their reception to which children should be introduced. They need to learn, not only why there are sacraments and why people think they are important, but also about equivalent celebrations in other religions and in the lives of people who have no specific link with any religion.[13]

12. Ibid., 141–42.   13. Ibid., 142

Underpinning Purnell's approach is a recognition that the average year's cohort in a Catholic school was made up of children from both practicing and
nonpracticing families; he was concerned to respect the integrity of both.
Particularly with regard to the latter group, he argued that the admission
to the sacraments of a child whose faith experience was not centered on the
worshipping community might have a deleterious effect:

In fact, the very sincere efforts of teachers and priest to make it possible for [a
child] to go to the sacrament may actually be harmful: it may damage his faith, a
faith which may not have a religious expression such as is enjoyed by his teachers
but is as real and deep as theirs; this faith has, at its heart, his parents.[14]

Purnell's approach is underpinned in a theology of sacraments that has become dominant within English catechetical circles, but that does raise a serious theological issue. Effectively, he absolutizes the well-established understanding that God's action is not limited to the sacraments.[15] However,
instead of being presented as the exception to the normal understanding
that the sacraments are occasions of God's action, this principle now becomes the interpretive key to understanding the sacraments themselves as
symbolic expressions of divine action that has already taken place in the life
of the individual. Thus,

Sacraments [. . .] presuppose and celebrate God at work in the whole of creation,
in every human being; wherever there is forgiveness, love, healing, efforts at building a real community, commitment and dedication, sharing, attempts at justice,
there is God. The sacraments celebrate these activities, purify our understanding
of them in the light of the Gospel and Christ's sacrifice, and empower us to act as
Christ acted. Sacraments do not bring God into the world; God is here at work in
everybody.[16]

Progressing on the basis of this principle, Purnell comes close to equat-
ing the extra-sacramental experience of a nonpracticing child with that of
its communicating peer. This, for him, justifies the severing of the gener-

14. Ibid., 141.
15. For example, Thomas Aquinas expressed this understanding in the following terms,
"God did not cause his power to be restricted to the sacraments in such a way that he could
not bestow the effect of the sacraments without the sacraments themselves." David Bourke
(trans.) St. Thomas Aquinas. Summa Theologiae, volume 56, The Sacraments (3a.60-5) (London:
Eyre and Spottiswoode and New York: McGraw-Hill Book Company, 1975), Part 3a, question
64, article 7, p. 125. See also 3a. 64, 3; 3a 66, 6; 3a. 68, 2.
16. Purnell, Our Faith Story, 139–40.

al link between classroom and sacramental cohorts. Purnell's approach undoubtedly represents a sincere attempt to formulate a theological position that engages with the realities of the variety of faith experience and religious practice contained within the classroom. However, while he admirably expresses the freedom and range of divine action, the resulting formulation barely engages with the traditional understanding of the internal dynamics of the sacraments—that is, with the formal ecclesiological discourse of sacramental grace.

Purnell's notion of the home-school-parish partnership was embedded in subsequent publications issued by the Bishops' Conference under the National Project—either in documentation providing broad outlines[17] or in resources for developing the parish catechetical teams that the partnership required.[18] Most significantly, it found its most widespread expression in the programs for religious education developed for use in Catholic schools.

The greatest impact on the celebration of first confession and Communion was felt with the primary scheme, *Here I Am*.[19] This highly developed and well-resourced program brings together Purnell's approach to religious education in schools and the graduated approach to religious education outlined in *Quam Singulari*. The program develops a limited number of themes, subdivided into topics, across all the primary years. It therefore engages with the same key issues at five different levels, permitting the child to follow a progressive cyclical path, with each year's material building upon what has gone before and preparing the ground for what will follow. At each level emphasis is placed on engagement with a child's own experience, the Christian tradition and cross-cultural/multifaith links. Across the child's primary school career the sacraments are explored under a number of topics selected by the school—thus, for example, the Eucharist is considered through engagement with the topics of communion, meals, memories, and thanksgiving. What is not envisaged is that this educational process should provide a complete, self-contained package for the preparation of any of the

---

17. James Gallagher and Bishops' Conference of England and Wales, *Living and Sharing Our Faith: A National Project of Catechesis and Religious Education—Guidelines* (London: Harper Collins, 1986).

18. Lynn Walker, *All Is Gift: Guidelines for Parish Catechists—Working with Children* (London: Collins, 1987); Paddy Rylands, *Sharing the Gift: Preparing to Celebrate the Sacraments with Families in the Parish* (London: Collins, 1989).

19. Anne Byrne and Chris Malone, *Here I Am: A Religious Education Programme for Primary Schools* (London: HarperCollins, 1992, 2000).

children for actual reception of the sacraments; that responsibility is understood as sitting with the other two members of the tripartite partnership—namely, families and parish working together.

The Ethnography of First Communion

The question remains, however, as to whether or not the home-school-parish partnership really operates in practice. As this was one of the questions that motivated my own ethnographic research, it is to my findings that I now turn. The locations for my research were selected on the grounds of the different approaches to the preparation of children to the event that were adopted in them. In the first, the school retained its traditional dominant position with regard to both preparation and celebration; the use of *Here I Am* was effectively suspended during the weeks leading up to First Communion celebration, to be replaced by a catechetical resource that breathed a rather different educational air. In the second parish, a more collaborative approach had been attempted, with a higher degree of parish involvement being aimed at.

Religious sisters had been appointed as catechetical directors in the third and fourth parishes, and each had attempted to withdraw the responsibility for sacramental preparation from the school. In both instances the parish Sunday Mass became the setting for catechesis, with attendance at Mass during the period of preparation obligatory for both children and parents. There was a radical difference, however, in the overall approach taken by the two sisters. One was content to maintain the underlying approach to the event found elsewhere in the archdiocese; the other had taken the far more drastic step of incorporating the celebration of confirmation into the process, administering it a few weeks before the First Communion day itself. As we shall see, this appeal to the "traditional order" of the sacraments has a growing attraction in some parts of the church.

In none of the parishes studied was the result unproblematic. The school-based approach of the first setting was challenged by the deanery catechetical coordinator (who was the religious sister of the third subject parish). She wished to extend her transfer of the focus of preparation from the classroom to the Sunday Eucharist across the deanery as a whole. In the second parish, problems were encountered particularly at the level of the First Communion event itself, with a clash of interests on two fronts—between the parents and the priest over the mode of celebration, and then between the priest and parishioners. The fourth setting was the most complex, and from an ethnographic perspective the most challenging. I progressively found that, in a situation of strained relationships between the parish catechetical team and the diocesan authorities, my very presence there was being used by the parish as justification for its shift in sacramental policy. I will discuss my findings from each of these settings in turn, beginning with the first, as it not only most closely approximates the traditional role played by the parish school, but also because it illustrates most clearly a dissonance between formal national policy and practice on the ground.

Preparation Carried Out by the Parish School

All the settings studied were located in broadly working-class areas of the archdiocese. This first was a long-established parish and school[20] in the inner city of Liverpool, in an area marked by high levels of unemployment. All responsibility for the preparation of the children for First confession and Communion lay with the school staff. Consequently, contrary to Purnell's expectation that the home-school-parish partnership would result in a discernment process wherein the parish and family rather than the school would bear responsibility for determining readiness for admission to the sacraments, I found that the chief power broker in the lead-up to the admission to these sacraments was the school's head teacher. This was a local woman who enjoyed considerable standing in the community and who described her role in the preparation process as being an intermediary between the parents and the priest in gaining access for the children to the sacraments. Speaking of parents who had not attended church for a long time and who consequently were unsure about the reception they might receive from the priest—especially in the light of the reported policy of other clergy in the district—she said:

They need to come to you first to see whether he was going to rant and rave. So they come to me and say, "Can I go to Communion when my child makes its first communion, and theses are my circumstances." Because they think you're church and they think you're holy, before they can get to the priest—because they hear horror stories.

20. The parish was founded in 1865, and its current church was built in 1878.

In other words, for the parents of the children in her school the only real point of contact with the parish as institution lay with the head teacher; there was no preexistent relationship with the priest that could possibly function as the framework within which the process of discernment envisaged by both Purnell and formal Catholic teaching could take place to any meaningful degree. This distance between priest and families was compounded by broader sociological factors that were clearly expressed in the priest's own analysis of the perception that families in the school would have of him in his formal capacity: a mistrust on their part of institutional authority of any kind whatsoever. As a result, his declared pastoral aim was to make the First Communion process as "non-threatening as possible," and consequently all Catholic children in the school cohort of seven- to eight-year-olds were admitted to First Communion without any formal discernment process.

The priest and head teacher did organize a series of four preparatory meetings for the children's parents, but these took place on the school premises and were chiefly led by the head teacher. This reinforced a sense that the school functioned as the primary agent in the event—underscored by the fact that the children's preparation was located entirely during their regular religious education classes led by the classroom teacher.

These classes, too, departed radically from the educational role of the school envisaged by Purnell. While the school generally followed *Here I Am* for its religious education classes, that program was dropped during the six weeks prior to First Communion, and an American resource designed for parish catechesis rather than for school use was followed[21] during the half-term leading up to First Communion. This program did not share the educational principles of *Here I Am*, and it cut across the graduated approach embodied in the National Project. Consequently, the teacher found that he was attempting to engage the children with concepts to which they had not been previously exposed and which therefore lay beyond their capacity for understanding—and indeed his own capacity for delivery. The problems that this engendered became apparent in an exchange I observed as he attempted to negotiate the subject of the Real Presence, which was far more explicitly presented in Leichner than anything the children had previously encountered:

21. Jeannine Timko Leichner, *Called to His Supper: A Preparation for First Holy Communion* (Huntington, Ind.: Our Sunday Visitor, 1992).

Now, I said that the wine is just normal wine. Well this here, this bread, this normal, it's just a normal host at the moment. This has not been blessed yet, so would this be the body of Jesus at the moment?

[Several children:] No.

No, it wouldn't. So it hasn't been blessed yet. It's just a normal host. So what would happen in Mass is the Father, the priest would bless the bread, and once the bread has been blessed then it becomes the body of Jesus and, of course, is shared out and we receive the body of Jesus. Same again, would this taste any different? Before it's been blessed and after it's been blessed?

[Several together:] No.

No, it wouldn't. But, is it different?

[Several:] Yes.

It is, isn't it. Yes. And remember we said, how's it different? Well, it's up to you really—it's here and here: in your head and in your heart, and what you believe in. And the priest will have said a special blessing to change it from just being a normal host into the body of Jesus. Now, it's, erm, no—I won't use that phrase.

The "phrase" he narrowly avoided using, he told me later, was, "It's magic." The movement outside the familiar educational framework to which children and teacher alike were accustomed thus resulted in confusion for both.

This encounter raises a broader question that extends beyond the classroom. For those locations in which a parish catechetical process has been developed, the National Project framework envisages a complementarity between the two settings of classroom and catechetical session. If instead there is dissonance between the school curriculum and the material upon which parish catechesis is based, then a seamless interface between the two will not be achievable, resulting in misunderstanding.

Parish-led Catechesis of Parents: The "A-Team"

I found in the second fieldwork site a development on the approach taken in the first. Here, too, the catechesis of children took place in the parish school—with the key distinction that the classroom sessions did not depart from Here I Am. Instead, the children prepared for First Communion by following the program topics selected for the period (special people, memories, energy, and freedom and responsibility), highlighting links to the Eucharist through focused worksheets. What was particularly interesting in this parish, however, was the involvement of a group of parents in hosting three preparatory meetings with parents. In the first parish the head teacher had performed a key intermediary role; here it was this group of women. They called themselves "The A-Team" after a TV series that had featured a band of desperados. All were mothers of young children, and most stood in an ambiguous relationship with the church and its teachings—not least with regard to marriage and regular Mass attendance. They certainly did not conform to the type of catechist required by formal church teaching—one with "a deep faith, a clear Christian and ecclesial identity."[22] On the other hand, they were representative of the body of parents with whom they were to engage.

From an educational perspective, the significance of the "A-Team" lies in the attempt to use them to mediate to parents the significance of the *Here I Am* topics that the children were studying at school. The underlying rationale was to equip families to continue at home a discussion of the issues that had been raised in the religious education class so that parents could help their children to relate those issues to the concrete events and circumstances of their lives. The idea of itself was sound, but in practice there was a dissonance between the realities of the parents' lives and the range of meanings that the priest expected the *Here I Am* themes to hold for them. This can be illustrated by two examples, the first drawn from the preparatory meetings that the priest held with the "A-Team," the second from one of the parents' sessions.

It was the "A-Team" who identified the dissonance. As they struggled to prepare the parents' sessions, one related an episode from an earlier year, when the theme under discussion had been meals. Speaking of the parents' session, she said:

We were talking about meals, like as a celebration—'cos if you're working all day and your husband works, that's when you sit and talk, isn't it, about how the kids' day's gone and what your husband's done at work, and what you've been doing yourself. We were with this group, and some of them—you couldn't, well, I couldn't get any response. And this woman went, "I don't sit at the friggin' table—have you seen the way he eats? He slobbers and everything!"

Quite simply, the expectation that a parallel could be drawn between the everyday experience of a family eating together and the Eucharist was fruitless in a setting in which many families did not own a dining table, let alone

22. *General Directory for Catechesis* (London: Catholic Truth Society, 1997), 237.

eat together on a regular basis. However, a further underlying presupposition of this discussion topic, namely that the first communicants were being raised in regular family settings, was further undermined in the subsequent parents' session on freedom and responsibility. In response to the priest's questioning, the majority of mothers present replied that the single factor that would most limit their personal freedom would be marriage to their present partners. The priest's attempts to stress the positive aspects of companionship and security were fatally undermined when he turned to one of the "A-Team" members for support, only to be told, "I've never been married. I don't want to be married. I don't want to lose my identity. I don't want to take his name—that gives him something of me." Such dissonances suggest that genuine and radically embedded enculturation may still be some ways away.

Catechesis in a Church Setting

At first glance the processes of sacramental preparation attempted in the final two parishes most closely approximated Purnell's vision for a parish-based catechesis. However, I believe that the factors that led to the transfer of sacramental preparation from the classroom were rather more complex than those envisaged by the authors of the National Project. This is most clearly evidenced by the fact that in neither location was there evidence of an ongoing and personal discernment process of either the preparedness of the child or indeed of the appropriateness of its admission to the sacraments. Rather, two sets of concerns appeared to feed into the procedure. The first, which was common to both, was to "normalize" the child's experience of First Communion by imposing a pattern of weekly Mass attendance ahead of the celebration—with the related hope that this would induce a lifelong habit. However, the experience in both parishes was that while parents were (albeit grudgingly) willing to attend Mass for several months in order to secure their child's participation in the First Communion event, once this goal had been achieved they rarely returned again. Indeed, one of the sisters admitted that the parents quite openly declared this to her early in the preparation process:

[One of the mothers said] "after the sixth of May we don't have to bother." So I looked, and she saw my face and said, "Oh, I'm just being honest." She will not be there—and she made it very clear—after he's made his communion. And there were some mums who looked askance, but I had the feeling they looked askance because this woman was honest, not the fact that she wouldn't be there. She was expressing in all honesty, "I'm only here for the beer," sort of thing. And I think that would be general.

A second factor played into the decision of the fourth parish to incorporate the celebration of confirmation into the celebration of First Communion. A number of dioceses across the English-speaking world have taken this step, justified as a restoration of the "traditional" order of the sacraments of Christian initiation.[23] In the context of England and Wales, the sole case is the diocese of Salford, centered in the city of Manchester and immediately adjacent to the Liverpool archdiocese; significantly, the current archbishop had been responsible as bishop of Salford for its introduction there. While the clergy and catechists in this fourth parish used the language of initiation to justify their adoption of the restored order, it was difficult to avoid the impression that a different anxiety was also at play—namely a concern that while the celebration of First Communion remained popular and at an age when children were relatively easy to engage with, the same could not be said of confirmation. Incorporating it into the First Communion process, therefore, not only ensured that the children received all the sacraments of initiation, but also relieved parish catechists from what many experienced as the thankless task of catechetical engagement with teenagers.

Conclusions

This last point introduces a critical issue. Despite the endorsement of a partnership approach in the underlying rationale for the National Project, in terms of resources and expenditure that partnership has remained singularly unequal. With the exception of the relatively small number of independent schools, the overwhelming majority of Catholic schools in England and Wales now receive 90 percent of their funding from government; nonetheless, the remaining 10 percent of costs that are met by the Catholic community represents a considerable and costly investment (this figure has gradually risen from 50 percent funding since the Second World War). It has not,

23. U.S. and Canadian dioceses that have set out on this path include Cleveland, Ohio; Fargo, North Dakota; Marquette, Minnesota; Portland, Maine; Saginaw, Michigan; Prince Albert, Saskatchewan; Prince George, British Columbia; and Saskatoon, Saskatchewan. The dioceses of Brisbane and Adelaide have pioneered the approach in Australia, while in Scotland a national consultation led to most of the eight dioceses adopting this revised pattern. In England and Wales, Salford alone has done so.

however, been matched by a corresponding investment in the training and employment of the skilled catechists required if Purnell's vision of parish-based catechesis is to flourish. The result has been one of disillusionment at the parish level—and of the kind of well-meaning but flawed catechetical attempts that my research has highlighted. This funding imbalance may not at all be reflected in many American settings, where the parish may take a more direct role in developing its own catechetical structures and in employing catechetical staff. However, the deeper issue of the relationship between the catechesis offered and the realities of the lives of the families catechized raises questions that surely need to be explored on both sides of the Atlantic.

6   Burning Hearts

Scripture and Adult Faith Formation

Stephen J. McKinney

The disciples said to each other, "Did not our hearts burn within us as he talked to us on the road and explained the scriptures to us?"

Luke 24:32

This chapter will examine how faith is communicated through adult education within the Catholic tradition and, specifically, using a case study, in a scripture study group held in St. Dominic's parish in the Archdiocese of Glasgow, Scotland. This chapter will begin with a brief overview of the approaches to adult faith formation within the Catholic Church in Scotland and, in particular, in the Archdiocese of Glasgow. The origins and history of St. Dominic's scripture study group will be explored in some detail, and there will be a concise personal profile of each of the members of this group. The next four sections, which draw on interviews I conducted with members of the group, will discuss the following: the reasons the members joined the group; the processes or methodology used in the meetings; the progression from group to community; and the impact the group has had on the Christian lives of the members. The concluding section will highlight a number of key points concerning this scripture study group that have emerged throughout the chapter.

Introduction

In recent years the Catholic Church in Scotland has identified a pressing need to continue faith formation beyond Catholic school. This is within the spirit of the "General Directory for Catechesis" (paragraph 29), which calls for the expansion of adult catechesis.[1] After a meeting of the Bishops' Conference on May 9 and 10, 2006, Archbishop Mario Conti of Glasgow and Fr. Paul Conroy, the general secretary of the Bishops' Conference, were asked to establish the Scottish Catholic Forum for Continuing Faith Formation on behalf of the bishops of Scotland. The aim of this national forum was to improve coordination and communication and act as a locus for the sharing of information and for future planning. The forum initially met on September 28, 2006. Representatives from all of the dioceses of Scotland and representatives from a number of major bodies concerned with Catholic education (Scottish Catholic Education Service, University of Glasgow) were invited. The purpose of the forum was ultimately to map out the opportunities available for adult faith formation, identify gaps in the provision, and discuss future possibilities. A small group was asked to undertake a mapping exercise that revealed that a wide variety of local initiatives have been developed within each of the eight Scottish dioceses, and that there are a number of ways of categorizing the adult faith formation that is available. One approach is to examine the range of providers: seminary, diocesan centers, universities, colleges, and parishes. Another is to list the range of methodologies used: lectures, seminars, study groups, peer study, and distance learning. This leads to distinctions that can be made between formal (award-bearing courses leading to some certification or qualification) and more informal types of learning. Further distinctions can be drawn between short-term learning and longer-term learning. This chapter looks at the ways in which faith can be communicated through long-term informal learning and engagement.

1. Congregation for the Clergy, "General Directory for Catechesis," in *An Anthology of Catholic Teaching on Education*, ed. Leonard Franchi, 313 (London: Scepter, 2007).

Adult Education in the Archdiocese of Glasgow

The Archdiocese of Glasgow is the largest diocese in Scotland in terms of estimated Catholic population (208,329 out of an estimated Catholic population in Scotland of 661,849). There are 99 parishes, and the weekly Mass attendance is approximately 52,347.[2] The archdiocese has developed a wide variety of opportunities for adult faith formation. These range from centrally organized major day events such as the archdiocesan congresses on the Eucharist (October 2005), on scripture (October 2006), and the permanent diaconate (2007) and short evening courses to longer-term certificated courses such as the LIMEX courses (with the Loyola Institute for Ministry, New Orleans) and the new catechist course (in conjunction with the University of Glasgow).[3] The Archdiocese of Glasgow offers the LIMEX Certificate in Religious Education or Pastoral Studies and the Masters in Religious Education or Pastoral Studies.[4]

Some of the opportunities are theological and aimed at intellectual development, while others are more directed toward spiritual development. Scotus College, the national seminary, is located within the archdiocese and provides a variety of theological and spiritual courses, including courses for Catholic teachers. There are also local parish initiatives. This chapter will focus on one long-term parish initiative, the scripture study group in St. Dominic's parish in Bishopbriggs.[5] Bishopbriggs is a small town adjacent to North East Glasgow. The first Catholic church to be established was St. Matthew's, which was opened in 1950 and is located in the center of the village. As the village grew rapidly in the 1960s and 1970s, a second Catholic church was needed, and St. Dominic's Church was opened in 1970. There are two large Catholic primary schools, St. Helen's and St. Matthews, and a Catholic secondary, Turnbull High School.

St. Dominic's is an active parish, and by the beginning of the new millennium had developed a strong tradition of devotional and social activities.

2. Archbishops and Bishops of Scotland, *Catholic Directory for Scotland* (Glasgow: Burns Publications, 2007), 570–73.

3. Archdiocese of Glasgow, *Adult Education*, available online at http://www.rcag.org.uk/education_adultintro.htm (accessed January 19, 2009).

4. Loyola Institute for Ministry Extension Program (Loyola University, 2009), available online at http://lim.loyno.edu/extension/prospectus.html (accessed January 19, 2009).

5. St. Dominic's Catholic Church, available online at http://www.st-dominics.org.uk/ (accessed January 19, 2009).

Like many parishes, a great deal of effort and energy was, and is, directed toward the preparation and celebration of the sacrament for the primary school–age children. This is planned and prepared in close conjunction with the local school. The attractive and modern parish hall has been frequently used as a venue for high-school retreats. There was a successful RCIA (Rite of Christian Initiation for Adults) group that still exists, but few other opportunities for adult faith formation outside the liturgical and devotional activities. As a lifelong student, teacher, and lecturer in scripture, I offered to present some form of scripture study for adults in the parish.

St. Dominic's Scripture Study Group

After lengthy discussions in 2001 and 2002 with Fr. Andrew Tolan, the parish priest, we decided to offer a six-week introduction to scripture for the parish. A number of models were considered, including *Contextual Bible Study* and *Lectio Divina*. *Contextual Bible Study*, based on the work of Gerald West in South Africa during the apartheid period, seeks to read the Bible in a "fresh and transformative way," with "marginalized groups and with those who work with the marginalized."[6] Facilitators are trained to be responsible for the running of the sessions "in accordance with the CBS principles and processes."[7] The Contextual Bible study approach, while offering many strengths, was deemed to be too structured and directed for the purposes of this short introduction. Many of the principles of CBS, such as the emergence of a "dynamic dialogue rather than a more passive expert-recipient style of relationship," and the "belief that all participants bring to the group their own special contribution of experience, insight and faith," were to develop in the St. Dominic's group as the group grew and evolved.[8] The practice of *Lectio Divina* is the ancient Christian practice that has been "kept alive by the Christian monastic tradition."[9] This is a process that begins with "reverential listening to the word of God" and leads to the reader finding a word or passage that speaks to him or her in a personal way; he or she ruminates on it and enters into prayer and contemplation. *Lectio Divina*

6. The Scottish Bible Society and the Contextual Bible Study Group, *Conversations: The Companion* (Edinburgh: Scottish Bible Society, 2006), 6.

7. Scottish Bible Society, 25.

8. Scottish Bible Society, 11.

9. Luke Dysinger, "Accepting the Embrace of God: The Ancient Art of Lectio Divina," available online at http://www.valyermo.com/ld-art.html (accessed January 19, 2009).

is described by the "General Directory for Catechesis" (paragraph 71) as an "eminent" form of the study of scripture.[10] It was felt, however, that a basic overview of how scripture had been written and structured and an overview of some of the main themes of the Old and New Testaments would be more appropriate for this short introduction.

The six sessions were planned for October and November 2002 and consisted of three sessions on the Old Testament and three sessions on the New Testament. The sessions were all held on Sunday nights in one of the parish hall meeting rooms between 7:00 P.M. and 8:30 P.M. The first few sessions, led by myself and Fr. Andrew, provided an overview of some of the main themes of the two testaments. After the first few sessions, it was decided to concentrate more on the shared study and reflection on the actual passages of scripture rather than focus too intensely on background information and comments from exegetes (although these were always included in each session to aid the reflection). The sessions proved to be very popular, attracting between fifteen and twenty people each night. At the end of the six-week introduction, a number of the regular participants asked if the group could continue on a weekly basis. It was agreed that the group could continue on Sunday nights during school term time, and that it would focus on a particular book of the Bible, rather than on a selection of biblical readings focused on themes. The book of Exodus was chosen as the first text to introduce the group to the idea of covenant. Since then the group has democratically chosen and studied Samuel, Kings, Mark, Matthew, Luke, Acts, and John. These choices have helped to maintain the attention of the members and sustain the life of the group.[11] During Advent and Lent the group examines the Sunday readings, and other parishioners are invited to join for the duration of the season.

In the last few years the role of the group has developed and diversified. In 2006 (repeated in 2007 and 2008) the group was asked to prepare and present one of the holy hours during the forty hours adoration. These holy hours were very well received and were perceived to be examples of the group providing a service for the spiritual life of the parish. The group was also asked to deliver a workshop at the archdiocesan scripture congress in October 2006. This was well attended and the seminar was featured in

10. Congregation for the Clergy, "General Directory for Catechesis," 341.
11. Frances Krumplemann, "Reading the Bible," in *The Modern Catholic Encyclopedia*, ed. Michael Glazier and Monika K. Hellwig, 717–18 (Dublin: Gill and MacMillan, 1994).

the archdiocesan newspaper, Flourish.[12] The group was asked in December 2007 to organize a scripture-based ecumenical service for the local Christian churches. At least three times a year (Easter, October, and Christmas) the group shares a communal meal, an *agape*, where we all bring food and drinks and share an evening together.

The average attendance is fairly steady at eight people per meeting. Groups never remain static, and the membership of the group has changed over the years. Some of the original members left the group after a number of years. Some members dropped out for a year or two but have returned. Some have joined in the last two years: Caroline, now a student at the University of St. Andrews, joined the group as a fifteen-year-old school girl because her mother, Trudy, spoke so much about the discussions that took place in the group. A number of people from the neighboring parish of St. Matthews had been attending for some time until Monsignor Bradley, the parish priest of St. Matthews, asked if the group could be advertised as a joint venture. One of the newer members is from a parish on the other side of the city. He heard about the group from archdiocesan publicity materials promoting adult faith formation, and has been a regular member for over a year.

One of the fascinating aspects of this history is that it was never intended to be a long-term group. Many of the original members of the group found the shared study of scripture quite challenging and, at times, a little intimidating, and it did take some time (possibly over a period of years) before all of the participants felt confident to speak freely and enter the discussion. The level of engagement with scripture has deepened, and the participants have become much more adept at contextualizing, examining, and interrogating passages of scripture. As the years have passed the role of the leaders has evolved into a facilitating role.

The success of a group such as this depends on the commitment of the participants to attend the sessions, but equally importantly, the willingness and courage to engage and share thoughts, ideas, and reflections. This group is on a shared journey of discovery that deepens their knowledge and understanding of Christian faith and their spirituality. While it would be incorrect to argue that a shared spirituality within the group had developed, it could be stated that all the members of the group have developed a greater understanding of the variety of approaches to spirituality.

12. Vincent Toal, "St. Dominic's Scripture Study Group," Flourish (October 2006).

The Members of the Scripture Study Group

Clearly many of the members have made a very serious time commitment to the group, but, equally clearly, they must feel that they gain something in their faith life from the sessions. At the archdiocesan workshop some of the personal faith reasons for their commitment emerged. In preparation for this written account of our group, I interviewed all of the members of the group, except for Caroline, to further explore these personal faith reasons. I used short, semi-structured interviews and conducted the interviews in October and November 2007. I asked questions to ascertain: why they joined the group in the first place; what motivates them to continue attending the group; what they enjoy in the group study; and, finally, what impact the shared study has had on their faith lives. The results of these discussions will be explored under the following sub-headings: the motivation to join the group; methodology used by the group; progress from group to community; and the impact of the scripture study group on the Christian lives of the members. A brief profile of each of the group members will precede this discussion.

Aileen, raised and educated in Bishopbriggs, is a physiotherapy manager based in Shettleston in Glasgow.

Fr. Andrew has been a priest in the Archdiocese of Glasgow for 51 years. He has been the parish priest of St. Dominic's since September 1995.

Caroline is Trudy's daughter. She is currently studying medicine at the University of St. Andrews.

Graham is a parishioner in Holy Cross parish in Glasgow. He is a day service worker with the Glasgow City Council Social Work department.

James is retired after thirty years as a joiner. He is married with adult children and grandchildren. He is a parishioner in St. Matthew's parish, Bishopbriggs.

John is the chief technician in the Department of Environmental and Evolutionary Biology at the University of Glasgow. He is married with three adult children.

Margaret is retired. She was the deputy head teacher of St. Helen's, Bishopbriggs, for over twenty-four years. She is married with one daughter.

Mary is currently a lecturer in the Department of Childhood and Primary Studies at the University of Strathclyde. She is married with three adult children.

Stephen is a lecturer in religious education in the Faculty of Education at the University of Glasgow. He is married with two school-age children.

Trudy is a math teacher at the local Catholic secondary, Turnbull High, and is married with two adult children.

The Motivation to Join the Group

From the conversations in the interviews it becomes clear that the scripture study group at St. Dominic's has provided a forum and a focus for people who already had a long-term desire to engage with scripture on a deeper level. John, for example, stated:

I am actually interested in scripture. How could I put it? I am interested in the depth of scripture, what's in the words. I am interested in the interpretation of scripture. I've always been interested in it.

However, they all commented that they had found it difficult reading and studying scripture on their own. Margaret stated:

Well, I had made several attempts to study scripture over the years in my adult life, mostly unsuccessful. I always had an interest and I was always anxious to learn more but private study did not seem to lead far.

James adds that reading scripture on one's own, without any assistance or direction, can be a bewildering experience:

I always just read the Bible and took it on face value. I always wanted to know something more. I would read something and take it as it was. I couldn't figure it out myself or I didn't even have the confidence to figure it out.

Aileen was prompted to join the group in St. Dominic's because she felt that her religious education in school had been inadequate:

Having been in school in the 1970s and early '80s . . . that was the stage when religious education was "God loves you" and nothing else and I knew nothing. I knew more about Muslims and Jews than Catholicism. That was my religious education. I wanted to know more.

Trudy also referred to her experience of religious education at school in the late '60s and early '70s, although for her it was probably more fruitful:

I've always liked discussions about RE and the Bible. When I was at school I was the only person who took RE seriously. . . . It would be me and the teacher talking while the rest were surreptitiously doing their homework.

Fr. Andrew had lived through the major changes in the weight attached to the importance of scripture in the Catholic liturgy in the Vatican II and post-Vatican II eras. He was heavily influenced by the introduction of the three-year cycle of readings in the lectionary:

The introduction to the lectionary was a great influence on me—feeling that this was a powerful source for my own prayer life and development and the church had produced a book of great authority. The church, at worldwide level, was saying that scripture is very important. The general introduction to the lectionary states: love of scriptures is the force that renews the entire people of God. This is very powerful.

The group has also provided a time and space in the week for this type of discussion. James states that this kind of space was absent in his working life:

The group is a good group. Everybody has their own ideas. I am a Catholic and I believe in it. I never studied it much. In the building trade there were Catholics, but they wouldn't really delve into the faith side.

Fr. Andrew, reflecting on the membership of the group, thinks that the scripture group has attracted a certain type of parishioner—the more regular attendee who feels desire for a deeper Christian life:

I think within the community of the parish, those who attend more regularly are gradually more aware of the wide range and wealth of scripture and recognize that there is a depth within scripture. Within the community there were people who had the thirst for a deeper understanding of scripture and how it could influence their lives. In a big parish, people are at all kinds of levels. Those who have come to the group are people who are very committed parishioners in terms of worship and the whole way of life in the parish.

This does not mean that the group was constructed to be elitist or exclude anyone, nor has it become so, as Fr. Andrew further states:

[. . .] but we have constantly made it clear—no expertise required. The meeting is open to every parishioner.

While the group is advertised in the parish bulletin and fellow parishioners are encouraged to participate, it is, nevertheless, the regular members of the group who have sustained the group by their perseverance and commitment, and arguably these are prerequisites for the sustained existence of such a group.

Methodology Used in the Group

As the group has developed, the methodology that has evolved in the meetings has been a crucial aspect of the continued existence of the group. The leaders have become facilitators and the conversation has changed from a question-and-answer format to a dialogue. Initially the background details (that is, the information about Jewish religious practices and the different religious groups) were explained by the two leaders, but some of the other members of the group, notably Margaret, have been able to undertake some research and have contributed background details of the passages that are being studied. The methodology of the meetings is a simple model of shared reading and discussion. The group discusses between thirty and forty verses per night. I divide the verses into passages for discussion (reflecting a piece of narrative, miracle story, or parable). The group reads the passage, pauses for silent reflection, and then discusses the passage. The group is often able to draw new meanings from familiar passages by locating passages within narrative and structural contexts. Often the passage is related to the life experience or life views of the members of the group, and this is reapplied to the passage, leading to a dynamic of orthopraxis and orthodoxy.[13] The scripture study helps the members to read his or her own lived experience in light of the Gospel and the revelation of Christ.[14]

One of the major advantages of studying in a group and systematically reading a Gospel is that the more difficult and challenging passages have to be examined and discussed and not ignored or glossed over. As Aileen comments:

The pace of it is ideal. You could skip over things on your own, but the group works through it slowly.

---

13. John Paul II, "Catechesi Tradendae," 1979, in An Anthology of Catholic Teaching on Education, ed. Leonard Franchi, 167 (para. 22) (London: Scepter, 2007).
14. Congregation for the Clergy, "General Directory for Catechesis," 407 (para. 152).

This has led to many hard challenges and, at times, an acknowledgment that the meaning of some passages has to remain unresolved for the group at that time.[15] Further, creating the right atmosphere for open discussion is very important. The relationship within the group must be one of trust and cooperation. Fr. Andrew points out that as the group has developed the members of the group have felt more comfortable:

People have developed and changed a great deal since first joining—when the group began some were content, and for a long time, just to be, reading and listening to what the others had to say. But because of the informal and welcoming atmosphere, everybody has felt relaxed and free to make their own contribution.

As the group has grown in confidence, people have become more comfortable in sharing their views on passages of scripture. The group has become, according to Mary, a forum where:

People are free to share their views and know they will be respected.

The openness to the views of the others creates the opportunity for a rich sharing of life and Christian experience that never loses the possibility to surprise and delight. John thinks it is good to hear how other people interpret scripture, and Graham comments:

You get the views of others. It expands one's insights into the texts. Yes, you are never quite sure what someone might come away with. Stories, life stories, experience, and how scripture relates. I like to listen to others . . . to other people's shared experiences.

James finds the sharing of views very beneficial:

The discussions are the best thing for me. I would never have thought of half the things that come up.

The members of the group, then, find that the meetings have some structure but are sufficiently informal to allow the free sharing of views. They find this interesting and stimulating.

The next section will explore the development of the group from a group of Christians to a community of Christians.

15. John Barton, "The Bible and Its Authority and Interpretation," in *The Oxford Companion to Christian Thought*, ed. Adrian Hastings, Alistair Mason, and Hugh Pyper, 69–72 (Oxford: Oxford University Press, 2000).

Progress from Group to Community

As we have seen, the openness to the view of the other has fostered a deeper understanding of different perspectives on scripture and on life and faith. Aileen comments

[. . .] it's good to understand how different folk tick.

As the group has developed in openness and trust, so too the friendships between the members of the group have grown, as Mary explains:

I've really valued the friendships I have made there and valued the supportive atmosphere.

This has not created some cozy, exclusive group for mutual self-support. As has been stated, it demands commitment from people with busy lives and professional careers. Mary's comments would be echoed by many members of the group:

It has been a great experience overall. Oh! I do get upset if I miss it. Sometimes I could see it far enough. Sometimes it's a real effort to get out the door, but it is always worth it.

There can also be differences of opinion. There is not always a consensus on how a passage is to be interpreted and, at times, members of the group can argue their case quite strongly and be single-minded. This, however, is seen as a strength of the group rather than a limitation.

As the years have passed, the bonds between the members of the group have strengthened. As the members have become more comfortable with the shared experience and with each other, the form of the group has moved from one of group to community. Fr. Andrew articulates this generation of community and states that the shared meal experience has been crucial in this process:

There has been a great spirit of community developed in the group and expressed and reinforced by fulfilling part of the Gospel message that we are invited to come together to enjoy a banquet here on earth and we've had some wonderful occasions of sharing a meal together, mostly in the chapel house. We have enjoyed being together and having very enjoyable meals. These have strengthened the bonds of fellowship.

All of the members of the group concur with this feeling that the shared meals contribute to the fellowship, including John:

Eating—this is bonding. It is so important that we do eat together, that we do socialize. It encourages good relations, makes you more and more comfortable and you're more willing to express an opinion without worrying if it's the wrong opinion.

Mary echoes this and states that the fact that all the members of the group contribute to the meal by providing food or drinks adds to the feeling of community. These two references to New Testament ideas on the importance and symbolism of sharing food—the prefiguring of the eschatological banquet (Lk 22:30) and the sharing of communal foodstuffs provided by the individuals (Acts 2:43–47)—emphasize the articulation of explicit (Fr. Andrew) and implicit (John and Mary) links between scriptural themes and the shared lived experience of the members of this community.

One persistent concern is the ability of the group to welcome new people to this community. Reassuringly, Graham, the newest member, identified the fellowship, the community spirit, as one of the reason he continues to attend the meetings:

I found a small group in a small room . . . two professional inputs providing good support. Some members are quite well qualified . . . teachers . . . ex-teachers. I found a quite affable informal atmosphere . . . good touch of humor . . . easier to relax into.

The group has grown and developed into a supportive community that is strengthened by shared purpose and communal meals. Fr. Andrew thinks that the dynamic in the group is very important, but this is not a dynamic that is exclusive to a small group, but one that is open to the newcomer from the parish or the stranger from another parish.

The next section examines the impact of the group on the Christian lives of the members.

The Impact of the Scripture Study Group on the Christian Lives of the Members

The impact of the scripture study group on the Christian lives of the members can be perceived in a number of ways. First, it has deepened the knowledge and understanding of scripture for all members of the group. Secondly, it has had implications for their participation in parish and church life.

The members of the group have a deeper knowledge and understanding of scripture. For Fr. Andrew it has helped his Christian life to develop:

For myself—it is helping to satisfy a desire for a deeper understanding of scripture—a deeper faith in the presence of our Lord Jesus Christ.

James states that attending the group has helped him in his search for knowledge and has prompted him to continue seeking:

Oh yes . . . it gives you a better understanding through the Gospels and of Our Lord. Gives a better understanding of the life and times of Jesus and better understanding of what you can do about it . . . better understanding that makes you go back. You are always looking for more answers. I suppose you keep looking. A thirst for knowledge on my part. Whether lack of education or understanding . . . but a thirst of knowledge for the life and times of Jesus.

John and Margaret have found that the group has helped them in their personal study of scripture. John has found that the group has helped his personal reading of scripture to become more meaningful:

I want to know what it is saying to me for that day, for that bit of my life. The group has bolstered my personal reading as well. When you're reading it personally, you are not expressing what you're taking from it until you come to our discussions, because you don't express it to yourself.

Margaret has found that her participation in the group has encouraged her to pursue a deeper personal study of scripture:

Also—apart from the discussions, I have tried to do deeper study, which I would never have done had I been left on my own. I use commentaries. I enjoy that too. It takes up quite a lot of time. It throws light on things.

The study has helped to inform her contribution to the group. The scripture study group has also had an impact on the participation of the members in different aspects of parish and church life. Margaret, for example, has found that the study in the group has helped her to have a greater confidence in hearing and receiving scripture during Mass:

It has given me a better understanding of scripture if I hear a reading on a Sunday we have done. If we have not done it—I can make a better shot of understanding the readings.

She feels that she has a better understanding of the genres of scripture and its cultural and historical contexts. Aileen states that the group has drawn her more into the life of the parish:

I would say it has. I feel more part of the parish community and I feel I can give more to the parish community.

This includes participation in the preparation and delivery of the holy hour—Aileen's attendance at the group gave her the confidence for this and gave her the confidence to write prayers for the services. James states that the group has helped him in his efforts to live a more authentic Christian life:

I mean you try a wee bit harder. Because of my age and I have time. You have the time. You can give it more time and thought. You've got to try. The scripture group helps—it helps you to try harder . . . to be a better Catholic.

Mary has found that a greater understanding of scripture has helped her in the ecumenical work she undertakes on behalf of the parish with other Christian churches in the Bishopbriggs Churches Together group. The scripture group, then, has helped the members deepen their knowledge and understanding of scripture and has helped some of them to develop their private study of scripture. It has also helped the members further their Christian life and participate more fully in parish life and ecumenical activities.

Concluding Remarks

A number of key points emerge from the discussion above and from discussions held in the scripture group over the last five years.

First, while acknowledging the strengths of *Contextual Bible Study* and *Lectio Divina* and recognizing aims and principles we share with these models, I recognize that one of the keys to the success of this particular group has been the rejection of fixed or prescriptive models of scripture study and the gradual development of a model that cohered with the needs and aspirations of the participants within this particular local church context—a model that contains an inherent flexibility that has allowed the group to shape itself, create its own aims, and direct its own activities according to its own methodology. This is a local form of adult faith formation, initiated by a local priest and a parishioner, that has not relied on external support or external "expertise" and guidance.

Second, although the reading and discussion does not lead to prayer and contemplation in the way that *Lectio Divina* does, a short prayer has been introduced in the last year at the beginning and the end of the meeting. However, the activity of the group could be described as a joint quest for a deeper understanding and intimacy with Jesus Christ, and this joint quest could be described as a joint prayer.

Third, this local model is a model that required the courage to allow scope for the expression of a strong ministry of lay leadership and collegiality. Fr. Andrew, despite his many other commitments, has seldom failed to attend the group, and while we share a joint leadership/facilitator role, he has always insisted that I be acknowledged as the leader. He actively sought the commitment of the group to take responsibility for the two holy hours and the ecumenical prayer service. He has hosted the shared meals in his own dining room, providing hospitality for the table fellowship.

Fourth, one of the points that has been debated over the last five years, and that was discussed at the archdiocesan seminar, is the feasibility of initiating a scripture study group in a parish where there are no identified "experts" in scripture. Many members of the group feel that the impetus and initial direction requires such input. Certainly, a group such as this cannot be started and cannot be sustained without the commitment of one or two motivated individuals. Fr. Andrew and I also remain resolute in our conviction that many Catholics are more conversant with scripture than they realize and that, with the aid of appropriate support, they should have the confidence in their own ability to engage meaningfully with others in the shared study of scripture.

Finally, this model has drawn on a spiritual need and desire of a number of people to deepen their faith and has allowed these people to express themselves in way that is appropriate and meaningful for them within their own local context. It has supported them in their personal Christian spiritual lives and in their contribution to parish and inter-Christian dialogue. It has not always been a comfortable process, nor a smooth process, but it has allowed a genuine community of believers to grow slowly and naturally.

The School Context

In many countries the churches have made a major investment in schools as a key institution for witnessing to and communicating their faith. In the UK context, Anglican and Catholic church-state relations differ significantly. This influences how Catholic schools perceive their roles and how these schools are perceived by others outside that church. Sullivan articulates how a Catholic worldview has implications for educational practice. Traditionally, Catholic schools have given high priority to conveying Catholic tradition to the next generation. This is a process that requires attention be given to the universal and enduring features of that tradition. These are outlined in Sullivan's analysis of the "text" of Catholic education. However, in keeping with other chapters in this book, he shows how the "text" must be presented in a dynamic and sensitive engagement with the context in which education takes place, and he exposes key aspects of the mediating processes entailed in conveying Catholic Christianity in schools. Between message, messengers, and recipients a complex range of factors are at play, and these need attention if the attempt to communicate faith is to be efficacious.

The context for communicating faith could be differentiated into four dimensions. First, there is the personal context of learners: their age, maturity, motivation, and needs. Second, there is the particular type of institutional setting. Sullivan describes one example, the Catholic school. Third, there is the contemporary cultural context. Fourth, none of these three aspects of context can be adequately understood without taking into account the legacy of history and without considering how individuals, institutions, and ideas are influenced by prior dilemmas, decisions and developments, challenges and choices. Gower analyses the third context: elements of our postmodern culture. Without attention to the influences exerted on people via the assumptions prevailing in their culture, the task of communicating faith may be carried out with a culpable blindness, and thereby become ineffective. Gower casts light on how broad cultural assumptions, some inimical to Christian faith, seep into the thinking of young people. This kind of cultural analysis and interrogation of the thought patterns and themes operating in children and teenagers provide a valuable aid for those charged with faith education (and not only in schools). Critical discernment of the categories and concepts that shape our perceptions is an essential prerequisite for the communication of faith.

McKinney picks up the fourth dimension of the context as a way into understanding religious education in Catholic schools in Scotland. He provides a double-pronged approach here. First, he sketches in the changing position of Catholic schools in Scotland since the early nineteenth century and up to the present day, showing the role and scope of religious education within these schools. Then he draws on insights from the personal history and experience of a key player within the changing scene of the past forty years, in order to bring out some of the major features and key priorities of school-based Catholic religious education. In doing so, the elements of doctrine, liturgy, pastoral care, spirituality, and personal witness are shown to be interwoven and mutually reinforcing.

Nobody can share what he does not already (at least partly) possess. No one can communicate confidently a form of life that she has not internalized, nor can she convey convincingly principles and practices for which she cannot claim ownership. Communicators of faith have to be able to translate a "language" that has become natural to them, one that is integrated into their thinking, feeling, deciding, loving, and acting. This is why the focus of Edwards' chapter is on promoting the spiritual development of staff in order to empower witnesses as a key component of Catholic educational leadership. Drawing on his experience in Jesuit education as well as in diocesan inservice activities, he brings out what is needed and why, and shows how these needs can be addressed.

It can happen that faith communicators offer answers to questions that have not yet been asked and neglect to address the questions that have been asked. Not only is there an art to questioning as part of the process of communicating faith; there is also the need to develop the capacity to question effectively, on the part of learners, if faith is to be owned, internalized, and lived out adequately, beyond the rule book and outside of familiar situations. The longer route to religious knowledge, via the process of questioning, can often lead to greater depth of understanding and a more lively faith. Topley derives from Bernard Lonergan an approach to questioning as a valuable dimension of faith communication, one that moves learners from attentiveness to responsibility.

7   Text and Context

Mediating the Mission in Catholic Schools

John Sullivan

The tasks of teachers in Catholic schools are many. They have to attract the interest of their pupils in what they think is important. Then they invite pupils to go beyond attention and to be ready to participate. By witnessing to and modeling how the various aspects of the curriculum can make a difference in our lives, teachers should challenge pupils to grow, learn new skills, deploy new concepts, become informed by new knowledge, adopt new attitudes, take on new stances, and act motivated by new values. By listening to, sharing with, and supporting pupils, teachers encourage them to adopt, assimilate, and deploy what they learn, as well as to question, criticize, extend, and reconstruct it in different ways in response to changing circumstances.

In doing all this, they serve two different constituencies, or, to deploy categories described by Joseph McCann, they address two different reference groups.[1] These reference groups—from which they take their identity and to which they look for guidance, and, at the same time, by which they expect

---

1. Joseph McCann, "Improving Our Aim: Catholic School Ethos Today," in *Reimagining the Catholic School*, ed. Noel Prendergast and Luke Monaghan, 160–61 (Dublin: Veritas, 2003).

to be judged—are the church and society. In addition to meeting the usual educational standards required by the state, teachers in church schools have to bear in mind the reference group—the church—that differentiates their schools from mainstream schools. Here I leave aside the important responsibility of teachers in Catholic schools to serve the common good and, as part of this, to meet the educational standards required by the state, having treated them elsewhere.[2] Instead I concentrate on suggesting some of the ways that their relationship to the church and their drawing upon its theology have a bearing on understanding the nature, purpose, and functioning of Catholic schools. Theology, however else it may be described, is about how we perceive the bearing of ultimate reality on our lives (as individuals and in community).

Educational practice, either explicitly or implicitly, draws upon a view of the world, an understanding of the nature of humanity, and a sense of priorities. It seeks to engage people with reality, impart a way of ordering this reality, and equip them to flourish (or at least cope) in the face of its demands. Questions about what is true, about how we might come to know this truth, and what we are to make of it in our lives are never far from the surface. A central thrust of this chapter is the dialectic between, on the one hand, the solidity and continuity of a particular religious faith and its theological resources and associated piety, and, on the other hand, the flexibility required if this faith is to respond ever less inadequately to the changing needs and contexts it encounters. The interplay between text and context is at the very heart of Catholic education, in schools as well as in other locations.

Thus behind the theology of Catholic schools to be employed here is an image of such communities as being places of conversation rather than of unilateral transmission. Mediation, reconstruction, risk-taking, reciprocity, and reception are required. This does not mean that there is no place for promulgation, orthodoxy, repetition, tradition, docility, or obedience. Indeed, any form of creative fidelity depends on both memory and imagination. It looks back to history and tradition for sources of wisdom, but it is not imprisoned in the past. It looks out sensitively and positively at the present, but is wary of being kidnapped by contemporary perspectives and cat-

2. John Sullivan, *Catholic Schools in Contention: Competing Metaphors and Leadership Implications* (Dublin: Veritas, 2000); Sullivan, *Catholic Education: Distinctive and Inclusive* (Dordrecht: Kluwer, 2001); Sullivan, "From Formation to the Frontiers," *Journal of Education and Christian Belief* 7, no. 1 (2003): 7–21. A modified version of this article appears in this book as Chapter 1.

egories. In the interplay between remembering and exploring, there should be discerning. The dimension of memory facilitates the emergence of both individual and collective identity; it also provides bearings and a framework for interpreting experience. This experience needs to be tested, sifted, extended, evaluated, and revised as it comes into contact with imaginative exploration of the new, the different, and the other.

In the first part of this chapter I spell out some features of the text to be deployed in Catholic schools, commenting on the theology that underpins this text. In the second part of the chapter, the notions of context, intermediate discourse, and mediating factors are explored and then related to the task of mediating the mission in Catholic schools.

Text and Theology

Catholic education rests on certain foundational principles and perspectives drawn from a theology of creation, an anthropology, a Christology, and an ecclesiology. That is, it builds on a belief in God and God's relation to the world, a view of human nature, convictions about the role of Christ, and an interpretation of the place of the church in human affairs. An economic rendering of these beliefs might be laid out as follows: God is our Creator, the source of our life, and its final goal. Ultimately we are called to share in God's life. Education is one context among others where we experience this invitation and have an opportunity to grapple with its implications. How do we get to know God and the nature of the divine life we are invited to share? Jesus the Christ revealed to us true humanity and divinity, embodied a pattern for worthwhile living, and offers us a personal relationship that is salvific. Education should be recognized as an invitation to continuous conversion into a more Christ-like personality, to personal holiness, and to social transformation. By learning, growth, development, and sacrifice (literally, "making holy" the substance of our lives), we shall be ready to enjoy eternal life with God and in communion with others. God's Holy Spirit is constantly available to us all in every circumstance of life as presence and power. We are called to enter into union with Christ, through accepting the presence of Spirit, through prayer, and through conversion of lifestyle, from one currently ruled by sin, into one modeled for us by Jesus in the Gospel.

All truth comes to us from God, whatever its mode of mediation. Part of coming to appreciate creation is to learn to see the interconnections of all reality. This entails developing a holistic, rather than a partial or fragmented, outlook. We do not attain this outlook in isolation, but in the context of experiencing life in community. Education is to be carried out within a harmonious relationship with the living tradition of the church. Her ecclesiology provides the Catholic Church with a particular way of bringing together her thinking about human nature, the person of Christ, and God as the source and goal of creation. It also establishes a context for understanding the relationship between the material and the spiritual, nature and grace, faith and reason, freedom and authority, discipline and development, and the individual and the community. The church is founded to carry on Christ's mission and to convey his word. Catholic schools are part of this mission.

In Catholic schools, religion is the core of the curriculum. Christ is the model for human life. The church is the medium of living tradition that cannot be bypassed. The spiritual dimension of life must receive due attention. Morality is to be seen in objective terms. Mortality should be kept in view. All areas of knowledge are to be interrelated. It is belief in the essential interconnectedness of the various elements of Catholic education that leads to a desire on the part of the Catholic community to establish and maintain separate schooling, rather than to provide additional teaching of those elements that have not been covered in mainstream schooling. Neither the explicitly religious nor the apparently secular can be properly appreciated if taught in isolation from the other.

One way of describing the nonseparation of sacred and secular is to refer to a sacramental perspective. In this perspective Catholics believe that God can be encountered in all aspects of our experience, not only in the explicitly religious moments of private prayer, the reading of Holy Scripture, and celebration of the Eucharist, but also, for example, in classrooms, in human relationships, in aesthetic expression, and in nature. Although the Catholic Church has traditionally emphasized seven particular moments when we are particularly conscious of an encounter with God's presence through Christ—baptism, Eucharist, reconciliation, confirmation, matrimony, holy orders, and sacrament of the sick—the sacramental perspective goes deeper than this; it facilitates in us a way of reading the whole world as the theatre of God's grace and presence to us.

The text to be deployed in Catholic schools must include pervading themes in the Christian Gospel such as faith, hope, love, justice, reconciliation, and community. It also includes pervading themes within Catholic educational thought that have emerged from reflection on the tradition's attempt to provide education that addresses the needs of both church and secular society. Among these themes we find Christ-centeredness, a community inspired by the Gospel, a sacramental perspective, and a nonseparation of sacred and secular, together with the integral development of the human person, a synthesis of faith, life, and culture, the autonomy of the disciplines, and interconnectedness between message, community, service, worship, and curriculum.[3]

Catholic theology in the past provided the authoritative texts that have to be conveyed. It has tended to operate as if theology should always come from above the cultural battleground and the dramatic interpersonal exchange that is the field of education, with its key concepts already fully worked out prior to the pedagogical encounter. Its focus of attention, on the divine, the supernatural, and the sacred, and its sphere of operation and manner of speaking, seemed far removed from everyday life and earthly concerns. Its teaching emanated from a center that purported to speak universally, to all contexts and times. Catholic theology in the future will have to pay considerably more attention to the contexts in which texts are taught and to how doctrine is being received and appropriated by people in diverse situations. It will also have to trust more in a theology that emerges from below, although doing so in a dialogue with traditional resources. Its construction will have to be more local, inclusive, and provisional.

Theological literacy and ecclesial belonging within the Catholic tradition are necessary ingredients in the equipment required for any worthwhile attempt to mediate the mission in Catholic schools, for the church is the primary reference point, and discipleship must be the ultimate goal, if the school is to claim with any justification to be grounded in Christ. It is difficult to imagine how the school's mission could be enacted without there being a critical mass of people working in Catholic schools who display knowledge about the life and teaching of Christ and a personal relationship with him. This depends upon an understanding of the scriptures, which are the privileged testimony to God's pattern of dealings with humanity, and it is fed by participation in the sacramental life and the worship of the church and a life of prayer, as well as by witness to Christian teachings and virtues.

3. Sullivan, *Catholic Education: Distinctive and Inclusive*.

Of course, it must be conceded that the grace of Christ and the workings of the Holy Spirit cannot be restricted by our plans and projects or confined through human limitations and deficiencies. Normally speaking, though, we cannot effectively teach Christ if we do not know him ourselves.

The person who seeks to live out the mission of Catholic schools must bear in mind the multiple dimensions of the Christian faith and be alert to its various languages. This means that attention should be given to the *kerygma*, or proclaiming the basic message about Christ, as conveyed in the Gospels and commented upon in the rest of the New Testament. This must be accompanied by attention to *leitourgia*, or the dimension of worship, which is the primary context for both proclamation and assimilation of God's word. Without the surrounding environment of *koinonia*, or of fellowship and communion, the word in both proclamation and worship could be heard in too detached a manner and come across as cold and isolating. To all these we must add *diakonia*, the spirit and practice of service, which expresses the Word in action, builds up the community, and is itself a form of worship, of the divine image in others.

Those who work in Catholic schools must monitor how well they keep these four dimensions in balance with one another, so that each feeds into and is enriched by the others. If this balance is kept, there should be mutual interaction, nourishment, and correction that will guard a school against distortions and narrowness in its use of the languages of faith. Of course it has to be acknowledged that when the surrounding culture changes, Christian activities such as proclamation, worship, community building, and service appear in a different light, both in relation to the culture and to each other. Cultural shifts, both in the church and in society, have led to new understandings, evaluations, and practices in matters of dialogue, outreach, language, upbringing, inclusiveness, liberation, and attitudes to authority. Furthermore, different contexts are sensitive to different aspects of the theological tradition. Catholic school teachers and leaders need to consider how this might apply in their context. Which parts of the tradition seem obscure, defunct, or difficult? Which parts seem particularly accessible, relevant, and attractive? In my own work I find that some groups, while very open to the "horizontal" aspects of the Christian message—for example, love of neighbor, tolerance of human differences, and care for community life—find it much harder to access the "vertical" aspects—for example, rejection of sin, readiness for conversion, openness to grace, dedication to worship, and acceptance of the otherness of God.

Context

Separate Catholic schools have been argued for traditionally because of the particular importance attributed to context in the learning process. If the communication of text alone had been their principal purpose, there would not have been a need for a system of separate schools. Catholics believe that they have a mission to communicate certain texts, scriptural and ecclesial, ones that have authority, that are essential for a true reading of our situation and that are ultimately necessary for our salvation. However, this mission does not require any particular form of delivery. Nevertheless, certain kinds of environment are more conducive to Christian learning in the Catholic tradition. Catholic schools, in the UK and elsewhere, were set up in the nineteenth century in response to what was seen as a hostile, Protestant-prevailing atmosphere. Catholic schools provided a safe environment in which the faith could be witnessed to, experienced, and transmitted, free from anti-Catholic prejudices and principles. By the end of the twentieth century the contrasting hostile environment was perceived to be materialistic and secularist. Again, separate schools provided an opportunity in which the faith tradition was allowed space and resources to be taught and experienced within the educational system.

Although this chapter considers the endeavor of mediating the "text" of Catholicism in ways that connect fruitfully with diverse, challenging, and changing educational, social, and cultural contexts from a UK perspective, the basic tasks entailed by such mediation are similar in many other parts of the world. The most substantial documentation of the challenges facing Catholic educators worldwide appears in Grace and O'Keefe's two-volume *International Handbook of Catholic Education*.[4] Grace and O'Keefe and their many contributors chart a range of issues that regularly surface in country after country. These include how features of the external world, for example, secularization, globalization, financial pressures, and relations between church and state, impact upon Catholic schools. They also include more internal is-

---

4. Gerald Grace and Joseph O'Keeffe, eds., *International Handbook of Catholic Education* (Dordecht: Springer, 2007).

sues—for example, student admissions, staff selection, leadership, spiritual formation, and curriculum provision. Developing the mission must take all of these into account. The recent *Carnegie Conversation on Catholic Education* provides an example of important discussions by relevant stakeholders in the U.S. on the prospects for renewing Catholic education in that country.[5] Helping to form Christ in the lives of others requires sophisticated pastoral theology and skilled practical application. "Regulative concepts like sacrament, vocation, forgiveness, beatitudes, and agape"[6] need to be brought into creative and sensitive contact with particular people and communities in service of Catholic education. They form part of its "text."

Text, however, is only part of the story. It is only ever encountered, experienced, received, understood (and misunderstood), appreciated (or rejected) in a wider context. Contexts affect the encounter with text and how it is interpreted. Context includes practices, the local and wider environment, sets of relationships, and the atmosphere or *ethos* of a school. Catholic schools seek to provide a context that is conducive to an optimal encounter with their underlying text, in contrast to the social context in which many young people are immersed. We live a society that prefers to focus less on the "hardware" of character, of personal formation, of long-term commitments, of irrevocable stances, and of objective truth claims and conversion of life in accordance with these truth claims. It relies more on what may be called "software." In a "software society" skills and competencies are often spoken of as if they could be identified, described, demonstrated, and practiced without reference to who you are, what else you are doing, what you are like as a person, who you are with, and your overall lifestyle. This leads to disconnections: of choices from consequences, of learning from living,

---

5. John Staud, ed., *Carnegie Conversation on Catholic Education* (Notre Dame, Ind.: Alliance for Catholic Education Press at University of Notre Dame, 2008). For complementary expressions of support for Catholic education and alternative readings of the priorities facing it, see also United States Conference of Catholic Bishops, *Renewing our Commitment to Catholic Elementary and Secondary Schools in the Third Millennium* (Washington, D.C.: United States Conference of Catholic Bishops, 2005); also see Notre Dame Task Force on Catholic Education, *Making God Known, Loved, and Served: The Future of Catholic Primary and Secondary Schools in America* (Notre Dame, Ind.: Notre Dame Task Force on Catholic Education, 2006); and Congregation for Catholic Education, *Educating Together in Catholic Schools: A Shared Mission Between Consecrated Persons and the Lay Faithful* (Rome: Congregation for Catholic Education, 2007). For historical perspective on structures of support for Catholic education, see John Augenstein, Christopher Kauffman, and Robert Wister, eds., *One Hundred Years of Catholic Education* (Washington, D.C.: National Catholic Educational Association, 2003).

6. Staud, *Carnegie Conversation*, 44.

truth from virtue, practices from people, head from heart and hand. It also leads to fragmentation: within the curriculum, within personal development, and within society. If our political, social, economic, and cultural location and our character greatly affect what we can take in, understand, and appreciate, Catholic schools aim to provide a more appropriate ambiance that facilitates faith development and a synthesis of faith, life, and culture.

Connections between a faith tradition and its mediating factors can be of several kinds. First, there can be unity, when it is very hard to distinguish what comes from the faith tradition itself and what comes from the surrounding culture. This can be comforting, but it can also be extremely damaging for the healthy growth of the faith tradition, which can fail to exercise its prophetic function, too readily accept the status quo, and confuse the fashionable with the essential. Second, there can be a clear distinction between our understanding of what is central to faith and our appreciation of the factors that might mediate it in any particular context. This could be healthy, but it could also slip into separated thinking and compartmentalized action, if our "rendering unto Caesar" is not informed (and challenged) by our "rendering unto God." Third, there can be opposition. While necessary in most contexts for some of the time, if fidelity is to be maintained, it tends to harden positions, drive people into separate camps, and stifle creativity, which is itself a (necessary) form of fidelity. The ideal connection, as with our understanding of the divine and human nature in Christ, avoids either confusion or separation between faith and its mediating factors, between text and context, between religion and culture.

An Intermediate Discourse on Catholic Education

Until recently a huge gap existed in discussions about Catholic education between authoritative exhortations (for example, from Rome and the bishops) and the daily decisions and practices of teachers, in whatever setting they were working. Rhetoric and reality seemed very far apart. Guiding principles issued at an international level necessarily are expressed in general terms and in abstract language. They speak of the ideal toward which all should strive. Educators have to relate these general principles to particular settings. They must bear in mind specific individuals and groups, and they are obliged to take into account the many diverse factors—historical, political, social, economic, philosophical, psychological, cultural—that influence both educational institutions and ecclesial life. Global statements about ideals need to be interpreted and appropriated by critical and reflective educators. Mere repetition, without meaningful mediation and sensitive application, leaves those who utter them vulnerable to the accusation that they are unduly simplistic in outlook, pious in aspiration, and irrelevant to the complex realities involved in communicating faith, whether in the home, parish, school, or university.

There is gradually emerging, through the cumulative work of scholars in many countries, an intermediate discourse about Catholic education, one that is neither abstractly universal yet platitudinous (who does not want loving communities?) nor merely operating at the local and practical level of "tips for teachers."[7] Head teachers of Catholic schools play an especially crucial role in developing this intermediate discourse, along with other partners, such as parents, pupils, teachers, academics, bishops, clergy, diocesan officers, advisers, inspectors, and policy makers. It is not a matter of a clear philosophy and theology, complete, readily available, waiting to be put into practice. This would be a display of one-way thinking. Rather, the intermediate discourse that grows up between text and context, between principles and practice, only emerges in the light of particular challenges: for example, those thrown up by admissions policies, curriculum decisions, assessment tasks, in partnership with various groups and in response to diverse pastoral situations. Only then do we come to see the meaning and purchase as well as the weakness or incompleteness of our starting philosophy and theology. As philosopher of education Terence McLaughlin says, "there is a limit to the extent to which any Catholic perspective on education (or indeed any other general educational perspective) can be abstracted from the practical circumstances in which the enterprise of education must be conducted at any particular time."[8]

7. James Arthur, The Ebbing Tide: Policy and Principles of Catholic Education (Leominster, UK: Gracewing, 1995); Anthony S. Bryk, Valerie E. Lee, and Peter B. Holland, eds., Catholic Schools and the Common Good (Cambridge, Mass., and London: Harvard University Press, 1993); James Thomas Byrnes, John Paul II and Educating for Life: Moving toward a Renewal of Catholic Educational Philosophy (New York: Peter Lang, 2002); James Conroy, ed., Catholic Education: Inside Out/ Outside In (Dublin: Veritas, 1999); Matthew Feheney, ed., From Ideal to Action: The Inner Nature of a Catholic School Today (Dublin: Veritas, 1998); Gerald Grace, Catholic Schools: Mission, Markets and Morality (London: Routledge Falmer, 2002); Thomas H. Groome, Educating for Life: A Spiritual Vision for Every Teacher and Parent (Allen, Tex.: Thomas More Press, 1998); Terence H. McLaughlin, Joseph O'Keefe, and Bernadette O'Keeffe, eds., The Contemporary Catholic School (London: Falmer, 1996).

8. Terence H. McLaughlin, "A Catholic Perspective on Education," Journal of Education and Christian Belief 6, no. 2 (2002): 122.

There are at least five (overlapping) dimensions to the task of developing an intermediate discourse in Catholic schools. For any particular teacher and leader these dimensions could appear in various kinds of order and with different levels of priority.

First, there is the working out of a balance between denominational integrity and addressing the ecumenical imperative. I have claimed elsewhere that Catholic education must seek to be both distinctive and inclusive.[9] One of the ways that Catholic schools are inclusive is in their embrace of ecumenism—in their thinking, in their professional action, and in their worship. Without being unaware of, indifferent to, or superficially casual about denominational differences, and while promoting and protecting a distinctively Catholic perspective in the educational endeavor, Catholic teachers and school leaders have a duty to make room for, to respect, to hear the voices of, and to learn from the colleagues, pupils, parents, and community members connected to the school who come from other parts of the Christian family. Without a deep knowledge of their own Catholic tradition to bring to the table of ecumenical discussion and sharing, it is unlikely that teachers in Catholic schools will contribute much to ecumenism in education. But if they only listen to their own tradition, it is likely that their understanding of it will be severely limited. Catholic schools offer a uniquely privileged arena for ecumenical effort; this is an opportunity that is, as yet, and despite some honorable exceptions, largely ignored.

Second, there is the task of relating a Catholic perspective to the language of secular education. There will be much in the literature and in professional discussions relating to curriculum, pedagogy, and assessment, to pastoral care and community building, that Catholic educators can learn from and also to which they can contribute something distinctive. Catholic educators can contribute to discussions about the nature of education for citizenship and of sex education. They can enter the debate as to the relative weighting to be given to the various elements of the curriculum—for example, the arts, sciences, and technology. They can assist in decisions about allocating resources to pupils with special needs or to curriculum areas that might give the school an advantage in the educational marketplace. In these ways and in devoting time, energy, and imagination to spiritual development, in serving the disadvantaged, Catholic schools can bring their

9. Sullivan, *Catholic Education: Distinctive and Inclusive.*

faith tradition into dialogue with mainstream "secular" education. Catholic schools should avoid either jumping onto every bandwagon or remaining in an educational ghetto, isolated from current developments, methodologies, and resources. Critical discernment is required in establishing the right level and quality of dialogue.

Third, Catholic teachers and leaders have to engage with the phenomenon of managerialism. As I have argued elsewhere, this is an inescapable responsibility for Catholic school leaders.[10] Wrestling with managerialism, if carried out properly, so that the Catholic "text" is creatively related to the managerial context, will tax the patience, challenge the ingenuity, extend the professional repertoire, and deepen the spirituality of those engaged with this struggle. Catholic schools should ensure that they are not swamped by the management tools at their disposal. This applies to institutional planning and evaluation, governance, management priorities, resource allocation, performance management, managing the place of one's school in the market and the overall drive for economy, effectiveness, and quality in systems and policies. Their primary purposes should be served and enhanced rather than suppressed or distorted by the approaches stemming from recent management thinking. For example, it is salutary to remember that we cannot plan, control, or measure everything that matters in education. If we could, what would the place of the unexpected, of delight, of serendipity?

Fourth, Catholic lay professionals have to develop a discourse between themselves and the institutional church. For many centuries, authority and education have been largely in the hands of clergy. Most Catholic schools were once led by clergy and members of religious orders. This situation changed many years ago, with Catholic schools today being led and staffed overwhelmingly by lay people. Although much progress has been made in articulating the lay voice in church circles, especially in education, it will still take some time before a mature dialogue can develop where each "party" can take the other seriously. This articulation of an intermediate discourse between Catholic lay professionals and the church is both a necessity and an opportunity for the healthy development of schools, for the wider church, and ultimately for the credibility of the church's engagement in the world.

10. Sullivan, "Wrestling with Managerialism," in *Commitment to Diversity*, ed. Mary Eaton, Jane Longmore, and Arthur Naylor (London: Cassell, 2000).

Fifth, there has to be dialogue between the different parts of the Catholic "system." Too often parishes, schools, seminaries, Catholic higher education, religious orders, adult educators in religion, the religious movements, and other agencies all act in isolation from one another. This means that good practice is spread less quickly than it would otherwise be, that lessons learned in one sector are not applied elsewhere, that unnecessary frustration arises about lack of progress. By focusing too closely on one particular type of context, the tendency to treat each part of the Catholic "system" in isolation tends to obscure the nature of the text to be communicated. It also tends to obscure the complex task of mediation itself. Thus, while some sectors may adequately take into account the nature of the "seed" to be broadcast, God's word, others may insufficiently allow for the nature of the "soil" in which it has to be planted. All sectors of the church and its educators need to be more appreciative of the multiple factors involved in mediating the mission and their interactive, mutually modifying nature.

Mediating Factors

The Catholic nature of a school is mediated by several factors. These include its geographical location, its history, its gender balance, its class composition, its academic intake, its curriculum mix, and its ethnic nature. For brevity I comment on only the first of these, but each factor could be explored for the many ramifications it could produce. A school's geographical location may present particular opportunities, as well as challenges. For example, the school may be in the inner city, urban, suburban, or rural. It could be remote from other Catholic schools or surrounded by them. It might be in an area that offers significant opportunities and support for enhancing learning or it may be relatively impoverished in this respect. The location may have a bearing on later employment opportunities, or the reputation of the school, or the intrusion of alien values. The environment may present challenges to accommodation, to expansion, to redevelopment, to boundary management, to recruitment of staff and/or pupils.

One must also take into account its particular position within the spectrum of Catholic tradition, the "instruments" and "melodies" it favors from among the "orchestra" and overall "repertoire" of Catholicism. For example, while the majority of Catholic schools are sponsored by a diocese, one marked feature of many Catholic schools is their link with one of the religious orders. Some schools are in the trusteeship of, for example, the Jesuits, the Salesians, the Sisters of Notre Dame, or the Congregation of Jesus, to name only a few of the many religious orders that have given so much to Catholic education. While all starting from the same Gospels, each stress their teaching in different ways, just as people cooking from similar ingredients can end up producing food that tastes significantly different. (Increasingly, religious orders seek to share their charisms with the laity.) Even in diocesan Catholic schools, which now comprise the majority, there is variety of interpretation and emphasis, a feature encouraged by the relatively strong diocesan, as opposed to national, basis of Catholic schooling. Thus, a religious education syllabus may be approved in some dioceses, but not in others. This is also true in matters of sex education. There is variety of interpretation between dioceses about the kinds of teacher behavior and lifestyle that might merit dismissal.

What I have not taken into account so far is the factor that most obviously creates differences within an organization: the sheer individuality of its members. We are all different in important ways and we bring to the school our own little world, with our particular histories, hopes and fears, strengths and weaknesses, perspectives and priorities. Christian mission may be universal in scope, addressed to all, and to be applied to all manner of people and situations, but it cannot escape the need for attention to particularity.

Mediating the Mission in Schools

In mediating the mission, teachers and leaders in Catholic schools do many things in relating text to context, in connecting the life of God to their human circumstances. We can use various verbs, closely overlapping in meaning, that are suggestive of the kind of activity such mediation involves. First, they *internalize* the text in its diverse features. They take it into themselves, so that it becomes a very part of them. This takes a considerable amount of time. They are not only informed by but also formed and indeed transformed by it. They do not simply consider the text at "arm's length," but let it impregnate their very being. Second, they *process* it, so that in rehearsing it, they connect it to other experiences, knowledge, and values that they have, so that it is owned by and can in future come *from* them rather than appear as something external that they have borrowed or put on as a disguise or mask. It no longer remains in the realm of the abstract but functions in a way similar to Newman's real assent (rather than merely as a formal notion).[11] Third, they *translate* it for others, taking into account different levels of cognitive understanding, personal maturity, and social circumstances. This entails finding alternative metaphors and establishing an imaginative outreach into the worldviews and conceptual schemes of those currently outside or only partly and falteringly inside the tradition. Fourth, they *remap* what they are mediating. That is, they locate it conceptually, in terms of intellectual idea, moral principle, or aesthetic sensibility, in relation to a "foreign" language or a culture that is outside the "wall" of the faith community. Fifth, they *integrate* the mission into the whole range of their pedagogical and professional duties. It is no longer an "add-on," but rather permeates all that they do. Thus purpose, motivation, general methods, and particular actions all blend together. Sixth, they *correlate* the mission with the whole range of their tasks, so that different purposes, constituencies, actions, methods, resources, concepts, priorities, ways of evaluation are all made to cohere rather than go off in different directions. In all these ways that are difficult to distinguish sharply from one another, they connect principles and practice to different levels and types of activity in the tasks of teaching and organizational leadership.

Conclusion

The theological teachings that underpin Catholic education, or, as I have called them collectively here, the text, might include the following beliefs. First, God is our Creator and permanently present to all creation. Second, in the person of Jesus the Christ, God has revealed both the depth of God's love for us and the capacity of humanity to receive and respond to God. Third, with the help of the Holy Spirit we can continue to respond to and be transformed by God's gracious offer of forgiveness and new life. Fourth, in personal prayer and in community worship we can draw nourishment from God for all our needs and be renewed in all our efforts. Fifth, in indwelling scripture, we can learn to become familiar with and discerning of God's will for us, aware that God is working out a purpose in the midst of our world. These are some elements of the "text" to be integrated into our professional work of education and related to our diverse contexts, personal, institutional, and cultural.

11. John Henry Newman, *A Grammar of Assent* (Notre Dame, Ind.: University of Notre Dame Press, 1979).

I have suggested that it is in the complex, critical, and creative relationship between text and context that the kind of learning aimed for in Catholic schools (both by children and by their teachers) is developed. This relationship is multidimensional, reciprocal, dynamic, dialectical, ongoing, and unfinished. Both text and context have to be taken into account if we are to understand the nature, purpose, and functioning of Catholic schools. Neither text nor context can be fully understood without reference to the other and without extensive reflection on the interplay between them.

8   The Challenges of Postmodernity

Ralph Gower

The Challenge

"I'm postmodern; I live in a postmodern age." So speaks many a person who is familiar with the term, normally meaning very modern, up-to-date, or simply "With it." What the term actually means depends on the context. It can mean "very modern" when applied to science, because in this context, to be very modern means holding the very modern belief that science has let us down. Such a view claims that instead of the simple explanations and basic principles we were promised, scientists are finding that the world is complex. Discoveries that were made for good (such as nuclear fission for energy production and genetic manipulation to defeat disease) have led to evil (nuclear weapons of destruction and biological weapons of fatal disease).

Not only does postmodernism differ from one area of cultural context to another, but it is not always very recent. The clearest statement about the nature of postmodernism that I have seen was written by Charles Jencks in the correspondence columns of the *Times*:

The first use of the term "Postmodernism" . . . extends to the 1870s when it was used by the British artist, John Watkins Chapman, and in 1917 when used by Rudolph Pannwiz. "Post-impressionism" (1980s) and "Post-industrial" (1914–1922) were the beginning of the "Posties" which flowered intermittently in the 1960s in literature, social thought, economics and even religion (Post-Christianity). "Posteriority," the negative feeling of coming after a creative age, or conversely, the positive feeling of transcending a negative ideology, really developed in the 1970s in architecture and in literature, two centres of post-modern debate (hyphenated half the time to indicate autonomy and a positive, constructive movement). "Deconstructive Postmodernism" comes to the fore after the French post-structuralists (Lyotard, Derrida, Baudrillard) became accepted in the United States in the late 1970s and now half the academic world believes post-modernism is confined to negative dialectics and deconstruction. But in the 1980s a series of new, creative movements occurred, variously called "constructive," "ecological," "grounded" and "restrictive" post-modernism. It is clear that two basic movements exist as well as the post-modern condition—"reactionary postmodernism" and "consumer postmodernism.". . . I should add that one of the great strengths of the word and the concept, and why it will be around for another hundred years, is that it is carefully suggestive about our having gone beyond the world-view of modernism—which is clearly inadequate—without specifying where we are going. That is why most people will spontaneously use it as if for the first time. But since "Modernism" was coined apparently in the third century, perhaps its first use was then.[1]

I have taken this a step further in defining postmodernism as a series of reactions against the authority that lies behind each system and that has been in existence over a period of time. Properly used in different areas of society (such as culture, economics, and religion), the term refers to the way in which traditional ways of doing things are being replaced because of a demand for change, often brought about by a challenge and opposition to the earlier form.[2] This can be demonstrated to be true by examining the meaning of postmodernism in several different areas.

Philosophy

Postmodern philosophy rejects the authoritative philosophical viewpoints of the past, a rejection that began when church teaching was the philosophy of the day. Church teaching had to be tested by rationality. Ordinary people could see that there were things wrong with a church in which one church group could fight against another in a Thirty Years' War, or where its

1. Quoted by Richard Appiananesi and Chris Garratt, *Introducing Postmodernism* (Cambridge: Icon, 1999), 3.
2. Ralph Gower, "How to Stop Churches Becoming Old Peoples' Clubs" (2007, unpublished).

teaching about the earth as the center of the universe was shown to be false by Galileo. Famous names in the history of philosophy contributed, too. Bacon (1564–1642) claimed that truth was not limited to the church and the Bible but was to be found in experiment and rational thinking. Descartes (1596–1650) replaced the idea that "God knows everything and I will pursue his knowledge" with "I can know things myself, without God, and can pursue my own knowledge." Locke (1632–1704) said that reason was the basis of truth; scripture and the supernatural needed to be tested by reason. Rationalism (or modernity) challenged supernaturalism and sought to replace it. Things did not stop there. The Romantics wished to emphasize the importance of human feeling, emotion, and intuition rather than reason, and more recently arguments have been put forward to claim that there is no reality, no truth, and even "self" is illusory. All are differing reactions against authoritative philosophical positions, from supernaturalism to rationalism, and as such are different forms of postmodernism.

Social Life

This involves opposition to past, rationally based life in three different forms.

First, if we believe that the rational (or classical) rules, associated with modernism, which have been foundational for art, music, theater, and architecture, should be resisted and replaced with complete freedom in culture, then we are adopting a postmodern position. In postmodern culture we have complete freedom to reject rules for art and so paint as we like, form a "sound mass" by mixing styles and sounds in music, mix styles in fashion from worldwide origins, seek to discard script or text in the theater, and break away from formal, geometric style in architecture.

Another form of postmodern opposition is with regard to oppression. At one level, if we believe that the way parents and grandparents brought up children was too narrow-minded, we therefore adopt a (postmodern form of) culture that expresses broad-mindedness. At another level postmodernism resists our current education system by seeking a move to independent computer learning, on the grounds that systematization of subjects and the social discipline of the classroom are oppressive. Postmodernism resists a legal system based upon "modern" values and in which people without money (for defense purposes) are disadvantaged. Postmodernism resists oppression of the disadvantaged in our society, such as women, "blacks," and homosexuals.

The third area of reaction against oppression is to make working-class (or "subjected") people aware of what is happening to them as part of the process of increasing the profits of management. This is done by making known what has happened in industrial society, from the point where individuals were gathered from home to work in factories or mills so that goods could be produced more cheaply by the factory owner. Currently, some goods are produced which are effectively out-of-date so that repairs are not available, which means that new goods have to be purchased. Factory owners also switch production overseas where labor is cheaper, or move "hands" from local factories to smaller, computer-based centers. Postmodernism opposes the change from a nation state into a market state.

(Christian) Religious Life

We have already noted the fact that opposition to the church and its teaching began, effectively, with the Renaissance, but it has not ceased. It currently involves the claim that there is neither absolute truth nor certainty, because "What is true is only true for me," and we cannot know whether our experiences are real. The message of Christianity according to such a view cannot therefore be absolutely true. This would rule out central Christian beliefs, for example, that in order to deal with human sin, God himself took human form in the person of Jesus, demonstrating how life should and might be lived, and made possible by his crucifixion death on our behalf and by indwelling the human life in spirit form. Beyond this, postmodernism claims that there is no historical truth; history is written by the "winners" and fitted into a particular viewpoint. Therefore there can be no truth in the biblical account of the life of Christ, nor in the explanation given, for example, in the letters of St. Paul. Still further, postmodernism claims that there is no truth in promises for the future; any thought of the intervention of Jesus Christ so as to rehabilitate the world is no more than wishful thinking. Postmodernism therefore offers spiritual alternatives to Christianity. Christians understand spirituality with reference to the Christian life made possible by closeness to God and indwelling by God-in-Spirit-form (the Holy Spirit). Postmodernism sees spirituality in terms of "New Age spirituality" or "Self spirituality." Such spirituality represents a belief in something beyond and outside of oneself and an emphasis upon "positive thinking" far removed from rationality or religion by emphasizing freedom to rely upon individual, personal experience and alternative explanations of suffering.

Christians claim that suffering is often the result of "sin," but postmodernism claims that such problems arise because of a refusal to make choices
and live by them. The Christian approach interprets sin as offending against
an objective, God-given order, while postmodernists emphasize the need for
authenticity in relation to self-chosen priorities and goals.

It is clear that many of the postmodern challenges to authority are likely
to affect people who seek to share their faith, or to come to faith because the
challenges meet the Christian faith "head-on." The authority of reason is of
greater importance than the authority of scripture, and truth in itself is not
real; what is true is what is true for me. Neither are there grounds for accepting the historical truth of the Bible, because all history writing is biased and
slanted. Since one of the key things from a postmodern perspective is for
human beings to think positively and to make choices, exploration of "New
Age" religion and "spirituality" is important. Such a challenge raises a number of problems.

First, how are ordinary church members to begin to understand the true
nature and complexity of postmodernism so as to be able to communicate
their faith in a way that is relevant to the present age? How many church
members (and clergy, too) really understand the nature of postmodernism,
and how many can actually meet the challenges to their faith that stem from
postmodernism? When I was very much involved in research into the way
the postmodern approach affects the attitudes of young teenagers to Christianity, I was dismayed to find that very few Christians understood the nature of postmodernism at all, and even fewer were able to answer the actual challenge questions made by teenagers against the Christian faith. When
preparing this chapter for "Communicating Faith," I noted an article in the
Baptist Times headed, "Teens and the Church." One statement cried out to me:

Post-modernism means absolutes are harder to define and comprehend.[3]

Perhaps it was not intended to define postmodernism, but simply to give
consequences of it; but it was confusing to read it in a leading denominational weekly.

Second, is there any link between the absence of answers to postmodernism by church members and the reason for departure of teenagers from the
church? There is little doubt about the disappearance. One report written at

3. R. Dickinson, "Teens and the Church," Baptist Times (September 20, 2007)

the beginning of 2007 by a reporter in the *Times* claimed that if the fall-away of teenagers and those who have grown out of their teens from churches continues, then thousands of churches will be closed during the next fifteen years. It is not simply a matter of a gap in church congregations. It is a matter of great concern that somewhere and somehow we are not communicating to the teenage group about our Christian faith in a way that God can use. Is there any way we can enter into the thinking, attitudes, and feelings of teenagers who have turned away from Jesus Christ and from the church so that at least we are aware of the problem from their point of view?

Meeting the Challenge—Step 1

One way is to design an attitude test that reveals the attitudes of teenagers to the church and to the Christian faith. In such an attitude test, teenagers would respond to a whole battery of statements, some of which are distinctively postmodern and some of which are "traditional." Included in the statements would be a section devoted to Christianity in which some statements were orthodox Christian and some reflect anti-Christian views associated with postmodern thinking. By using a five-point scale of +/−2 for statements with which they strongly agree or strongly disagree, +/−1 for statements with which they agree or disagree, and a zero score where the respondent was neutral, it is possible to get a measurement of their attitudes.

Therein lies a problem. Where can we find large groups of teenagers who will participate in such a test? It is no good trying in churches, because those who react against Christianity will already have left. (There are indications that by sixteen years old, those who reject Christianity and the church have already left.) Neither is it normally possible to administer such a test in schools, because of the interruption this would cause to the normal syllabus. I was one of those in an *abnormal* position. I was privileged to be given the opportunity to look into the attitudes of eleven- to fourteen-year-old children in North Merseyside schools with the support of the University of Liverpool, the University of Bangor, and Sefton Education Authority, with the support and cooperation of one of the authority's senior advisors.[4]

4. Full reports of the work with children in schools in Sefton, Merseyside, were provided in Gower, *Conversations with Children* (Bootle, UK: Sefton Education Authority), 2003; and Gower, *The Effect of Postmodernism upon Children and Their Religious Education* (Bootle, UK: Sefton Education Authority), 2005.

The first problem was how to write the statements. What language would teenagers use in understanding and responding to such statements? Which statements would be relevant to their experiences? With the help of the senior advisor and the support of head teachers, it was arranged that I would talk with groups of five children at a time for twenty minutes per group in a number of schools throughout the Authority. I was able to interview 180 children in such a way, in places that varied from an empty classroom to a school library and a medical inspection room.[5] Another possible problem was whether the children would feel free to respond to me. It helped to be a qualified and experienced teacher, but somewhat to my surprise, age helped as well. I corresponded somewhat to a grandparent. Relationships between the children and their family grandparents were generally very good, and they treated me in the same way. It also helped that I was fairly deaf, because it resulted in the children wanting to help me to overcome the problem, and this influenced their desire to help me in other ways. So how did the conversations go? What follows is an element from conversations with three different groups of children.[6]

Eleven-Year-Olds, about to Move Up to Secondary School

Gower: We've talked about things which are right and wrong; now let us talk about things that are real. This table is real (knocks it) because I can feel it, see it and I suppose I could smell it—at least I could when it was first made; I could cut it. And if I dropped it on the floor I could hear it too. Does that mean that everything is real if we can see it, hear it, feel it, or are there other things that are real that you can't do that with?

Eleven-year-olds: No; Dreams.

Gower: Ah! But are dreams real?

Eleven-year-olds: No, because they're dreams aren't they? You can't touch them. You can't smell them.

Gower: But they are real, dreams, aren't they? If you've had a really nasty one it frightens you, doesn't it?

Eleven-year-olds: Ah! Yes!

5. This created a theoretical problem. Would the children be safe with me? Further, would I be safe from possible and untrue complaints from the children? In order to eliminate any such possibility everything was sound-recorded, from the group's entry into the room with me until their departure.
6. Each child's contribution is separated by a semicolon.

Gower: So they're real, but not in the way you can touch them, feel them or smell them. But you have lived through it.

Eleven-year-olds: You can see them, and do everything else, but you can't touch them.

Gower: Can you think of anything else that you can't touch or feel or smell that is real?

Eleven-year-olds: Fire!

Gower: What about the thoughts you have in your head? Are they real?

Eleven-year-olds: Yes and no, because you know that you've got them, and no because you can't touch them; You can't handle them.

Gower: So when you talk about things that are real, there are some things that are real because you can touch them, but there are other things that are real like our thoughts or our dreams. What about when you're afraid of something; is fear real?

Eleven-year-olds: Yes, it's horrible.

Gower: You can feel that though, can't you, in a special way? And you can say that love is real, but that is different too, isn't it?

Eleven-year-olds: Yes.

Gower: A religious person feels that God is real, don't they? How do you think you could tell if God is real or not?

Eleven-year-olds: Because you could see him; You'd phone him [Laughter]; if your dad was down at the pub having a drink, you'd know he was there because you could phone him and you could hear him; Growing up in a society where the parents tell their kids that a God is real and someone came up to them and said "God isn't real," then they just wouldn't believe it because they're used to it that God is real.

Gower: Do you think children believe what they do because of their parents?

Eleven-year-olds: Yes; As we grow up we think a thing is right because that's what we've grown up with.

Gower: So you think that if parents are religious then their children become religious, too.

Eleven-Year-Olds: Yes.

They are already moving toward the postmodern position that there is no reality, and that beliefs at their stage of life are parental.

*Twelve- to Thirteen-Year-Olds: A Conversation Starting with
Rules in Football*

Gower: One of the rules which was made a long time ago is that a good
rule is one which brings the greatest happiness to the greatest number of
people. Suppose you had rules that always did that. Do you think it would
work?

Twelve- to thirteen-year-olds: Then everybody would be the same and nobody would be different; There wouldn't be any difference between people;
If it was for every single person, some people would be happy but some people wouldn't be.

Gower: The idea is the "greatest happiness of the greatest number." But
do you think everybody can be happy?

Twelve- to thirteen-year-olds: Probably.

Gower: What would you say to a person who said that the only person who
could make the really right rules was God (like religious people)?

Twelve- to thirteen-year-olds: It depends how they hear them; Some people
of Islam are religious but they interpret their ideas of Islam in a different
way. They think they should kill, but we think they're wrong; Kamikaze—
they kill themselves for their country and they think it's good!

Gower: You've actually said something very important. When you get religious rules, people have to interpret them in their own way to know what is
right and wrong. Do you think that is right about every rule—that we have
to decide for ourselves whether they are right or wrong for us? Or can rules
be right or wrong in themselves?

Twelve- to thirteen-year-olds: We have to decide for ourselves because some
people think it's right and some people think it's wrong.

Gower: So suppose one of your friends says something is right and you
think it's wrong, how do you decide between you?

Twelve- to thirteen-year-olds: Argue with them; Some families, well most
families, ground their kids and some people just don't think it's right and
others think, like, stopping smacking is wrong, but I personally don't get it
[laughter]; Not smacking hard, because you try and discipline the child to
keep them from lying.

They recognize one of the postmodern claims, that right and wrong are personal issues and not absolute and external.

Thirteen- to Fourteen-Year-Olds: Postmodern Approach to Employment

Gower: Has anyone any idea of the work they are going to do when they leave school?

Thirteen- to fourteen-year-old: Yes, I want to be an engineer.

Gower: What kind of engineer?

Thirteen- to fourteen-year-old: Designing computer-controlled domestic equipment—like fridges, which will order what you need when you begin to run out.

Gower: Sounds great; but where will you do that?

Thirteen- to fourteen-year-old: There's already some design companies that are working on it.

Gower: What do the rest of you think of a job like that?

Thirteen- to fourteen-year-olds: You have to get good exam results.

Gower: Anything else?

Thirteen- to fourteen-year-olds: You have to be prepared to move; and work overseas.

Gower: Why? What do you mean?

Thirteen- to fourteen-year-olds: Well, the big companies will build factories where they can get cheaper workers overseas, so that they will make more money; Yes, just like Dyson's are taking their factory to Malaysia and putting a lot of people out of work in this country; My dad says business always does that.

Gower: Does the advertising ever tell you about this? What would be the truth?

They clearly understood some of the postmodern approaches to capitalist/consumerist power.

In all, 180 children were interviewed in groups of five, thirty-six groups in all, with discussions that varied from Harry Potter to ghosts and experiences with the Ouija board. Overall it gave guidance on what language the children used, what themes were relevant to them, and how far they were influenced by postmodern thinking. It was therefore possible to begin to bring things together in a four-page attitude test. Page 1 recorded details about the children—age, sex, school and area where they lived—and gave instructions to tell them how to proceed. Pages 2 and 3 contained ninety-six statements, half reflecting different aspects of postmodernism and half different aspects of traditionalism. The questions were brought together under the headings of culture, commerce, religion (which was about Christianity), and thinking. Page 4 gave space and opportunity for the children to say what they thought about the paper and invited them to do so. Experts in the field confirmed the validity of the test. In all, 426 children completed the test in five different secondary schools. The following statements are taken at random from Section 24 in the "religion" section of the test:

53. There's no difference; all religions worship the same God.
55. God can help people to live better lives.
56. Stories in the Bible about Jesus are exaggerated.
57. Someone had to create the world; it must have been God.
62. Jesus was only a man and didn't rise from the dead.
68. "Spirituality" means ghosts and spirits.
75. Christianity is the only true religion.

Scores on any one section could vary from 24 (if every response was strongly negative) to 120 (if every response was strongly positive). So what did we find?

1. Scores for "culture" were very similar to scores on "thinking." Whether children were able to think things through or whether they simply absorbed attitudes from contemporary culture, the result was the same. Further, children in school Years 7 and 8 were mostly neutral to postmodernism as a reaction against rationality in the areas of culture and thinking, but some were beginning to adopt a postmodern approach.

2. The same children (from county and denominational schools) reacted more strongly against the power and authority lying behind present-day "commerce," and were beginning to adopt a postmodern approach. They understood the issues—which were real in the homes and communities where they lived—and this stimulated reaction.

3. More children held negative (postmodern) attitudes toward Christianity (241) than positive ones (173); there were 12 children who did not complete or who spoiled this section of the attitude test. The statement that gained greatest approval was, "It does not matter what religion one believes in." Other statements that gained general approval included "Christianity is not the only true religion," "People who pray are not stupid," "Christians do not live better lives than other people," and "I don't often go to church." The children had already come to agreement about a number of factors in

religion. Although they had ceased to attend church, they had a respect
for Christianity and for other religions, although they did not believe that
Christianity helped people to live better lives, nor that it was the only true
religious faith. They believed that religions were different and that one's religious faith was a personal choice. In short, they were on course for adopting a [moderate] postmodern position toward Christianity but had not yet
arrived at a typical postmodern position that had no place for Christianity
at all.

Page 4 of the test paper gave children an opportunity to respond to the invitation, "Now, if you wish, tell us what you think about the paper." There
were a few comments like "I didn't have enough time," or "This is a waste
of time," but most of the written comments were used by the children to express their doubts about the Christian faith. They were genuine questions,
but they took the form of typical postmodern "challenge" questions that demanded answers, and the comment was frequently made that they had not
received the answers they needed. There was a veiled threat that if Christian
leadership could not or would not provide the answers, then there was no
point in them following Christianity.

If we bring together (1) the negative reactions to the attitude statements,
(2) the comments made on page 4 of the test paper, and (3) comments made
during the preliminary interviews, it is possible to draw up a list of key questions that are a direct challenge to the Christian church, and which are not
being answered to the satisfaction of the children:

—How can you make sense out of what Christians call "the Trinity"?
—What, exactly, is a Christian?
—How can Christianity be true if people who call themselves Christians
do not believe and practice the same things, and even attack one another?
—If God is real, how come some prayers are answered and some are not?
—If God is real, as Christians claim, how is it that scientists deny it?
—Why can't Christians do some good in the world instead of just sing-
ing hymns and reading the Bible?
—If God is good, why is there so much evil in the world?
—Can you prove what the church teaches about Jesus?
—Why is it always wrong to steal and always wrong to tell a lie?
—How is it that if Christianity was started by a Jew who lived 2,000 years
ago and 2,000 miles away, Great Britain became a Christian country?

Meeting the Challenge—Step 2

Some of the challenge questions are more than mere questions; they are deeply important and emotional to the children who raised them, such as the one, "How can you make sense of the Trinity?" It was a Year 5 girl in a Church of England school who stood up from her group of five and demanded, "How can God have a son if he cannot have sex?" The others in the group gave her a clap. It was a Year 9 boy from a secondary school who, having been taken by his R.E. teacher with a class to see some of the local churches, stood beside a baptistery in the Baptist church and said to the minister, "Look sir, we have been to the Church of England and seen the font where children are baptized and become Christians (although they have to be confirmed or something). Then we went to the Methodist church which was simpler but more or less the same. And now we come here to something quite different but which is still called "baptism." How on earth are we to understand Christianity if Christians differ so much from one another?"

It seems clear that children at the lower end of secondary schooling will not come to faith unless answers are given to the fundamental postmodern challenge questions that they are beginning to ask. Some children in this age group go even further. They believe that the claims of Christianity are ridiculous, and use their challenge questions to prove it! It is clear that unless Christian leadership is able to give answers and communicate faith, then teenagers will give up, find the meaning to life elsewhere, and leave the church. That's the simple answer to the challenge.

I was given an opportunity to see how well Christians and Christian leadership could communicate their faith by accepting invitations to explain what I had found, in groups from Churches Together, Ministers' Fraternals, and conferences, so as to answer some of the pupils' questions in churches in England and in the U.S. I was severely shaken. Not only were most people in church congregations totally unable to answer the questions, but neither were many clergy able to answer them. They were able to organize camps, weekends, youth church, activities, and music that met some of teenagers' social and cultural needs and indicated that the church was "with it," but they did not answer the postmodern challenges to Christianity that were fundamental to the teenagers concerned. It was clear that unless Christian leadership was able to answer the challenge questions in the way that teenagers needed, then this age group would soon be absent from the church (which, of course, they are).

One way of being able to meet the problem is for Christians to be taught the answers to these and similar questions through their church, through conferences, and through reading, although my impression is that this is not normally happening.[7] I have noted some current attempts to answer the question, "Why does God sometimes hear our prayers and at other times does not," and most attempts to answer this would not convince a teenager. Another major question that asked, "How can God have a son if he cannot have sex?" leads to the question about the nature and reality of the Trinity. If only Christians understood that while in our culture, a "son" means "the offspring of the father," by contrast, in Israel at the time of Jesus, a "son" meant "the revelation of the father." Because God in Absolute form could not be personally known, God revealed himself in human form in the person of Jesus, and he now indwells every Christian in Spirit form. This is language and concept a teenager can understand, but where do they hear it?

Another way of being able to meet the problem is for Christians in different groups to give the same answers, or at least acknowledge that revelation is so vast that different groupings would have different interpretations, just as different individuals would suggest different routes so as to complete a major journey. The trouble is that instead of one group saying, "God has led me this way," while another group says "God has led me a different way" they say, "I am right and you are wrong!" If you were a teenager and asked "What, exactly is a Christian?" and the many answers varied from "One who is baptized into the church as a child" to "One who follows the teachings of Jesus Christ" or "One who asks Jesus into his heart," is it not to be expected that the church would be held up to ridicule by intelligent young people?[8] Add to this multitudes of differences between those Christians who celebrate the Eucharist and those who keep the Lord's Supper, those Christians who believe there is a hell and those who do not, those who worship in

7. In a recent BBC "Songs of Praise" broadcast where there were large numbers of young people in the congregation, the interviewer asked one girl why there were so many teenagers. "Because we are allowed to ask questions here which you are not allowed to ask in other churches," she replied.

8. Children gave five different definitions: Christians are people who follow the teachings of Christianity; a Christian is a person who believes in the Bible; Christians are people who believe in God; a Christian is a person who goes to church; Christians believe they will go to heaven when they die.

quietness and those who shout, raise their arms, and sing in tongues, those who believe that the ministry should include women and those who do not, and those who believe that homosexuality is not a sin while others believe the opposite, then is it really any wonder that teenagers react as they do? The simple answer is that Christians of every persuasion should (quote, teenager) "Get their act together!"

For many years I was the inspector responsible for children's religious education in schools throughout the whole of inner London, and I had the opportunity not only to meet with and talk with children and their teachers within a very large area, but was able to talk with children who had settled in London and had come from other parts of the world. It became clear that reaction against Christianity due to postmodern challenge is not simply a local or even a national issue, but an international one.

One is sometimes tempted to despair, but it is no small comfort to remember that Jesus gathered a completely diverse group of disciples, from tax collector to fishermen, and (except for one!) they found unity together.

9 Communicating Faith through Religious Education

Stephen J. McKinney

This chapter aims to look at how faith can be communicated through religious education within the specific context of Catholic schools in Scotland. This will be achieved by a critical review and reflection of the history of religious education within the post-Vatican II era and through the application of insights gained from a series of extended expert interviews with Bill Horton, recently retired advisor of religious education for secondary schools in the Archdiocese of Glasgow. The interviews provided a wealth of background information and fascinating insights into the development of religious education in the Scottish Catholic secondary schools. Bill's personal and professional journey as teacher and advisor in religious education and his archdiocesan and national leadership roles meant that he was involved in many of the major initiatives of the late twentieth century. The initial sections of this chapter will, then, sketch a brief history of Catholic schools in Scotland and provide an overview of the unique nature of these Catholic schools, including the post-Vatican II history of religious education within Catholic schools. The chapter will then examine some key ideas drawn from

Bill Horton's comments on this history and his vision of religious education and the future of religious education.

Catholic Schools in Scotland

There is a rich diversity of national-cultural heritages within the post-Reformation Catholic community in Scotland: Italian, Lithuanian, Polish, Irish, and indigenous Scots Catholics.[1] The critical mass for the establishment of post-Reformation Catholic schools, however, came from those of Irish origin.[2] The geographical proximity between Scotland and Ireland has historically facilitated frequent crossover and interchange in both population and culture. At the beginning of the nineteenth century, increasing numbers of Irish Catholics, procuring employment in agriculture but also increasingly in industry, had settled in Scotland, especially in the West.[3] Those Irish Catholics who sought schooling for their children encountered the bewildering variety and somewhat chaotic mosaic of school provision in Scotland that predated the establishment of the national school system and compulsory school education.[4] A small number of voluntary Catholic schools were established in the west of Scotland to preserve religious identity and culture for Catholic children.[5] The number of Catholic schools grew steadily throughout the early nineteenth century, but demand for Catholic schooling dramatically increased with the influx of the Catholic Irish immigrants who arrived as a result of the series of famines in Ireland in the period of 1845–1849.[6] Despite attempts by the government to standardize school education in 1872, the Catholic schools remained substantially self-funded because the Catholic Church was concerned that the distinctive con-

---

1. Stephen J. McKinney, "Immigrants and Religious Conflict: Insider Accounts of Italian, Lithuanian and Polish Catholics in Scotland," in *Global Citizenship Education: Philosophy, Theory and Pedagogy*, ed. Michael A. Peters, Harry Blee, and Alan. Britton (Rotterdam: Sense Publishers, 2007).

2. Robert Anderson, "The History of Scottish Education, Pre-1980," in *Scottish Education Post-Devolution*, ed. Tom G. K. Bryce and Walter Humes, 219–28 (Edinburgh: Edinburgh University Press, 2003).

3. Martin J. Mitchell, *The Irish in the West of Scotland 1797–1848* (Edinburgh: John Donald Publishers, 1998).

4. Martha Skinnider, "Catholic Elementary Education in Glasgow, 1818–1918," in *Studies in the History of Scottish Education 1872–1939*, ed. Thomas R. Bone, 13–70 (London: University of London Press, 1967).

5. James E. Handley, *The Irish in Scotland 1798–1845* (Cork: Cork University Press, 1943).

6. Robert F. Foster, *Modern Ireland 1600–1972* (London: Penguin Press, 1988); Thomas M. Devine, *The Scottish Nation* (London: Penguin Press, 2006).

fessional nature of Catholic schooling should be preserved.[7] This was resolved by the 1918 Education (Scotland) Act, which enabled the Catholic schools to be recipients of full state funding but retain denominational status, Catholic religious education, and the right to appoint Catholic teachers (subject to approval from the Scottish hierarchy).[8]

This early history of Catholic schooling has been presented by insider academic sources as an arduous struggle to educate an impoverished immigrant community that experienced sectarian hostility and resentment. Arguably, the sectarianism and resentment were focused on certain periods of history—for example, the economic recession between the two world wars.[9] Perhaps this history requires contemporary revision within broader conceptual frameworks of immigrant typologies. Some recent historical accounts have, perhaps more helpfully, focused on the heroic and invaluable contribution of a number of religious orders and congregations to Catholic schooling, and to Scottish education as a whole, in the nineteenth and twentieth centuries.[10] The influence of the Marists, Sisters of Mercy, Sisters of Notre Dame, and the Franciscans of the Immaculate Conception declined in the 1980s and the 1990s. The Jesuit school remains in Glasgow, and there is a Jesuit chaplain, but there are no Jesuits involved in management and teaching. The Catholic schools are now almost exclusively managed and staffed with members of the Catholic laity and, in some cases, especially in secondary schools in the east of Scotland, a fairly high percentage of non-Catholic teaching staff.[11]

Currently, there are 55 secondary, 327 primary, and 6 SEN (Special Ed-

7. Thomas A. Fitzpatrick, *Catholic Secondary Education in South West Scotland before 1972* (Aberdeen: Aberdeen University Press, 1986).

8. Anderson, "The History of Scottish Education, Pre-1980," in *Scottish Education Post-Devolution* (see note 2), and in Lindsay Paterson, *Scottish Education in the Twentieth Century* (Edinburgh: Edinburgh University Press, 2003).

9. Brother Kenneth, *Catholic Schools in Scotland 1872–1972* (Glasgow: John S. Burns and Sons, 1972); Tom Gallagher, *Glasgow—The Uneasy Peace: Religious Tension in Modern Scotland* (Manchester: Manchester University Press, 1987); Lindsay Paterson and Cristina Iannelli, "Religion, Social Mobility and Education in Scotland," *British Journal of Sociology* 57, no. 3 (2006): 353–77; and Devine, *The Scottish Nation.*

10. Francis J. O'Hagan, *The Contribution of the Religious Orders to Education in Glasgow during the Period 1847–1918* (Lampeter, UK: Edwin Mellen Press, 2006); John Watts, *A Canticle of Love: The Story of the Franciscan Sisters of the Immaculate Conception* (Edinburgh: Birlinn, 2006).

11. Fitzpatrick, "Catholic Education," in *Scottish Life and Society: A Companion to Scottish Ethnology*, Vol. 11, ed. Heather Holmes, 435–55 (East Linton, UK: Tuckwell Press, 2000); Fitzpatrick, "Catholic Education in Scotland," in *Scottish Education Post-devolution*, ed. Tom G. K. Bryce and Walter Humes, 272–81 (Edinburgh: Edinburgh University Press, 2003).

ucational Needs) state-funded Catholic schools in Scotland.[12] There are three private Catholic schools, two in Glasgow and one in Perthshire. The state-funded Catholic schools are comprehensive and coeducational (with the exception of Notre Dame High School for Girls in Glasgow).[13] Approximately 124,000 children attend Catholic schools, accounting for over 21 percent of the overall school population.[14] According to the Scottish Bishops' Report, approximately "5 percent of Catholic students attend non-denominational state schools and around 10 percent of students in Catholic schools are not baptized Catholics."[15] Catholic schools are inclusive of all members of the Catholic community, and admission is not determined by any criteria of public practice. Further, Catholic schools have become attractive to members of other Christian denominations and other faiths, and the figure of 10 percent proposed by the Bishops' Report is probably a conservative estimate for the Catholic secondary schools. Catholic schools are located primarily in the postindustrial west central belt, where many of the Irish immigrants and their descendants had worked and settled, but there are a small number of Catholic secondary and primary schools in Dundee, Perth, and Edinburgh, and primary schools in Aberdeen, Inverness, parts of the Highlands, and the Borders.[16]

Religious Education in Catholic Schools in Scotland

The pre-Vatican II approach to religious education in Scotland's Catholic schools is probably best summed up by some of the titles used, "Religious Knowledge" and "Religious Instruction," which contain clear indications of a transmission model of education that belongs to an age of greater certainty and possibly greater self-confidence. There was probably also more confidence in the level of parental practice and support for the faith formation of the children. The children's catechism was used in most primary schools,

12. Scottish Catholic Education Service (SCES), available online at http:www.sces.uk.com (accessed January 19, 2009).
13. McKinney, "The Faith School Debate: Catholic Schooling in Scotland," *Pastoral Review* 3, no. 4 (2007): 28–34.
14. SCES online.
15. Bishops' Conference of Scotland, *Religion in Scotland's School: A Report to European Council of Episcopal Conferences (CCEE)*, 2006, available online at http://www.chiesacattolica.it/cci_new/PagineCCI/AllegatiArt/30/Scozia_ingl.doc.
16. McKinney, "Catholic Education in Scotland," in *Scottish Education beyond Devolution*, ed. Tom G. K. Bryce and Walter. Humes, 3rd ed. (Edinburgh: Edinburgh University Press, 2008).

and various books of Christian doctrine were used in the secondary schools. The early stages of the post-Vatican II era coincided with a developing crisis in morality and spirituality in society that created an initial vacuum in the vision and provision of religious education.[17] A working party was set up by Bishop Thompson in the early 1970s to respond to the "General Catechetical Directory" (1971), and this resulted in The Approach to Religious Education in the Catholic Secondary School (1974).[18]

A number of interrelated external factors acted as additional catalysts for the development of religious education in the Catholic schools. First, the Catholic schools were to benefit enormously from the endeavors to improve and develop religious education in the nondenominational sector. This began with the Millar Report (1972), which presented the findings of a group established to audit the provision of religious education in nondenominational schools in Scotland.[19] They discovered that religious education in Scotland often reflected a rationale and methodology that were anachronistic and ineffectual, usually overly concerned with a historical approach to Christianity and biblical study. They raised major concerns: Education authorities demonstrated little interest; religious education was allotted insufficient time and was poorly resourced; no internal/public exams and no inspections existed; teaching often lacked imagination and relevance; many teachers lacked motivation and confidence to teach religious education; and the quality of the teaching and learning varied enormously. This has to be viewed within an educational context that contained no specialist teachers and no departments of religious education (there was no teaching qualification for religious education).[20] This further meant that schools were often poorly resourced for the teaching of religious education. This situation can also be contextualized within a complex sociocultural and religious context.[21] The practice rate in the established Church of Scotland had be-

17. Fitzpatrick, "Catholic Education in Scotland."
18. Sacred Congregation for the Clergy, "General Catechetical Directory" (1971), in Vatican Council II More Postconciliar Documents, ed. Austin Flannery, OP (Leominster: Fowler Wright Books, 1982); Scottish Catholic Bishops, The Approach to Religious Education in the Catholic Secondary School (Edinburgh: SCB, 1974).
19. Scottish Education Department, Moral and Religious Education in Scottish Schools (the Millar Report) (Edinburgh: HMSO, 1972).
20. Alex Rodger, "Religious Education," in Scottish Education Post-devolution, ed. Tom G. K. Bryce and Walter Humes, 600–605 (Edinburgh: Edinburgh University Press, 2003).
21. McKinney, "Symbol or Stigma? The Place of Catholic Schools in Scotland," The Catalyst 7 (2007): 12–14.

gun to fall in the 1950s–1960s, and the influence of Christianity began to decline in public and private spheres.[22] One of the consequences was that the general knowledge and understanding of religious language and concepts, especially within families from Christian traditions, were also declining.[23] Ethnic and religious diversity became more marked as increasing numbers of Asian immigrants (from the 1960s onward) enabled the establishment of vibrant Muslim, Sikh, and Hindu communities in the larger cities such as Glasgow.[24]

The Millar Report recommended that the rationale and methodology for religious education be revised to reflect contemporary thinking in the understanding of the nature and purpose of learning and religion—thinking influenced by developmental psychology and the phenomenology of religion. The report advised that teachers of religious education, at all levels, should be adequately trained and that specialist teachers of religious education should be trained for secondary schools. Courses were established at teacher training institutions and inspections introduced in 1983.[25] Further progress in the development of religious education was marked by the SCCORE (Scottish Central Committee on Religious Education) documents. *Bulletin 1* (1978) and *Bulletin 2* (1981) mapped out the aims and outcomes of a religious education designed to respond to the complexity of the new sociocultural and religious context.[26]

This created a climate of greater expectation of professionalism in religious education in both denominational and nondenominational sectors. A teaching qualification for Catholic secondary teachers was introduced in 1974, and the Catholic secondary schools responded quickly to these initiatives.[27] Catholic schools in the east of Scotland were the first to introduce principal teachers of religious education in Catholic schools in the mid-1970s. Catholic schools in the West would introduce principal teachers of re-

22. Callum G. Brown, *Religion and Society in Scotland since 1707* (Edinburgh: Edinburgh University Press, 1997); Brown, *The Death of Christian Britain: Understanding Secularisation 1800–2000* (London: Routledge, 2001).

23. Alex Rodger, "Religious Education."

24. Bashir Maan, *The New Scots* (Edinburgh: John Donald Publishers, 1992).

25. Fitzpatrick, "Catholic Education in Scotland."

26. Scottish Central Committee on Religious Education (SCCORE), *Bulletin 1: A Curricular Approach to Religious Education* (Edinburgh: HMSO, 1978); Scottish Central Committee on Religious Education (SCCORE), *Bulletin 2: Curricular Guidelines on Religious Education* (Glasgow: Consultative Committee on the Curriculum, 1981).

27. Fitzpatrick, "Catholic Education in Scotland."

ligious education in the early 1980s, and by the late 1990s almost every Catholic secondary school in Scotland would have a principal teacher of religious education. With an expectation that each pupil (S1–S6) should receive two periods (approximately fifty-five minutes each) of religious education per week, very few Catholic schools were able to staff religious education departments with sufficient specialist teachers. Hence, teachers continued to be recruited from other subject areas (generalist religious education teachers) and were asked to be responsible for one religious education class for the academic year.

The next key moment in the development of religious education in Scotland was the publication of the *Religious and Moral Education 5–14 National Curricular Guidelines*.[28] This curricular approach to all subjects for children aged 5 to 14 was prompted by huge concerns about the transitions between primary school and secondary school and transitions within primary and secondary schools. There were concerns that the progression in learning between these stages was not taking place and, if anything, pupils were regressing. This was perceived to be particularly problematic in the transition between primary and secondary schools.[29] Religious and Moral Education was included in the 5–14 curricular guidelines, which used a common structure, concepts, and language for all subject areas.

The importance of this document cannot be underestimated, because it represents the first set of national curricular guidelines and programs for religious education from primary level 1 to secondary level 2 in the nondenominational sector. Initially, the denominational schools were to be issued the same document with an appendix at the back. This was rejected by the Scottish Catholic Education Commission for a number of reasons. First, the Catholic school sector questioned the separation of the *religious* and the *moral dimensions*, arguing that, for Catholic Christianity, morality stems from religion. Second, Catholic schools have an explicit faith formational dimension. This was not reflected in the document. Third, while Catholic schools have a responsibility to teach about other Christian denominations and

28. Scottish Office Education Department (SOED), *Religious and Moral Education* (Edinburgh: Scottish Office Education Department, 1992), 5–14, available online at http://www.ltscotland.org.uk/5to14/htmlunrevisedguidelines/Pages/RE/Main/recontents.htm (accessed January 19, 2009).

29. Frank R. Adams, "5–14: Origins, Development and Implementation," in *Scottish Education Post-devolution*, ed. Tom G. K. Bryce and Walter Humes, 369–79 (Edinburgh: Edinburgh University Press, 2003).

world faiths, the focus for Catholic schools is primarily Catholic Christianity. Fourth, it was argued that there was insufficient emphasis on liturgy and the sacraments. Finally, there were concerns about the nature and understanding of personal search (the element that allowed for personal religious or spiritual development).

This process acted as a catalyst for an internal review of the rationale for religious education in Catholic schools in Scotland, resulting in the publication of a separate document: 5–14 *Religious Education (Roman Catholic Schools)* (1994).[30] This document is introduced by a rationale that presents religious education (not religious and moral education) in the context of the mission of the Catholic Church and the Catholic school. While the other world religions are treated with great respect and are taught, the main focus is on Catholic Christianity. Some of the strands for Christianity were changed to include sacraments and liturgical cycle, and the concept of personal search was presented within the context of Catholic Christianity and the Catholic community. Arguably, the rationale for religious education in this document was more focused on a rationale for Catholic schools in Scotland rather than religious education, but this document was to be very influential in Catholic educational thinking in Scotland. Further documentation was specifically developed for the upper school in the late 1990s (e.g., the *Framework for S5/6 Religious Education*, 1998).[31] This document reflected the influence in Scotland of the thinking of the prominent American religious educator, Thomas Groome (Groome's two day National Conference, "Education for Life," in 2002 at the University of Glasgow, was a great success). An updated, coherent and comprehensive rationale for Scottish Catholic religious education 3–18 was to be undertaken in the middle of the first decade of the twenty-first century.

Religious education was supported by the appointment of full-time chaplains and the establishment of the Catholic Education Commission (1972).[32] A national Catholic syllabus for religious education was produced in 1980. This provided structure and direction and assisted in the selection of appro-

30. Scottish Office Education Department/Catholic Education Commission (SOED/CEC), 5–14 *Religious Education (Roman Catholic Schools)*, 1994, available online at http://www.ltscotland.org.uk/5to14/htmlunrevisedguidelines/Pages/re_rc/main/rerccontents.htm (accessed January 19, 2009).

31. Catholic Education Commission Scotland, *A Framework for S5/6 Religious Education* (Glasgow: Catholic Education Commission Scotland, 1998).

32. Fitzpatrick, "Catholic Education in Scotland."

priate resources. In the Catholic primary schools, the adoption and adaptation of the Irish Veritas program "Children of God," while not without its critics, proved to be generally successful. The introduction of the successor to "Children of God," the Alive-O! Program (published by Veritas), has been more controversial. It would be crude and divisive to attempt to identify different "camps" or "schools of thought" concerning a vision of religious education for the Catholic primary school, because this would suggest a polarization of views. There is, however, at times a robust debate, and some have questioned the child-centered and developmental approach favored by Alive-O! and its supporters and the lack of doctrinal content. Perhaps a useful lens for understanding this debate is the application of Groome's (1996) ontological/epistemological framework for education to religious education in the Scottish scene.[33] There is a balance between what the children should *know* (epistemological) and how they should *be* (ontological). This can be a creative tension, but if a group decides to focus too intensely on one aspect, for example, epistemology or knowledge, it can be to the detriment of the other, ontology or being, and this can create imbalance and tensions.

In recent years, the Catholic secondary schools have employed a wide range of resources, including published materials, resources designed for Catholic schools within Higher Still national qualifications, and some sophisticated programs created within religious education departments. At the time of this writing, the Scottish educational community awaits further developments in the *A Curriculum for Excellence* initiative, which aims to "improve the learning, attainment and achievement of children and young people in Scotland."[34] Bill Horton, working in Catholic education in Scotland between 1971 and 2006, has been a key figure in the implementation of many of these developments.

Bill Horton: A Short Biographical Sketch

After gaining a science degree from Strathclyde University in 1965, Bill Horton worked in industry until 1970. In 1970–1971, he retrained as a sec-

33. Thomas H. Groome, "What Makes a School Catholic?" in *The Contemporary Catholic School*, ed. Terence H. McLaughlin, Joseph O'Keefe, and Bernadette O'Keefe, 107–25 (London: Falmer Press, 1996).

34. Learning and Teaching Scotland (LTS), *Curriculum for Excellence*, 2009, available at http://www.ltscotland.org.uk/curriculumforexcellence/ (accessed January 19, 2009).

ondary teacher of science and math at Notre Dame Catholic Teacher Training College in Glasgow. He taught in John Ogilvie High School, Blantyre, between 1971 and 1973. In 1973, he was appointed assistant principal teacher of guidance at Sacred Heart in Paisley, where he was later promoted to principal teacher of guidance in 1975. Between 1971 and 1975, Bill had pursued further qualifications in religious education and was appointed principal teacher of religious education at St. Modan's Stirling in 1976. In 1979 he was asked to accept the post of religious education advisor for secondary schools in the Archdiocese of Glasgow, becoming effectively the first full-time advisor for religious education in Catholic secondary schools in Scotland. He retired from this post in 2006. I conducted a series of lengthy interviews with Bill in August and September in 2007. These semi-structured interviews were constructed as an extended expert interview.

Religious Education and Faith Formation

Bill Horton does not explicitly quote international or local church documentation on Catholic religious education during the interviews, but his vision is the result of many years of reflection on these ideas and the implications for the specific (some would argue unique or idiosyncratic) socio-historical, ecclesial, and educational context of Scottish Catholic schools. His thinking on the importance of support for the lay teachers, for example, is deeply rooted in his understanding of documents such as *Lay Catholics* (1982).[35] He has a broad conception of religious education as a process that aims to educate and form children so that they can understand and realize the fullness of their humanity, and within this process, be encouraged and free to engage in a personal and communal relationship with God. This religious education is not limited, then, to a curricular subject, but should underpin all activity and relationships in the Catholic school.

Although Bill Horton never aligns himself with any academic thinker, his vision is very similar to the "realistic optimism" articulated by Groome (1998).[36] While Bill clearly understands the challenges faced by Catholic

---

35. Sacred Congregation for Catholic Education, *Lay Catholics in Schools: Witnesses to Faith*, 1982, available at http://www.vatican.va/roman_curia/congregations/ccatheduc/documents/rc_con_ccatheduc_doc_19821015_lay-catholics_en.html (accessed January 19, 2009).

36. Groome, *Educating for Life: A Spiritual Vision for Every Teacher and Parent* (Allen, Tex.: Thomas More Press, 1998).

school communities in Scotland, he retains a positive vision of religious education and Catholic schools as Christ-centered, inclusive, and able to meaningfully engage all those who attend Catholic schools:

I think the whole future of Catholic education and its growing acceptance and acknowledgement in the wider community is dependant on us . . . dependent on making ourselves open and welcoming to those who do not practice and also to those of other denominations and faiths.

Perhaps Bill Horton's vision is one that has been partly molded by the exigencies of the Scottish Catholic schools—in other words, the vision of religious education has been reconfigured to respond to the increase of those who do not practice and the rich, and sometimes eclectic, mix of other denominations and faiths. The dynamic of the catechesis-evangelization model that is often proposed, for example, by the 5–14 document (1994), becomes more weighted toward evangelization (my insert in brackets):

Do we want to have schools that are just for the support of these families and young people or are Catholic schools evangelizing communities that seek to bring the message and presence of Christ alive and active in the wider community? This is perhaps the central question for the future of Catholic schools and religious education in Scotland. If we lack faith in God's action and presence, then I think the temptation would be to go down the same road as some schools have done in England [select a high percentage of practicing Catholics].

It is important to reemphasize that Catholic schools in Scotland have not adopted practice as criteria for selection, but also that he is not denying the importance of practice:

This is not to say we don't think practice is important. We do, but practice flows from free will and desire to worship and acknowledge God's presence.

Underpinning his arguments is the conception of the space and time accorded to the formation of an authentic faith that is a personal commitment that can be freely expressed within a diverse and rich community. This contrasts with the dangers of the adoption of the public external expressions of faith to gain admittance to a Catholic school. He is, however, fully aware of the challenges that face the model that he has proposed for Scottish Catholic schools.

Faith Formation within the Context of the Challenges of Twenty-First Century Scottish Society

There are two main strands to his perception of the challenges faced by Catholic religious education in contemporary Scotland. First, there has been a change of religious culture and religious structures. He argues that Scotland has moved to a post-Christian society, and that this has affected the Catholic community. He also identifies serious deficiencies in the vision of the home-school-parish triangle, where the school becomes the major focus for faith formation of young people. He argues that processes have to be established in an attempt to reinstate some kind of effective working relationship between home-school-parish:

There has to be dialogue and cooperation between parish, home, and school communities, so that the responsibility is a shared one. The schools have a lot to offer and could be assessed as being more successful than many parishes and home in the present time.

Second, he indicates that the fall in practice rate that has affected both staff and pupils in Catholic schools has a number of consequences, but should not necessarily result in a lack of purpose and confidence in the promotion of faith formation within the school setting. Catholic schools are called to encourage staff to witness to their faith, but also to support staff in their faith journey:

We have to be compassionate as well in helping staff who have faith challenges in their own personal lives.

It has been more common to focus on the support required by pupils, and possibly presume that teachers do not require the same level of support, but he recognizes that the Catholic school as a Christian community has a responsibility to support all members of the community in their faith. He prioritizes the needs of the staff because he perceives them to be key figures in the process of faith formation. I will return to this below.

The Faith That Is to Be Formed

The conception of faith proposed by Bill Horton is not just the intellectual assent to a set or system of beliefs, but the engagement with God in a personal, loving relationship:

We are seeking to nurture a first-hand faith, not a second-hand faith, for each of these young people. This is what is required in today's world—that they start to own their faith, not the faith of their priests, parents, and grandparents. The development of their own personal relationship with God is what is being nurtured and developed in this way.

This personal loving relationship has a communal aspect in a shared spirituality and shared spiritual purpose:

This is what we mean by faith. We mean that God has an interest, a love, a care, and concern for all, and that calling on this help can and does bring vision and direction and hope into the life of a school community.

This approach, however, contains internal challenges, as it can be very difficult to measure the progress a child might be making. This is particularly challenging in the present educational climate of increased accountability and the requirement to produce measurement of success in nearly all aspects of school life. He warns against the temptation to intervene in the faith formational process to create indicators of success:

At times, it will appear that we are failing and we will be tempted to tell them and direct them, but what approach to faith development is this? As long as we seek to give them an understanding in a personal way of the love of God the Father, the compassion of Jesus his son, and the power and presence of the Holy Spirit.

He also has a clear understanding of certain prerequisites that must be in place for this faith formation to be successful.

The Prerequisites for Faith Formation in the Catholic Secondary School

Bill Horton identifies a number of starting points for faith formation in the secondary school. First he perceives the approach to religious education in the Catholic primary schools as an appropriate and effective means of faith formation:

There is growing evidence of spiritual hunger among our young people and this is being nurtured and developed by primary RE programs. They are therefore going to be better equipped and receptive to prayer, mediation, and reflection in the secondary school.

He does, however, question whether the process of faith formation in the primary school is continuous with the secondary school and does actually progress in the secondary school:

It would be tragic if this openness and awareness of Jesus Christ alive and active was not given expression and recognition in the secondary school.

His vision, then, for the starting point in the secondary school is to continue the process and, crucially, the rationale and methodologies utilized in the primary schools. This could be perceived by secondary teachers as challenging, because they would be called to be more open and share their own faith, as their primary colleagues are, to continue this process of faith formation for young people:

Where does it start? With us as teachers and nonteaching staff ourselves. At senior management, departmental level there should be a focus, from time to time, for prayer and reflection when getting together to look at contemporary policy procedures and strategies. Doing it together as staff will encourage us to do it naturally and appropriately with the pupils. You cannot really ask for pupils' participation and involvement if staff themselves are not prepared to commit themselves to it with their own peer group. Nonteaching staff in a school have a role as well and should not be excluded from such activities. Their inclusion will help to create a climate of care, love, and support that complements the achievement and excellence that are central to the Catholic school.

Inviting Jesus' power and presence alive and active in this task transforms our actions in this regard.

As is consistent with his realistic optimism, he recognizes that progress has been made in the developments in the spiritual programs in the faculty of education, University of Glasgow (where the majority of teachers for Catholic schools are educated), but he perceives this as a long-term, continuing personal development.

How Is Faith in the Catholic Secondary to Be Formed?

As has been mentioned, he does not envisage religious education as a purely academic engagement, but as a process and an integral part of school life:

You are really sowing or planting in the head and the heart in order to help young people understand their humanity.

This humanity is clearly based on a strong sense of humanity rooted in Christian anthropology. With reference to the religious education class itself, he, once again, highlights the necessity for teachers to persevere and have courage:

Pupils in religious education often don't enthuse the way they would about other subjects that interested and excited them. But this does not mean that you are not dealing with key questions and deep emotions in their lives.

He understands these key questions and deep emotions as opportunities to engage in the mystery of God's revelation and in the shaping of these communal and personal relationships with God. He further argues that teachers should be constantly aware of the opportunities for encounter with God in everyday events. He believes that the school community has a vital role to play in faith formation, and lists the kind of faith formational activities that are typical in a Scottish Catholic secondary school.

I believe that faith formation centers on the recognition of God's presence and action within the school community. This can take place in formal ways through assemblies, religious education classes, visits to the oratory, outside speakers, and partnership in charitable activities. These have a place and are important and should be placed within the school calendar.

He points out that many schools have created pastoral support/liturgical and spiritual support/charitable support teams:

In many schools now there is a group representative of different people in the school—teaching staff, nonteaching staff, chaplains, and, where appropriate, pupils, too, that has the responsibility of putting in place activities, celebrations, and themes that provide a focus for the faith development of all within the school community.

While recognizing the importance and value of these activities and these support structures, he thinks they are in themselves insufficient. He argues that the focus should not simply be directed by the liturgical seasons, but the schools should be constantly focusing on Christological values and themes that emerge from the Gospels, and these should be studied, debated, and meditated on throughout the curriculum and life of the school:

But I do think this needs to be extended as well. Themes such as forgiveness, repentance, justice, hope, compassion, generosity could be chosen and explored and developed throughout the school for a particular session. This would help religious education to have a focus across the curriculum. So that, for example, the theme of forgiveness could be explored through subject areas such as English, history, modern studies, etc.

He also thinks that prayer must be at the heart of school life to sustain the Christian community:

More needs to be done, especially with regard to encouraging the more informal times of prayer and reflection, where teaching and nonteaching staff use their own initiative and desire to pray and reflect with young people in different circumstances within the school community. In fact, this would take the least effort and preparation, but does take courage and faith to witness and seek participation and involvement in this way.

He provides a realistic appraisal of the absence of a consistent prayer culture in many schools, but argues that it is a culture that can be nurtured and that, with more imagination and resources, can be readily supported:

There are lots of prayer resources to help us that are interesting, attractive, and user-friendly. The chaplain is a resource, and the use of the oratory and the influence of staff, including religious education staff in this regard, are all important resources, along with local priests, church organizations, and movements. All are available to assist and help bring alive Jesus Christ's presence and action at the heart of the school community.

His comments are ultimately evangelical in the sense of a call back to a live and communal Christian faith, expressed in rich and varied prayer practices, that empowers the Catholic school to be an inspiring Christian community full of hope and possibilities. This is a community that is confident and open enough to welcome those of other denominations, other faiths, and those of no religious faith.

Concluding Remarks

This vision of faith and faith formation requires great commitment and courage and could be easily misunderstood and misrepresented to lack intellectual rigor and be overly liberal and relaxed. There can be a genuine fear that allowing children time and space and opportunities to grow in their faith cannot be measured and quantified in the same way as a more systematic knowledge and understanding of the teaching of the church. Some Catholic educationalists can feel anxious that the Catholic schools have failed if young people do not have a solid grounding in church teaching to enable them to face the challenges of an increasingly secular world. It would be invidious to dismiss their view as a misguided overemphasis on epistemology as it arises from genuine concern. Perhaps a clearer articulation of views like that of Bill Horton is more helpful? Bill Horton's approach necessarily includes equipping young people with the intellectual and spiritual tools to engage with life and the next stages of the faith journey, whether that is a continuation of the journey, a return to faith, or even a rejection of faith. The young people grow in their knowledge and understanding of the teaching of the church as they experience intellectual, emotional, and spiritual growth—a process he perceives as iterative. His reflections, at the end of a long career of service to religious education and Catholic schools, call for a transformation of the individual and the community. His vision of religious education is contextualized within his vision of the Catholic school as aspiring to be an authentic Christian community that is a prayerful and spiritual community, and one that supports all of its members in their personal and communal relationship with Jesus Christ.

10 Leadership and Transmission

Empowering Witnesses—An Ignatian Perspective

Michael Edwards

A few years ago I was asked to speak to a group of committed Catholics about young people, the faith, and Catholic secondary schools. The premise of their conversation was as follows: the primary purpose of Catholic education is faith formation; fewer and fewer young people attend Mass on Sundays; therefore, Catholic education is a failure!

I was at pains to point out that, from my experience, the longing for a sense of the spiritual and faith identity among our young people is strong. Our schools are doing some excellent work in spiritual and faith formation for young people, and, for a significant number, the school is their only real experience of church. We talked about a vision and mission for Catholic education. We talked about the need for witnesses of the faith. We talked about the need for a sense of belonging, of community, of welcome. In this context I aired the idea of the need for parishes to do even more to meet the needs of our young people and to make them feel welcome and part of the worshipping community. This is a problem for our schools, one gentleman objected, because schools no longer teach the faith. I was told that we should forget about "welcome" and teach the children that if they didn't go to Mass on Sunday they would go to hell and that would solve the problem! As I left the meeting somewhat disheartened, I remained confident that our Catholic schools are not failing in their mission as part of the church, but only me, in failing to explain our purpose and convert a very narrow-minded view.

It is not the remit of this chapter to rehearse the rationale, however it might be contested, of Catholic schools. A key principle, which I believe is becoming more and more urgent, is about leadership and faith transmission in the context of the school community. How do we nurture leaders and how do we empower them? There is a crisis in terms of succession planning for Catholic school leadership. We are very conscious of this, and a number of strategies are being implemented through the Catholic Education Service (for England and Wales), dioceses, our Catholic colleges, and support given by the Centre for Research and Development in Catholic Education at the Institute of Education, University of London. One such piece of relevant and recent research, *Theological Literacy and Catholic Schools*, looks at issues facing the Catholic church in England and Wales with regard to the recruitment of suitable qualified teachers, the diminishing number of teachers who have experienced a Catholic tertiary education, and the need to articulate the role of Catholic schools, which is both authentically Catholic and theologically coherent.[1]

Yet there is another and perhaps even more fundamental dimension that we need to continue to explore. It is the link between faith transmission and staff spiritual development in schools. Bearing in mind that a significant and growing number of staff in our schools is neither of the faith nor practicing the faith, there is a need to enable all those working in our schools to understand that they have a vital contribution to make with regard to the mission and vision of the school as a Catholic community. In short, we need to be able to empower them as witnesses to that mission that is rooted in the faith. There can be no second-class citizens in this matter—namely, those who are and those who are not of the faith. Theological formation is, of course, essential, but we still need to be focused on empowering all those working in our schools to be essential witnesses to the Catholic school as a faith community.

1. Gerald Grace and Nick Weeks, *Theological Literacy and Catholic Schools* (London: Centre for Research and Development in Catholic Education, Institute of Education, University of London, 2007).

Parallel concerns about teachers and leadership for Catholic schools—preparation and prior training, support and development, especially the need to integrate spiritual development with professional development—arise elsewhere, not least in the U.S. Ronald Nuzzi, from the University of Notre Dame, has commented recently, "In a previous generation, pastors, parents, diocesan officials, and universities did not concern themselves with the spiritual formation of Catholic school educators. Such formation was typically supplied via religious communities and congregations through their induction processes leading to religious profession or vows."[2] Nuzzi's view that prospective leaders of Catholic schools "are relatively unaccustomed to professional theological discourse in relation to the operation of K–12 education"[3] applies as much in the UK as in the U.S. Theological literacy and personal faith formation are rarely part of the repertoire of Catholic educators, despite the fact that they are integral to the tasks required. Without attention to this dimension of teacher and leadership preparation and ongoing development, the distinctiveness of Catholic education will be lost. As Fordham University's Gerald Cattaro reminds us, we should not think of the Catholic school as just like other educational organizations (though there will, of course, be similarities): "as an apostolate of the Church" [it has] its own unique knowledge base.[4]

I am conscious of the fact that faith development and spiritual development are not necessarily the same things. However, in terms of ensuring

---

2. John Staud, ed., *The Carnegie Conversation on Catholic Education* (Notre Dame, Ind.: Alliance for Catholic Education Press at the University of Notre Dame, 2008), 31.

3. Ibid.

4. Ibid., 59. For complementary studies emphasising the integration of spiritual formation with professional development, see Maria J. Ciriello, *The Principal as Spiritual Leader* (Washington, D.C.: United States Catholic Conference, 1994); Congregation for Catholic Education, *Educating Together in Catholic Schools: A Shared Mission between Consecrated Persons and the Lay Faithful* (Rome: Sacred Congregation for Catholic Education, 2007); Patricia Earl, "Challenges to Faith Formation in Contemporary Schooling in the USA: Problem and Response," in *International Handbook of Education*, ed. Gerald Grace and Joseph O'Keefe (Dordrecht: Springer, 2007); C. Hunt, Thomas Oldenski, and Theodore Wallace, *Catholic School Leadership* (London: Falmer, 2000); James Mulligan, *Catholic Education: Ensuring the Future* (Ottowa: St. Paul University/Novalis, 2005); Merylann Schuttloffel, "Contemporary Challenges to Recruitment, Formation and Retention of Catholic School Leadership in the USA," in *International Handbook of Education*, 85–102; Paige Smith and Ronald Nuzzi, "Beyond Religious Congregations: Responding to New Challenges in Catholic Education," in *International Handbook of Catholic Education*, 103–24; John Sullivan, "Addressing Difference as Well as Commonality in Leadership Preparation for Faith Schools," *Journal of Education and Christian Belief* 10, no. 1 (Spring 2006): 75–88; United States Conference of Catholic Bishops, *Co-workers in the Vineyard of the Lord* (Washington D.C.: United States Conference of Catholic Bishops, 2005).

that the mission of the school becomes a lived reality that permeates every aspect of its being, it has everything to do with who we are and what we are, and this is our spirituality as a community of faith. We need to empower all teachers, regardless of their personal faith stance, to recognize themselves as collaborators in the mission of the school and the church and thereby recognize their role in spiritual leadership as witnesses to that mission. Spiritual leadership is a task that many staff in schools tend to disassociate themselves from and see as the role of a chaplain or the religious education team. Although there are specific elements of spiritual leadership that may appropriately belong to the head teacher, the chaplain, or indeed the religious education team, there is a sense in which all staff are entrusted with the spiritual formation of students, if we mean by "spirituality" one's way of life. In the Christian sense, our spirituality is realized in how we live our day-to-day lives.[5]

It is, therefore, important that schools include aspects of staff spiritual development as part of their professional development and formation, which Rogus and Wildenhaus suggest in the context of the changing role of religious in schools and the shifting context of the church.[6] In the past, schools run by religious such as the Jesuits maintained their particular charism or religious identity by the fact of the presence of large numbers of the particular religious order working within the school. This is no longer the case. The challenge for today is to enable each member of the staff to reflect upon his or her ministry as a teacher so as to empower him or her to participate in spiritual leadership and to promote the particular religious and Catholic character of the school and the process of communicating faith.

In the first part of this chapter I would like to offer some reflections on this idea of developing spiritual leadership, which articulates the mission of the school as a Catholic faith community. I shall consider first some general principles that should be of relevance to any Catholic school, and in so doing, review what we might mean by "spirituality," so that we might understand this context of spiritual development for staff in school. Over the past few years I have had the privilege of leading staff in-service days on vision

5. Thomas H. Groome, *Educating for Life: A Spiritual Vision for Every Teacher and Parent* (Allen, Tex.: Thomas More Press, 1998), 330.

6. Joseph F. Rogus and Colleen A. Wildenhaus, "Ongoing Staff Development in Schools," in *Catholic School Leadership*, ed. Thomas C Hunt, Thomas Oldenski, and Theodore Wallace, 167 (London: Routledge, 2000).

and mission as a Catholic school in a number of institutions. Some of these have been with schools founded in a particular religious order tradition. I have found that it is often easier to articulate the vision and mission when an additional factor such as the tradition and story of a religious order or congregation is present: for example, St. Ignatius and the Jesuits or St. Angela Merici and the Ursulines. Therefore, in the second part of this chapter I will say something about St. Ignatius Loyola, his spirituality, and its links with Ignatian pedagogy as an example of a process of articulating the mission and vision of a school that has at the heart of its mission the communication of faith. It is my hope that this model may be of some use to any Catholic school reflecting on these issues.

Spiritual Development Programs

The principles that underpin the aims and objectives of a staff spiritual development program are founded in the need to enable all to participate more fully in the mission of the Catholic school. The Sacred Congregation for Catholic Education in *The Catholic School* states:

By their witness and their behavior teachers are of the first importance to impart a distinctive character to Catholic schools. It is, therefore, indispensable to ensure their continuing formation through some sort of pastoral provision. This aim must animate them as witnesses of Christ in the classroom and tackle the problems of their particular apostolate, especially regarding a Christian vision of the world and of education.[7]

We need to see the links between the mission of the Catholic school as part of the church apostolate and the vocation of the individual teacher, and to see how these are related to the need to develop the spiritual formation of each member of the community. This seems to be a matter of helping teachers to clarify and "to become ever more mindful about *why* they do *what* they do, in order that they might be inspired to fulfill more perfectly the personal requirement of their vocation."[8] Louise Moore, in writing about the characteristics of staff development in Catholic schools, says that they re-

7. Congregation for Catholic Education, *The Catholic School* (Rome: Sacred Congregation for Education, 1977), no. 78.
8. Richard M. Jacobs, *The Vocation of the Catholic Educator* (Washington, D.C.: National Catholic Educational Association, 1996), 71.

quire a unique dimension in addition to those of personal and professional growth.[9] She underlines the idea that teaching in a Catholic school is more than an occupation—it is a vocation—and poses the question of how Catholic schools support and encourage the important spiritual work of their teachers. This is linked with the ideals of "The Declaration on Christian Education," *Gravissimum Educationis*, which declares that the distinctiveness of the Catholic school is found in the relationship of its religious dimension in the educational climate and the personal development of each student in the tension between culture and Gospel.[10]

The synthesis of faith, culture, and life is a theme taken up in *Lay Catholics in Schools*, in the context of how to live one's personal identity in a way that involves the whole person.[11] The development of the whole person is the underpinning principle of spiritual formation; therefore, Catholic school principals and heads have a responsibility to enhance the spiritual formation as well as the professional development of teachers.[12] Rogus and Wildenhaus go on to consider spiritual formation as crucial, particularly in the climate of the diminishing role of the religious in schools and the importance of enabling lay staff to become spiritual leaders. They list spiritual formation categories along with action approaches that are a useful checklist. The categories include: changes within the Catholic Church; personal religious formation; commitment to Catholic education; religious development of the young; and involvement with social justice.[13]

The recurring theme here appears to be "the whole person." This is the key to what we might mean by spirituality in the context of spiritual formation.

The Meaning of Spirituality

Thomas Groome gives a useful insight, saying that "spirituality is one's way of life." He says that our spirituality is realized in how we live our day-to-day lives and that its essence is found in our relationships—with God,

9. Louise Moore, "Staff Development in the Catholic School," in *Catholic School Leadership*, 96.

10. Ibid., 97.

11. Congregation for Catholic Education, *Lay Catholics in Schools* (Rome: Sacred Congregation for Education, 1982), nos. 25–31.

12. Rogus and Wildenhaus, "Ongoing Staff Development in Schools," 158.

13. Ibid., 168.

self, others, the world—and is therefore necessary for human wholeness. He goes on to say that "a vibrant spirituality lends a foundation for integrating all the bits and pieces of our lives, helping us to live a whole and balanced life."[14] Helga Neidhart, admitting that spirituality is not easy to define, reiterates Groome, saying, "spirituality is an essential dimension of being human. It encompasses our understanding of God, self, other, the universe, and the actions and relationships that flow from these understandings." She goes on to say that "spirituality refers not just to an aspect of life that is 'religious,' but rather to the search for God's presence in every dimension of life, and the integration of the whole life in terms of ultimate values."[15]

It is worth noting at this point, bearing in mind that many people might feel uncomfortable with the term "spirituality" because they find it too disembodied, exacting, or focused only on religious faith, that it is possible to make a distinction between human spirituality and devotional spirituality. In many cases they may overlap or complement each other, but not necessarily. John Bradford clarifies and articulates the distinctions well. He says "it is essential to see religion—devotional spirituality—as giving order to, articulating and endorsing human spirituality." He considers that devotional spirituality refers to the "formation of a corporate and personal religious life."[16] In the context of the Catholic school community there has to be some adherence to devotional spirituality. It is crucial that making such distinctions does not alienate a significant number of staff in our schools who value the ethos and mission of the school but are not of the Catholic faith. What I consider important in what he says is that the foundation-stone of spirituality is human spirituality, as each person has human-spiritual needs, whether he or she has religion or not. He says that the process by which devotional spirituality builds upon human spirituality is profound. He develops the point by saying:

What we call devotional-spiritual needs will be human-spiritual needs expressed in the culture and language of a particular religion and which enhance attunement to the Divine. A religion makes the invaluable contribution of providing

14. Groome, *Educating for Life*, 330–31.

15. Helga Neidhart, "Leadership Spirituality in the Context of Catholic Education," in *Leadership in Catholic Education 2000 and Beyond*, ed. Patrick Duignan and Tony D'Arbon, 87 (Strathfield, NSW: Australian Catholic University, 1998).

16. John Bradford, *Caring for the Whole Child: A Holistic Approach to Spirituality* (London: Catholic Children's Society, 1995), 13.

a language, culture and tradition within which the significance of personal and ultimate issues (e.g., the purpose of life) can be articulated, shared and reflected upon.[17]

Alex Rodger, in his chapter "Human Spirituality: Towards an Educational Rationale," makes some useful comments on the meaning of human-spiritual needs. He writes in the context of our spiritual questioning as human beings, which stems from the fact that we are mysterious to ourselves and that we find it impossible to give up the search for meaning, value, and purpose in life.[18] He says that "spirituality involves everyone: being a person means being a spiritual being; spirituality has to do with living life to the full and discovering how to become more fully human; spirituality is about self-discovery, discovery of others and discovery of the world; spirituality is not synonymous with religion, nor is it opposed to it; we are feeling our way in attempts to understand spirituality; we will need to learn what spiritual development is and how we can foster it; spirituality covers a wide range of human experience; spirituality can be experienced in awareness, in response and in ways of life."[19] This thinking appears to find its roots from Macquarrie, who says:

Fundamentally spirituality has to do with becoming a person in the fullest sense. . . . It can be described as a capacity for going out of oneself and beyond oneself; or again as the capacity for transcending oneself. . . . It is this openness, freedom, creativity, this capacity for going beyond any given state in which he finds himself, that makes possible self-consciousness and self-criticism, understanding, responsibility, the pursuit of knowledge, the sense of beauty, the quest for the good, the formation of the community, the outreach of love and whatever else belongs to the amazing richness of what we call "life in the spirit."[20]

Part of our challenge is to enable colleagues to realize that every member of the school community is able to make a valuable personal spiritual contribution that builds up the community regardless of his or her own faith stance or lack of it. Also, implicit from what he says, would be the need in the Catholic school context to initiate or induct all staff into the language of

---

17. Ibid., 14.
18. Alex Rodger, "Human Spirituality: Towards an Educational Rationale," in *Education, Spirituality and the Whole Child*, ed. Ron Best, 45 (London: Cassell, 1996).
19. Ibid., 60.
20. John Macquarrie, *Paths in Spirituality* (London: Harper and Row, 1972), 40.

the school as church so that each may realize that his or her personal contribution builds up the devotional spirituality of the school. My experience is that the school as a Catholic community becomes enriched when staff from other faith-traditions, or of none, feels empowered through the realization that its contribution matters.

Patricia Sullivan and Timothy Brown, in their book *Setting Hearts on Fire: A Spirituality for Leaders*, write about how spirituality transcends the particular faith to which one subscribes and that it has more to do with moving inward to examine core values, moral commitment, and care for the soul.[21] This has links with the observations made by Bradford. They go on to say:

The fundamental source of being human is spirituality—an awareness of God's Spirit in one's life. Spirituality involves being aware of relationships with others, with thoughts, words and actions. It controls beliefs, attitudes and practices by which people give witness to Christ and acknowledge God in their lives.[22]

We need, therefore, to focus our use of the term "spirituality," at least in the Christian sense. In admitting that spirituality is a word that is sometimes difficult to pin down, we need to consider a working definition, in Christian terms, and how it can be expressed in worship, fundamental values, and lifestyle. In this context, spirituality is therefore "the whole of life viewed in terms of a conscious relationship with God, in Jesus Christ, through the indwelling of the Spirit and within the community of believers,"[23] or as something "to do with the ways and means of attuning oneself to the presence of Jesus and to make an appropriately generous response to that presence."[24]

Having looked at some general ideas about what we might mean when we talk of spirituality in the context of the Catholic school, I shall now focus more specifically on Ignatian spirituality and Ignatian pedagogy as an example of a way of proceeding.

---

21. Patricia Sullivan and Timothy Brown, *Setting Hearts on Fire: A Spirituality for Leaders* (New York: St. Paul's, 1997), viii.

22. Ibid., xi.

23. Adrian Thatcher, "Spirituality as an Academic Discipline," in *Spirituality and the Curriculum*, ed. Adrian Thatcher, 57 (London: Cassell, 1999).

24. Michael Holman, SJ, "The Christian Ministry of Teaching," in *Contemporary Catholic Education*, ed. Michael Hayes and Liam Gearon, 70 (Leominster: Gracewing, 2002).

The Link between the *Spiritual Exercises* and Ignatian Pedagogy

The *Spiritual Exercises* of St. Ignatius act as a foundation to Ignatian pedagogy and spirituality within the context of the school. This is fundamentally based on the Ignatian Paradigm of *experience-reflection-action*, which not only serves as a model or structure for the *Spiritual Exercises* themselves, but also for the teacher-learner relationship and indeed the whole rationale of Ignatian education.

The essential power of the *Spiritual Exercises* of Ignatius is the call to reflect upon experience in prayer in order to discern where the spirit of God is leading, and the vital dynamic is the individual person's encounter with the spirit of Truth. The principles for directing others in the *Spiritual Exercises* become a perfect description of the pedagogical role of the teacher, whose task is not merely to inform but to enable the student to progress in the truth.[25] It is clear that this role is one of leadership and even more essentially one of spiritual leadership, in that the teacher is privileged in a primary role of facilitating the growing relationship of the learner with truth. This is in parallel with the *Spiritual Exercises*, which is intended as a method to guide others through experiences of prayer, wherein they meet and converse with the living God, come honestly to grips with the truth of their values and beliefs, and make free and deliberate choices about the future course of their lives. If teachers are to use the Ignatian pedagogical paradigm successfully, they not only need to be sensitive to their own experience, attitudes, and opinions, but they need to be suitably inducted into the characteristics of Jesuit education with ongoing formation, which includes spiritual formation, since, it seems to me, they are integrally bound into the whole educational enterprise.

Through all this we must keep in mind that Ignatius did not seek to impose a spirituality on the world, but rather to find a way of discerning the presence of God already active in the world. The most concise encapsulation of this spirituality is the phrase "finding God in all things." This is a synthesis of matter and spirit, namely that the human and the divine become

25. For further information and commentary on the characteristics of Jesuit education, see the International Commission on the Apostolate of Jesuit Education, "Ignatian Pedagogy: A Practical Approach," in *Foundations*, ed. Carl E Meirose, SJ, 237–71 (Washington, D.C.: Jesuit Secondary Education Association, 1993).

inseparable. This theme is one that is taken up in the Catholic Education Service (CES) document *Spiritual and Moral Development Across the Curriculum*, where it says:

The nature of Catholic education rests on one of the fundamental aspects of the Church's teaching. It is the insistence, in the Catholic synthesis, that the human and the divine are inseparable: in the person of Christ, in the action of God in our lives, in the task of exploring and understanding revealed truth. Catholicism sees no separation of the human from the saving action of God.[26]

This indicates that this fundamental principle is not exclusive to Ignatian education, but is something that can be applied universally to Catholic education.

For the students we teach, all too often they will have a limited understanding as to where God may be found, which in their minds may be confined to church or formal prayer. Teachers are in the privileged position of helping students to authentically interpret ways of finding the presence of God in all that we do. It is therefore vital that teachers are given the opportunities to develop this understanding for themselves, through programs of staff spiritual development, so that they may more fully understand their crucial role in enabling their students to find the greater meaning and purpose in their lives. We need to be aware that, although it is proper that the school provides opportunities for the traditional encounters with God through formal prayer and liturgy, their experiences of this outside of the school context may be very limited. There is scope, in the context of the school, not only to provide quality prayer and worship, but to develop the experience of God to be encountered in all that is done.

In the same way that young people in our care need to be developed in academic matters, their spirituality also needs cultivation. We know that they can recognize goodness, truth, or beauty, so we should work to enable them to understand that these are in some way indicators of the source and author of these qualities. With Ignatian spirituality, the whole of the curriculum, indeed the whole world, is an opportunity for encounter with the Divine. So when students are touched by beauty, awe, wonder, and mystery, that can be interpreted as an experience of God. Since God is also a Trinity of love and

---

26. Catholic Education Service, *Spiritual and Moral Development across the Curriculum* (London: Bishops' Conference of England and Wales, 1995), no. 5.

relationship, any experience of relationship that builds people up is an experience of the love of God working in their lives.[27]

This theme of finding the presence of God in all things and experiencing
the love of God working in our lives, indeed in every moment and opportunity, is clearly "sacramental." It makes sense to develop this way of thinking as
a model for understanding how the school community may be considered as
"sacrament," as a way of realizing this powerful dimension that enables our
Catholic schools to be distinctive. The Catholic Education Service (for England and Wales) discussion paper "Spiritual and Moral Development Across
the Curriculum" devotes the whole of its introduction to the theme of the
sacramental reality of the school; therefore, it is worth pointing out that this
is not something exclusive to Ignatian education, but something that can be
appropriately unraveled and developed to help all those working in the context of the Catholic school have a clearer understanding of its mission.[28]

Ignatian Pedagogy and the Characteristics of Jesuit Education

Although The Characteristics of Jesuit Education gives a description of the
goal of Jesuit or Ignatian education, Father General Peter-Hans Kolvenbach,
SJ, in an address at Georgetown in 1989, amplified it, saying:

The pursuit of each student's intellectual development to the full measure of God-
given talents rightly remains a prominent goal of Jesuit education. Its aim, however, has never been simply to amass a store of information or preparation for a
profession, although these are important in themselves and useful to emerging
Christian leaders. The ultimate aim of Jesuit education is, rather, that full growth
of the person which leads to action—action, especially, that is suffused with the
spirit and presence of Jesus Christ, the Son of God, the man-for-Others. This goal
of action, based on sound understanding and enlivened by contemplation, urges students to self-discipline and initiative, to integrity and accuracy. At the same
time, it judges slip-shod or superficial ways of thinking unworthy of the individual
and, more important, dangerous to the world he or she is called to serve.[29]

27. Australian Jesuit Education Office (AJEO), "Finding God in All Things," in Ignatian
Foundational Insights (Sidney: Jesuit Education Office, 2000), 25.
28. Catholic Education Service, Spiritual and Moral Development across the Curriculum, 7–8.
29. International Commission on the Apostolate of Jesuit Education, Ignatian Pedagogy,
241.

This goal, which Father Arrupe summarized as "forming men and women for others,"[30] which requires a full and deeper formation of the whole person, which is part of the spiritual quest, requires its teachers to be likewise formed in this approach in order to participate fully in the collaborative nature of the Jesuit apostolate in education.

Daven Day, SJ, in his paper "Ignatian Education: From Foundational Insights to Contemporary Praxis," states that our generation has witnessed a remarkable flowering of activity centered on the spiritual insights of Ignatius, and that once again lay people have taken rightful ownership and leadership of Ignatian spirituality. He goes on to say that "this same burgeoning of creativity has occurred in education when educators revisited the traditional insights of Ignatius."[31]

The Characteristics of Jesuit Education first of all explains its rationale and how it came about. It then makes connections between the characteristics of Jesuit education and the spiritual vision of Ignatius. The statements upon which it builds come directly from the world vision of Ignatius, reflecting on that vision and applying it to education in the light of the needs of men and women today. It seems appropriate, therefore, to present an outline of what the booklet describes as Jesuit, or Ignatian, education, since this is essential to formulating an understanding of its rationale along with the possibility of comparison with the general principles of Catholic education. These ten statements have subsequently been designated as "Ten Dimensions of a Jesuit School and Ignatian Leadership."

First, since for Ignatius, God is creator and Lord and present in our lives in all things, and since he can be discovered, through faith, in all things, it states that Ignatian education: is world affirming; assists in the total formation of each individual within the human community; includes a religious dimension that permeates entire education; is an apostolic instrument; and promotes dialogue between faith and culture.[32]

Second, since for Ignatius, each person is personally known and loved by God, this love demands a response, which to be authentically human, must be an expression of radical freedom. Therefore each person is called to be

---

30. Ibid., 241.

31. Daven Day, SJ, "Ignatian Education: From Foundational Insights to Contemporary Praxis," in Briefing Papers: Occasional Readings on Topics That May Be of Particular Interest to Ignatian Education (Australian Jesuit Education Office, 1994), no. 1 (December 1994).

32. Society of Jesus, Characteristics of Jesuit Education (London: Irish and British Provinces of the Society of Jesus, 1987), 12–17.

free to give of oneself, accepting responsibility and consequences for actions, and free to work in faith toward true happiness, which is the purpose of life. Therefore, Ignatian education: insists on individual care and concern for each person; emphasizes activity on the part of the student; and encourages lifelong openness to growth.[33]

Third, because of the effects of sin, the freedom to respond to God's love is not automatic, and so we need to be aided and strengthened by the redeeming love of God. This freedom requires genuine knowledge, love, and acceptance of self. It requires freedom from distorted perceptions of reality and therefore the need to recognize and deal with the influences that either promote or limit freedom. Therefore, Ignatian education: is value-oriented; encourages a realistic knowledge, love, and acceptance of self; and provides a realistic knowledge of the world in which we live.[34]

Fourth, since Ignatius' worldview is centered on the historical person of Jesus Christ as the model for all human life as persons for others in the service of God, Ignatian education: proposes Christ as the model of human life; provides adequate pastoral care; and celebrates faith in personal and community prayer, worship, and service.[35]

Fifth, since for Ignatius, a loving and free response to God's love cannot be merely theoretical, and that action is required by love being shown in deeds, Ignatius asks for total commitment to imitate and be more actually like Christ. We are called to put these ideals into practice in the world of the family, business, social movements, political and legal structures, and religious activities. Therefore Ignatian education is: preparing for active life commitment; serving a faith that promotes justice; seeking to form "men and women for others"; and manifesting a particular concern of the poor.[36]

Sixth, for Ignatius the response to the call of Christ is made through and in the Roman Catholic Church, which is the instrument through which Christ is sacramentally present in the world. Mary, the mother of Jesus, is a model of this response. Ignatius and his companions were ordained priests and put the Society of Jesus at the service of the Vicar of Christ. So, Ignatian education is an apostolic instrument, in the service of the church as it serves human society, and prepares students for active participation in the church and the local community, for the service of others.[37]

33. Ibid., 18–21.
35. Ibid., 26–29.
37. Ibid., 37–40.
34. Ibid., 22–25.
36. Ibid., 30–36.

Seventh, Ignatius insisted on "magis," the "more." His concern was for greater service of God. Therefore, Ignatian education pursues excellence in its work of formation, and is to be a witness to excellence.[38]

Eighth, as Ignatius came to know and love God through Christ and responded by giving himself to the service of the kingdom of God, he wanted to share this experience with others as companions. The strength of a community working in the service of the Kingdom is greater than that of an individual. Therefore, Ignatian education: stresses lay-Jesuit collaboration; relies on a spirit of community among teaching staff and administrators, the Jesuit community, governing boards, parents, students, former students, and benefactors; and takes place within a structure that promotes that community. This structure requires a good degree of shared responsibility in its leadership.[39]

Ninth, Ignatius and his companions made decisions on the basis of an ongoing process of individual and community discernment in the context of prayerful reflection in order to review past decisions and make adaptations in a constant search for the "magis" or greater service to God. In response to this, Ignatian education seeks to: adapt means and methods in order to achieve its purpose most effectively; be part of a "system of schools with a common vision and common goals"; and assist in providing the professional training and ongoing formation that is needed, especially for teachers. Also, in order to achieve genuine collaboration and sharing of responsibility, lay people need to have an understanding of Ignatian spirituality and Jesuit traditions, in the same way that Jesuits need to have an understanding of the lived experience of lay people.[40]

Finally, the tenth dimension is that of Ignatian pedagogy. Although *The Characteristics of Jesuit Education* does not deal effectively with this tenth dimension, it does at least make the links with the *Modus Parisiensis* and *The Spiritual Exercises* and draws some analogies between the methods of the *Exercises* and traditional Jesuit teaching methods. A later document produced by the International Commission on the Apostolate of Jesuit Education (ICAJE), called *Ignatian Pedagogy: A Practical Approach*, emerged in 1993 as a response to the internationally positive reactions to *The Characteristics of Jesuit Education* in terms of the need to make *The Characteristics* more accessible to teachers.

---

38. Ibid., 41–43.   39. Ibid., 44–51.
40. Ibid., 52–55.

The document gives a clear explanation of Ignatian pedagogy in terms of the way in which teachers accompany learners in their growth and development as the art and science of teaching, which cannot simply be reduced to methodology. This approach must include a worldview and a vision of the ideal human person to be educated as in *The Characteristics of Jesuit Education*.[41]

Conclusion

I have proposed that there needs to be a clear link between faith transmission and staff spiritual development in schools as a means to helping teachers to recognize their role as leaders and witnesses to the mission of the school as part of the faith community. This also has implications in terms of the early formation of future senior leaders. It is through reflection on the idea of spiritual leadership that the mission of the school as a Catholic faith community can be articulated. In order to do this effectively, we need to clarify what we mean by spiritual development in the context of the Catholic school. I have presented the Spiritual Exercises and Ignatian pedagogy, along with the characteristics of Jesuit education, as a way of living out this leadership and transmission and empowering witnesses. It is my hope that these reflections may be of use beyond schools founded in the Ignatian tradition.

41. International Commission on the Apostolate of Jesuit Education, *Ignatian Pedagogy*, 241.

11   Questioning for Faith Commitment

Raymond Topley

The goal of Christian religious education is Christian discipleship. The basis for this claim is to be found toward the close of St. Matthew's Gospel, where Jesus directs his followers to go and make disciples, teaching them to observe all that he has commanded them (Mt 28:19). The church has no option than to do likewise. This raises the question as to the nature of Christian discipleship. A scanning of the tradition from the time of Christ to the present leaves one in no doubt that there are two distinct, yet related, elements that contribute to discipleship. One is hearing the word of God, the other is doing the Word. I think the contrast meant is between hearing and doing, rather than the Word and the word of God. Authentic Christianity, like much of human life, is possessed of both a cognitional and a behavioral element. This attention to faith in action presents a particular challenge to Christian religious education. The challenge may be articulated in the following question: How can one form and communicate faith in such a way that the faith in question is not just something that is held in the head and the heart but is something that extends, additionally, to the hands? I propose that only an approach to religious education and catechesis that assigns a central role to questions and questioning will suffice in meeting the challenge of holding

in tension the knowing and doing dimensions of Christian faith and discipleship. A beginning to this task may be made by considering, first of all,
the practice of questioning in education generally.

Questioning in the Classroom

It is frequently noted that the mark of an effective teacher is the ability
to manage questions skillfully in the achievement of intended educational goals. Little wonder that this claim should be made when research reveals that in the average classroom up to 400 questions are asked every day![1]
However, not all questions are of equal value. In educational parlance some
are referred to as lower-order questions, while others are deemed to be of a
higher order. Such a dualistic categorization is somewhat simplistic. Distinguishing among the various types of questions that surface in educational
activity is a much more sophisticated task. Mastery of the art of questioning
requires a more subtle differentiation of the wider range of question types
and techniques that are available to the interested teacher. Simple recall
questions of the "who, what, where, and when" type need to yield and lead
to the more subtle probing and penetrative questioning of the "why, where-
fore, whence, and whither" genre.[2] To appreciate how these all fit together
and relate to each other requires an insight into how questioning can lead to
the student's ongoing intellectual, moral, spiritual, and religious development. Before considering this further, however, there is need now, in keeping with the overall purpose of the chapter, to note the importance and role
of questioning in religious education itself.

Questioning and Religious Education

While the issue of questioning is as important for religious education as
it is for all education, it is particularly relevant to Christian religious education. The reason for this is that Christianity is not just a religion of knowing. It is also a religion of doing. Christian knowing is meant to issue forth
in Christian doing. The words of Jesus himself bear out this point, for in-

1. See Edward C. Wragg and George A. Brown, eds., *Questioning in the Primary School*, new
revised edition (London: Routledge Falmer, 2001), 16.
2. See Bernard Lonergan, *Insight: A Study in Human Understanding*, vol. 3 of *The Collected
Works of Bernard Lonergan*, ed. Frederick E. Crowe and Robert M. Doran (1957; Toronto: University of Toronto Press, 1992), 197.

stance, from his remarks to the lawyer when concluding his telling of the parable of the Good Samaritan, "Go and do the same yourself" (Lk 10:37). Scripture scholar A. M. Hunter, commenting on the purpose of Gospel parables, observes, "Every parable of Jesus was meant to evoke a response and to strike for a verdict."[3] In other words, those learning the ways of discipleship—as catechumens, retreatants, or religious education participants—are called upon to make both judgments and commitments in response to hearing the message of Christ. This linking of religious doing with religious knowing is echoed throughout the 2,000-year history of Christianity. It was well summarized by German Jesuit Johannes Hofinger, one of the great religious education voices of the mid-twentieth century:

We not only have to give our students a thorough knowledge of their faith, but we must also form true Christians who truly live their Christianity. Religious knowledge in itself is not the real goal of our teaching, it is only a means. The goal of religious instruction is religious living.[4]

In responding to the educational challenge that the knowing-doing linkage entails, there are two ways in which the teacher or catechist may proceed. One could be described as the shortcut, the other as the long way 'round. The shortcut methodology is operative whenever an adult (parent, teacher, priest) merely directs a child or young person what to think and how to act. Little or no educational processing occurs on the part of the learner, as it is the weight of authority that is the sole operative principle in such instances. When, in time, the authoritative presence is removed from the scene, there can remain very little to inspire and sustain the learner for the long haul of life. An alternative to this approach involves the learner as an active educational agent from the very start of the process and right up the time when the desired conclusion is realized. To teach in such a manner requires an effective teaching strategy. Such a strategy, in turn, needs to be undergirded by a solid theory of knowledge and learning. It is to one such theory, drawn from the work of Bernard Lonergan, S.J., that attention is now directed. Marrying Lonergan's theory of knowing with educational questioning provides a versatile teaching tool capable of seamlessly linking the knowing-doing axis required by Christianity and Christian religious education. Before looking

3. Archibald M. Hunter, *Interpreting the Parables* (London: SCM, 1964), 12.
4. Johannes Hofinger, *The Art of Teaching Christian Doctrine: The Good News and Its Proclamation* (London: Sands, 1961), 17.

in some detail at what Lonergan has to offer in this regard, a word of introduction to the man and his method will help contextualize what is to follow.

Lonergan and His Cognitional Quest

Bernard Lonergan (1904–1984) was a renowned philosopher and theologian with considerable expertise also in the areas of mathematics and economics. Lonergan's initial fascination was with the issue of knowledge. Writing as a student from Heythrop College in England to a confrere back in Canada, he revealed, "The theory of knowledge is what is going to interest me most of all."[5] He eventually recorded the results of his quest in his lengthy volume, *Insight: A Study of Human Understanding* (1957). Lonergan derived inspiration from many sources, including Augustine, Aquinas, and Newman. For instance, he confessed to having devoted eleven years of his life to the study of the mind of Aquinas[6] and to having read Newman's *A Grammar of Assent* several times over in order to understand what the author was getting at. Apart, however, from the influences upon him that he generously acknowledged, Lonergan was very much his own man, the lone scholar, forging an independent furrow. He dedicated himself completely to the task he had set himself, delving into the human mind and "working out an empirical theory of human understanding and knowledge."[7] In his other great work, *Method in Theology* (1972), he extended his theory of knowing to embrace human action and behavior, also. It is the completed structure that promises most in our pursuit of a methodological approach to the communication of faith, understood comprehensively as embracing knowing and doing.

In pursuit of his cognitional clarification goal, Lonergan famously posed for himself three fundamental questions, only the first of which need occupy us here: "What am I doing when I am knowing?" Lonergan commentator Tom Daly, from Australia, has suggested an alternative and, arguably, improved wording for this: "What am I doing when and as I am coming to know?" or, better still from an educational perspective, "What am I doing as

---

5. Pierrot Lambert, Charlotte Tansey, and Cathleen Going, *Caring about Meaning: Patterns in the Life of Bernard Lonergan* (Montreal: Thomas More Institute, 1982), 142.

6. Frederick E. Crowe, *Lonergan* (London: Geoffrey Chapman, 1992), 40.

7. Bernard Lonergan, "The Form of Inference," in *Collection*, vol. 4 of *The Collected Works of Bernard Lonergan*, ed. Frederick E. Crowe and Robert M. Doran, 15 (Toronto: University of Toronto Press: 1988).

I am learning?" as "coming to know" is but another expression for "learning." So Lonergan set himself numerous exercises to try to isolate the experience of how one comes to have "an insight." In answer to his initial question and as a result of his understanding of how the human mind works, he identified three levels of consciousness through which a person traverses in arriving at true and certain knowledge of anything. He later added a fourth level to account for the movement from knowing to doing. I survey these four levels as preliminary to seeing how they might serve the purpose of communicating faith and the making of disciples. In light of Daly's analysis, these levels of consciousness might legitimately be labeled "Lonergan's Levels of Learning,"[8] even though he himself never used this particular phrase.

Lonergan's Levels of Learning

Lonergan was happy to be described as a "methodologist."[9] Particularly with his interest in mathematics and science, he was partial to a methodical way of going about his own scholarly and professional work, and he liked to say from time to time, "It never hurts to know what you are about."[10] In the opening chapter of *Method in Theology*, he outlines his search for what he terms a "transcendental method," which he describes as "a basic pattern of operations employed in every cognitional enterprise."[11] He finds such a pattern in the operations of the human mind, an examination of which leads him to the conclusion that the human subject, in coming to know and act, progresses along four distinct levels of consciousness. It should be noted that, in addition to naming and commenting on the levels, each of them also requires the observance of a particular imperative, or "must do," if the human subject or person is to participate as genuinely and as authentically as is required by the level in question. Accordingly, in the accounts of the levels that follow, the respective imperatives will also be noted. Though he named

8. See Tom Daly, "Learning Levels," in *Australian Lonergan Workshop*, ed. William Danagher (New York: University Press of America, 1993), 233–48. For a more detailed treatment of Lonergan's levels of consciousness theory, see Lonergan, "Cognitional Structure," in *Collection*, vol 4 of *The Collected Works of Bernard Lonergan*, ed. Frederick E. Crowe and Robert M. Doran, 205–21 (Toronto: University of Toronto Press: 1988); Lonergan, *Method in Theology* (Darton, Longman, and Todd, 1972), chap. 1, "Method," 3–25.

9. See Lambert, Tansey, and Going, *Caring about Meaning*, 220.

10. Terry Tekippe, *Theology: Love's Question* (London: University of America, 1991), 124.

11. Lonergan, *Method in Theology* (1972; Toronto: University of Toronto Press, 2003), 4.

these levels as the experiential, the intellectual, the rational (or reasonable), and the responsible, I will adopt more educationally and user-friendly terms for the purposes of this chapter.

1. *Level of Data.* Many pedagogical lessons begin with a presentation of new data to the class by the teacher. This can take the form of a story, some information, a poster, a picture, or a puzzle. The principal operations at this level pertain to the human senses, such as seeing, hearing, tasting, and touching, or, alternatively, remembering sense experiences from the past or imagining them in the future. The only requirement on the part of the learners is that they *be attentive.*

2. *Level of Understanding.* Once attentiveness has been achieved, the next step entails a search for meaning. This is arrived at through the exercise of intelligence by means of which the learners wonder and puzzle over the data presented in the previous level. Hopefully and eventually, through this engagement they will acquire some understandings and insights as to the deeper meanings and significance of whatever was presented. This level is driven by curiosity, which may be understood as the natural drive to uncover and reveal what is hidden and unknown. The restless searching for coherence and connections is satisfied with nothing less than a solution. The requirement at this level, therefore, is that learners *be intelligent.*

3. *Level of Checking.* At this level a reality check is taken. Questions such as, "Is it so?" or "Is it not so?" "Is it true?" or "Is it false?" are asked. The operations here are those of checking, weighing the evidence, judging the facts and the procedures. The required answer is a simple yes or no. If the person is not sure and unable to make such a judgment of fact, then there is no option but to return to the previous level and renew the search for insight. At level three the person sets some conditions that need to be fulfilled in order for an affirmative answer to be given. Among the concerns here are not just the answers arrived at from the previous level, but also the question of proper procedure. So one wonders, "Did I leave anything important out in arriving at the solution I arrived at?" In other words, bias has to be detected and eliminated if the truth of a situation is to be arrived at. Once the person can honestly and authentically declare, "It is so" or "It is true," then the work of the level is complete. The search is over. The importance of this level resides in the fact that it provides a platform for decision making that is the principal task of the next and final level. At level three, therefore, the imperative for learners is that they *be reasonable.*

4. *Level of Response.* This is also referred to as the moral level, for it is at this level that the person deliberates on the various courses of action that are possible in light of the truth apprehended at the previous level. This, in turn, leads to decision, which only reaches fulfillment when it results in corresponding action. The main operations are those of deliberating, evaluating, deciding, and doing. At this level Lonergan understood human subjects as constituting themselves and their worlds. Here, truth finds its natural fulfillment in the doing of the good. The required imperative is, *"be responsible."*

Essential to the success of the process is the faithful observance of the transcendental imperatives or precepts, as they are the key contributory ingredients to the realization of the task of each level. As such, they are the soul of the process. Their importance is attested to by Hugo Meynell, who, in his 1976 address to the Philosophy of Education Society of Great Britain, noted:

The cultivation of these four dispositions, the inculcation of what Lonergan has called "the four transcendental precepts," "Be attentive, Be intelligent, Be reasonable, Be responsible" is, I shall argue, the basic aim of education."[12]

This is quite a claim, and it derives directly from Lonergan's analysis of the human condition and the struggle entailed in knowing the truth and doing the good. If this claim can be sustained, then there arises a question as to how, practically and effectively, these imperatives may be delivered on in the classroom. The answer proposed here is straightforward enough, but potentially very effective. The imperatives may be activated by a distinctive type of question at each of the four levels. They might well be termed "trigger questions," as they are designed to trigger in learners the required imperatives, one for each level. It remains to be seen just how such skillful educational questioning can be undertaken by the teacher so as to enable the fruitful fulfillment of these imperatives on the part of learners. I begin by reviewing the first three levels and the kind of questioning needed to elicit true and certain knowledge. Following that, I consider the kind of educational questioning needed at level four, where moral issues are tackled and decisions made. Finally, consideration will be given to what is required, at this level also, by way of questioning for faith commitment.

---

12 . Hugo Meynell, "On the Aims of Education," in *Proceedings of the Philosophy of Education Society of Great Britain*, 10 (July 1976): 81.

Questioning for Knowledge (The First Three Learning Levels)

Theories of learning have little value unless they are workable in practice. Accordingly, the picture painted above is merely academic and idealistic unless it can be shown that it can be operated efficiently in the achievement of educational growth and change. The proposal being made here is that the key to realizing such change and effective progression from one level to the next is the simple construct of teacher questioning. Just as each level has its own learner imperative, so, too, each level has its own specific type of question, by means of which the teacher can test and ensure that the necessary transcendental imperative has been undertaken and completed. At level one, for instance, after the telling of a story or parable, the use of simple recall questions, such as who, what, where, when, and how, can enable the teacher to test if attentiveness has, indeed, occurred. If these questions cannot be answered satisfactorily by the learners, then the original data may need to be revisited and re-presented.

At level two the search for meaning occurs and so questions at this level may be referred to as search or research questions. Teacher questioning here may be formulated along such lines as "What do you think was really going on here?" "Can you see or make any connections between what is in the story and what is outside and beyond the story?" "Are there any questions coming into your own mind concerning what we have been discussing?"

Then at level three, as learners are being invited to make judgments about their own insights and discoveries and to differentiate between truth and falsehood, reality questions are posed such as, "Is what we have discovered so far in the lesson true?" "Is it really so?" If such questions as these seem somewhat philosophic and removed from the everyday lives of children, one has but to recall that children, especially in the context of storytelling, frequently challenge adults with the simple but arresting words, "Is it true?" and the even more emphatic version, "Is it *really* true?" At this learning level the answer given is in the form of either a simple positive or a simple negative, a "yes" or a "no." Responders should always be expected to offer a reason for monosyllabic answers. If none is forthcoming, however, the teacher should gently challenge further by means of the justifying "Why?"/"Why not?" construct. This then sets in place all that is necessary for progression to the fourth level, where response questions take center stage.

Questioning for Commitment (Learning Level Four)

While each of the learning levels is an essential part of the overall structure, level four requires particular attention and treatment. The reason for this is that at this level several layers or stages of questioning are necessary if learners are to be guided toward the kind of commitment that moral, spiritual, and religious education requires. The essential task of level four is the making of a decision regarding the issue under discussion. However, this needs to be preceded by the making of a value judgment. For instance, in respect to the parable of the Good Samaritan, treated, initially, solely as a human interest story with no religious overtones, learners are asked, "Was the Samaritan right to help the injured man?"[13] Whichever answer is forthcoming is a value judgment. Presuming the answer is in the affirmative and that an acceptable justification can be offered for the response, the next step is that of decision making. This particular task needs to be handled with skill and sensitivity.

With children especially, it is advisable not to jump immediately into the matter of personal commitment by posing, at this juncture, a question such as "What are you going to do in your own life and experience as a result of hearing this story?" Such a way of proceeding is too direct, too raw, too upfront. Rather, it is preferable, and developmentally advisable, first of all, to situate the learners in the imaginary scene or story and ask a question along the following lines: "*If* you had been there, what might you have done?" This opens the way to posing a more generalized question, such as "*When* you find yourself in a situation like this one, how do you think you might act or like to act?" The final stage of questioning at this level deals with the particular: "*Name* the circumstances (who, how, where, and when) in which you feel you might be able to act in a 'Good Samaritan' way."[14] Responses to such questions, as already indicated, ought always be age- and developmental stage–appropriate. An example of a positive, practical, and particularized response would be something along the following lines: "I could help

---

13. Note how this differs from the key question at the previous level, which is concerned with knowledge and veracity of same: "Is it *true* that the Samaritan in the story helped the injured man?" This invites a judgment of fact (level three). The level-four question invites a judgment of value: "Is it *good* that the Samaritan helped the injured man?"

14. Lonergan once referred to method as a crutch. Here, these three highlighted words, "If," "When," "Name," fulfill a similar function. They provide useful scaffolding in assisting the teacher move the learners along from the imaginative to the particular via the general.

my little brother who is not very good at math. I could do this after tea in the kitchen by teaching him how to add and subtract."

By this stage the comprehensive or "long way 'round" educational journey from data to doing is about to be completed. In summarizing the steps suggested above one may recall, by way of example, that at level one the story of the Good Samaritan is related and tested by recall questions; that at level two the story is explored and insights and meanings sought with the help of research questions; that at level three, checking, by means of reality questions, occurs to ensure that a correct judgment has been arrived at regarding the meaning and truth of the story; while at level four a personal decision is made in respect to whether or not to imitate and emulate the praiseworthy action portrayed by the main character in the story of the Good Samaritan. The questioning part of the exercise is now complete.

The lesson itself may be brought one step further and concluded optionally with some element of educational or artistic expression of the decisions made. For instance, the learners might have recourse to drama, art, or creative writing by way of expressing how they might see themselves imaginatively implementing their own particular decisions. However, the actual carrying out of the decisions in question usually occurs at a time and a place beyond the confines of the classroom walls. There may, consequently, be merit in the teacher suggesting that at some stage in the not-too-distant future the topic will be returned to and an opportunity afforded the participants to report, should they so wish, on their efforts at translating their decisions into action. For instance, in a moral education lesson, utilizing the above approach on a topic such as "confronting global warming," one can imagine how enthusiastically children, individually and collectively, might report on their innovative efforts at addressing this particular contemporary problem.

Questioning for Faith Commitment

The methodology of questioning outlined above can serve equally well the needs of both moral education and religious education. Indeed, it is an effective instrument for any kind of education that requires on the part of learners the exercise of judgment and the making of decisions or commitments in light of the judgments made. What then, one may legitimately ask, differentiates a religion lesson from a, strictly speaking, moral lesson?

Moral lessons deal with issues in their own right. For instance, learners are faced with a range of topics that have to do with interpersonal relationships such as honesty, bullying, and respect for others, and with human living generally. What religion introduces to the mix is transcendental motivation, by which is meant going outside oneself and looking to a religious Being, for instance, as source of motivation in the doing of the good.

The religious dimension of a lesson of this nature proposes that one acts not just out of self-interest, but out of regard and love for a religious figure such as Christ. This line of thought is concisely articulated by St. Paul when he declares unequivocally that "the love of Christ compels us" (2 Cor 5:14). This is particularly relevant when the believer is faced with the dilemma of knowing the right decision but being unable to deliver on the corresponding action. The transcending of self-interest and the overcoming of considerations such as fear are what is at issue here. Religion in this respect can help close the gap between admirable intent and actual execution and thus enable the Christian believer, for example, to act honorably and responsibly out of love for God and in the knowledge that this is in line with what Jesus requires of his followers.

An illustration of this may be seen in respect to the topic and virtue of forgiveness. It is a common experience that when someone has been deeply hurt by another—sometimes unjustly so—it is often quite difficult to find within oneself the strength and natural ability to forgive. Faced with the seemingly impossible demands of the teaching of Jesus in this area, such as forgiving and loving others, including one's enemies, the offended person can feel quite helpless. It is here that Christianity offers the possibility of self-transcendence. This it does by proposing that the motivation to exercise forgiveness, and other virtues, can be sourced from within the person's own faith in the love that Jesus has for them.

Accordingly, in the methodology that is being proposed and applied to religious education, as distinct from moral education per se, participants are challenged at level four to bear in mind their own personal relationship with Christ, rather than dealing solely with the actual existential issue under consideration, such as forgiveness. The essential question is whether or not they would be prepared to do the difficult action demanded by the Christian message solely or principally out of acceptance of Christ's love for them and their own love for Christ. When faced with such a challenge it can sometimes transpire that the believer does not, at this particular point in time, have a strong enough personal relationship with the person of Christ to enable and sustain the desired Christian decision that needs to be made and subsequently implemented. What this points to is a realization of the need for religious educators and catechists to assist believers in developing a strong personal relational bond with Christ through prayer and contemplation. Thus, the kinds of lessons deriving from a question-based approach to religious education need to be complemented regularly by what might be termed "relational lessons" that focus on the person of Christ and that are affective as well as informative by nature. By means of such lessons, one's affective relationship with Christ is built up and can then be appealed to and brought into play motivationally at level four when required.

All of these positions are premised on a belief in the reality of God's grace. It is interesting to recall Lonergan's observation toward the end of his life that his book Method in Theology was "principally concerned with the fourth level on which the grace of God, and faith, hope and charity, are exercised."[15] So the role of divine assistance in the form of God's grace in the religious development of the young learner and believer must always be borne in mind, particularly at this stage of the lesson. God's grace is required not only in the deliberating and deciding stages but throughout the whole process. One needs always to remain open to the possibility of divine assistance. It can be appreciated, however, that it is at level four that the question of God's grace comes into play in a quite particular and explicit way. It is this factor that makes a lesson religious as distinct from one that is merely moral or simply experientially exploratory.

Workable, Worthwhile, and Welcome

By way of conclusion, three questions need to be considered concerning the approach to religious education and faith formation being here proposed: Is it workable? Is it worthwhile? Is it welcome?

Is it workable? It is indeed workable.[16] The basis for so claiming emerges from valuable practitioner feedback garnered over a ten-year period in three colleges of education.[17] After participating in a Lonergan-based preparato-

15. See Lambert, Tansey and Going, Caring about Meaning, 90–91.
16. This approach to teaching is particularly effective for lessons utilizing stories or that aim to culminate in decision making.
17. For a more detailed treatment and identification of the quotes offered, see Raymond Topley, "Bernard Lonergan's Levels of Consciousness Applied to Christian Religious Educa-

ry course these primary (elementary) student teachers each prepared several religion lessons utilizing this form of structured and scientifically sequenced questioning. Even a short selection of the feedback gives a flavor of the promise and possibilities of this approach to teaching.[18] "At first I was a bit skeptical about this method. However, I find it to be a very child-centered approach to teaching religion. What the child says becomes the basis for the next question." "The method was a revelation. It transformed religion class into a forum for debate and forming of thought-out opinions. I thought it was excellent" (teacher of nine-year-old students). "Lonergan's methodology applied to the teaching of religion is quite brilliant. If it is followed carefully then the children are doing more than learning about God. They are learning to live with God. They will be living like God wants them to." "Using this method brought with it a terrific sense of achievement. I could see when the children made the connections and had 'insights'—their faces lit up." "The Lonergan method gave me a whole new insight and perspective into the delivery of a parable and story and really focused the children's minds" (teacher of twelve-year-olds). "The evaluation section (level four) was the most successful and the class showed they were able to apply the main points of the story by deciding what they should do in future similar situations and how they would go about it" (teacher of eleven-year-olds).

Is it worthwhile? It is indeed worthwhile. In saying this, my reasons focus on the making of judgments and commitments. These are essential to the religious nurturing of the developing Christian who is called upon incrementally to make decisions in favor of Christ and the adoption of a corresponding Christian lifestyle. Without these elements religious education can be somewhat anemic and "soft" in avoiding the challenge of personal judgment and decision. Prominent religious educators of our time insist on the importance of this critical dimension to education. For instance, Thomas Groome maintains that "critical reflection needs to be encouraged from the beginnings of intentional education."[19] In the same vein, Luigi Giussani, founder of the religious renewal movement *Communion and Liberation*, declared that

---

tion" (Ed.D. diss., 2004, Graduate Theological Foundation, Indiana, appendices 5–8), copies housed at St. Patrick's College, Drumcondra; The Lonergan Centre, Milltown Institute; The Lonergan Institute, Boston College; and The Lonergan Research Institute, Regis College, Toronto.

18. Feedback comments here pertain to lessons taught to children of primary/elementary school age, particularly in the age range of 9 to 12. In some cases the specific average age is indicated.

19. Thomas H. Groome, *Christian Religious Education: Sharing Our Vision and Story* (London: Harper and Row, 1980), 237.

True education must be about an education in criticism. Up to about the age of ten (maybe even sooner these days) a child is allowed to say, "Because the teacher said so, because mommy said so. . . ." What one has been told must become a problem! Unless this happens, it will either be irrationally rejected or irrationally kept but will never mature.[20]

Is it welcome? Finally, is this approach welcome, in the sense of being timely? It seems that Christian parents who, in the past, have been admirably proactive in the Christian nurturing of their children are, in increasing numbers, leaving it to their children to "make up their own minds" regarding the religion of their choice.[21] If this is so, then it is a matter of urgency that church leaders and religious educators take note. It follows from this that Christian religious education will need to be more focused on developing the child's ability to make informed judgments and meaningful commitments. This is an agenda for the immediate present as well as the emerging future. The approach to questioning in religious education suggested here can contribute substantially to the realization of this agenda and the consequent ongoing formation of Christian disciples. It may even earn for the dedicated teacher the accolade: "You taught me to think for myself."[22]

The value underlying such a pedagogical approach can be appreciated not only in respect to general education, but to religious education and faith formation in particular. Such education will need to continue to push beyond the safe terrains of the merely didactic and stretch toward the riskier waters of the interrogative. The essential thrust of the interrogative pertains to the present—what one can and should do here and now for the development of oneself and one's world and, in respect to a Christian, for one's faith and one's community of believers. The particularity of decision making, be it in general education or faith education, is well attested to by Cardinal John Henry Newman, when he explains what he calls the illative sense as

A capacity sufficient for the occasion, deciding what ought to be done here and now, by this given person, under these given circumstances. It decides nothing hy-

20. Luigi Giussani, *The Risk of Education* (New York: Crossroad, 2001), 10.

21. See, for instance, the findings of an RTE/MRBI poll airing April 16, 2009, on an RTE (Irish National Television) program, "Thirty Years a' Praying," produced by Kevin Cummins, indicating that over 80 percent of Irish parents intended leaving such a decision exclusively to their children.

22. See Groome, *Educating for Life: A Spiritual Vision for Every Teacher and Parent* (Allen, Tex.: Thomas More, 1998), 292–93.

pothetical, it does not determine what a man should do ten years hence, or what another should do at this time. Its present act is for the present, not for the distant or the future.[23]

Intentional methodological questioning, as outlined in this chapter, can play its part in the fulfillment of this task and so make a worthwhile contribution to the communication of faith understood, albeit as being more interrogative than didactic.

Appendix

Table 11-1 presents a summary of the Lonergan-based method, showing each level's "must-do" or imperative and indicating clearly where the trigger questions come into play. This table is outlined for a general or moral lesson. Religious data, along with attention to the "grace of God window" at the decision stage of level four, will make it a religion lesson. God's grace, of course, cannot be managed and can surface anywhere.

Table 11-1. Questioning for Commitment Grid

Learning level	Learner imperative	Type of question	Examples of questions
1. Data	Be attentive	Recall	Who? What? Where? When? How? What happened in the story?
2. Understanding	Be intelligent	Research	What is the meaning of it all? What do you think?
3. Checking	Be reasonable	Reality	Is it true? Why/why not? Is it so? Why/why not?
4. Response	Be responsible	Response	
		a. Evaluation	Is what was done by the main character right and good?
		b. Decision	
		i. Imaginary	If you had been there, how might you have acted?
		ii. General	When in a similar situation, how will you act?
		iii. Particular	Name a situation in which you will act out your decision.
		c. Doing	Artistic expression in classroom. Actual expression in everyday life.

23. John Henry Newman, *An Essay in Aid of a Grammar of Assent*, ed. Ian T. Ker (Oxford: Clarendon, 1985), 226.

PART 4

Higher Education

The following three chapters focus on the university as a setting for communicating faith (and for communicating *about* faith). Two concentrate
on pedagogical considerations, while one advocates a particular line on the
complex and contested relations between theology and religious studies.

In "Plasticity, Piety, and Polemics," Sullivan suggests three desirable
qualities or features of teaching that seek, respectively, to highlight and
hold together three different priorities. First, there is the task of reaching
out to students and inviting them into active engagement with the material
of study. Second, there is the responsibility that teachers have of adequately
representing the religious traditions, in such a way that their distinctive nature and demands come across clearly. Third, there is the duty to promote
critical questioning and acknowledgment of the contested nature of religious claims (contested within, between, and beyond religious traditions).
Living traditions persist, despite continuity, as unfinished, still developing
responses to the world around them, and displaying the capacity to reach
fresh interpretations of what they are about and what they entail.

There is an echo here of the triple dimensions of rhetoric, of *pathos*, *ethos*,
and *logos*. Sullivan's advocacy of plasticity on the part of the teacher offers
a way of identifying with and addressing the *pathos* of students, their interests and concerns, their perspectives and priorities. Without this, they experience no connection with the act of teaching. His reminder to teachers
that, as trusted representatives of a tradition and as stewards of a discipline,
they should seek to do justice to that way of life and those ways of thinking,

finding out and acting (a quality described here as "piety"), bringing out the demands it makes on learners and adherents, might be interpreted as a concern with the *logos* or central messages(s) of a faith tradition. His emphasis on polemics serves as a mechanism for promoting independent, critical, discerning responses among students—an appropriate *ethos* in the classroom, facilitating a shift in attention away from the authority of the teacher toward the need for authentic responses, whether commitment or rejection, on the part of students.

Aquino deepens this pedagogical exploration by proposing ways to help students to move back and forth between the personal and communal dimensions of faith and to consider material being studied in both religiously specific and more secular ways. He thereby shows how bridges can be built between claims to authority by teachers and traditions and a desire for authenticity and ownership on the part of students. Promoting the capacity to make judgments is key here. Aquino plots a path that links the nurturing of intellectual virtues with personal formation. At the same time, he brings into conversation thick and thin commitments—that is, tradition-specific, comprehensive, and integrated ways of thinking and those that seek to avoid reliance on particular beliefs and practices and to appeal to the widest possible constituencies. He demonstrates how, in mediating between the conflicting demands of authority and autonomy, the teaching of theology and philosophy in a university can make a valuable contribution to the emergence of communities of informed judgment. His chapter provides a philosophical underpinning for the pedagogical ideals outlined by Sullivan, especially offering a way of linking piety and polemics, an intellectual integrity that is compatible with religious fidelity.

D'Costa, too, is seeking ways to facilitate an engagement at the university that opens up access to both intellectual integrity and to religious fidelity, with these envisaged as partners rather than as opponents. Defining theology as an ecclesial activity, faith seeking understanding, he explores the complex and uneasy relationships that have developed between theology and the newer discipline of religious studies. Articulating a position informed by Roman Catholic perspectives, D'Costa examines prevailing assumptions that influence the position taken by scholars on the relative position of these academic neighbors. Both offer windows into faith, but from different vantage points, with different goals and employing different tools. No discipline can be properly understood without reference to its own history, and all histories reveal a power struggle. "Windows into Faith" offers an interpretation of that history and an insight into tussles about authority and power. Although on his own admission controversial, D'Costa's version of the relationships between theology and religious studies casts light on some of the issues at stake, and it deserves serious consideration. Two documents from Pope John Paul II are mined by D'Costa for their bearing on how one might perceive the relationship between theology and religious studies; these are Ex Corde Ecclesiae (1990), which provided a raison d'être for a Catholic university in the contemporary world, and the encyclical Fides et Ratio (1998), which invited scholars to revisit the relationship between faith and reason and to come to appreciate better their mutual need one of the other, without collapsing one into the other. It follows from D'Costa's chapter (on my reading of it) that, although religions should be understood in their own terms, this does not rule out the value of also studying them from alternative perspectives.

12   Plasticity, Piety, and Polemics

Communicating a Faith Tradition in Higher Education

John Sullivan

In this chapter I bring out the tensions that underlie three tasks that are too often treated in isolation from one another, but which I believe should be held together as regulating parts of the teacher's intentions. These tasks should be considered as intimately connected and mutually qualifying aspects of effective religious teaching in an academic setting. The first task is that of adapting to the needs of students, here called "plasticity." The second task is that of displaying the virtues required, epistemologically as well as morally, by the religious tradition, here called "piety." The third task, described here as "polemics," is that of rendering this tradition problematical and controversial in order to show that an engagement with it can be intellectually serious and at the same time a contribution to its ongoing development. While the focus here is on the university, the tension between the three tasks—and the qualities associated with them—has application (to a lesser extent) in other settings.

An earlier version of this chapter was published as "Plasticity, Piety and Polemics," *Journal of Religious Education* 49, no. 2 (Spring 2001). The material appears here with permission of the journal's editor.

The exercise of plasticity on the part of the teacher entails a willingness to adjust classroom activity, the topics covered, the methods employed, and the relationships established in such a way as to accommodate the diverse needs of learners. Such plasticity or flexibility displays a willingness to bend, to make allowances for the real starting points and current perspectives of students. It treats students as important; it aims to create a hospitable space for them, so that they willingly become fully engaged. The novelty encountered by students will be experienced as benign rather than malign. Students' freedom will be enhanced rather than diminished as a result of participation.

By piety in the classroom I mean a set of responses (to something—or someone—outside ourselves) that acknowledges that if we are to have any chance of getting near the topic of study, we have to approach it in such a way as to take seriously its "otherness." If plasticity is about the adjustments the teacher makes to create inclusive classrooms, piety is about the adjustments both teacher and students have to make in order to appreciate the distinctiveness of the subject matter. Without preparing themselves, without following the necessary discipline, they will not be equipped to travel the journey to this "foreign" place. Such piety may entail learning a language or set of concepts. It may require becoming adept in the use of certain tools. It may call for the development of particular qualities, attitudes, or virtues. If teachers do not press for such respect and readiness on the part of students, there is the danger that they mislead, that they betray the truth they have been authorized to protect, that they have failed in their duty of stewardship. The stress on piety ensures that a teacher's emphasis on students' freedom, rights, and needs is tempered, and it prevents students from remaining imprisoned within the limited perspectives of their own immediate experience.

My focus on polemics is intended to qualify the demands made by the content and the communities from which it emerges. The stress on piety calls on students to be ready to change and to distance themselves, to some degree at least, from where they are, if they are to come near what is different and special about the topic under study. My emphasis on polemics calls upon communities (in this case religious communities) to be ready to change and to distance themselves from where they currently are, if their tradition is to remain alive. Effective teachers make accessible and less forbidding what at first seems difficult and strange, not just by the clarity of their explanations and by their mastery of subject matter, but also by reaching out to students and inviting them to engage appropriately with it. They reduce the apparently complex to something simple. It is, however, also the responsibility of teachers to render the familiar unfamiliar, so that it can be seen in new ways and from fresh angles. Sometimes they must stress complexity rather than simplicity, create problems as well as show how to solve them, and raise questions rather than provide answers. These are some of the ways they engage in polemics.

Plasticity

One of the marks of inclusive teaching is a quality of hospitality in the classroom. A hospitable teacher makes students feel welcome, respected, and appreciated. He sees students as they really are (even though at the same time he must always be able to see their future potential as far outstripping their present performance). Students know that what they bring to the classroom will count for something and will be heard. If they are to take ownership of and responsibility for their own learning, then several prior conditions are necessary. They have to feel that they have made a mark with us. Their ignorance, fear, uncertainty, and tentativeness must be treated sensitively. Their experiences of life must be acknowledged; otherwise they cannot build on them. Students need to feel that they can "be themselves" in the classroom, before they can be asked to become somebody different, to be open to change, perhaps even to conversion, that is, really turning toward the subject matter of study. Hospitable teachers facilitate such integrity rather than pretense on the part of students. They make room for a larger rather than a limited self to become involved in the classroom. "Hospitality in teaching involves asking the 'right' questions of others. These are questions that 'draw out' students so that their own experience becomes a valuable and respected resource enabling them to find their own voices, to be true to their own experiences, talents and identity."[1]

The teacher is charged with inviting students to enter unfamiliar worlds as opened up by "texts" of various kinds. In religious studies the teacher must lay out pathways toward new understandings of God and human beings. Plasticity on the part of the teacher will help in this process; it will prevent approaches to students that are either too automatic or too uniform. Account will be taken of what students bring to the classroom in terms of

1. John Bennett, "The Academy and Hospitality," *CrossCurrents* 50, nos. 1–2 (Spring/Summer 2000): 26.

their religious knowledge and experience. Some of this is positive, while some will function as an obstacle or as "baggage." In order for the teacher to discern what students bring and "where they are coming from," and in order to facilitate students' access to one another, she must attend carefully to the factors that foster effective conversation.

Martin Buber speaks of education as having an ascetic character, where the teacher seeks to separate herself from the instinct to dominate and to experience the person "on the other side" of the teaching relationship, the pupil.[2] The kind of understanding and insights sought for in religion do not develop properly in an atmosphere of manipulation or of control. Too methodical an approach rushes students, bypasses their present particularities, fails to wait for questions or to weigh them properly, and can slip into pushing for a premature commitment or self-definition. "A good teacher will know when to withdraw, so that she does not take up too much space in order to let the students come to their own conclusions."[3]

Teachers who display plasticity treat their students as important, as making legitimate demands on them, as individuals, each at different stages in their journey of life (and faith), each possessing experience, insights, and feelings that must be taken into account. They "bend" toward them; they reach out rather than impose; they invite rather than compel. In doing so they display a flexibility of response that acknowledges the need for readiness on the part of students. The sensitivity shown in the exercise of plasticity also serves, at least in part, to acknowledge and to respect the inalienable freedom of students. If responsible, critical, and creative commitment to a way of life is a desirable outcome from theological teaching, then the fullest space needs to be left for the development of student freedom of judgment, decision making, and practice. "The religious educator who attempted to 'paint on' faith, or to force it in any way, could well be the greatest enemy of all to the development of true faith. . . . Religion may require an even more explicit regime of freedom than any other [learning area], so sensitive and profound is its potential effect on its learners."[4]

It is not just that consent—and therefore integrity and authenticity—

---

2. Martin Buber, *Between Man and Man* (London: Fontana, 1974), 123.

3. Donna Teeven, "Philosophical Hermeneutics and Theological Education," *Teaching Theology and Religion* 3, no. 2 (June 2000): 85.

4. Terence Lovat, "The Support Text and the Public Syllabus: A Case for Integrity," *Journal of Religious Education* 48, no. 2 (2000): 35.

cannot be imposed; even understanding cannot be "driven in" from outside. Understanding is "interior, immanently received and personal."[5] It is part of a set of dynamic and *internally* generated mental operations, as Bernard Lonergan pointed out in *Insight*.[6] The "health" or effective functioning of these mental operations will be influenced, positively or negatively, by the pattern and ordering of emotions in students. An approach by the teacher who displays plasticity toward students is one that is willing to consider seriously and without condemnation new perspectives, however tentative, awkwardly expressed, or unorthodox. "Fear of error is not an ideal condition for growth in understanding."[7] The teacher who reaches out to or "leans toward" students creates a hospitable space for learning where all voices receive a respectful hearing. Often the willingness to bend, to accommodate in a nonjudgmental way, is the crucial factor in eliciting into speech a voice that otherwise did not even know it had something to utter.

Piety

Starting where students are, however, is merely that, an introduction to their task. If plasticity can be interpreted as a form of partial surrender to students, then a different kind of surrender, by both teacher and students, is required when they face the subject matter of the religious lesson. Just as athletes have to train so that their bodies are put in readiness for the rigors of a race, so the spirits of learners need exercise to prepare them to be both receptive and responsive to the realm of religion.

What we know depends on what we like, in the sense of what we are attached to, and it is also intimately dependent on what we are like, the qualities and virtues that comprise our character. We cannot "master" or dominate the subject matter of religion, but must be ready to be changed by its demands if we are to get near to knowledge of what is offered. Coming to know any religion will entail spiritual and moral exercises that "awaken, test, train, deepen and even strain the student."[8]

5. Christopher Cotter, "Integrating Tradition and Experience," *Journal of Religious Education* 48, no. 2 (2000): 9.
6. Bernard Lonergan, *Insight* (London: Longmans, Green, 1958).
7. Cotter, "Integrating Tradition and Experience," 10.
8. Thomas Martin, "Aristotle's *Confessions* as Pedagogy: Exercises in Transformation," in *Augustine and Liberal Education*, ed. Kim Paffenroth and Kevin Hughes (Aldershot, UK: Ashgate Publishing, 2000), 43.

To dispose ourselves to be open to and capable of recognizing religious truth we need the cleansing virtues of purity and humility. These will help us to leave behind some of the obstacles to spiritual wisdom: damaging alternative attractions and false images of self. "The practice of purity is a discipline, an *ascesis* of turning away from pleasure (for example, turning off television to do homework)."[9] Purity releases us from too much personal baggage and allows us to attend with more of our real selves. Humility, on the other hand, makes us docile, facilitates a readiness, at least temporarily, to accept authority and opens us up to the possibility that we are both ignorant and in need of conversion.

A combination of purity and humility on the part of the teacher is also needed. First, such a combination prevents him or her from loading the subject matter with too much personal "freight" and from pursuing his or her own agenda under the guise of dispassionate scholarship. Second, it reduces the temptation to invest too much hope in the teacher's own repertoire of skills and methods and leaves some "space" for the subject matter to work its own way into the mind, heart, and life of the students. Although good teachers should be committed to what they teach, and ready to witness to the difference it has made in their own lives, prudence suggests that often a degree of detachment is also required; some expressions of enthusiasm on the part of teachers can be counterproductive in the classroom.

In emphasizing piety I seek deliberately to turn attention away from the self of students and also away from the self of the teacher. The religious teacher should aim to focus instead on how we might establish a right relationship with the object of our study, which, in the case of religion, is ultimately God. For this, personal authenticity is not enough. Just as any attempt to get to know someone only on our own terms is likely to lead to our missing something vital about the other person, so approaching a religion only on our own terms is likely to lead to misinterpretation and a failure to take its full measure. We have to allow ourselves to be called into question by what we are studying; we have to let it stand *over* us if we are to get near understanding it.

The still-too-neglected religious thinker von Hügel once described an experiment required of a prospective student by the Unitarian preacher James

9. Phillip Cary, "Study as Love," in Paffenroth and Hughes, *Augustine and Liberal Education*, 65.

Martineau.[10] The student, already strongly analytical, sharply critical of religion, and highly cerebral in his approach to his studies, was asked to spend two periods of six months with very different communities. The first was to be with uncultured, narrow-minded but believing peasants in Westphalia. Then he was to spend six months with highly intelligent and skeptical medical students in Berlin. His reflection on how best to approach the study of religion was to be informed by his experience of how these two vastly different communities coped with their hopes and fears and how they responded to the successes and problems they encountered. The student took the view that the piety of the former, despite all its limitations and prejudices, took them further toward wisdom for a worthy life than the skepticism and freedom of the latter group. For all their shortcomings, the believing peasants acknowledged the givenness and objectivity of religious truth. They knew they stood (whether in darkness or in light) under its authority. They knew that they should allow themselves to be conformed to the reality that stood over them, even if their progress was faltering and erratic. On the other hand the medical students, in their intellectual pride and self-confidence, stood over a religion they cut even further down to the scale and meaning allowed it by their conceptual apparatus and methodology.

I am not arguing that we should abandon our critical faculties when studying religion, as I will make clear. I am, however, suggesting that we should help our students to harmonize their moral and spiritual lives with the disciplines of academic life. The intellectual historian Mark Schwehn employs the notion of "the *manners* of learning," meaning both the methods and the virtues that underpin a particular discipline; the task of the teacher is one of developing an "ethos of inquiry" that fosters the virtues that are constitutive of any field of learning.[11] This is to acknowledge the Aristotelian view that cognition and character are mutually implicated. "It is a mistake to think that just by virtue of being a rational agent an individual has the realized capacity for a correct grasp and appreciation of ethical considerations."[12] There are intellectual vices as well as virtues; vices inhibit our access to ethical and spiritual truth; virtues facilitate such access.

10. Friedrich von Hügel, *Essay and Addresses on the Philosophy of Religion*, 2nd series (London: Dent, 1926), 126–29.

11. Mark Schwehn, *Exiles from Eden* (New York: Oxford University Press, 1993), 44, 34.

12. Jonathan Jacobs, "Theism, Blame and Perfection," *Heythrop Journal* 41, no. 2 (2000): 142.

Among the former could be listed the two excesses of gullibility and close-mindedness, together with willful naivety and superficiality, dishonesty and arrogance. In contrast, an intellectually virtuous student is inquisitive, attentive, persevering, and circumspect.[13]

To reach truth in religious matters often requires a lengthy and difficult search, one calling for serious commitment and strength of character. Self-control allows a student to focus her energies in close attention. Perseverance in the face of difficulties and a willingness to face opposition keep one "on track." A clear sense of priorities helps us to avoid distractions. Our willingness to be taught needs to be tempered by vigilance with regard to the sources of instruction. Even our desire for knowledge is subject to moral scrutiny: our appetite for it must be constrained (for it is not the only good and must not be pursued at the expense of other duties and dimensions of life). Our motivation too must be worthy, for it is possible to seek knowledge merely to impress others or for the sake of material gain, rather than because of love of truth.[14]

One might say that thinking well is an essential ingredient in the flourishing life, and at the same time that only through a virtuous life is thinking well made possible. "Exercising care over the formation of our minds is not a purely academic pursuit; it is also a spiritual one."[15] Without such care we cannot grow into the full stature required by our Christian calling.[16] The philosopher David Hume derided the "monkish virtues," believing that they "stupefied the understanding." Others, however, have seen humility, self-denial, faith, and charity as indispensable to higher education, preparing for learning by "a disposing of the soul toward an inner readiness to lose the self for the sake of the truth."[17] In defending the claim that charity has cognitive implications, Schwehn suggests that the exercise of this virtue should make his historical work "more cautious in appraisal, more sympathetic with human failings, less prone to stereotype and caricature."[18]

Of course, such a claim has to be backed up by personal example, if it is to have credibility. Credibility has to be both earned and granted. Part of what I mean by the teacher's piety is a concern (in his presentation of infor-

13. W. Jay Wood, Epistemology (Leicester: Apollos, 1998), 47, 35.

14. Gregory Reichberg, "Studiositas, the Virtue of Attention," in The Common Things: Essays on Thomism and Education, ed. Daniel McInerny (Mishawaka, Ind.: American Maritain Association, 1999).

15. Wood, Epistemology, 18.   16. Ephesians 3:16–19; 4:23–24.
17. Schwehn, Exiles from Eden, 46–49.   18. Ibid., 51.

mation and selection of resources) to do justice to the tradition that he represents and to the disciplines or pathways that make access to this tradition possible. Beyond this, it includes a vigilant self-awareness of the degree to which he consistently and earnestly seeks to exemplify the appropriate moral qualities and to embody the required intellectual virtues. A question that is perhaps even more crucial for the teacher of religion than for other areas of the curriculum is: "am I the kind of human being they want to be influenced by?"[19] Can students trust teachers so that they take the risk of giving themselves willingly to the learning process?

In fact, two different kinds of trust are required for the effective teaching of a religious tradition. The first form of trust has more chance of being granted and is the hoped-for fruit of their practice if teachers display the kind of hospitality and inclusiveness I have summarized (above) under the heading of plasticity. The second form of trust depends on the degree to which a teacher's knowledge of and fidelity to a tradition reflects it sufficiently accurately for a religious community, at least through its authorized leaders, to treat him or her as both an exemplar and elder. Such recognition is the fruit of piety. Can other members of the tradition trust the teacher to represent it authentically and in its integrity? The second form of trust is shown in the kind of authority granted to a teacher.

It is dangerous for a tradition to rely too quickly on the second kind of trust—that granted to teachers on account of their piety by a religious community—without sufficient attention being given to the first kind of trust, elicited from students by teacher plasticity. Any resulting affiliation by students is likely to be experienced as alienating and inauthentic. It is also dangerous for teachers to expect a high degree of personal trust without attention being given to the demands, the canon, and the criteria (intellectual, moral, and spiritual) of the tradition. Any resulting personal loyalty shown by students to teachers can easily be misplaced and ultimately be limiting (and therefore disempowering), because no single person can adequately reflect all the dimensions of any particular religious tradition or community. Trust in the classroom functions as a kind of bridge between where students start and where the teacher aims to take them. If this is the case, then the place on the other side, that territory toward which trust in the teacher is

19. Miriam Peskowitz, quoted by Stephen Webb, "Teaching as Confessing," *Teaching Theology and Religion* 2, no. 3 (1999): 150.

only a prerequisite for movement, must be something more than the teacher's personal interpretation and appropriation of the tradition. One of the ways that we communicate the view that the tradition stands in judgment over us is by encouraging student assessment of the extent to which we practice the intellectual (and other) virtues that we teach in the classroom.

I ended the section on plasticity by speaking about the need to make allowances for the realities of student readiness for learning and to respect their freedom, suggesting that, without consent, religious affiliation becomes domination. In stressing the need for attention to piety, as described above, I want to qualify the importance I gave there to student perceptions and priorities. If they are to learn, students must dispose themselves appropriately; that is, they must allow themselves to be docile or teachable, to acknowledge, even if only provisionally, that there are legitimate demands on them other than those coming from their own nature and needs. Without such docility they will be imprisoned in the parochialisms and prejudices stemming from the accidents of their particular experience; their world will be confined and their options prematurely foreclosed. The religious teacher's role is to draw students' attention to aspects of reality of which they may be unaware, aspects that have a claim on them. The religious teacher has to bring out the strength of the call (inherent in the tradition and that toward which it points) to constant conversion, intellectually, morally, and spiritually. Without such conversions, which confront the negative elements within us of hate, pride, envy, and laziness, access to religious truth is not possible. As one commentator put it, part of the religious teacher's responsibility "is often to speak against what is already inside students."[20]

In the Christian tradition our recognition of the need for conversion and, following this, our capacity to engage in it, depend radically on the grace of God. Our insights and our responses are not the result of personal will or effort alone, though they have a necessary part to play. Stephen Webb claims that "the most significant task for the Christian teacher is to make room in the classroom for God, to remind students that God is more than just an object of discussion, and to prepare students to think about themselves in relation to their creator and sustainer."[21] Our growth also depends on other people. Moira Lee draws our attention to the scriptural injunctions that foster

20. Lake Lambert, "Active Learning for the Kingdom of God," *Teaching Theology and Religion* 3, no. 2 (2000): 78.
21. Stephen Webb, "Teaching as Confessing," 152.

mutual learning: "giving honor to one another (Romans 12:10), admonishing one another (Romans 15:14), serving one another (Galatians 5:13), building up one another (1 Thessalonians 5:11), lovingly bearing with one another (Ephesians 4:2), and forgiving one another (Colossians 3:13)."[22] By piety, then, I am referring not only to the development of certain qualities that make access to the realm of religious truth a possibility for us, but also an openness both to the grace of God and to the collective wisdom of God's people.

Polemics

The gift that God wants to make available to us can be received only by an act of the whole person. The plasticity of the teacher with regard to students ensures that their real self is reached, touched, and engaged. The kind of piety described above calls into being a larger self at the same time as it both develops and invites an active receptivity. Effective and authentic religious pedagogy has two principal sources. It flows partly from our commitment to students, as exemplified in plasticity. It also flows from our ecclesiological commitments, as exemplified through piety. Each of these qualifies, corrects, and completes the other. Our piety prevents our plasticity from leaving students with weak (and therefore misleading) impressions of the otherness and distinctiveness of a religious tradition. Such piety leads us to do justice to what is currently beyond the students, but beckoning them. Our plasticity ensures that, in doing justice to the tradition, we neither leave students behind nor damage them; nor do we take them "into custody" by prematurely appropriating their commitment. Plasticity and piety, even when combined, however, are insufficient.

The religious teacher is more than a facilitator of student growth and also more than a representative of or spokesperson for a religious tradition. A teacher must call into question where students are at any particular time, in the interests of their continuing growth and ever deepening maturity. Here piety qualifies and directs plasticity. The teacher must also call into question the tradition at any particular stage of its history. This task serves (modestly) to assist the tradition to ensure, first, that it really does contribute to the flourishing of its members, and second, that it never ceases striving to reduce

---

22. Moira Lee, "Experiencing Shared Inquiry through the Process of Collaborative Learning," *Teaching Theology and Religion* 3, no. 2 (2000): 111.

the gap between the ideals and current attainment. Even the most highly developed religious tradition is immersed in historical compromise, limited by the shortcomings of its members, inadequately converted in some dimensions of its life, and therefore not yet in full or secure possession of the truth. Our reverence and respect for a tradition must not blind us to the fact that it remains a vehicle, not a destination. Our openness to the prompting of the Holy Spirit should remind us that the tradition has a future as well as a past. Without critical openness, our commitment and affiliation can slip into idolatry. This is where the teacher's polemical role has a part to play.

To speak of teaching as polemical is to envisage it as an act of provocation. Such provocation should be aimed neither at diminishing students nor at boosting the ego of teachers. It serves to inject into the classroom moments of liveliness, moments that hint either at the provisionality of the knowledge so far attained (by any of us) or that suggest the potential "bite" or purchase that the religious ideas might have in our lives. It invites students to look again at what they thought was familiar and see it in a new way. It deliberately disturbs them so that they feel the inner tensions and conflicting priorities and voices within a tradition. Perhaps such provocation reveals a distortion in the tradition or the misuse of a concept.

Provocation can also show the need for change, either in students or in the religious tradition. Students should not rest easy or feel comfortable all the time. Nor should a religious tradition be allowed to slip into complacency. Both students and adherents of a tradition should expect some features of religious teaching to confront them with awkward questions; they should expect their lives, in some respects at least, to be called into question. The sources of evidence and the reliability of arguments used to buttress the tradition will be scrutinized thoroughly. Inconsistencies will be exposed. Religious teachers will be sensitive to the political dimension of all knowledge claims, bringing home to students that these claims can be interpreted as serving the interests of some while ignoring or perhaps even suppressing the interests of others. It can be unsettling to ask students to consider Cicero's question, "*cui bono?*"—who stands to gain from this claim?—and its correlative, who stands to lose? A variation on this might be to ask: on whose experience is this founded and whose experiences have been discounted? Such questions are potentially polemical and have a capacity to modify the way that students understand a concept, doctrine, a rule, or a practice.

Of course, criticism must be balanced by confidence, if it is not to be corrosive either of the tradition or of the personhood of the student. Commitments and questions about such commitments need to be nurtured alongside one another, rather than in different institutions. Religious communities must be vigilant about the ideological implications of employing certain techniques of inquiry, lest they undermine the tradition from within. They cannot afford, however, to ignore all legitimate "angles of approach," simply because such methods come from "without the camp."

Just as plasticity that is not qualified by piety leaves students in an impoverished world, and just as piety that is not qualified by plasticity threatens to dominate them, so a polemical approach that is not qualified by piety runs the risk of betraying the nature and mutilating the meaning of a religion. When this happens, much of the scope and power of religion, both attractive and repelling, gets entirely lost or becomes incomprehensible. In engaging students in the practice of criticism, and in bringing out the polemical nature of religious discourse and practice, the teacher must help them to go beyond skill in analysis and deconstruction. Teachers should help students to sense the capacity of religion to touch their lives in its depths, while leaving them the psychological space to develop their own responses.

Teachers of religion need to integrate the task of polemics with the tasks of plasticity and piety. This will require of them a high degree of self-awareness, a consciousness of their modus operandi and the effects of their methodological repertoire in the classroom. How well does it connect to where the students are? Does it do justice to the religious tradition being studied? Does it promote independent, critical, and creative thinking by students? Does it treat the tradition as if it is one that is closed and merely reproducing itself, or does it communicate this tradition as one that is living, open to new questions and perspectives, capable of further development?

Here our methods, our relationships, and the tone we set will be as influential as the material we put before students. It will be through the medium of the teacher's example, rather than through the texts in the foreground of study, that students come to learn what are perhaps two of the most crucial things in academic religious education: "how judgment is made within an assenting community" and "how knowledge grows within an assenting community."[23]

23. Sheryl Burkhalter, quoting Kenneth Bruffee, in "Four Modes of Discourse," in *Beyond the Classics? Essays in Religious Studies and Liberal Education*, ed. Frank Reynolds and Sheryl Burkhalter (Atlanta: Scholars Press, 1990), 160.

Conclusion

I have argued that the communication of a religious tradition in higher education requires of the teacher careful attention to—and a balanced integration of—three tasks that mutually qualify one another. This implies that, outside the specific learning community in front of him or her, the teacher must hold constantly in mind both the religious tradition and the wider community of scholars. These latter will overlap, in varying degrees, with membership of the religious tradition, but they should never be wholly identified with it. It will be clear from my earlier comments that there are limits to the potential of each of the three tasks described here. None is sufficient on its own. Each requires the other two for the healthy communication of religion in a university setting. Just as each student experiences the learning of religion in the classroom differently, inevitably any particular teacher will interpret differently how to respond to the triple pull of relevance to students, fidelity to tradition, and openness to truth.

There are several implications of the preceding analysis. First, students need to meet these two different communities, the religious tradition and the community of scholarship, on the terms set down by these communities. Second, they should see that these two communities are not coextensive. Third, they need guidance in recognizing how these two communities critique each other. Fourth, they need help in becoming sufficiently insightful, self-critical, and resilient to acknowledge and to cope with how these two communities critique them. Finally, they also need sufficient confidence in themselves and in the academic tools at their disposal to believe that both of these communities would benefit from critique by them.

13 Thick and Thin

Personal and Communal Dimensions of Communicating Faith

Frederick D. Aquino

As Maximus the Confessor once said, "We who plague people with words are many nowadays, while those who teach or are taught by actions are few."[1] This observation captures a profound disconnect between words and actions in our contemporary learning environments. However, the problem runs deeper, stemming from a persistent concern over how to handle intellectual challenges, conceptual differences, varied kinds of cognitive dissonance, and wide-ranging forms of epistemic anxiety. By now, most of us have tried different epistemic proposals to heal the intellectual wounds of our past. Yet we continue to participate in and feel the impact of a long-standing crisis of authority (both religious and nonreligious) in our current settings, and the wounds remain open. The effects of the crisis are evident in our struggle to navigate a sustainable intellectual path, thereby hoping

I wish to express appreciation to Derek Neve and John Sullivan for their valuable comments on this chapter.

1. St. Maximus the Confessor, *Capita de caritate (Prologue)*, in *The Philokalia: The Complete Text Compiled by St. Nikodimos of the Holy Mountain and St. Makarios of Corinth*, Vol. 2, ed. G. E. H. Palmer, Philip Sherrard, and Kallistos Ware, 52 (London: Faber and Faber, 1981).

to secure some epistemic closure or, at least, find an appropriate salve to relieve the level of pain.

With these challenges in mind, how does one engage in the ongoing task of forming people intellectually and communicating faith within a university context? What links people from radically different starting points and commitments? How does one constructively work through the relationship between personal and communal dimensions of faith? In this essay, I take up these questions in three brief meditations. More specifically, I highlight the reality of our situation and put forth a proposal for thinking about a new, or perhaps not so new, course. I include my own personal and professional experiences as a graduate professor of theology and philosophy, and I draw insights from broader publics and other fields of knowledge (e.g., history, ethics, and epistemology). However, I am not particularly interested in offering and defending a full-blown vision of theological education. Rather, I argue that finding viable and concrete ways to connect thick and thin commitments is fundamental to the task of aptly communicating faith in diverse academic settings. My claim is that a robust set of intellectual virtues fits such a task; they are regulative pointers to how one *ought* to inquire about matters, regardless of intellectual differences.

In the first meditation, I explain how the modern crisis of authority precipitates the quest for epistemic certainty and how the subsequent divide between public (e.g., secular) and private (e.g., religious) modes of discourse complicates the task of communicating faith in a university (public) context. This meditation is by no means an exhaustive account of the crisis of authority; it simply points out that the epistemic dilemmas of Luther, Calvin, Descartes, and others (pick your figure and/or your ecclesial tradition) are still with us, and such awareness warrants deeper reflection about the implications for communicating faith. The second meditation stresses the importance of the intellectual virtues for guiding the educational process and for working through the tensile relationship between autonomy and authority. Those charged with the task of communicating faith need to pay greater attention to the intellectual formation of persons, and not simply to state-of-the-art techniques and learning outcomes. The third meditation argues that communicating faith within a university context in its varied forms (e.g., religious, secular) requires what I call an embodied particularism of informed judgment. This kind of particularism has a synthetic component in that the concrete self draws insights from an expansive range of sources and therefore is able to move from the particular to the more comprehensive. A proposal of this sort challenges accounts that insulate thick commitments from broader conversations or those that strip human agents of their particular habits, practices, and beliefs under the guise of thinly conceived forms of public discourse. Conversely, informed judgment calls for a richer conception of intellectual formation that includes rigorous communicative, philosophical, moral, and religious practices.

Meditation One: The Crisis of Authority as Persistent Problem

The modern crisis of authority affects a wide variety of intellectual issues, fields of knowledge, and areas of life. For example, one can see its impact on contemporary debates about theories of knowledge, truth, rationality, warrant, consciousness, human selfhood, meaning, value, and perception. However, the aim of my first meditation is not to cover the entire conceptual landscape. Rather, I highlight briefly the epistemic underpinnings of the crisis of religious authority in the Protestant Reformation. More importantly, I try to show how the gradual bifurcation of public and private modes of discourse shapes the current challenge of communicating faith, especially when thick (e.g., tradition-specific ways of thinking) and thin (e.g., generally shared principles, independent of reliance upon tradition) commitments of people seem incommensurable. Furthermore, the current climate of students shows that the crisis is still very much with us and that such a focus is both timely and relevant—so much so that I have included philosophical counseling as a growing part of my teaching responsibilities.

The Protestant Reformation is a fitting example.[2] The Reformers essentially claimed that scripture, not the teachings of the church, was the locus of authority for adjudicating theological claims. However, their flight from the primacy of ecclesial authority fits within the larger quest for epistemic certainty. With the emergence of competing authorities, the basic Reformation plea (doctrinal claims are Christian if and only if they are grounded in

2. My narrative, though not exactly the same, has been shaped by Jeffrey Stout's historical account of the crisis of authority in *The Flight from Authority: Religion, Morality, and the Quest for Autonomy* (Notre Dame: University of Notre Dame Press, 1981) and William Abraham's work on the epistemic crisis of authority, and its implications for contemporary theology, in *Canon as Criterion in Christian Theology: From the Fathers to Feminism* (Oxford: Clarendon Press, 1998). In my estimation, Abraham's analysis is a nice complement to Stout's historicist narrative and vice versa.

scripture) became less and less effective. What initially weakened the Reformation's appeal was the extent to which internal disagreement occurred over the interpretation of scripture, and broadly speaking, the inability to provide a criterion for settling public issues. Questions about securing the right interpretation of scripture, the freshly appointed epistemic norm, quickly surfaced. By what standard do people adjudicate between conflicting interpretations of scripture? Who is the authoritative interpreter of scripture? Is it Calvin, Luther, and/or the internal witness of the Holy Spirit confirmed in the elect? In the end, claims of inner illumination only complicated the search for the criterion of knowledge. What began for the Reformers as "as an appeal to a single authority of scriptural revelation now seems to recognize, implicitly at least, ten authorities in every pew."[3]

However, the interpretive disagreements of the Reformers were simply another example of the impending crisis of authority in broader circles. The problem of acquiring a general method of knowledge inevitably changed the conversation and the landscape of theology, science, and philosophy. All discourse that failed to provide an assured methodological standpoint belonged in its proper place, namely, the realm of the private. Thus, the point here is not to single out the Protestant Reformation as the only victim of the crisis of authority. In fact, what starts as a regional problem in the Reformation eventually becomes a larger problem of securing a criterion or general method by which people can adjudicate claims of knowledge (e.g., Descartes' internal appeal to the *cogito* as the clear, distinct, self-evident foundation for all other beliefs).[4] The same kind of crisis also can be seen in claims of papal infallibility, ecclesial infallibility, reason, and experience. The failure to agree on the locus of authority for judging theological and nontheological issues has certainly intensified and continues to fuel the long search for new grounds of epistemic certainty.

Today, we see similar levels of anxiety materialized in various attempts to canonize particular theories of interpretation, knowledge, scripture, church, and human beings. Such moves have privileged certain dimensions of the Christian tradition and broader philosophical perspectives while fostering a crisis of authority from which we are currently reeling. Students,

---

3. Stout, *The Flight from Authority*, 44.

4. For a fuller treatment of the regional and universal dimensions of the problem of the criterion in the Reformers and Descartes, see Abraham, *Canon as Criterion in Christian Theology*, esp. chap. 7.

professors, staff, administrators, and the broader publics very much recognize the crisis; a current example is the hot topic of religion's role in the public and, more specifically, the question of whether it is detrimental to human flourishing.[5] The list of issues is pretty extensive!

Obviously, the modern crisis of authority gives rise to different responses. I mention two general tendencies. One option tries to transcend the contingencies of history and tradition, thereby removing the shackles of ignorance, wish fulfillment, and outdated cosmologies. The goal is to identify hindrances steeped in the particular and move toward a thinner mode of discourse. Reason, experience, education are some of the candidates for purging and healing cognitive impurities. An aim of this kind is admirable, noble, and relevant. Yet, proponents of such projects occasionally receive a grave reminder of the human potential to engage in dehumanizing activities. In this regard, Jonathan Glover masterfully captures the tension between the human quest for enlightenment and the human potential for the tragic:

At the start of the century there was optimism, coming from the Enlightenment, that the spread of a humane and scientific outlook would lead to the fading away, not only of war, but also of other forms of cruelty and barbarism. They would fill the chamber of horrors in the museum of our primitive past. In the light of these expectations, the century of Hitler, Stalin, Pol Pot, and Saddam Hussein was likely to be a surprise. Volcanoes thought extinct turned out not to be.[6]

My point here is not to belittle the Enlightenment project (a popular move), but simply to underscore the humane and inhumane facets of such an effort and to remind us of the lingering effects of the epistemic crisis.

Another option fully embraces irony, contingency, and play. A hermeneutical posture of this sort constitutes a radical move toward the thick (the particular). The inclination is to emphasize the rooted nature of so-called "authoritative" texts and authors, undermine epistemic finality, widen the ugly

5. E.g., Richard Dawkins, *The God Delusion* (Boston: Houghton Mifflin, 2006), and Christopher Hitchens, *God Is Not Great: How Religion Poisons Everything* (New York: Twelve Books/Warner Books, 2007).

6. Jonathan Glover, *Humanity: A Moral History of the Twentieth Century* (New Haven: Yale University Press, 1999), 6. Glover provides an eye-opening account of humanity in the twentieth century. He offers a chastened but deeply committed project of the Enlightenment, moral history of the human situation. In fact, Glover tries to "replace the thin, mechanical psychology of the Enlightenment with something more complex, something closer to reality." Yet, an additional aim "is to defend the Enlightenment hope of a world that is more peaceful and more humane, the hope that by understanding more about ourselves we can do something to create a world with less misery" (7).

ditch of human interpretive dilemmas and sources of meaningfulness, and claim that access to the real is an illusion. From this perspective, the stress is on the importance of communally (or individually) established practices and narratives. Consequently, people recognize the separation between our inherited epistemic solutions (whether in a text, person, or magisterium) and the very real levels of cognitive dissonance in their own lives. The thick nature of this response is simply the other side of the philosophical coin.

Both responses are shaped, whether negatively or positively, by the long-standing quest for autonomy from tradition, contingency, and received dogma. The result is the so-called spatial distinction between the private (e.g., religious discourse) and the public (e.g., secular discourse). The problem of competing religious authorities, traced back to at least the sixteenth and seventeenth centuries, led to a search for a better way of achieving agreement in the public arena. Appeals to accepted opinions of religious authorities eventually played a diminished role in matters of public discourse.

The irony, however, is that the conceptual moves of the past quest (and perhaps the current versions) for autonomy were shaped by antecedent historical traditions (e.g., Descartes' indebtedness to the Platonic-Augustinian tradition). The attempt to purify thought of its historical contingency represents a failure to account for antecedent historical traditions. Furthermore, the fact that we still suffer from some of the same forms of epistemic anxiety as our intellectual ancestors seems to imply that we have failed to see such proposals in their proper context. For example, understanding Descartes' project in its context might help us to determine whether his "problem is, in any important sense, our problem and, therefore, whether his response still demands the kind of attention it once did." This approach just might free us from our "compulsion to be Cartesian."[7]

To some extent, our current epistemic questions and problems are similar to those of our intellectual ancestors, but in other ways our situation is different. One difference, for example, is that we live in a time in which appeals to epistemic finality make less and less sense. How, then, does one proceed under the current epistemic dilemma? For some, the price of admission, under the quest for autonomy, entailed losing a thickly conceived locus of authority; for others, the crisis simply confirmed the impression that incommensurable standpoints were inevitable; for still others, the situation warrants a

---

7. Stout, The Flight from Authority, 37.

new call for more robust accounts of how public space is to be renegotiated.

The point here is not to map out fully the details of the crisis. I simply note that the effects of the crisis seem to be very much with us, especially as we try to navigate a course that stipulates the conditions for handling the tensile relationship between authority and autonomy. How, then, *ought* we to proceed? Do we simply adhere to the intellectual strategies of our own community, fortify the walls, or, at least, add thicker layers of insulation? Or do we seek to overcome the rubbish of the ages, and thereby try to find some pristine and authentic expression of our humanity? What role does epistemic dependence play? Do we opt for the stance of radical autonomy, refusing to trust any claim until we have the preponderance of evidence, independent of appeals to authoritative sources?

Meditation Two: A Matter of Regulative Practices

The problem of adjudication certainly precipitates the human aspiration for a solution that enables cognitive agents, whether religious or nonreligious, to take on challenges such as relativism, competing claims of authority, and interpretive differences. A desire of this sort is not unique to any one field of knowledge. History, for example, is replete with various attempts to crown plausible candidates as the queens and kings of public discourse. Perhaps this is a sign of unwillingness to acknowledge our finitude, contingency, and tradition-specific ways of being in the world. In saying this, I am not suggesting a Rortian overdose of irony and contingency, but rather my analysis essentially agrees with Jeffrey Stout that the modern flight from authority seeks to find an uncontaminated epistemic space. It is within this context that I offer my constructive proposal.

A shift in emphasis may generate new possibilities for thinking about epistemic reflection/conduct within a pluralistic setting. Changing the focus to regulative practices, however, does not bypass meta-questions about authority and autonomy; it simply targets the normative question of how people *ought* to conduct themselves epistemically in a pluralistic setting. Thus, I want to give greater attention to the actual processes, materials, and intellectual virtues that guide epistemic reflection. As I hope to show, extreme forms of individualism (exaggerated claims of autonomy) and authoritarianism (unhealthy appeals to authority) impede this kind of inquiry. Both stances reflect the ongoing influence of the crisis. One tries to find a thinly agreed-upon rationale without the baggage of the past, while the other seeks to thicken its narrative.

A possible antidote to these extremes may be found in what I am calling an embodied particularism of informed judgment.[8] The concrete self, with its particular commitments, engages in an extended conversation with radically different people and communities. However, informed judgment does not hide behind the walls of authority, nor does it deny its tradition-specific ways of being in the world. Rather, it tries to map out an alternative understanding of the relationship between the thick and the thin aspects of epistemic reflection/conduct.[9] A proposal of this sort also envisions the educational process as a combination of discourse (e.g., disseminating information, acquiring communicative skills) and intellectual formation (e.g., internalizing the relevant intellectual virtues).

In my context as a graduate professor of theology and philosophy I invite students to participate in a process of philosophical reflection and intellectual formation, rejecting the assumption that the latter is essentially unrelated to the former. In other words, the intellectual virtues fit within the broader framework of forming cognitive agents. I have found that students, whether religious or not, find a delineated set of intellectual virtues a more helpful avenue for guiding the intersection of thick and thin commitments. Knowing how to think about, reason through, and understand complex issues comes through induction into a set of practices, commitments, virtues, skills, and dispositions. The assumption here is that books alone are insufficient for addressing difficulties of life and forming people. Ultimately, teachers strive to form communities of inquiry, inviting students to explore a shared world of learning. Accordingly, people within this learning environment endeavor to develop critical skills of reflection, internalize praiseworthy dispositions (e.g., humility, desire for truth, intellectual honesty), interact authentically and openly with one another, broaden epistemic horizons, and make crucial connections. Ultimately they learn to function as a community of inquiry without ignoring and/or collapsing the reality of competing claims.

8. See Frederick D. Aquino, *Communities of Informed Judgment: Newman's Illative Sense and Accounts of Rationality* (Washington, D.C.: The Catholic University of America Press, 2004).

9. See Joseph Raz, *Engaging Reason: On the Theory of Value and Action* (Oxford: Oxford University Press, 1999); Raz, *Value, Respect, and Attachment* (Cambridge: Cambridge University Press, 2001); Michael Walzer, *Thick and Thin: Moral Argument at Home and Abroad* (Notre Dame: University of Notre Dame Press, 1994); Thomas Nagel, *The View from Nowhere* (Oxford: Oxford University Press, 1989); and Nagel, *Equality and Impartiality* (New York: Oxford University Press, 1991).

Cultivating this kind of inquiry requires a social context in which people desire to acquire knowledge, understanding, and wisdom, follow the ongoing conversation about fundamental issues, learn how to evaluate different arguments and interpretations, and form their own understanding of things. On a university level, the social dimension consists of inducting students into a set of practices, materials, and people. Restricting the intellectual virtues to the material content of specific fields of knowledge is not my concern here, especially since methodological procedures, first principles, levels of training, conceptual commitments, and pedagogical goals are certainly bound to differ. The intellectual virtues are no replacement for domain-specific forms of training, but they seem especially "relevant to any discipline, and *ought* to be of interest to anyone who seriously seeks to transmit knowledge,"[10] cultivate the life of the mind, acquire understanding, and pursue wisdom. Thus, agreement on a set of intellectual virtues (e.g., interest in truth, intellectual honesty, concern for evidence, capacity to listen to and follow counterarguments, and the ability to see how things hang together) opens up the possibility of exchange between people of differing commitments.

A regulative approach to education, then, focuses on the question of how epistemic agents *ought* to engage in and guide the process of intellectual inquiry.[11] So, my emphasis here does not intend to squelch the autonomy of the intellectual agent; in fact, its concentration on how the pursuit of intellectual excellence *ought* to be guided implies protecting people from the ongoing challenge of intellectual vices (e.g., arbitrary appeals to authority, fudging the evidence, unwillingness to hear challenging and alternative arguments in and outside of a classroom). A properly formed person deciphers when relying on the insights of others is necessary, how to respond to criticism, and how to develop one's own thinking (which is never really in isolation). In other words, intellectually virtuous practices ideally make epistemic freedom possible.

A person of informed judgment does not assume that one size fits all, given that diverse educational settings (e.g., a seminary, a religious studies department, a religious university, a secular university, various ecclesial communities, and broader publics of society) call for domain-specific levels of

10. Robert C. Roberts and W. Jay Wood, *Intellectual Virtues: An Essay in Regulative Epistemology* (Oxford: Clarendon Press, 2007), 324.

11. For a helpful discussion of regulative epistemology, see Roberts and Wood, *Intellectual Virtues.*

training, different methodological procedures, and wide-ranging modes of public discourse. In addition, informed judgment does not suggest servile deference to authorities as the solution to an epistemic crisis within a pluralistic context. Quite the opposite, it demands the capacity to form arguments, map out questions, and pursue greater levels of understanding. Intellectual cloning is foreign to what I have in mind here. Epistemic dependence—gathering insights from others—is certainly fundamental to intellectual formation, and in fact it seems unreasonable to see this phenomenon as detrimental to one's intellectual integrity.

Part of intellectual formation, then, entails showing people that the desire for truth, the love of knowledge, the search for understanding/wisdom involve determining whether belief-forming processes, practices, and people yield true beliefs over false ones and contribute to expanding the locus of one's knowledge and one's understanding. The hope is that people motivated in such a way will be more likely to conduct thorough inquiries, scrutinize evidence carefully, investigate numerous fields of study, and consider alternative explanations. Yet, another part of intellectual formation requires that cognitive agents recognize sources of informed judgment as crucial to their intellectual development. Rarely do people form apt judgments about particulars in isolation. On the contrary, they take into account feedback from other sources of informed judgment, and proceed to see how things hang together in relation to the particular issue or question at hand. As noted earlier, epistemic dependence is not a subtle version of authoritarianism; it simply refers to the maturation process in which epistemic agents, under the tutelage of recognized experts, learn to assess arguments, evaluate evidence, and form their own conclusions.

The pedagogical process includes other intellectual virtues. I mention four. First, people who strive to be intellectually honest tackle difficult questions without seeking simple answers; they acknowledge the limits of their knowledge and their understanding while tenaciously trying to expand both. However, people who ignore complex and difficult questions only solidify epistemic vices such as intellectual dishonesty, close-mindedness, and rash judgments. These vices preclude the possibility of refining our thinking and of participating in conversations with others. Second, people who desire to be open-minded take seriously different ideas and counterarguments, recognizing that impulsively assessing evidence fosters intellectual deficiencies and hinders intellectual growth, both personally and communally. They realize that amassing and presenting knowledge includes persistence, discipline, patience, and wisdom. Third, intellectual courage requires, among other things, the willingness to defend one's position while considering other perspectives. Tenacity certainly plays a role in sustaining one's position, but it should not be confused with closed-mindedness. Last, people who pursue understanding seek to grasp how insights from various fields of knowledge hang together, and they decipher how to incorporate these insights into their current base of knowledge. Thus, understanding entails the urge to connect various pieces of data, practices, and experiences into a synthetic judgment.

Obviously, the goals of education are multifaceted. As the brief observation about the importance of intellectual virtues indicates, students and professors agree to engage in a set of regulative practices. Though they may be related, each virtue has a distinct aim. For example, the desire for truth may involve virtues such as intellectual honesty, epistemic humility, tenacity, and courage, but the primary concern is deciphering whether a belief is true. Understanding certainly includes the desire for truth and thereby presupposes knowledge (a person knows that p) as an important component. However, the goal of understanding is to see how various pieces of data hang together in light of one another. A person "can know many unrelated pieces of information, but understanding is achieved only when informational items are pieced together by the subject in question."[12] Acquiring propositional knowledge (one aim of education) involves knowing "*a relatively isolated proposition*" or a set of propositions, and that for any proposition (or set of propositions), a person either knows or does not know it (or them). In this regard, one can understand a theologian's or philosopher's particular work "without its being true, but one cannot know that p without p's being true. Very commonly we understand propositions, stories, and theories that we take to be false. We would be in quite a fix intellectually if we couldn't."[13] The

12. Jonathan Kvanvig, *The Value of Knowledge and the Pursuit of Understanding* (New York: Cambridge University Press, 2003), 192; see also Wayne D. Riggs, "Understanding 'Virtue' and The Virtue of Understanding," in *Intellectual Virtue: Perspectives from Ethics and Epistemology*, ed. Michael DePaul and Linda Zagzebski, 203–26 (Oxford: Oxford University Press, 2003).

13. Roberts and Wood, *Intellectual Virtues*, 47. For a fascinating account of the connection between knowing that and knowing how, see Stephen Hetherington, "How to Know (that Knowledge-that is Knowledge-how)," in *Epistemology Futures*, ed. Stephen Hetherington, 71–94 (Oxford: Clarendon Press, 2006). Essentially Hetherington argues that "to know that p is to know how to perform various actions. . . . For knowledge is an ability to perform various actions: to represent or reply or respond accurately" (72, 89). It seems especially relevant to the task of communicating faith to recognize such a connection without necessarily and always confusing knowing p with knowing how to do p.

result is the expansion of one's epistemic horizons, not simply an accumulation of isolated pieces of information. Thus, both knowledge and understanding are crucial to the process of intellectual formation. They are especially important for equipping people, as much as possible, to acquire truth and to see beyond their own perspective, thereby making the crucial connections among diverse ideas and resources (as an embodied particularism of informed judgment envisions in the third meditation).

We have met countless people who know that p but fall short in the areas of understanding and wisdom. We have also met people who have profoundly internalized the virtues of humility, courage, and intellectual honesty but fail to acquire knowledge that p. Ideally, we hope that the subjective and the objective come to together in the epistemic agent. Yet, this goal does not imply that intellectual virtues are necessary and sufficient for acquiring knowledge. However, intellectual formation is an important part of the educational process, especially in our effort to guide how people *ought* to engage in the process of learning. We have met the student who has no desire to operate with a virtuous motivation, and yet can spout off mathematical knowledge. The other side of the equation is to help students to foster the requisite dispositions or motivation for learning and to become more humane.

Meditation Three: An Embodied Particularism of Informed Judgment

My account of informed judgment, then, envisions the university as a place that endeavors to cultivate epistemic agents who can move from particular commitments to broader forms of discourse, both within a community and among radically different communities. The urge to connect the thick and thin or the personal and communal is at the heart of an embodied particularism of informed judgment. Accordingly, informed judgment entails linking new and existing knowledge to relevant questions, issues, and subject matters at hand. As meditation two shows, practices, habits, and persons are fundamental to guiding various aims of the educational process. It is hard to imagine professors and students naturally or innately up-to-snuff when it comes to deciphering truth, evaluating evidence, and following arguments. Nuanced accounts of faith and, for that matter, other fields of knowledge require a constructive vision of how the intellectual virtues *ought* to contribute to cognitive development.

An embodied particularism of informed judgment, therefore, zooms in on the social conditions under which epistemic agents actualize the urge to connect. However, my use of the term "social" does not suggest the overextended view that desiderata such as knowledge, truth, rationality, justification, understanding, are simply a social construct or simply what our peers will let us get away with. On the contrary, my proposal focuses on the requisite evaluative capacities of cognitive agents within a particular context. In this regard, the social dimension challenges the "Cartesian image" in which people inquire, evaluate arguments, and pursue knowledge as autonomous agents. Such an image "ignores the interpersonal and institutional contexts in which most knowledge endeavors are actually undertaken."[14] Consequently, it makes sense to expect students to operate from particular starting points, but it does not follow that their beliefs should be protected from being interrogated. In fact, people who are interested in pursuing truth, knowledge, understanding, and wisdom *ought* to extend their particular claims to the varied public spaces of human discourse.

As a result, informed judgment challenges extremes such as authoritarianism and individualism. It seems reasonable, at least *prima facie*, for people to trust select individuals and associated communities that have shaped their current way of thinking and being in the world, but it also makes sense to operate with some level of suspicion about these thick commitments. However, it does not follow that either option alone fully captures the ongoing task. On the one hand, a radical conception of autonomy (a person acquires knowledge independently) fails to explain both how our intellectual training actually occurs and the extent to which others have contributed to a person's knowledge and understanding of things. On the other hand, a radical appeal to tradition-specific forms of belief-formation is equally problematic. Such a posture rarely enables people to get out of the house, view the broader landscape, and explore critically both internal and external claims. As noted earlier, we start from somewhere in terms of our training, our knowledge of various subject matters, our different methodological com-

14. Alvin I. Goldman, *Knowledge in a Social World* (Oxford: Clarendon Press, 1999). As Frederick F. Schmitt, "Social Epistemology," in *The Blackwell Guide to Epistemology*, ed. John Greco and Ernest Sosa, 354 (Oxford: Blackwell Publishers, 1999) points out, a contemporary question in epistemology is "whether, and to what extent, the conditions of knowledge include social conditions. Is knowledge a property of knowers in isolation from their social setting (and in what sense of 'isolation'), or does it involve a relation between knowers and their social circumstances?" For further consideration, see Schmitt, ed., *Socializing Epistemology: The Social Dimensions of Knowledge* (Lanham, Md.: Rowman and Littlefield, 1994).

mitments, and our awareness of interpretive issues. Nevertheless, an important goal of university education is to help people learn to think, write, and argue in ways that show healthy respect for other sources of knowledge while making informed judgments of their own. Consequently, what I am after here is a philosophy of education that is deeply particularistic and genuinely committed to a more expansive form of human discourse.

The cultivation of aforementioned intellectual virtues demands a host of critical interlocutors, and therefore presupposes the capacity to extend personal judgments to communal spheres of discourse. For example, if pursuing truth is a personal matter, what prevents ideological distortions and epistemic vices from setting in or becoming entrenched in one's own thinking? However, these same tendencies can be systemic in communities. In fact, an appeal to the communal over against the personal or to the personal over the communal is not an immediate remedy for intellectual vices. We have seen intellectual abuses on both personal and communal levels.

Instead, informed judgment calls for the intersection of the communal and the personal, undergirded by a persistent commitment to intellectual integrity. For instance, intellectual freedom is a valued good, but it does not imply exemption from engaging others in honest and open discussion, nor does it mean that acknowledging dependence upon other sources of informed judgment necessarily shrinks the space of one's intellectual freedom. Both individual and communal dimensions need regulative processes. The virtues function as regulative pointers about how both individuals and communities *ought* to conduct the process of intellectual inquiry. The importance of communal learning is the capacity to extend the self into a more expansive way of seeing, knowing, and understanding things, and the importance of autonomy is for individuals to learn to incorporate insights from others without such a process turning into something like groupthink or authoritarian dictates from on high.

My suggestion here is not really new; it is steeped in a long-standing tradition, both in its Christian and non-Christian versions (e.g., Aristotelian, Stoic, Christian). It also calls us to revisit the rich contours of religious and philosophical traditions and explore ways in which these resources may serve as resources of healing. Pursuing a proposal of this sort may be a painful experience, especially given the ongoing manifestations of the epistemic crisis, but it may result in profound forms of transformation in the various publics of reflection.

However, we must resist the temptation to equate any one methodology, epistemology, or approach with the content and identity of the Christian faith. The narrowing of perspective that accompanies such an equation partly explains the current resistance to and criticism of religion, and I think eventually results in commensurate forms of scientism, secularism, and fundamentalism. Canonizing an epistemological theory is not the answer; it simply exacerbates the crisis. Rather, reconnecting our intellectual practices with the healing practices of religion seems more promising. This does not imply backing away from rigorous thinking; rather, it simply locates our intellectual projects within a set of vibrant materials, persons, and practices.[15]

My proposal of informed judgment seeks to unpack the conditions under which formative practices, people, and habits transform the self, thereby identifying a process for cultivating human excellence. It is not simply about following rules or duties, but entails the ability to make connections that are not obvious. Informed judgment is deeply needed, given current manifestations of the ongoing crisis of authority. Such a move requires the power to discern what matters and what is relevant for our context. Moreover, it calls for teachers to decipher a proper fit between the subject matter and the particular kind of audience they encounter. Again, a person of informed judgment will resist the reductionistic mentality. This kind of informed judgment is not something that can be transmitted simply as a rule-governed process of decision making; it is a honed taste or cultivated judgment about making relevant connections, disseminating the content of faith, and extending one's commitments to a broader conversation.

Digesting isolated pieces of information is no replacement for the synthetic component of discernment, understanding, and wisdom. The capacity to connect various insights and experiences into a coherent understanding of how they fit together is an acquired habit. With this in mind, one challenge ahead is to come to grips with the crisis, find the appropriate resources of healing, and, more importantly, foster human agents of informed judgment. The urge to connect is at the center of an embodied particularism of informed judgment.

15. For a fuller discussion about the relationship between the ontology of Christian identity and epistemic reflection, see *Canonical Theism: A Proposal for Theology and the Church*, ed. William J. Abraham, Jason E. Vickers, and Natalie Van Kirk (Grand Rapids, Mich.: Eerdmans, 2008).

14   Windows into Faith

Theology and Religious Studies at the University

Gavin D'Costa

The Context

In examining course offerings in theology and religious studies at the university, we need to focus on the terms, assumptions, and historical contexts in which our questions are raised. In writing as a Roman Catholic I define theology as an ecclesial activity. By this I mean that theology is faith seeking understanding, and faith takes place in a communitarian context that is accountable to the Bible, tradition(s), the magisterium, the theological community, and the people of God.[1] This leads to a tension between the teaching of theology in a secular university and the self-definition of many secular universities, which hold that teaching and research must be carried out with the sole prerequisite of high-level intellectual skills and abilities, thereby excluding religious faith and ecclesial authority. In practice in secular universities, things are far more complex and fluid. However, the tension is not only between this definition of theology and its practice in secu-

---

1. See Joseph Cardinal Ratzinger, *The Nature and Mission of Theology* (San Francisco: Ignatius Press, 1995), 45–120.

lar universities, but also between this definition of theology and its practice within faith-based Catholic universities in Europe and the United States. Many Catholic theologians in these countries have seen ecclesial account-ability and authority as a theological ideal that they are happy to accept, but a practice that they find intolerable if it means any interference with theo-logical faculties and any real involvement of the church hierarchy with the practice of academic theology.

This is illustrated in the complex dispute about the mandatum introduced in 1990 with the publication of *Ex Corde Ecclesiae* by Pope John II. The man-datum required by the Vatican in Catholic universities meant that the local bishop or his delegate must formally approve any teacher of Catholic theolo-gy—an approval that could be withheld and an approval that is the condition of teaching in the faculty. The point is also illustrated in the U.S. university sector, when non-Catholics and Catholics mounted fierce opposition to the requirement of the mandatum on the grounds of compromising intellectual freedom, of unacceptable interference with university integrity, and the dan-ger of ruining the hard-won reputations of some Catholic institutions. The entire process required protracted negotiations by the U.S. bishops to satisfy the Vatican, a complex story that I have partly recounted elsewhere.[2]

The tensions between this ecclesial definition of theology and its prac-tice in secular universities have led to the secularizing of theology. This pro-cess began in Berlin in the nineteenth century with the establishment of the modern research university.[3] All disciplines within the research university had to conform to the scientific model of study: objective, detached, non-partisan (thus nonecclesial), and conducted with skills and abilities that could be cultivated in any man (and eventually any woman), irrespective of religious faith. This meant that theology's anomalous place in the university forced it slowly to become a form of "religious studies"—our second impor-tant term, to which I now turn.

Religious studies as a discipline began at the same time as the secular-izing of theology, and there is no accident in this telling coincidence. There are four significant factors worth noting. First, some of the founding fathers of the history of religions were keen to overcome "the Christian view of oth-

2. See further in Gavin D'Costa, *Theology in the Public Square: Church, Academy and Nation*, (Oxford: Blackwell, 2005), 105–10.
3. See the excellent study of Thomas Albert Howard, *Protestant Theology and the Making of the Modern German University* (Oxford: Oxford University Press, 2006).

er religions" as condescending and biased because of the assumed uniqueness and exclusive truth of Christianity. They hoped to ensure that a neutral
objectivity prevailed, in keeping with the Enlightenment *Wissenchaft*. Ninian
Smart, a key figure in the introduction of religious studies in the UK, exemplifies this when he writes that the "theological establishment is therefore,
a problem in that it is a kind of conceptual albatross around the neck of religious studies."[4] One major question that has been raised against this kind
of approach is whether there is a neutral place from which to view religions.
Are all forms of investigation biased in some sense or other? Second, some of
the founding fathers of the history of religions were wanting to relate Christianity positively to other religions, and thus studied them with an underlying template that conformed them to Christianity: doctrines, practices, ethics, holy book(s), and holy founder(s).[5] This inevitably led to a mode of study
that eventually assimilated the study of Christianity with the study of any religion in particular, thereby slowly relegating theology to something that had
no place within the university, as Christianity was being studied in a way that
was not privileging or pejorative toward other religions. Both these forms of
history of religions were imbued with particular ideological colorings, even
if both envisaged an escape from such biases and confessionalisms. Third,
the history of religions, the study of ancient languages, and the examination
of ancient civilizations all contained methodologies that were highly respect-
able in the modern research university: history, languages, and classics now
form the backbone of most humanities faculties. Compared to theology's
sectarianism, which required adherence to a church and an authority that was
outside the university, religious studies seemed to offer a proper *Wissenchaft*
for the newly conceived institutions. Fourth and finally, during the secularization of Europe in this period, students increasingly wanted a type of intellectual discipline that catered to their faith—and found it in religious studies.

Religious studies, thus conceived, has a firmly established place in the
secular university and increasingly so in the faith-based universities of the
United States and Europe, while theology struggles in both university contexts.[6] The erosion of the discipline of theology is not limited to Christian-

4. Ninian Smart, "Religious Studies in the United Kingdom," *Religion* 18 (1998): 8.
5. See Tomoko Mauzawa, *The Invention of World Religions, Or, How European Universalism Was Preserved in the Language of Pluralism* (Chicago, Chicago University Press, 2005).
6. I have tried to give empirical fleshing out to these claims in *Theology in the Public Square*, 38–76.

ity alone, but can be found amongst all the world faiths, insomuch as they become imbricated into an educational system shaped by modernity.[7] Inevitably, modernity perpetuates itself (and its parasitic offspring, postmodernity) through its institutions: educational, financial, governmental, and military. The question of communicating faith is inextricably tied to this complex cluster of issues.

I acknowledge that this telling of the story of theology and religious studies is contested. There have been developments in the study of religion that claim to have transcended the type of divide I have outlined, where religious studies imitates scientific objectivity and sees, in contrast, theology as problematically confessional. Two points are important here. First, this move in religious studies has come from scholars who have drunk deeply from postmodern critiques of the modern: that there is no neutrality, every tradition of inquiry is historically and culturally situated, and there is thus no grand narrative as modernity presumed. Second, insomuch as religious studies entails a confessional self-reflexivity, some of the antagonism between it and theology dissolves. Let me briefly inspect some of these claims. Timothy Fitzgerald, for example, has argued that the dominant confessional bias behind religious studies for the last hundred years has often been liberal forms of Protestant theology—in the assumption of a single divine reality that is being responded to within the different religions.[8] Fitzgerald's argument is that the very construct "religion" is shored up by ideological presuppositions held by scholars, primarily religious, not always Christian, but always deeply Western. He seeks to show how religious studies "imposes on non-Western institutions and values the nuance and form of Western ones, especially in distinguishing between religion on the one hand and, on the other hand, either society, the secular, politics, or economics. In addition, and in pursuit of its construction of the other religions, it draws up typologies of Judaeo-Christian monotheistic categories such as worship, God, monasticism, salvation, and the meaning of history and tries to make the material fit those categories."[9] Fitzgerald has a point in showing how religion in the West became privatized, and this privatization was then exported to

7. See James Arthur's fine study, *Faith and Secularisation in Religious Colleges and Universities* (London: Routledge, 2006).
8. See Timothy Fitzgerald, *The Ideology of Religious Studies* (Oxford: Oxford University Press, 2000).
9. Ibid., 9.

the world religions. Fitzgerald is a healthy reminder to be careful that we do not simply see what we would like to (either negatively or positively). He also reminds us not to smuggle in theological or alien interpretative categories *without being clear* that this is happening. But all this presupposes some vantage point that will allow things to eventually appear as they really are.

Where is this vantage point for Fitzgerald? "My proposal is that those of us who work within the so-called field of religion but who reject the domination of ecumenical theology and phenomenology should reconceptualize our field of study in such a way that we become critically aligned with theoretical and methodological fields such as anthropology, history, and cultural studies."[10] And the greatest of these is "cultural studies," or more precisely, cultural anthropology. It would seem that, at the crucial pressure point, Fitzgerald creeps back into the modernist camp. Why should cultural anthropology provide a nonideological platform, a pure, rather than interpreted, viewpoint, when Fitzgerald has already earlier acknowledged in his argument that "ultimately all our attempts at understanding are based on metaphysical assumptions and articles of faith."[11] But at the final step Fitzgerald does not acknowledge his own metaphysics and articles of faith; he simply assumes this is the best perch from which to view the world. Anthropology has been strongly criticized for just this evasion by the distinguished anthropologist Bernard McGrane.[12] Fitzgerald is aware of McGrane's work and cites it approvingly. He adds, with reassurance, "a great deal of the most cogent criticisms that have been made against the culture concept, and indeed against anthropology itself, have come from within the discipline itself."[13] This reflexivity does commend the discipline, but it does not show how Fitzgerald is going to escape the trap of ideological constructivism. He is too intelligent to ignore this, but never shows us the way out, except for commending the endless reflexivity claimed by most intellectual disciplines within the academy. In the end, Fitzgerald is guilty of cultural anthropological ideological reading strategies that are quite distinct from a theological reading—which is what I seek.

Is theology, as I understand it, doomed to extinction in secular universi-

10. Ibid., 10.

11. Ibid., 43.

12. See Bernard McGrane, *Beyond Anthropology: Society and the Other* (New York: Columbia University Press, 1989).

13. Fitzgerald, *The Ideology of Religious Studies*, 237.

ties and even in confessional, faith-based universities? Must it inevitably become a type of religious studies, even if the faith basis of religious studies is usually hidden and in its secular guise promotes forms of secularized readings of religion?[14] Whose faith will be communicated in the universities of today and tomorrow?

Our Mission

I shall draw upon Roman Catholic ecclesial documents to develop this next section, but this simply locates my practice rather than suggesting that only Roman Catholics should find this section of use. I hope that all Christians can share from each others' traditions. Given my diagnosis of the problem, I must either abandon my definition of theology (which I could not, as it is not my invention but part of a long ecclesial tradition), or instead argue why theology as I understand it is not only important within the university (both secular and faith based), but a prerequisite to the university, insomuch as the development of knowledge is itself predicated upon theology—and in the classical tradition, theology working with its handmaiden, philosophy. I want to argue that the Christian tradition actually provides for a sense of the interconnectedness of all knowledge and a *telos* for all learning, both of which are actually missing from the secular university (and admittedly many faith universities). The very attractiveness of this vision both implies the rehabilitation of faith universities and poses interesting questions for Christians working in secular universities; but this is for the conclusion.

There are three general statements that can be distilled from two very important documents on this matter, both published by John Paul II: *On Catholic Universities* (subsequently referred to as CU) and *On the Relationship between Faith and Reason* (FR), that help establish an orientation to the question of the relationship among theology, philosophy, and the intellectual disciplines, and more importantly, how they might be re-visioned within a Catholic university. I shall state a brief proposition derived from the documents and offer a brief commentary regarding their implications.

First: all creation is God's creation, so that, in principle, no form of authentic

14. See the very perceptive and fine critique offered by Fitzgerald, *The Ideology of Religious Studies*, although Fitzgerald's own alternative anthropological approach simply replicates the patterns he criticizes: an alien discourse describes the "religions."

knowledge properly gained from any discipline will contradict the truth of Christianity. Indeed, all such knowledge will in fact illuminate, deepen, and develop our understanding of both the created world and the Creator.

CU succinctly expresses the dialectical tension within this claim: "A Catholic University's privileged task is to unite existentially by intellectual effort two orders of reality that too frequently tend to be placed in opposition as though they were antithetical: the search for truth, and the certainty of already knowing the fount of truth."[15] Clearly, while the truths of the disciplines are not revealed truth, their fount is. Put like this, the distinction between theology and the other disciplines is properly highlighted, but not in terms of affording theology special knowledge properly due to biologists, physicists, and economics. Hence the dialogue between the disciplines takes place with a proper confidence of their respective integrities and fields: "While each academic discipline retains its own integrity and has its own methods, this dialogue demonstrates that methodological research within every branch of learning, when carried out in a truly scientific manner and in accord with moral norms, can never truly conflict with faith. For the things of the earth and the concerns of faith derive from the same God."[16]

It is in the relationship between theology and such disciplines that many interesting questions arise, rather than whether there is any such relationship. There are thus a number of important points that result from this proposition. First, it allows for a confidence that the intellectual search for truth, properly undertaken, in whatever discipline, should not and need not be feared by the church. The church's own mission is advanced through the university's learning, and without such learning the church's incarnation in all aspects of human life, analogically following the full incarnation of the Word in flesh and social reality, is compromised. In this respect, the intellectual defense and elaboration of Christianity and its relation to all human culture is entrusted to intellectuals within Christianity, and there is no better structural gathering for such a task than a Christian university. Clearly, those who are not Christian are often as "good" if not better economists, biologists and so on—technically, and in terms of research productivity. And insomuch as they properly pursue their disciplines, there should be no conflicts between their work and the truth of Christianity. This leads to a second point.

15. John Paul II, *On Catholic Universities* 1 (1990).
16. Ibid., 17.

Whenever there are conflicts between theology and other disciplines, and proper legitimate conflicts, one critical issue is this: should either pole of the tension have priority in determining the outcome? Put differently, is there any priority or normativity given to truth, theologically understood, when it comes into conflict with the findings of any discipline? Or does each discipline, including theology, have equal standing, given that each discipline is acting properly within its remit? At this level of generality, it might be said that properly speaking, no such conflict is possible if each discipline is legitimately pursued, for it would not make claims outside its proper limitations and contexts. Those within the discipline are usually best at spotting tendentious claims. However, this dramatically highlights the question as to who defines the legitimate object of study, the appropriate methods of inquiry, and the research questions within that field. Alvin Plantinga puts the matter well when he argues that in any discipline: "should we not take for granted the Christian answer to the large questions about God and creation and then go on from that perspective to address the narrower questions of that discipline? . . . To what sort of premises can we properly appeal in working out the answers to the questions raised in a given area of scholarly or scientific inquiry? Can we properly appeal to what we know as Christians? . . . Must the Christian community accept the basic structure and presuppositions of the contemporary practice of that discipline in trying to come to an understanding of its subject matter? Must Christian psychologists appeal only to premises accepted by all parties to the discussion, whether Christian or not? I should think not. Why should we limit and handicap ourselves in this way?"[17]

Theology has a priority or normativity when it comes to a legitimate clash between itself and other disciplines. But this normativity is not one that can question the competence and findings of a scientist or sociologist within the parameters of his legitimate discipline. This point requires elaboration if such researchers are not to complain against inappropriate interference. Hence, it is necessary to clarify the possible contexts of these clashes and the very limited cases where normativity can obviously be affirmed.

J. G. Hagen makes three important distinctions: When a religious view is contradicted by a well-established scientific fact, then the sources of rev-

17. Alvin Plantinga, "On Christian Scholarship," in *The Challenge and Promise of a Catholic University*, ed. Theodore M. Hesburg, 267–96, 292 (Notre Dame, Ind.: University of Notre Dame Press, 1994).

elation have to be reexamined, and they will be found to leave the question open. When a clearly defined dogma contradicts a scientific assertion, the latter has to be revised, and it will be found premature. When both contradicting assertions, the religious and scientific, are nothing more than prevailing theories, research will be stimulated in both directions, until one of the theories appears unfounded.[18]

Hagen's model has more porous lines than he acknowledges, but his claim is right. One might still cite the current understanding of the Galileo case to be an example of the first category. The second might instance a scientist claiming on scientific grounds that there was no creator of the world. Admittedly, but not in this case, the understanding of a dogma may develop so as to later allow for a scientific view that was earlier excluded. The third category might relate to a very wide field indeed, and here matters are rightly left open. Hagen, writing in 1912, cites Copernicus, Kepler, and Galileo as examples of conflict in this category. Hence, a scientist, sociologist, or psychologist who is a Christian should, in principle, find these distinctions reassuring, as they indicate no abuse of academic freedom and a position to which they probably implicitly subscribe.

The third and final point is to note that the first principle assumes a metaphysics that requires further elaboration. *Faith and Reason* rightly assumes that God's creation is intelligible, rational, and indirectly reflects God. Properly investigating this creation can therefore indirectly lead to God, can never exclude God, and within a Christian context, the existence of God harmonizes all forms of knowledge, for, *a priori*, there is a unity to creation, for it was created for a single purpose: to give glory to God. Further, this means that belief in God is an appropriate context for the proper and fullest understanding of the various objects of study, not always necessarily in terms of the objects themselves (as this would compromise the genuine autonomy of each discipline), but certainly in relation to discerning when a discipline has illegitimately made claims, and also in relating the discoveries of each discipline to moral, epistemological, and ontological issues. This is precisely what Plantinga's comment above proposes. Wolfhart Pannenberg, in the context of a specific science-religion debate, puts this strongly, nicely drawing out these implications:

18. J. G. Hagen, *Catholic Encyclopaedia*, "Science and the Church," (1912), 21 of 27 pages (http://www.newadvent.org/cathen/13598b.htm [accessed July 2007]).

If the God of the Bible is creator of the universe, then it is not possible to understand fully or even appropriately the processes of nature without any reference to that God. If, on the contrary, nature can be appropriately understood without reference to the God of the Bible, then that God cannot be the creator of the universe, and consequently he could not be truly God and could not be trusted as a source of moral teaching either. To be sure, the reality of God is not incompatible with all forms of abstract knowledge concerning the regularities of natural processes, a knowledge that abstracts from the concreteness of physical reality and therefore may also abstract from the presence of God in his creation. But neither should such abstract knowledge of regularities claim full and exclusive competence regarding the explanation of nature, and if it does so, the reality of God is thereby denied by implication. The so-called methodological atheism of modern science is far from pure innocence.[19]

The *second* general proposition that follows on from the first and its various implications is this: *All knowledge should be pursued primarily out of love for the world as an object of God's creation, and only secondarily for instrumental or functional ends. Only through the primary can the secondary be best determined. In this sense, the primary end of all forms of knowledge is contemplation of and glory to God. Likewise, the means of pursuing these different sciences, while determined by the object of inquiry, should never be in conflict with the ends of all inquiries.*

This proposition might initially sound both pious and useless, but its operation can be impressively discerned in Oliver O'Donovan's profound theological critique of modernity's technological instrumentalism leading to constructivism and atheism.[20] This proposition offers a platform from which to criticize the trend to harness universities to industrial and economic ends, thereby judging all disciplines in terms of economic productivity. It also is able to question the liberal's defense of the university as preserving knowledge for knowledge's sake, which in the end fails hopelessly to identify what that "sake" is, given that the conceptions of knowledge are so diverse in the modern arena. Such liberalism eventually relates (and often leads to) postmodernism's love of endless play and plurality, which is late capitalism's hidden exaltation of knowledge for its own sake, the production of culture for the enjoyment of the bourgeoisie.[21] Of course the liberal and the utilitarian

19. Wolfhart Pannenberg, "Theological Questions to Scientists," in *The Sciences and Theology in the Twentieth Century*, ed. Arthur R. Peacocke, 3–16, 4 (London: Oriel Press, 1981).

20. Oliver O'Donovan, *Begotten or Made?* (Oxford: Clarendon Press, 1984).

21. See Fredric Jameson, *Postmodernism, or, the Cultural Logic of Late Capitalism* (London: Verso, 1990).

both hold important elements of what is being asserted here. The utilitarian is right in seeing that knowledge is power to be harnessed, but the *telos* of the good and the *means* of securing that *telos* are "questions" always requiring the help of the social sciences and natural sciences. This is precisely why CU specifies as one of the essential characteristics of a Catholic university the ethical dimensions to all knowledge: "Because knowledge is meant to serve the human person, research in a Catholic University is always carried out with a concern for the *ethical and moral implications* both of its method and of its discoveries. This concern, while it must be present in all research, is particularly important in the areas of science and technology."[22]

Note that the ethical concerns are not simply about the use of discoveries and the fruits of knowledge, but also the means and methods employed. Also to be noted is the cyclical nature of the purpose of knowledge: it serves the human family and the natural and cultural world within which it subsists, but it *only* does so because God's redemption is concerned with the human person, and also, therefore, the natural and cultural world. Rather than human ends at the center, we have God's glory, and from that follows the purpose of humankind. In FR this is given specification when the Pope writes: "In the field of scientific research a positivistic mentality took hold which not only abandoned the Christian vision of the world, but more especially rejected every appeal to a metaphysical or moral vision." This led, in some scientists, to the exaltation of "market-based logic" and also "the temptation of a quasi-divine power over nature and even over the human being."[23] The need is for scientists to work again within "the *sapiential* horizon."[24]

Hence, only when we affirm the glory of God in prayer and praise can the purpose of the human family be fully discerned, and thus the ethical criteria by which to judge the methods and contents of the various disciplines. It is precisely when power is replaced by love, understood as service to the powerless, that the church's sense that all knowledge is at the service of the kingdom of God enters the contemporary debate about the university. Put bluntly, the purpose of the university is to find love at the heart of all things, for love is the cause of the world. This does not mean that the study of atoms is going to show that love rather than neutrons and protons are to be found, or that the meaning of pi is love rather than approximately 3.14159. Rather, once the

22. On Catholic Universities, 18.
23. John Paul II, On the Relationship between Faith and Reason 46 (1998).
24. Ibid., 106

atomic structure or the structure of mathematical formulae has been expli-
cated, the question of how such ordering analogically facilitates the possibilities of love, harmony, beauty, and truth is vital, and is another way of recognizing the ethical and methodological dimensions of the disciplines.

Historically, Christian universities have often fallen short of this task and
even perverted it, but that would be no argument against the basic vision
being advanced here. David Schindler makes the point very incisively when
he writes that the task of the Catholic university is twofold: "(1) to show,
from within each discipline and in the terms proper to each discipline, how
that discipline is being guided by a worldview—in the case of liberalism, by
mechanism and subjectivism; and (2) to show how a Catholic worldview (of
the cosmos as created in the image of Christ's [eucharistic] love, hence of a
cosmos wherein order and love are mutually inclusive) leads to a more ample
understanding of evidence and argument, already within the terms proper
to each discipline."[25]

To summarize: within the context of a Christian university, knowledge
is first about contemplation, wonder, and awe, and only then, because its
proper context is situated within God's creation and creative purposes, can
its instrumental value be judged. In both method and conclusions all disciplines must value and protect the dignity of the human person. The ethical context of the intellectual enterprise is properly regarded only within the
overall religious framework of the university.

The third proposition is implied in the first and is related to the manner
of the second's operation: *theology has a central role to play in the Christian university and must function as a servant "queen of the sciences."* First, the integration
of knowledge central to the Catholic university, in contrast to the modern
research university, requires the Catholic intellectual vision to be articulated in some detail by theologians in harmony with natural scientists, social
scientists, and the human sciences. This is clearly a collaborative and long-
term task. Since the truth of God is the center of this unification, theology
with philosophy is central to this attainment. CU puts it succinctly, and is
worth quoting in detail: "Integration of knowledge is a process, one which
will always remain incomplete; moreover, the explosion of knowledge in recent decades, together with the rigid compartmentalization of knowledge
within individual academic disciplines, makes the task increasingly diffi-

25. David Schindler, *Heart of the World, Center of the Church* (Edinburgh: T. and T. Clark,
1996), 171.

cult." But a university, and especially a Catholic university, "has to be a 'living union' of individual organisms dedicated to the search for truth. . . . It is necessary to work towards a higher synthesis of knowledge, in which alone lies the possibility of satisfying that thirst for truth which is profoundly inscribed on the heart of the human person."[26] Aided by the specific contribution of philosophy and theology, university scholars will be engaged in a constant effort to determine the relative place and meaning of each of the various disciplines within the context of a vision of the human person and the world that is enlightened by the Gospel, and therefore by a faith in Christ, the Logos, as the centre of creation and of human history."[27]

Second, not explicitly stated or developed in my sources, is that all students and teachers in every discipline should at least have some training in theology and philosophy. This is important for a number of reasons. Theologians are simply not competent to develop this integration from their side alone, and while there are some very able intellectuals who were or are trained to a high degree in both theology and another discipline (Teilhard de Chardin and John Polkinghorne, for example), one cannot rely on such individuals alone. Whole research communities need to be working within such a paradigm, where highly trained physicists, economists, and psychologists are already thinking about these issues themselves, rather than theologians in any way policing matters.

There is a correlative requirement upon theologians. All theologians should gain some grounding in the social, human, and natural sciences, as well as philosophy, at least to an elementary level, if they are able to contribute to the task of a Catholic university. If these difficult demands are not structurally implemented, Catholic universities will revert to what many of them tend to be at present: places where liturgies and social service characterize the campus, but the intellectual scene is no different from its secular counterparts. The point I am stressing is not the lack of good intentions by Catholic institutions regarding their Catholic identity, but the lack of intellectual implementation into the curriculum regarding the implications of what it is to be a Catholic university.[28]

26. On Catholic Universities, n. 19.

27. Ibid., 16, n. 19. Note 19 cites John Henry Cardinal Newman's The Idea of a University (London: Longmans, Green, 1931), 457: the university "professes to assign to each study which it receives, its proper place and its just boundaries; to define the rights, to establish the mutual relations and to effect the intercommunion of one and all."

28. See further my Theology in the Public Square, 38–56; and since then the extensive and

How to Get There

I have outlined a kind of mission statement above that is appropriate for a Christian university, in which theology plays a major role. How far such Catholic universities explore these questions in the future remains to be seen, but is clearly required. In the recent past they have a poor record in some countries such as the United States, but it is also in that same country where new experiments are growing regarding the Catholic identity of both older and newly founded institutions. However, there are two further questions to be addressed: what is the role of theology in a secular university, given this ecclesial university mission statement? and what is the role of religious studies in both types of universities, given an acceptance of this definition of theology?

Theology has a role in the secular university that is sometimes afforded it on secular grounds (free speech for all and openness to intellectual ideas from any provenance), although this hospitality cannot be institutionally translated such that the formal requirement for students studying theology be ecclesial membership, nor can the interface between theology and philosophy outlined above be given institutional development. While this emasculates theology to a considerable extent, there is still a role for theology in at least asking these questions within the secular university as a form of evangelization. That is, theology must remain a thorn in the flesh of the secular university, always asking questions of method, presupposition, object, and *telos* in the disciplines—entering into engagement even when the institution does not formally facilitate or privilege theology (which can lead to a quite robust and healthy theology). And it must remain a thorn in the flesh within its own subject area, for it must seek to uncover the eradication of ecclesial theology within the university and try to show the advantages of its restoration as proper to the university, insomuch as the university is the place for the search for truth. In this sense, my use of the word "evangelization" above is not misplaced, for surely one goal of theology within the secular university is to eventually make it a Christian, faith-based university.

The second question is far more complex. In the first section of this chapter I tried to indicate that religious studies is in my view a spurious disci-

---

helpful work of Melanie Morey and John Piderit, *Catholic Higher Education* (Oxford: Oxford University Press, 2006).

pline, insomuch as it is an amalgam of other disciplines (history, linguistics, and classics)—and thus does not merit the title of a discipline; and is spurious insomuch as it is driven by a hidden ideology (secularism or liberalism) and cannot attain the neutrality that is its justification.[29] Hence, the notion of a theological religious study is required—that is, a theological evaluation and understanding of other faith communities that would supplant religious studies as a self-standing discipline. If the objection is made that this would be a return to Christian imperialism, then one serious element of this objection needs to be addressed. It is important to understand religions in their own terms. If theological examination means sidestepping this, then objectors are right to object. However, I would argue that it is important to understand religions in their own terms prior to any theological engagement and evaluation, but on theological grounds—not on the grounds that one can arrive at a supposed neutral understanding. I cannot expand this claim here but have tried to elsewhere.[30] I would even contend that this would make the subject matter far more interesting and relevant in our contemporary society. This type of theological religious studies is vital to interfaith pluralism. Such a theologizing of religious studies should happen at a faith university, for this is precisely one way of following the mission statement outlined above. Implementing it in a secular university is more problematic, but not in principle impossible. There are many courses about the view of religion X in the eyes of religion Y, even if this is most often done historically, rather than theologically. There is no reason this could not be developed as part of a theological curriculum, although lots of reasons this might fail.

There are huge tasks ahead, with serious institutional and personal challenges at every level—but we would expect little else from the daunting task of communicating the faith in every aspect of our pedagogy and practice.

29. I defend this claim in my book *Theology in the Public Square*, 1–36; and in D'Costa, *Christianity and World Religions: Disputed Questions in the Theology of Religions* (Oxford: Blackwell, 2009), chap. 3–4. My argument is that there is no actual discipline *per se* that constitutes religious studies and that historically it has been the co-opting of the sacred through alien disciplines such as psychology, literary studies, and historicism. This is not to say that there is a problem with the relationship of these disciplines with theology (Christian or otherwise), but that they are not to be privileged in defining "religion."

30. See D'Costa, *The Meeting of the Religions and the Trinity* (Edinburgh: T. and T. Clark, 2000), 127–31.

PART 5

International Perspectives

In the missionary nature of the church, witness remains central. As a vicar general of a religious congregation, Frances Orchard was asked to focus on religious congregations as major agencies deeply engaged in communicating faith. Such religious carry out their work across many countries and in deeply contrasting situations. This means that the triple task of understanding, living out, and sharing their charism will require modification and adjustment in order to take account of these diverse contexts. Constancy and flexibility, continuity and change, fidelity and adaptation are always at play as efforts are made to relate charism and context in ways that are harmonious and creative. This is despite the fact that, in this dispensation, there will always be a huge gap between who and where we are at any particular moment and who and where the Gospel calls us to be. Orchard has been instrumental in helping some religious orders attend more carefully to the relatively recent priority of developing ways to share their charism with lay people not intending to join their ranks, but who are willing to associate themselves with their mission and the priorities of a congregation as they work in some professional capacity in institutions that were once staffed mainly or entirely by religious. Her experience of helping religious share their charism is reflected in "Charism and Context."

The dialectic between mission and context and the tasks entailed by inculturation are taken up by the Congolese Notre Dame Sister, Victorine Mansanga, who reflects on changes of emphasis across time in the way that

Christian faith has been communicated on the African continent. Without attentiveness to context and to the life situations of the people addressed, communication misses its mark. Without sensitive inculturation, the Gospel conveyed remains alien and inaudible. Proclamation of the good news must be experienced as life-giving and liberating from real, not projected, predicaments, if it is to be received as salvific.

Issues raised by Mansanga, and by Topley in Chapter 11, surface again in Byrne's chapter on communicating faith in Ireland. Here he brings together attentiveness to a rapidly changing setting, where former, long-established certainties are eroded, and the need to embrace willingly a new emphasis on critical questioning of the way faith has been understood, explained, and passed on. Difficulties are acknowledged and treated seriously rather than dismissed either as signs of bad faith or as inevitable by-products of increasing secularization. A new context for communication prevails, and Byrne addresses this new context with discernment and hope. His analysis provides insights into the different needs of young people and adults when faith educators seek to build bridges between the lives of those they try to reach, on the one hand, and, on the other hand, the living tradition of Christianity and, more specifically, Catholic Christianity. He shows how the communication of a universal faith requires attention to the zeitgeist and to particular cultural contexts if it is to be welcomed.

A strong and secure sense of personal identity allied with a confident and warm openness to others seems essential for effective communication of faith, in any context. Teachers of faith always have to be contemplatives in action, combining inner depths and stability with a capacity for effective outreach. Schuttloffel's deployment of the contemplative principle in the context of the American Catholic Church offers a way to integrate faith, leadership, and communication. Paralleling other contributions in this section, she provides a sketch of recent changes in the context for communicating faith in the United States. Factors affecting Catholic identity are indicated before she turns to the need for leadership. The kind of leadership called for is one that facilitates the effective communication of faith in institutions and communities. Leaders should attend deeply to the messages they convey, across time and via even minor decisions. As mediators of the mission and as bearers of the vision, leaders in schools, parishes, and higher education should heed her case for a contemplative and collaborative style of ministerial leadership that promotes true learning communities in the church.

Boeve engages with language problems emerging from some recent cultural developments. Relations between the church and the wider societies in which she is located can be bedeviled by misunderstandings on both sides. This hampers the effective communication of faith in the public domain. At the same time, communication within the church is also undermined by language problems, especially when the mentality and conduct of life of so many church members is so deeply formed (usually unconsciously) by perspectives, norms, and patterns of behavior that prevail outside the church. Cumulatively these cultural forces create expectations that can work against the way of life that disciples are called to embrace. Boeve's analysis helps us to recognize the nature and functioning of such cultural developments as detraditionalization, individualization, and pluralism and to ascertain what kind of response thoughtful Christians should make to these. In service of effective communication of faith within the church (*ad intra*) and within the broader society and culture (*ad extra*), Boeve argues that these two tasks should be carefully distinguished. Effective communicators need to know, not only what they want to say, but also who they are speaking to and what they can and cannot assume about these people and their current understanding and concerns. Knowing one's interlocutors will more likely lead to appropriate communication rather than assumptions that, because a message is true, all people need to hear it in the same way.

15   Charism and Context

Frances Orchard, CJ

Communicating faith, as stated in the 1990 encyclical letter *Redemptoris Missio*, requires a diversity of activities arising from the variety of circumstances in which that mission is carried out. First, there is the mission *Ad Gentes*, where "missionary activity addresses peoples, groups and socio-cultural contexts in which Christ and the Gospel is not known."[1] Secondly there are established Christian communities, fervent in their faith, where the church is active in pastoral care. Thirdly, there are societies with ancient Christian roots that have lost a sense of living the faith and where a "new evangelization" is needed. Communicating faith is therefore much more than a classroom activity. The religious congregations, which operate at the sharp end of the church's mission, came into existence to meet a variety of different needs, and have adopted a variety of different strategies. Before exploring some of these strategies it is good to be reminded of the words of Pope John Paul II: "people today put more trust in witnesses than in teachers, in experience than in teaching, and in life and action than in theories."[2] It is for this

---

1. John Paul II, *Redemptoris Missio* (Rome: Libreria Editrice Vaticana, 1990), 33.
2. Ibid., 42.

reason that religious congregations, the main focus of this chapter, see all their members as "missionaries," in the contemporary sense of "those who are sent," the elderly or sick members, those whose ministries are primarily administrative or domestic, as well as those more evidently in the church's missionary activity.

In order to focus on the more formal aspects of communicating faith, this chapter will limit its scope to the actual apostolic works of religious congregations on an international level, the importance of *witness* being a given. It will also focus on communicating the *Catholic* faith, as this is the ecclesial task of religious congregations, always bearing in mind the significance of multiculturalism and the interreligious dimension. The nature and meaning of *charism* will be explored in some detail, so as to give an understanding of what it is that gives variety to religious congregations, which in turn characterizes their mission. Strategies for conveying that *charism* to the laity who now play a major role in the educational mission of the religious congregations will also be covered. To fit this all into an international, global context, the chapter has been divided into three sections: *Understanding the Charism*, *Living the Charism*, and *Sharing the Charism*.

Understanding the Charism

The context within which religious congregations operate has changed radically over the past half century. We now live in a rapidly globalizing, pluralist, secular, multicultural, environmentally fragile, polarized, postmodern world characterized by a widening gap between rich and poor and challenged by a resurgence of fundamentalism. There are also huge paradigm shifts taking place in the world as the economic hegemony shows signs of shifting from West to East, and in the ecclesial sphere church membership shifts from North to South. The Constantianian model of a westernized Latin Church proclaiming one true faith to so-called unbelievers is giving way to a church that respects the religious beliefs and traditional cultures of other non-Christian faith groups. The church sees the need to teach not only *ad gentes*, but also to be present *inter gentes*.

The religious congregations have always been at the forefront of the church's missionary activity, but they should not be regarded as agents of the church. They were not founded by the hierarchical church, but by men and women called by God, whose new foundations may or may not have been initially welcomed and approved by the church. Ignatius of Loyola was not at all sure that his new "company," the Jesuits, would receive ecclesiastical approval; and Mary Ward, the seventeenth-century pioneer of apostolic women's religious congregations using the Ignatian model, was imprisoned by the church for her efforts and her congregation suppressed. The charism given to these founders, as to others, although a gift to the church, may not always be recognized as such initially. Antonio Romano maintains that foundations happen at "critical periods of history . . . a sort of shock therapy for the Church . . . and often emerge at a time of disorientation and insecurity for the Church."[3] However, "shock" can either galvanize or paralyze, and it took three hundred years and the apostolic letter *Conditiae a Christo* (1900) before the church recognized apostolic congregations for women.

As the phrase "charism of the religious congregations" is central to this chapter, a deeper reflection on its origin and meaning is required. The word *charism* comes from the Greek root *char*, indicating something in the nature of well-being. *Char* is best translated as "to grant grace, to give, to lavish." The word *charism* appears sixteen times in the letters of St. Paul, but is unknown in classical Greek, prompting experts to believe that St. Paul might have created it. Most appearances are in the letter to the Romans (1:11, 5:15, 6:23), and in First Corinthians (1:7, 7:7, 12:4–31). Paul also gives several lists of charisms (1 Cor 12:8–10 and 28–30; Rom 12:6–8 and Eph 4:11). What characterizes all the uses is that *charism* is a gift of grace, offered lovingly and freely by the Holy Spirit in order to build up the community of believers. A gift that does not build up the community is, for Paul, passing and fruitless, and this prompted his well-known letter to the Corinthians: "and if I have all faith so as to remove mountains, but do not have love, I gain nothing" (1 Cor 13).

After a gap of centuries the Second Vatican Council reintroduced the concept of *charism* and applied it to religious life. The Council documents *Perfectae Caritatis*, *Lumen Gentium*, and Paul VI's apostolic exhortation *Evangelica Testificato*, apply the notion of charism to religious life itself, to the evangelical counsels, to various forms of religious life, to particular institutes, to founders, and to the personal vocations of individuals. This has led to a difficulty in locating *charism*. If St. Paul is speaking of charism as a gift received and exercised by individuals, can one speak of *charism* as a group charism

3. Antonio Romano, *The Charism of the Founders* (Slough: St. Pauls, 1994), 136.

bestowed on a particular congregation, let alone of "sharing charism with the laity"? Whatever difficulties in definition this gave rise to in the post-Vatican II period as religious congregations sought to rediscover their original charism, the important point is that the primary focus of concern was distinctiveness or uniqueness. What makes one religious congregation different from another?

Sandra Schneider, in an article entitled "The Charism of Religious Life,"[4] proposes that there are three interrelated levels of charism operative in religious congregations. First, and most important, is the charism of religious life itself. As it is not a form of life to which all the baptized are called, it is a distinctive gift to the church. However, religious life is not part of the hierarchical structure of the church, but a realization of its life and holiness. The hierarchy did not invent it any more than the founders invented it. It is a gift of the Spirit to be used by and for the church.

At a second level there are different types of religious life—eremitical, monastic, and apostolic—to which the term charism can be applied. An apostolic or ministerial form of religious life does not mean it arose solely in response to a particular social need—education, health, social work. Many Christians have responded to these needs without being called to religious life. Rather, virtually all religious congregations were founded to enable the members to give themselves to God in and through service of Christ in one's neighbor. What is characteristic of this form of religious life is a powerful sense of the absolute oneness of the great commandments of love of God and of neighbor. Service of neighbor is the love of God in action. It is not simply an overflow from the love of God. In this sense it is erroneous to try to define the charism of a religious congregation in terms of its corporate ministry, as was usual before the Second Vatican Council, when the terms "teaching order" or "nursing order" were current.

A third level of charism is to try to identify what gives different religious congregations among other congregations of the same type a special character. Few congregations have a distinct charism. Most belong to one of the main traditions: Augustinian, Benedictine, Carmelite, Franciscan, Dominican, Ignatian, to name the better known. Distinctiveness can perhaps best be seen in the special fourth vow taken by many religious congregations and

---

4. Sandra Schneiders, "The Charism of Religious Life," in *Loving the World as God Loves*, 7–15, Twelfth U.S. Religious Formation Conference, 2001, available online at http://www.smnz.org.nz/maristlibrary/religiouslife.pdf.

which gives a special character to that institute. However, what is essential is living, and being seen to live, as Christ lived. Probably what distinguishes one apostolic congregation from another is less the particular qualities than the totality—the complex shared story of all who belong to that particular unique congregation. As Romano writes: "it is not the great things that distinguish one religious family from another, for these must be held in common by all, but rather the characteristic way in which these great things are developed and put together."[5] In this sense, from the original charism of the founder a religious congregation develops a "culture," defined here as the core beliefs, values, traditions, and symbols that give identity and distinctiveness.

Schneider contends that the most salient feature of ministerial or apostolic religious life is mobility. Each member has responded to the call to "leave all and follow Christ." S/he follows the itinerant Jesus who had no place to call his own. The formation of new religious focuses strongly on "inner freedom," "non-possessiveness," disponibility, in order to be really free to follow the Lord. This inner availability is crucial if the religious is to be free to respond generously to the call to go "wherever the need is greatest." This has been a particular difficulty for women's congregations, who were not officially recognized by the church as apostolic congregations until the end of the nineteenth century. Most such groups struggled to come into existence, and survived by becoming semi-enclosed, quasi-monastic institutes constantly having to compromise on their spirituality and lifestyle. However, this did not prevent them from making numerous hazardous journeys into new continents during this period. There are stories of women religious crossing the plains of north India by buffalo cart to reach their mission station with the curtains of the cart constituting the enclosure required by church law. The quasi-monastic religious life into which women's religious congregations were confined, however, has disguised this need for mobility both from themselves and others. The supports of institutionalized religious life—corporate ministry, uniformity of lifestyle, stability of dwelling, regularity of prayer and practice—can all too easily replace mobility.

The Second Vatican Council, by inviting religious congregations to return to the charism of their founders and reflect on what that meant in to-

5. Romano, *The Charism of the Founders*, 136.

day's world, started a review of apostolic religious life that is ongoing. In general such reviews have brought about a deeper understanding of the spirituality of the founder, a rediscovery of the need for greater mobility, and a more genuine desire to serve the poor so as to witness to the prophetic nature of religious life focused on the person of Jesus Christ and his salvific mission. Prioritizing ministries was part of that ongoing review, and has usually been conducted within the context of diminishing vocations in the developed world, the "graying" of religious congregations, the opening up of a range new ministries, especially in the spiritual and social fields, and the call to give a "preferential option to the poor."

The consequence of this, particularly in the developed world, is that religious have been less evident in the traditional school's ministry. This has been a cause of considerable regret for the traditional clientele of such schools, often prestigious institutes. The church too has reemphasized the continuing importance of the schools' ministry: "consecrated persons are called to revive their educational passion living it in school communities as a testimony of encounter between different vocations and between generations."[6] Nonetheless, the trend away from the traditional schools' ministry, particularly in the developed world, has continued.

It is, however, worth remembering the context in which the traditional educational apostolate of the Catholic school started and flourished. From the beginning of the Middle Ages, as the church began to evangelize the invading tribes of northern Europe, it recognized "that civilizing and Christianizing must go hand in hand, that all education should have a humanizing effect."[7] Hence the great Celtic monastic schools and the great Benedictine monasteries taught the classic humanist traditions of Greek and Rome as well as Christian faith "with the purpose of promoting wisdom and humane living." In this way was forged an enduring partnership between faith and culture. The Augustinians, Dominicans, and Franciscans were renowned for their humane approach to teaching. The Jesuits put great value on the personal development of each student, and in helping him to think for himself—an important quality in the Reformation period. The great women founders of the sixteenth and seventeenth centuries were also remarkable

6. Sacred Congregation for Catholic Education, *Consecrated Persons and Their Mission in Schools* (Rome: Libreria Editrice Vaticana, 2002), 82.

7. Thomas H. Groome, *Educating for Life: A Spiritual Vision for Every Teacher and Parent* (Allen, Tex.: Thomas More Press, 1998), 234.

educators: St. Angela de Merici and the Ursulines; St. Jeanne de Lestennac and the Sisters of the Company of Mary; St. Jeanne Francis de Chantal and the Visitation Sisters ; Louise de Marillac and the Daughters of Charity; and Mary Ward. Despite the requirement for enclosure, reinforced at the Council of Trent, these women managed, some more successfully than others, to circumvent the discouragement of the church to develop an educational ministry for women. These women too were dedicated to the humanist tradition of education. In Mary Ward's schools her progressive pedagogy included art and drama, classics, and modern foreign languages, as well as moral tuition and the customary domestic subjects. Moreover, her sisters were forbidden to use physical punishment, but rather were to teach in ways marked by gentleness and respect for each student.

In the centuries that followed many hundreds of religious congregations dedicated to the educational apostolate as expressed in schools came into existence; to name just a few: the Congregation of Christian Brothers, the De La Salle Brothers, the Marists, the Congregation of the Holy Cross, the Brigidines, the Society of the Sacred Heart, the Sisters of Notre Dame, the Sisters of Loreto. The demand for education, the need to provide a sound moral and religious education in a rapidly changing industrializing world, led to a rapid expansion of the schools apostolate from the mid-nineteenth century. The church, as still happens today, when faced with a choice of building a church or a school, generally chose the latter. Cardinal Manning, Archbishop of Westminster, wrote in his journal of "the destitute, uncared for, untaught, running wild in the streets, without knowledge of the faith, a prey to apostasy or immorality," and actually used money raised for church construction to found schools manned by religious. He defended his action by saying: "could I leave 20,000 children without education and drain my flock to pile up stones and bricks?"[8]

The Catholic school system developed by religious congregations came into existence at a time when there was little or no state or diocesan school provision. Moreover, it was one of the few ministries the church allowed women religious to undertake, as it could be conducted within a semi-monastic lifestyle. Without an educated Catholic laity only the Religious Congregations could meet this need. Now, a century or so on, there exists in most developed countries a well-educated Catholic laity, and faithful to

8. Vincent Alan McClelland, *Cardinal Manning* (Oxford: Oxford University Press, 1962).

their charism to be mobile, the religious congregations are ready to move on to serve where the need is greater. Often it is not a question of schools or no schools, but of what schools and where?

Living the Charism

Mary Ward's congregation typifies what has happened within many such congregations. As recently as thirty years ago the focus of our apostolate would still have been girls' schools in the developed world. These were prestigious, highly regarded educational establishments in the United States, Canada, Australia, Ireland, England, Germany, Austria, Italy, Spain, India, Latin America—and before 1945 in Romania and Hungary, too. They fulfilled a need to give a quality education to predominantly middle-class Catholic girls. Education is still a priority, but the scope has broadened beyond schools, and the resources are shifting to the developing world. So in India, for example, alongside the traditional, middle-class schools there will be free schools for the poor; literacy classes; vocational centers, especially for women in the rural areas, where tailoring, agricultural, and other trade skills and basic health care will be taught; adult literacy programs; and teacher training. The presence of religious even where the state or circumstances prohibits evangelization is no deterrent to the desire to serve and witness to Christ. So we have schools in Nepal, a college for Palestinian girls in Jerusalem, and catechetic and pastoral projects in Cuba, and are exploring new openings in China and Mongolia. In Zimbabwe, Romania, and parts of India, where the social and economic circumstances are very different, we are still developing primary schools to ensure that children can access a quality Catholic education. Under the umbrella of the schools' ministry, which provides a communal center, other sisters work in local social and catechetical projects especially for women and children. Even as I write, a bishop from the southern Philippines has sent his vicar general with a request to consider making a foundation in his diocese. The purpose would be to provide a spirituality center for the catechists who work in the parishes and the schools, and as such it would fit our criteria for new missions—where there is a recognizable need and the laity are not yet ready to take on this ministry.

The particular educational needs of girls receive high priority where we work in the developing world. If parents have difficulties in finding fees, or money for uniforms and books, it is the girl in the family who drops out first. In rural areas where children need to cover long distances to attend school there are issues of safety and accommodation for the girls. Families are also more reluctant to send the girls to school where they also have a role in the local domestic economy, helping the women to collect firewood and water and look after the animals. Education and all the benefits it brings with it in job opportunities, higher life expectancy, better health standards, more self-sufficiency for women—all enhance the human dignity of the person made in the image of God.

The imperative of mobility for apostolic religious congregations, always seeking "the greater good," is challenging for a variety of reasons. Education requires resourcing—the training of members, the building up of an institution to provide continuity of service, sustainability—all of which require a considerable long-term commitment. At the same time parents want a quality education for their children, and if they are fee-paying, that something extra—the better facilities, the smaller classes, the pastoral care, the out-of-school activities, the exclusivity. This is as true in India and Africa as it is in the developed world. Of course, not all religious work in the private sector, but where the religious congregation pioneered the establishment of the school, before the advent of either the diocese or the state, many such schools are still in the ownership of the congregation. With the stability such institutions require comes the danger of the religious themselves settling for immobility. It is very easy for religious congregations to be cushioned from social reality by the success of the very schools they struggled to found. The problem can be as real in parts of urban India as on the Eastern seaboard of the United States.

In the post-Vatican II period some religious congregations made deliberate decisions to pull out of schools as a main ministry; others to be selective as to which schools they should retain, and which should be closed or handed over; others drifted, unsure how to "read the signs of the times"; others waited until the decreasing number of religious forced the decision on them. At the same time the religious strove to ensure that whatever the future brought, the particular charism of their congregation should be made more explicit to those with whom they shared their educational ministry. And this raises the question: can a charism be shared?

According to Romano, "the charism of the founder ends with his/her death, but lives on in the charism of the order . . . however, it is never disconnected from the people in whom it is incarnated."[9] It cannot operate apart from the lives of those people who have been chosen to receive it. It is a lived reality; it cannot be processed and packaged and simply handed on. A charism is not a philosophy to be pondered but a spirituality to be lived. Just as religious congregations that fail to live the charism of their founder can easily become ossified as theory and abstraction replace the living community, so too the charism cannot be passed to the laity unless they are prepared to live it. This constitutes a real challenge that religious congregations have tried to meet in diverse ways.

One of the problems for religious who have made their charism their own is that it is so much part of them that they are often unpracticed in reflecting on it in the public domain, and in articulating it clearly and confidently within a changed cultural context. There are congregations that have done this well, but others have tended to fall back on what is best described as "a packaged process." Examples of the latter would be splendid publications on the founder and on the history of the congregation: carefully worded mission statements that incorporate the distinctive characteristics of the particular founder; conferences and workshops given to school staff by members of the congregation; and special school celebrations; but one wonders just how deep this goes. Lay head teachers will absorb the material avidly as they wish to demonstrate continuity with the past. Their ability to absorb different charisms and cultures as they move from one headship to another is admirable. But what about the wider school community?

Sharing the Charism

If the charism is the special grace received by the founder of a religious congregation, the culture is what emerges as the body develops. All organizations have a culture—the core beliefs, values, traditions, and symbols that give the organization its particular meaning and purpose. Culture shapes the relationships or experience that members of an organization have with one another. Just as the task of the religious congregation is to ensure that the culture of the congregation is a genuine reflection of the charism of the founder, so the culture of the school that originated as a religious foundation needs to reflect that same charism. In an article entitled "Handing over

9. Romano, Charism of the Founders, 153.

the Baton: From Religious to Lay Administration," Paul Starkey draws a distinction between two paradigms used by religious congregations to inculturate the charism of the founder. The first paradigm he calls "the paternal paradigm" and describes it as "members of the Religious Congregation conveying to their lay colleagues key insights and symbols . . . so that the lay staff give expression to them in the culture of the school." The second paradigm, which Starkey calls "the partnership paradigm," has "members of the Religious Congregation working with their lay colleagues to discover what the congregation's traditions might look like when they are allowed to find expression in a lay context."[10] In the first paradigm the religious congregation "has possession of the tradition and tells the laity what it is." In the second paradigm a partnership has been formed to "discover" together what that tradition might look like in a new context, and there is no knowing in advance how it will develop. Although the second paradigm might appear risky to the religious congregation, it is in keeping with the fact that a charism is a gift given at a particular time to a particular person for a particular reason; it is not a possession, nor a code of practice, nor a philosophy, but a spirituality to be lived.

The packaged approach of the first paradigm can be seen as an attempt to impose particular formulas of the traditions of the congregation canonized at some point in history. The partnership paradigm regards the traditions of the congregation as alive and rich, and members of the congregation work with the laity to help discover together how old truths might find expression in new settings. The latter takes courage and trust as well as a great deal of mutual listening, reflection, and creativity. Where it works, the results are evident in the ability and willingness of lay men and women to speak, often spontaneously, knowledgeably and publicly, about the charism of the founder and the traditions of the congregation in a way that is compelling. The spirituality has been grasped and made one's own.

A charism unlived is a dead charism, and how reasonable is it to expect lay staff who have not made a commitment to religious life to try to live the charism? The sisters of the Society of the Sacred Heart would be a good example of one religious congregation who has reflected seriously and resourced generously their determination to make the charism of their con-

---

10. Paul Starkey, "Handing Over the Baton: From Religious to Lay Administration," *Catholic School Studies* 70, no. 2 (1997): 62.

gregation alive for their school communities. In the 1970s they set up a Schools' Network in the United States with a central office, board of directors, and trained members of the steering committees, whose task it was to draw up and review periodically the *Goals and Criteria* that are mandatory for all schools within the network. They also have a useful tool for delivering their *Goals and Criteria*, a website appropriately named SOFIE, to create community and enable the sharing of programs. Significantly, as the result of one review the *Criteria* were altered to "make it clear that the adults in the schools were 'to model' the values of the *Goals and Criteria*. The adults were 'to live' these values themselves, not just instruct the students to do so."[11]

The Society of Jesus, which has played a major part in the educational mission of the Catholic Church since its foundation in the sixteenth century, is another good example of a congregation that has been deeply committed to the traditional schools' ministry and that has sought to make the *charism* a reality for the laity who now play a major role with the Jesuit educational ministry. In an essay entitled "*The Experience of Ignatius Loyola: Background to Jesuit Education*" that appeared in the 400th anniversary volume of "*Ratio Studiorum*," Fr. Howard Gray, SJ, identifies three main elements in the influence St. Ignatius had on Jesuit education. First, for Ignatius education was a personal experience or "event" "from above, from within, and from outside himself."[12] In his autobiography Ignatius wrote of "God dealing with him in the same way a schoolteacher deals with a child." This was not a momentary event in the life of Ignatius, but a permanent feature of the way God dealt with him, and will deal with all who genuinely seek God. The primacy of experience—of finding God in all things and trusting in that experience—is a central element in Ignatian spirituality. Second, this Ignatian insight was codified for his followers initially in the *Spiritual Exercises* and then in the *Constitutions of the Society of Jesus*, ensuring continuity down the centuries. And third, for Ignatius education was an *apostolic enterprise* that would have an enormous influence on church and society. Wherever his companions went they taught, whether at universities, or as papal advisors at the Council of Trent, or to the Indies, even before the first of the many Jesuit colleges was founded in 1548.

11. Network of Sacred Heart Schools, *We Hold in Trust 2006–2007*, 2007, available online at http://www.sofie.org/ftm/introduction/.

12. Howard Gray, "The Experience of Ignatius Loyola: Background to Jesuit Education,"in *The Jesuit Ratio Studiorum: 400th Anniversary Perspectives*, ed. Vincent J. Duminuco, SJ, 1–21 (New York: Fordham University Press, 2000).

The early Jesuit colleges had a decidedly humanist as well as religious purpose, as can be seen in the curriculum. And a letter of one of the early Jesuits, Pedro Ribadeneira, to the King of Spain states: "the proper education of youth will mean improvement for the whole world," what today we would term "the common good."[13] In other words, the Ignatian phrase "to help souls" was not just designed to help souls to get to heaven, but had a noteworthy concern for the created world and man's God-given place in it. At the same time these schools were to be "open to rich and poor alike, without distinction."

In the aftermath of the Second Vatican Council the Jesuit general superior set up an International Commission on Apostolate for Jesuit Education. Its prime task was to produce a contemporary identity statement on Jesuit secondary education; in 1986 *The Characteristics of Jesuit Education* was published as the basis for renewed reflection on the experience of the educational apostolate. It became a guideline not just for Jesuit educators, but also for the many religious congregations established in the Jesuit tradition. Essentially, the booklet concentrated on goals and principles. This was a useful development, but it failed to address the pedagogical realities of how the goals and principles could be translated into daily classroom practice in the interaction between teacher and student. Methodology was important to Ignatius, as can be seen in his *Annotations* to the *Spiritual Exercises*, and four years later the International Commission produced *Ignatian Pedagogy: A Practical Approach.*

The significant factor of this new publication was the way it emulated the same spiritual path along which Ignatius himself felt drawn by God, and which he codified in the *Exercises* and *Constitutions*. The key lies in the Ignatian practice of *reflection.* Just as in the *Exercises* the person is drawn to reflect on his/her experience so that s/he discovers meaning and comes to understand what is a truth for him/her, so this same methodology is used in the classroom. The teacher, within the context of the students' lives, fosters a broad base of experience that requires analysis, synthesis, and evaluation so that learners become attentive to the human reality that confronts them. This they then reflect on, helped by carefully formulated questions and guided discussion, journal keeping and reflective papers to enable the stu-

---

13. John W. O'Malley, "How the First Jesuits Became Involved in Education," in *The Jesuit Ratio Studiorum*, 56–74.

dent to discover meaning. The experience of making the truth his/her own impels the student to act upon his/her convictions for the well-being of society. Teachers then encourage the student to reflect on and evaluate this experience, and this in turn becomes a circular learning methodology—experience, reflection, action.

The *Ignatian Pedagogy* is a comprehensive methodology for teaching and helping teachers and students alike to get in touch with Ignatian spirituality. In following the same path of discovery as Ignatius himself followed it shows the seriousness with which *charism* is taken. The challenge is whether the *Ignatian Pedagogy* can be effective in contexts where there is an over-directive national curriculum.

As with other religious congregations, the Jesuits have reviewed and extended their understanding of the educational apostolate and placed it more within the context of "doing justice." As part of their post-Vatican II review the Jesuits set up the Jesuit Relief Service (JRS) as an international organization in 1980. It now operates in over fifty countries, and an important part of its provision is education—in this case, education to the very poor—those who have lost everything, home, livlihood, family members, and a hope for the future. One of the main concerns of refuges and displaced persons as they enter the security of a refugee camp is that their children should continue with their education. This even takes priority on occasion over the request for food and medicine. Schools start up spontaneously with a blackboard under a tree, or drawing with one's finger in the sand of the riverbank. The process of learning can instill pride in refugees for what they can achieve in their hopeless present and gives them an expectation for a better future.

Often such schools are makeshift—a few tree stumps around a blackboard—but they can still give a reassuring sense of normality. Even in emergency situations a priority of the JRS teams is to get education going at the nursery and primary levels. Often it is the parents who will turn their hands to building a school if materials can be found. JRS will also train teachers in the camps; provide special needs teaching such as for children with visual or auditory impediments; run sponsorship schemes; set up adult literacy classes; provide vocational and income generating programs; and create computer and language courses.

The charism given by the Spirit to each founder is given for a purpose: namely, to respond to new situations in which to proclaim and witness to the Gospel of Jesus Christ. John Paul II reminds us that "the proclamation is to be made within the context of the lives of the individuals and peoples who receive it."[14] Whereas in the past members of religious congregations could usually be found either doing missionary work among peoples far from their own country and culture of origin or carrying on pastoral and/or educational work within their own country of origin, now the picture is much more complicated. Many religious now labor among people of other faiths and cultures that include their neighbours and fellow citizens within their own country, while others live in culturally diverse communities in either their own or another country. If communicating faith is to be effective in today's multicultural world, where witnesses are more valued than teachers, then the role of the religious is to be just that. In this they will be living truly according to the charism of their founders, who were called, first and foremost, into a special relationship with God.

14. *Redemptoris Missio*.

16 Communicating Faith in Africa

Yesterday and Today

Victorine Mansanga, SND

Go out to the whole world; proclaim the Good News to all creation.

Mark 16:15

Go therefore, make disciples to all the nations; baptize them in the name of the Father and of the Son and of the Holy Spirit, and teach them to observe all the commands I gave you.

Matthew 28:19–20

You shall be my witness . . . till the end of the earth.

Acts 1:8

This is how Jesus passed on to his disciples the mission he has received from his Father: he asked them to carry forth the mission to the end of the world. From these verses it is clear that Jesus entrusts his disciples with a mission and that this mission is fourfold: to go all over the world, to make disciples, to baptize them, and to teach them the good news. Guided by the Holy Spirit, the apostles accomplished faithfully their mission.[1] They organized the

---

1. See Second Vatican Council, *Lumen Gentium* [Dogmatic Constitution on the Church], 1965, 4; and *Gaudium et Spes* [Pastoral Constitution on the Church], 1965, 10.

church, and "by their oral preaching, by example, and by ordinances"[2] they entrusted to the bishops the divine mission they received with two recommendations: to hold fast to the traditions that they had learned either by their preaching or by letters and to defend and keep the faith.[3] Today Jesus continues to call disciples and send them all over the world for the same mission. His words echo in the hearts of his chosen disciples "to go and make disciples." The church holds fast to her mission and in her turn she sends forth disciples to communicate the good news. It is a circular movement of evangelizing and being evangelized, of being on mission and being sent forth for mission. Many people have accepted Jesus' mission and have gone out to the end of the world to bring the good news. *Agentes* (1965) recognizes the grandeur of the church's mission and highlights the characteristics of her missionary activity. The document states that "the church is missionary by nature"[4] and that the main purpose of her missionary activity is evangelization and implantation of the church in new places for her expansion. Her main "means of implantation is the preaching of the gospel of Jesus Christ."[5]

The spreading of the good news of Jesus Christ is not implemented in the same way everywhere. It takes into account the local church, the people, the culture, the traditions, and the signs of the time. In other words, it is shaped according to its social, religious, cultural, economic, and political context. It follows therefore that the good news is more and more being communicated in a world in mutation and of great upheavals and that the "high tide" moves people from North to South and vice versa. Consequently, the cultural encounter between different peoples becomes a great challenge in many different parts of the world. Thus, the issues relating to Africa that are dealt with here apply in many other countries.

This chapter sets the context in which faith is communicated in Africa. It attempts to demonstrate how the church has accomplished her mission of communicating faith and the effect this has had on African people and societies. It claims that to be effective in Africa, faith should evidently be communicated as "good news." That is, it should follow the footsteps of Jesus the master and the Sender who proclaimed the good news of the kingdom

2. Second Vatican Council, *Dei Verbum* [Dogmatic Constitution on Divine Revelation], 1965, 7.

3. See *Dei Verbum* 8; *Gaudium et Spes* 11.

4. Second Vatican Council, *Ad Gentes* [Decree on the Church's Missionary Activity], 1965, 5, 35.

5. *Ad Gentes* 6.

in words and deeds. To be able to meet this objective, I shall do three things. First, I analyze the context in which faith is communicated in Africa. Second, I scrutinize inculturation, which is one of the main challenges of communicating faith. I assert that to be successful the message of the Gospel should be incarnated in African cultures. Third, I outline the way the good news is proclaimed in Africa. As elements within this outline, first I examine the nature of evangelization, before scrutinizing the proclamation of the good news.

Setting the Context

There is a growing recognition that Christianity entered the African soil at the apostolic age. However, the history of how faith has been communicated since then is peculiar to each country. All African countries passed through a period of colonization, during which faith in Jesus Christ was either introduced or reinforced. Christianity in Africa has had a long journey. After many attempts, faith in Jesus Christ is deeply rooted in Africa as a result of being communicated, welcomed, and inculturated. This is not to say that faith is warmly welcomed everywhere or lived by everybody in Africa, since many acts of violence, imposition, resistance, hostility, and arrests are identified throughout the Christian history in Africa. But the fact is that today the church of Jesus Christ is implanted in Africa and bears fruit. The encounter was not without difficulty, but God's Spirit who was already present in Africa worked in such a way that many people welcomed faith.

Where people are coming from, who they are living with, and what has shaped them all have an impact on how they engage with and interpret Christian faith. There is a fundamental understanding that God was already present in Africa before the arrival of the evangelizers and that he had prepared them to receive the good news of his kingdom. In African cultures and traditions missionaries found some positive values that helped or could help Africans to welcome and live Christian faith. This is not to say that Africans' encounter with Christianity was easy. But it is evident that African culture has a strong religious sense and values that could easily match the Gospel values. Albeit Africans did not know about the Gospel, their knowledge about God was deep and profound. This religious sense could be explained in different ways.

First, Africans have a strong sense of the sacred. They knew about the existence of God, the Almighty God, Father and Creator of the universe before the arrival of missionaries. They knew that their ancestors derived from God the origin of their existence. They repeated in many circumstances that "God created our nails and fingers" to mean that God is our Creator. They knew his name, which is expressed differently in African languages as "Nzambi Mpungu," "Mungu Baba," "NkuluNkulu," "Chukwu Okike."[6] What these appellations have in common is that in all these languages the name of God is followed by a qualifier that means "Almighty God" or "God the Father" or "God the Creator." What is important for Africans is the knowledge that the Almighty governs heaven and earth. He is the only and unique God for both the visible and invisible worlds. It is striking to notice that God's presence imbued Africans' life. This is shown, for instance, by the fact that God's name was used in their exclamations such as "Ah! Almighty God Creator!" and in some of their educative proverbs, such as: "Seya n'kweeno; Kaluunga mwaasi kéna!" Kalunga is one of the attributes of God that means "omnipresent." It is not good to laugh at the other, since God is present. What happens to him may also happen to you. The second proverb makes direct reference to the name of God. It reads, "A Nzaambi nkéba; nge mosi ukikéba";[7] that is, when you ask God to take care of you, also take care of yourself. This proverb reminds people of their personal and individual responsibility for their own life. Each person is talented to build his own life and the life of all those who are under his/her responsibility. These two proverbs exemplify the argument that Africans know about the existence of God in their life. This awareness of an omnipresent God in their life is a sign that Africans were ready to welcome faith and the good news of Jesus Christ, the Son of God. They also know that this Almighty Father is above everything. His goodness is shown in the beauty of all creation. They recognized God's power over them. They feared him and could not talk directly to him, though they knew that he could give them anything they asked. They pray to their ancestors who see him in the invisible world to intercede for them. The eldest, chief of the family, is the only one allowed to get into contact with the invisible world.

Second, Africans believe in the world of the spirits called the invisible world. These are the spirits of their ancestors, who have shared life with

6. Nzambi Mpungu: Kikongo (D. R. Congo), Mungu Baba: Swahili (Kenya and Democratic Republic of Congo), Nkulunkulu: Ndebele (Zimbabwe), Chukwu Okike: Ibo (Nigeria).

7. Proverbs from D. R. Congo.

them in this world and who are alive in the other world. Death is considered as the rebirth in the invisible world. That is, they believe in life and rebirth after death. Life is a perpetual circle of being born and reborn after death. As *Ecclesia in Africa* has put it, "They believe intuitively that the dead continue to live and remain in communion with them."[8] There is a strong conviction that the dead are not entirely dead. They continue their life in the other world and remain in communion with them. Their belief in the power of their foremothers and fathers who live in the invisible world is so strong that they communicate with them and associate them with family events: problems, joys, and important ceremonies. They also ask them for protection and permission to carry out important ceremonies in the family. They know that spirits are everywhere, but also that they could easily locate them in the forest, in water, in the wind, the cemetery, and near their houses. People are prepared for new responsibility by taking them to sacred places such as the forest, where they are invigorated with the force of the spirit to acquire wisdom, the language and techniques that will help them to lead family matters effectively. This context could be used to explain the message about the existence of saints.

Third, Africans have a strong sense of family, community life, solidarity, and hospitality. They share life together in the family. A child is born, educated, and brought up in the family. Old people also enjoy life within the family environment. Each family is led by their eldest member, who exercises authority, having received from the ancestors the power to govern it. His role is to protect the family. In Africa the view is taken that one should find food for everybody, even for the stranger, and that it is better to have a little for each than have much for some and nothing for others. What is important for them is to share together the small amount of food they have. They share joys, suffering, hope, and fear together in the family. It goes without saying that this experience of community life in the African culture is the way by which the good news should be communicated.

These are some elements of the African socioreligious context. These cultural aspects influence the teaching and understanding of faith. As the theologian Adrian Hastings put it, "the way of teaching any set of ideas depends upon the context within which they will be understood."[9] It is in their

---

8. John Paul II, *Ecclesia in Africa* [Post-Synodal Apostolic Exhortation], 1995, 43.
9. Adrian Hastings, *Church and Mission in Africa* (London: Burns and Oates, 1997), 59.

social and cultural context that Africans are called to welcome faith. The more that evangelizers and teachers of faith understand these aspects, the better the message is received. This understanding helps them to recognize both the richness and the limitations of the culture and find in it those values that need to be affirmed and strengthened and those that should be resisted or modified.

As far as African values are concerned, it is worth noting that there has been a shadow side. Missionaries were confronted by habits such as polygamy, sorcery, slavery, fetishism, idolatry, and tribal division that challenged both the evangelizers and those evangelized. Despite the need for critique of what undermines the Gospel, it is important to emphasize the positive features of a culture. The evangelizer should confirm and reinforce in the minds of the people they address those signs of the kingdom that are inherent in their customs and traditions. Saint Paul's strategy in Athens is instructive here. Paul reminds the Athenians that they are very religious and that they already worship an unknown God. This warming up is followed by his announcing that he has come to tell them about their unknown God.[10] Similarly, evangelizers must be discerning about elements in a culture that they build upon.

Inculturation

The great challenge of communicating faith in Africa is inculturation. In her pilgrimage around the world to communicate faith, the church has always been involved in the process of inculturation. There is a great deal of literature on inculturation in church documents such as *Evangelii Nuntiandi* (1975), *Redemptoris Missio* (1990), *Ecclesia In Africa* (1995), and *General Directory for Catechesis* (1997), and in theology books such as those by Shorter (1994), Healey and Sybertz (1996), and Hastings (1997). But here I will say that inculturation is an important process of evangelization, a dynamic in which the message of the Gospel is rooted and incarnated in a culture; that is, it is embedded in people's social being, doing, thinking, behaving, and worship. The reason the Gospel message should be inculturated is that the Word was made flesh.[11] Accordingly the message to be communicated should be incar-

10. See Acts 17:16–33.
11. Jn. 1:1–14.

nated in the culture of the people in which it is being transmitted. *Evangelii Nuntiandi* (1975) insists on the evangelization of people's cultures. The document states that "what matters is to evangelize [people's] culture and cultures . . . in the wide and rich sense."[12] Commenting on this call, Arbuckle underlines that "the call for the evangelization of cultures makes no distinction between the First and the Third Worlds"[13] and that it is an essential feature of success everywhere. Inculturation is a worldwide task for Christians, whether they seek to communicate faith in Africa, Europe, in North America, or elsewhere.

In fact inculturation is a sign that the mission of the church is alive and flourishing. In many circumstances, to communicate faith is also to receive new values from the new culture. In this context it could be said that communicating faith enriches not only the learners but also the teacher, who receives in return the enriching experience of the new culture. In his recent address to the bishops of Kenya, Pope Benedict XVI underlined that "the church is one throughout the world, yet at the same time she is marked by a rich diversity of traditions and cultural expressions."[14] It is worth noting here that, although this diversity enriches the church, it should also be remembered that such enrichment is not automatic; that is, these diversities could only be worthy if the church makes use of them. They could not enrich "the tapestry of Christian culture worldwide"[15] if they are not introduced in the church. It follows that there is a need for local churches to make use of cultural richness to enrich the church.

In Africa, to inculturate the Gospel message means to Africanize it and to insert it into African cultures. It should be embedded in their socioreligious life by using the richness of African culture such as languages, images, proverbs, symbols, songs, joy, art, dance, and values. Missionaries who

12. See Paul VI, *Evangelisation in the Modern World* (Apostolic Exhortation *Evangelii Nuntiandi* of his Holiness Pope Paul VI) (London: Catholic Truth Society, 1975), 20, available online at http://www.vatican.va/holy_father/paul_vi/apost_exhortations/documents/hf_p-vi_exh_19751208_evangelii-nuntiandi_en.html (accessed November 13, 2007).

13. Gerald A. Arbuckle, *Earthing the Gospel: An Inculturation Handbook for Pastoral Workers* (London: Geoffrey Chapman, 1990), 16.

14. Benedict XVI's address to the bishops of Kenya during their visit in Rome, http://www.Catholic.org/featured/headline.php?ID=52448page=1 (accessed on November 2, 2007).

15. John Paul II, *Redemptoris Missio: Encyclical Letter of the Supreme Pontiff John Paul II on the Permanent Validity of the Church's Missionary Mandate* (London: Catholic Truth Society, 1991), 52, available online at http://www.vatican.va/holy_father/john_paul_ii/encyclicals/documents/hf_jp-ii_enc_07121990_redemptoris-missio_en.html (accessed November 25, 2007).

arrived in Africa understood quickly that to be effective, the message should be communicated in an African language. Their first effort was to learn the local language and compose a catechism in an African language that could be understood by the majority.[16] They were aware that faith is much better communicated in a language in which people think and transmit their thought. It was for this reason that the Bible has been translated into many African languages.

Despite their effort to translate the message in local languages, the liturgy remained in foreign languages for many years. People were obliged to repeat and memorize parts of the Mass, prayers, and songs in a language they did not understand. It would be fair to note here that African bishops understood quickly that their church could not really be Christian if she did not use an African language. Today the Gospel message is communicated in African languages. Although their churches are still full of foreign arts, their liturgy is animated with African cultural values and objects such as songs, dance, drums, gestures, offering, and ways of preaching and listening to the word of God. The first and best-known African liturgy is the Congolese rite inaugurated by the late Cardinal Joseph Malula, the first person who inculturated Catholic liturgy and religious life in Africa.

Another means of inculturating the message in Africa is the use of proverbs, myths, songs, and parables to communicate faith. It is widely known that African traditional societies have a long experience of an oral literature. They educated and communicated their heritage, for instance, through stories, proverbs, and songs. Today, many religious educators use this language to communicate faith mostly during homilies, retreats, and other important ceremonies. Many people like this method, since it helps them participate in the message that is being communicated. In this method, the preacher starts the first part of the sentence and lets the listeners complete the second one. This is not to say that everybody understands this language of proverbs and songs. What is essential is that people know that what is important in the song is not the song as such, but the message that lies behind it.

I would like to recall here that I was attending a celebration where the Gospel was being explained by the use of proverbs and songs. On the one hand, the old generation was happy and excited, since the message was significant for them. On the other hand, I heard a group of young people who

16. Africans have many dialects. The language to learn depends on local churches.

did not understand the message ask one another, "why are they laughing, what did the priest say?" The contemporary generation, used to the language of the city, finds it difficult to understand proverbs. Thus they need a contemporary language adapted to their age and time. In fact a proverb can only be well explained and understood in its local language. But the use of local language is becoming difficult in communicating faith, since churches are full of multilingual people. To sort out the problem of language in Africa, churches organize many liturgies in different languages—for example, French or English and the local language.

It should be remembered that to inculturate does not mean to reject but, on the contrary, to discern which values in the culture are in harmony with the Gospel values and how the Gospel values can be inserted into the new culture. The process is not easy, for it requires both a willingness to adapt and at the same time respect for the integrity of the Christian faith.[17] One should stress here that inculturation has two polarities: on the one hand it transforms cultural values by integrating them into Christianity, while on the other hand it incarnates the Gospel message into the culture. It could be said that Christian faith and a specific culture walk hand in hand. There is a link between faith and culture. Some cultural values cannot be dissociated from faith. There is at the same time insertion of Christianity in the African culture and transformation of African values through contact with Christianity. For faith to be rooted in any society, these two concepts should be taken into consideration. I would like to emphasize that the meeting of both faith and culture is a "*kairos* time," a time of adaptation and transformation. It is a time of making important decisions, such as whether to abandon a way of life or to adopt a new way of being, doing, thinking, or behaving. It is a difficult time that requires values such as courage, patience, discernment, prayerfulness, humility, openness, flexibility, courage, and love of others.

These values facilitate both the communication and the reception of faith. They are essential in the process of communicating faith, since they help adapt the teaching to new situations and to the need of people and their society; to listen to the cry of the people who are suffering from different kinds of oppression. Courage, for instance, is needed to confront difficult situations. It motivates people to announce the good news and to denounce unjust situations and values that contradict the Gospel, to promote

---

17. *Redemptoris Missio* 52.

peace and liberate people from all forms of oppression, to carry the good news. Discernment keeps people in tune with new needs of societies. Flexibility and creativity assist in adaptation, finding new ways to express and to embody faith. Those who communicate faith need to put themselves at the school of Jesus the master to learn about these values, to wait for God's action that helps transform the hearts of people to live a new life. It is in this way that the good news should be proclaimed.

Proclaiming the Good News

Proclaiming the good news is "the permanent priority of the mission."[18] All missionary activities should be directed to this aim. The good news has been communicated in Africa for centuries. The faith that the evangelizers had handed on to Africa is being transmitted from generation onto generation. The first step of this transmission is evangelization. Evangelization is concerned first with the proclamation of the Word and witness of life, and second with an interior individual change and social transformation. The evangelizers are called to "bear witness to the faith, hope, and love which dwell in them."[19] It is not surprising that the church in Africa has played an important role in the integral development of the human being and society. She stays in the forefront of conflict situations and promotes peace and justice. The African bishops are aware that the encounter with Jesus Christ transforms and refreshes individuals and society as a whole. Saint Paul's meeting with Jesus is a convincing case.[20]

There is a profound connection between evangelization and promoting human development. If the kingdom of God is about love, freedom, and beatitude, then evangelization should be about promoting love, liberation, justice, and peace. It is not surprising that there was no way for missionaries who brought the good news of Jesus Christ to Africa to speak about the kingdom of God and ignore the situation of poverty, misery, oppression, ignorance, and all kinds of suffering that surrounded Africans in the past and perhaps even more today. Guided by the Holy Spirit, they attempted to dignify Africans by trying to civilize them and liberate them from all kinds of oppression and ignorance. The church is aware that human development is central to her work of evangelization. Her concern is expressed as follows:

18. *Redemptoris Missio* 44.   19. *Ecclesia in Africa* 55.
20. See Acts 9:1–21; 1 Tim 1:12–16.

Nothing that concerns the community of men and women—situations and problems regarding justice, freedom, development, relation between peoples, peace—is foreign to evangelization, and evangelization would be incomplete if did not take into account the mutual demands continually made by the Gospel and the concrete, personal, and social life of [people].[21]

The church in Africa has played an important role in the development of individuals and society throughout her history. She contributes to the spiritual well-being and integral development of African countries. Today it is widely recognized that evangelization has renewed Africa, socially, religiously, economically, and culturally. Missionaries linked the teaching of the good news with education, help for the poor, and care of the sick. The faith they proclaim is expressed in the building of schools, clinics, and hospitals. The church also struggles to promote justice, peace, and reconciliation in Africa. She has played an important role in many situations of conflict between nations and in political civil wars. In this context the Gospel message is indeed presented and welcomed as good news. Pope Benedict XVI recognizes that the church in Africa has contributed to the progress of society. Talking to the bishops of Kenya, he stated that "the church in Kenya is well known for the fine contribution made by its educational institutions in forming generations of young people in sound ethical principles and in opening their minds to engage in peaceful and respectful dialogue with members of social or religious groups."[22] It could be fair to note that the church takes action for justice, peace, and liberation in Africa. The following quotation exemplifies the church's concern for the dignity of human being.

We are saddened and concerned about the suffering of our sisters and brothers in Zimbabwe. . . . We strongly appeal to the government of Zimbabwe, in the name of Jesus, to immediately stop the violence. And we urge all the political leaders of Zimbabwe to be fair, just and compassionate in governing their people, peace, good governance and respect of human rights should always be the overriding principle.[23]

21. Pontifical Council for Justice and Peace, *Compendium of the Social Doctrine of the Church* (Rome: Città del Vaticano: Libreria Editrice Vaticana, 2004), 66.
22. Benedict XVI: address to the bishops of Kenya during their visit in Rome, 2.
23. A Message from the Symposium of Episcopal Conferences of Africa and Madagascar (SECAM) on the State, 2007, available online at http://www.sceam-secam.org/newsInfo.php?id=58 (accessed November 25, 2007).

I would like to recall here that Jesus accomplishes his mission by preaching the Gospel in word and deed. He reminds people that he is aware of his mission[24] and also that he has come to proclaim the good news. At different circumstances he reveals that he is himself the good news. He describes himself as Good Shepherd, Life, Love, Path, Truth, salvation, Bread of Life. The communication of faith in Africa should similarly come across as positive in parallel ways. Since the word Gospel itself means "good news," accordingly, it should be communicated and welcomed as "good news." But it is well known that "Africa is full of bad news."[25] The African synod fathers asked themselves how Christians could introduce its good news in a place where there is always bad news. This awareness leads the African bishops constantly to find ways to support people who are suffering so that bad news could be transformed into good news. This requires structural as well as individual change. In an unsettled continent, Africans need a message that heals, strengthens, and buoys them up, a message that liberates and gives meaning to life.

The proclamation of the good news must be linked to concern with human liberation. Evangelizers in Africa were confronted with the need for different kinds of liberation. In many parts of Africa the first work of evangelization was to liberate children from the slave trade, then to liberate women from all kinds of oppression. First, liberation brought relief to women who were oppressed and considered as slaves in their marriage and whose role was limited to motherhood. Little girls or young women were often forced to marry a much older man chosen for them by fathers or uncles. Evangelization dignified and liberated women, who today rejoice in a free marriage with a man of their choice and a role as equal partners with their husband. Second, when Africans understood the importance of studies, priority was given to boys. Women missionaries worked hard to get girls into school. Today people understand the importance of education for girls. Schools are full of girls, and many women hold important positions as equal partners with men. It follows that good news for Africa should offer hope for a better life, for peace in their countries, for good education. In his encyclical letter *Spe Salvi*,[26] Pope Benedict XVI reminds us that there is no distinction between faith and hope. The communication of faith entails necessarily the

24. See Luke 4:43; 4:14–21.
25. See *Ecclesia in Africa* 40.
26. Benedict XVI, *Spe Salvi* (London: Catholic Truth Society, 2007), 2.

communication of hope. Those who are dying with hunger, suffering from injustice, homeless, or naked hope not only for a message of love but also that action should be taken to help them in their desperate situation. *Ecclesia in Africa* puts it as follows: "to Africa, which is menaced on all sides by outbreaks of hatred and violence, by conflicts and wars, evangelizers must proclaim the hope of life rooted in the paschal Mystery."[27] Thus, for the theologian Shorter,

> To those suffering from injustice and oppression, evangelization must involve the material transformation of society and release from those things which dehumanize and victimize them; for the sinner and the wounded evangelization must involve news of forgiveness and healing.[28]

These comments suggest that the Gospel should be adapted to particular contexts but also seek to transform those contexts. Communicating faith in Africa has undergone several stages throughout its history. The methods of communicating faith included the memorization of prayers and a certain question-and-answer technique. At its very beginning faith was communicated through prayers, which are one of the most efficient techniques of communicating faith. Teaching people to learn prayers by heart was an initial way of communicating faith. This was in fact the best way of teaching at the outset, since there was no written material, and because Africans were used to oral tradition.

To conclude, I would like to stress that communicating faith should take into account the signs of the time and use language that is sensitive to and appropriate for each particular context. God still speaks to people in events of their lives. Every new experience offers a fresh insight into the message of the Gospel. Fidelity to tradition must be combined with openness to new developments and new needs. Communicators of faith must acknowledge the readiness on the part of many people to question, rather than to receive passively; and, in a world of social, cultural, political, and religious upheavals, they should be as ready to be pioneering in how faith is communicated today as were their forebears in the past.

27. *Ecclesia in Africa* 57.
28. Aylward Shorter, *Evangelisation and Culture* (London: Geoffrey Chapman, 1994), 13.

17 Communicating Faith in Ireland

From Commitment through Questioning to New Beginnings

Gareth Byrne

Faith in Jesus Christ is never easy. Modern Western culture in particular seems to encounter faith in Jesus Christ as especially difficult. . . . Faith in Jesus Christ is not just a matter of the formulae of doctrine, but of a community which encounters Jesus Christ as a real person, a real person who reveals to us in his life and mission that *God is love.*

> Diarmuid Martin, Archbishop of Dublin, "Second Sunday of Easter 2007: Dedication of New Altar, St. Gabriel's Church Dollymount," Dublin, April 15, 2007

Communicating Christian faith, within the particular context that is Ireland today, is, it seems, a complex process that raises many issues worthy of exploration and investigation. Wherever one lives, be that in North America, Europe, or Asia, for example, reflection on communicating faith in other local churches can contribute to a fuller understanding of one's own experience and needs and situate personal knowledge within the broader worldwide experience of church. Some people in Ireland may feel that things were simpler in the past, when clarity and commitment were the order of the day.

Certainly, Irish society is conscious of a rich tradition of lived Christian faith. Though some remember a narrow-minded adherence to rules and regulations, many can recount instances of those they have known and loved, within family, parish community, and religious congregation, who lived a simple life, committed to Jesus Christ, and did so with great joy. Their journey gave witness, in very ordinary ways, to a deep sense of belonging to God and belonging to their brothers and sisters in the church and in the world.

In our time, for a variety of social, cultural, and ecclesial reasons, it seems that committed Christians in Ireland are often unsure how to express their faith, at least in public. They have become wary of letting it be known that they believe in Jesus Christ and that they have formed a deep personal bond with him. They seem to lack confidence in communicating their experience of a loving relationship with Jesus. They cannot explain their close connection with Mary, the mother of Jesus, and with the church, the community of those who, with Mary, live together in the presence of Christ day by day. Some, too, have let go of regular attendance at religious services. Good questions, which might have been understood as promptings of the Holy Spirit designed to strengthen faith, have in our time often instead been read as overwhelming faith and undermining it. Yet, research repeatedly shows that there is still a great sense of the spiritual, of belief in core Christian doctrines, and of fidelity to the importance of God, religion, and prayer in the lives of Irish people.[1]

Communicating faith today is something about which there are at least as many questions as answers, at least as many unresolved dilemmas as easy solutions. Nonetheless, Pope John Paul II repeated the claim made by Pope Paul VI that at present "in the Church we are living an exceptionally favorable season of the Spirit."[2] It can be suggested that there are at least seven deeply rooted questions that must be acknowledged first and addressed if there is to be a renewed understanding, in the Spirit, of what it means to live and communicate Christian faith in Ireland at this time: What is the faith context in Ireland today? What kind of communication is being considering? What is to be communicated? How can faith be communicated among

---

1. See Eoin G. Cassidy, "Modernity and Religion in Ireland: 1980–2000," in *Measuring Ireland: Discerning Values and Beliefs*, ed. Eoin G. Cassidy, 17–45 (Dublin: Veritas, 2002); see also Andrew M. Greeley and Conor Ward, "How Secularised Is the Ireland We Live In," *Doctrine and Life* (December 2000): 581–617.

2. Paul VI, *Evangelii nuntiandi* 75 (1975); John Paul II, *Catechesi tradendae* 72 (1979).

adults? How is faith to be shared with young people today? Can communication in faith be hospitable to all? And in what ways should communicating faith best be structured and resourced? These are the same questions, in fact, that must be asked in the church anywhere in the world, in any place or time, in any culture or circumstance.

The Faith Context in Ireland Today?

The first question that arises concerns the context that is Ireland at the beginning of the twenty-first century, with all its beauty and desolation, anxieties, hopes, and dreams. While acknowledging its Celtic and Christian roots, modern Ireland has emerged as a society intensely connected with a wider, varied, global, yet fragmented world, at times deeply fearful, at times fearless and unconcerned.

The confidence of the church in Ireland to live and breathe its Christian faith, something it did in the past even in times of persecution and famine, is in our time being questioned. Over the generations, the divisions that emerged in the church at the time of the Reformation had continued to scar the people of Ireland.[3] Yet the Irish Church persisted in strongly affirming Christ's love, bringing that message with conviction to all the nations of the earth. With Vatican II came a greater sense of dialogue with the modern world. New things were not only possible; new beginnings were already in the air. In Ireland, by the final decade of the twentieth century, the peace process in Northern Ireland and strong economic performance in the Republic provided a framework within which a great new optimism could emerge. Immigration, unheard of in Ireland even while Britain was developing an increasingly multicultural society, suddenly and quickly became an integral part of Irish life. At the beginning of the new millennium, migrants and other newcomers, in search of work, freedom, and fulfillment, rapidly established themselves and their rich traditions as contributors to a fresh and varied understanding of life in Ireland. It remains to be seen how the worldwide recession being experienced at the time of this writing will contribute to the movement of peoples and affect their quality of life and sense of well-being.

3. For a general historical overview of the church, highlighting the impact of major themes and events in Ireland, see Ciarán O'Carroll, *Church History*, 2 vols., Theology for Today Series (Dublin: Priory Institute, 2007).

For people who live in Ireland, communications technology and the globalization it brings have rapidly been assimilated into daily life experience. Recognition of the rights of a variety of peoples, religions, and traditions has led to acceptance of a new pluralism in defining Irish society.[4] Secularization, too, has come knocking loudly at the door. The inclination to drop traditional religious responses to life seems to be seductive, but there is evidence, too, of some resistance.[5] The pace of life and the stress it causes, the lack of time for family, friends, and parish community, and the ongoing place of religion in Irish society are topics talked about as much as the weather in Ireland these days. One of the real challenges seems to lie in finding new ways of living, at least some of the time, quietly, in silent wonder, present to self, others, the world, and God.[6]

Amidst all this cultural change there has resulted in what Dermot Lane refers to as the "presence of a hidden but deep crisis of faith among a growing number of adults."[7] In particular, the revelations in the 1990s of child sexual abuse in Irish society, and among priests, religious, and lay members of the Catholic Church, have had a sobering effect at a time when people were coming to question the role and authority of institutions generally and of the church in particular. The Catholic Church in Ireland, at the very moment when it might have felt itself legitimate at last, looking out into the world positively, found instead its understanding of itself and its position in society undone.[8] The enormous devastation felt by victims in the first place, and then by members of the church and of society, has been well publicized. Research shows, however, that the contribution of very many priests and religious, working within their local communities, has continued to be admired and appreciated.[9] The provision now of child protection policies and

4. See Irish Catholic Bishops' Conference, *Catholic Primary Schools: A Policy for Provision into the Future* (Dublin: Veritas, 2007), 5.

5. See Tony Fahey, "Is Atheism Increasing? Ireland and Europe Compared," in *Measuring Ireland: Discerning Values and Beliefs*, ed. Eoin G. Cassidy, 46–66 (Dublin: Veritas, 2002).

6. See Mark Patrick Hederman, *Anchoring the Altar: Christianity and the Work of Art* (Dublin: Veritas, 2002), 93–95.

7. Dermot A. Lane, "Challenges Facing Catholic Education in Ireland," in *From Present to Future: Catholic Education in Ireland for the New Century*, ed. Eithne Woulfe and James Cassin, 131 (Dublin: Veritas, 2006).

8. See Louise Fuller, *Irish Catholicism since 1950: The Undoing of a Culture* (Dublin: Gill and Macmillan, 2004).

9. See Eilis Monaghan, *Faith and Disadvantaged Youth: A Sign for the Future* (master's thesis, Mater Dei Institute of Education, Dublin City University, 2002); see also Greeley and Ward, "How Secularised Is the Ireland We Live In?" 591–92.

procedures in the Catholic Church may in time confirm the possibility of new beginnings, emphasizing the need for all to live their Christianity truly, deeply, and humbly.[10]

What Kind of Communication?

The second theme to be confronted with regard to communicating Christian faith in Ireland is the type and style of communication. From the time of St. Patrick, generations of Irish people have learned to share their Christian faith with each other and with their young people. From high crosses to hedge schools, from reciting the rosary at home to the development of highly organized Catholic schools, the Catholic Church in Ireland has had a strong tradition of catechesis. In the past, communicating faith in Ireland meant helping one another come to know Jesus more personally, more fully, more perfectly. A deep sense of church, and of the local parish as a community in love with Christ and supporting one another, was at the heart of faith. Christian life was never lived alone. It was embraced within the prayer, kindness, and care of neighbors and friends, united together as a worshipping and concerned community, seeking within its own limits to live in justice, love, and peace.

Today one cannot presume that everyone is ready for, or interested in, catechesis. Leading one another to develop a mature faith is still central to Christian life and to the communication of Christian faith. There is a great need, however, to respond to and take on board the complexity of life in Ireland today, and in particular to be aware of the different levels at which the population now relate to or are even aware of Jesus Christ. There can be no presumption of Christian faith, even in Ireland. Any consideration of communicating Christian faith today must begin with the broader concept of evangelization, proclaiming the saving love of God, made known in Jesus Christ.[11] The Crucified and Risen Lord will first have to be introduced to those who have never heard of him. His significance will have to be made known to individuals who recognize his name but have never understood his healing message. He will need to be reintroduced to those who have for-

---

10. See Irish Catholic Bishops' Conference, Conference of Religious in Ireland, Irish Missionary Union, *Our Children, Our Church: Child Protection Policies and Procedures for the Catholic Church in Ireland* (Dublin: Veritas, 2005).

11. See *Evangelii nuntiandi*.

gotten him or have been alienated from him, often by the very church that hopes to profess him to the world.

Communicating Christian faith in Ireland today must admit of different moments and different approaches, according to the variety of faith needs experienced by people in our time.[12] For some the witness of a Christian life, and conversation focused on committed relationship with Jesus, will constitute an initial proclamation, making Christ known for the first time. Following on from such an awakening, Christian initiation, after a time of preliminary investigation, may be requested. For those preparing to join the Christian community through the sacraments of initiation, and for those who are growing toward maturity in their Christian faith, catechesis will seek to provide appropriate formation and ongoing, deepening of faith, as the person learns to walk with Christ.

Some speak, also, of the need for a new evangelization to help those who wish to recover the Christianity they learned long ago but from which they have found themselves separated, or which they never really made their own. Pope John Paul identified the need, in the culture of our time, to seek to communicate faith in new ways, in order to help Christians who have become disconnected to develop a renewed, and more personal, relationship with Jesus and with the church.[13]

For those who are fully committed members of the Christian community, trying to live the fullness of the reign of God here and now despite their doubts, weaknesses, and mistakes, there is need for continuing reflection, nourishment, and the renewal that faith-filled action can bring about. The communication in faith that takes place among such individuals, within their local Christian community, has been referred to as theological reflection. As well as the study of theology, what is envisaged here is the creation of an informed space in which reflection, action, and renewed reflection can take place within the faith community, contributing in a very real way to the ongoing revitalization of the church and all her members.[14]

12. With this in mind the Irish Catholic Bishops' Conference is in the process of developing a National Directory for Catechesis.

13. See John Paul II, Novo millennio ineunte 40 (2000); John Paul II, Veritatis splendor 107 (1993).

14. See Eamonn Conway, Bairbre de Búrca, Denis O'Callaghan, Oliver Maloney, and John Littleton, "The Value of Theology," The Furrow 53, no. 6 (2002): 323–39.

Communicating What?

A third question that raises itself early in this discussion is what is meant by faith when we speak of communicating Christian faith. Humanity generally experiences faith in its broadest sense: the conviction that we should live each day positively with the confidence that there is something rather than nothing. Such an understanding, rooted deep within the human heart, leads to an affirmation that trust and love and happiness can be ours, and to the belief that there is meaning in all we see in life, even if we cannot find that meaning now. While many know times of personal suffering, doubt, and even depression, experience leads humanity to the great philosophical questions concerned with freedom, truth, beauty, and love, to a deep theological contemplation of God's place in all of life, and of the journey toward human fulfillment in God, lived both here and in the life to come: "Human dignity rests above all on the fact that humanity is called to communion with God."[15]

While some can make no sense of a God who creates and sets humankind free to respond to Truth and Beauty and Love, the Christian has met Jesus Christ and in his love has found his or her home. The communication of Christian faith, then, is more than an assent to a positive view of life or even to belief in God. Christian faith emerges out of relationship with Jesus Christ and with the community of his followers. In Jesus Christ, God's love is revealed as the love of the one who gives his very life for humankind: "For all eternity he remains the one who loves us first."[16] In Christ, too, the Christian understands, human potential is fully revealed, and we are invited by the grace of the Holy Spirit into the everlasting love of God. For the Christian, Jesus Christ speaks fully of God's love for us and our love for God. He cannot be surpassed. He cannot be denied. He cannot be resisted: "He himself is the treasure; communion with him is the pearl of great price."[17]

Communicating Faith among Adults?

The fourth question that must be addressed brings us to those who are participating in the discourse of faith: who is communicating and with

15. Second Vatican Council, *Gaudium et spes* 19 (1965).
16. Benedict XVI, *Sacramentum caritatis* 14 (2007).
17. Benedict XVI, *Jesus of Nazareth: From the Baptism in the Jordan to the Transfiguration* (London, New York, and Berlin: Bloomsbury, 2007), 61.

whom? In the past, on the understanding that all were Christian in Ireland, sharing faith with another or passing on the faith was usually considered an activity to be entered into with children and young people. Increasingly, schools became the focus of faith formation, and religious education was catechetical in nature. Much of this work was left in the capable hands of the teachers in the Catholic schools, Church of Ireland schools, and other national primary schools.

In our time there is a renewed sense that communicating faith must, in the first instance, be an adult activity. It involves adults, in adult conversation, celebrating the freedom that crowns human life and encourages genuine interpersonal dialogue: "God is free: therefore the human person, created in his image, is also free."[18] Religious faith is chosen as a way of life. The *General Directory for Catechesis* insists that adult catechesis is the primary form of catechesis.[19] Opening the adult heart to engage with Jesus and to communicate with others a sense of his significance in one's life, even in simple ways, can be dramatic, refreshing and life-giving.

Christianity is in the first instance a religion for adults. It is in adulthood that Jesus is fully chosen and chosen again and again as a companion for the journey. Young adults make many choices that give direction to their lives. They too can choose to live life within the worshipping, serving, community-building People of God. In married life or in the vocation to the single life, as a priest or as a member of a religious community, each Christian person learns what it means to live with Jesus, comforted, yes, and confronted by what he has to say about just and loving relationships with others. Parenthood and family life involve individuals in communicating their faith in new ways, taking on new responsibilities, and in particular learning to share their faith in the family. Middle life has its own challenges, as the younger generation grows up and becomes independent and life changes once more. This is often a period when space is found again and time can be given to God, to the community, and to those in need. In middle age and as one grows older, through good times as well as bad, darkness as well as light, sickness as well as health, Christians are asked, repeatedly, to express within their community and to one another the value of their personally

18. Jonathan Sacks, *To Heal a Fractured World: The Ethics of Responsibility* (London and New York: Continuum, 2005), 133–34.

19. See Congregation for the Clergy, *General Directory for Catechesis* (1997) (Dublin: Veritas, 1998), 20.

owned and active faith. By the way they live and love they respond to all the questions put to them in life, in the only way they can, by being responsible.

From commitment through questioning to new beginnings, each person is challenged again and again by the Holy Spirit to responsibility, conversion, transformation, and new life. This is lifelong learning.[20] It suggests the need for lifelong teaching as well. All who belong to the Christian community are invited to spend their whole life learning and teaching, playing their role in the ongoing communication that brings Christian faith alive.

Sharing Faith with the Young?

Having found once more the significance of ongoing adult faith development, a fifth theme for discussion comes to light concerning the sharing of Christian faith with young people today. Where and how do Christian adults communicate with their children and young people about faith? In Ireland the answer to the first part of the question has clearly been: "in school." The role and effectiveness of faith-supporting schools in Ireland has been noteworthy. In the Republic of Ireland these are, by and large, Catholic schools run as an extension of family and parish. Yet, parents and parish have somehow been persuaded that school is where all learning takes place, including spiritual, moral, and religious learning. In fact the Catholic school should be understood as supporting the family and faith community in educating the young in their religious life, spirituality, and prayer. It is the family, nourished and strengthened by the parish community, that provides the child's first experience of lived Christianity, introducing him or her to reflection, prayer, and ritual, providing a sense of what is considered sacred by those in whom the child places all her trust:

The *Christian family* is the first place of prayer. . . . For young people in particular, daily family prayer is the first witness of the church's living memory as awakened by the Holy Spirit.[21]

Irish primary schools, established as national schools nearly two hundred years ago and supported by local Christian communities of whichever de-

---

20. See Gareth Byrne, "Lifelong Faith Development in Home, Parish and Other Educational Environments," in *Exploring Religious Education*, ed. Anne Hession and Patricia Kieran (Dublin: Veritas, 2008).

21. *Catechism of the Catholic Church* (London: Geoffrey Chapman, 1994), 2685.

nomination, usually with the local bishop as patron, have played a great part in the religious education and formation of pupils, according to the Christian beliefs and values of their parents. The policy of state support for denominational education in the Irish Republic is based on the constitutional right of parents to choose the type of education they wish for their children, and is long established.[22] The state does not commit itself to an endorsement of the Christian or any other view of human destiny,[23] but it does facilitate denominational schools, among a variety of other schools. Teachers in the Catholic primary school sector participate generously in the religious education and formation of Catholic pupils, noting sometimes, however, that they feel isolated in catering to the sacramental preparation of children without the full commitment of parents.[24] They take on their role, and are employed so to do, not as sole witnesses to the faith of the community, but to support the faith of parents who have sent their children to the school. These teachers are a vital outreach of the parish to which the school belongs. Recognizing the variety of pupils under their care, they treat each of them as a unique and whole person. Such teachers, even when dealing with what might seem like ordinary learning, spark off extraordinary responses, "allowing the classroom to function as a holy place."[25]

Religious education in Catholic primary schools traditionally provides encouragement for Catholic pupils in their faith, helping them to connect with Jesus and to ask good questions about their own religious tradition, experience, and commitment, while introducing them to the faith of others in their school community. The first commitment of such schools is to the faith formation of Catholic pupils. Parents of children confessing other religions are encouraged to provide appropriate faith formation for their children, too, rather than seeking to reduce religious education simply to a study of various religions:

The religious education of primary-school children should therefore focus on helping the child become aware of and grow into the religious community to

22. See Gerry White, "Education and the Constitution," in *Religion, Education and the Constitution*, ed. Dermot A. Lane, 84–117 (Dublin: Columba Press, 1992).

23. See Kevin Williams, *Faith and the Nation: Religion, Culture and Schooling in Ireland* (Dublin: Dominican Publications, 2005), 89.

24. See Irish National Teachers' Organisation, *Teaching Religion in the Primary School* (Dublin: INTO Publications, 2003).

25. John Sullivan, *Catholic Schools in Contention: Competing Metaphors and Leadership Implications* (Dublin: Veritas, 2000), 198.

which they belong while promoting openness and mutual respect for others from a different cultural, ethnic, national or religious background. . . . What is required is support for children along their respective journeys rather than an abstract comparative overview of religions.[26]

What is of greatest importance is the encouragement of the individual to live out his or her faith with enthusiasm, while traveling contentedly together through life with those of other faiths and with those who have no religious faith to confess.

With the variety of pupils now coming to the Irish primary school, from different races, cultures, and religions, as well as those from homes where religion is not practiced, a variety of new forms of patronage is being suggested for new primary schools.[27] This opens up important questions about religious education and formation in these schools. The way forward seems to lie, as the Department of Education and Science points out, in providing clear definitions of the ethos of a school, its mission statement, and its religious education policy:

It is the responsibility of the school to provide a religious education that is consonant with its ethos and at the same time to be flexible in making alternative organizational arrangements for those who do not wish to avail of the particular religious education it offers. It is equally important that the beliefs and sensibilities of every child are respected.[28]

In the Republic of Ireland, under the system described above, the syllabus for religious education and formation at primary level has been seen as the legitimate concern of the schools' patrons rather than of the state. In Northern Ireland a core syllabus provided by the four main Christian churches and endorsed by the state provides the approved minimum religious education course to be followed in their schools for key stages one through four.[29]

26. Gareth Byrne, "Children's Religious Education: Challenge and Gift," in *Nurturing Children's Religious Imagination: The Challenge of Primary Religious Education Today*, ed. Raymond Topley and Gareth Byrne, 243–44 (Dublin: Veritas, 2004).

27. See Irish Catholic Bishops' Conference, *Catholic Primary Schools: A Policy for Provision into the Future* (Dublin: Veritas, 2007), sect. 5.2.

28. Department of Education and Science, *The Primary Curriculum: Introduction* (Dublin: Stationery Office, 1999), 58; see also Catholic Primary School Management Association, *Management Board Members' Handbook* (Dublin: Catholic Primary School Management Association, 2004).

29. See Department of Education, *Revised Core Syllabus for Religious Education* (Dublin: Stationery Office), available online at http://www.deni.gov.uk.

Other material, particularly in light of the arrival of children of other cultures and religions, can be added by the school. In both jurisdictions the significance for most Irish people of a religious perspective on life is affirmed, once the rights of those who do not believe are also recognized. As Andrew McGrady puts it:

School-based religious education should neither ignore faith nor presume faith: it should acknowledge faith as a key learning resource.[30]

At second level, adolescents are encouraged to come to know themselves and to review and critically assimilate their surroundings. They begin to understand their own identity and the importance of relationships in all things. The Christian community to which they belong, even remotely, responding "to the restless and critical minds of the young,"[31] seeks to ground them and contribute to their understanding of how to live in and relate to the world. Religious education at this level provides a forum for young Christians to test the message, values, and commitment of Christian discipleship, as well as to look at life from the perspective of other faiths. In the Irish context, religious education for this age group seeks to enable young people to rediscover and engage with their own spiritual and moral development. They are invited to bring their religious sensibilities, beliefs, questions, and practices with them into the classroom while acknowledging and respecting the convictions of the other.[32]

In recent years the Department of Education and Science in the Irish Republic has for the first time recognized religious education as a subject for state certification. The Junior Certificate Religious Education Syllabus[33] (at about 15 years) and Leaving Certificate Religious Education Syllabus[34] (before leaving school at 18 years) suggest a formula that, while respecting the

30. Andrew G. McGrady, "The Religious Dimension of Education in Irish Schools at the Start of the Third Millennium," in *From Present to Future: Catholic Education in Ireland for the New Century*, ed. Eithne Woulfe and James Cassin, 182 (Dublin: Veritas, 2006).

31. Congregation for Catholic Education, *The Religious Dimension of Education in a Catholic School* (Rome: Vatican Polyglot Press, 1988), 23.

32. See Gareth Byrne, *Religious Education Renewed: An Overview of Developments in Post-Primary Religious Education* (Dublin: Veritas, 2005), 20.

33. See Department of Education and Science, *Junior Certificate Religious Education Syllabus* (Dublin: Stationery Office, 2000); Department of Education and Science, *Religious Education: Junior Certificate Guidelines for Teachers* (Dublin: Stationery Office, 2001).

34. See Department of Education and Science, *Leaving Certificate Religious Education Syllabus* (Dublin: Stationery Office, 2003); Department of Education and Science, *Religious Education: Leaving Certificate Guidelines for Teachers* (Dublin: Stationery Office, 2005).

religious faith and tradition of all pupils, encourages and supports individuals in growing into their own faith with its spiritual and moral commitments.

As well as their most recent pastoral letter on the catechesis of children, *Nurturing Our Children's Faith*,[35] the efforts of the Irish Catholic Bishops' Conference in reaching out to young people at second level should be noted. Using the school programs as their starting point, the bishops have provided a series of documents supportive of the faith development aspects of religious education from a Christian perspective:

—Guidelines for the Faith Formation and Development of Catholic Students: Junior Certificate Syllabus.
—Towards a Policy for RE in Post-Primary Schools.
—Guidelines for the Faith Formation and Development of Catholic Students: Senior Cycle.[36]

In some dioceses young people have also been invited to become involved in project work at senior cycle level, particularly in transition year (between the Junior and Leaving Certificates), to help them understand more clearly what commitment in church might signify for active members of the Christian community. The connection among school, parish, and family is highlighted in this way, with young people encouraged to research and become involved in various forms of neighborly service suggested by Christian faith. These might include, for example, care for the poor, visiting the sick, liturgical ministry, faith friends projects with younger children, and various efforts at building up the parish community. This outreach seeks to help the young person recognize the responsibilities and values implied in the choice to belong to church. It comes at a time when many will decide whether or not to become more fully involved in their local Christian community.

35. Irish Catholic Bishops' Conference, *Nurturing Our Children's Faith* (Dublin: Veritas, 2006), available online at http://www.catechetics.ie.
36. See Irish Catholic Bishops' Conference, *Guidelines for the Faith Formation and Development of Catholic Students: Junior Certificate Syllabus* (Dublin: Veritas, 1999); Irish Catholic Bishops' Conference, *Towards a Policy for RE in Post-Primary Schools* (Dublin: Veritas, 2003); Irish Catholic Bishops' Conference, *Guidelines for the Faith Formation and Development of Catholic Students: Senior Cycle* (Dublin: Veritas, 2006).

Hospitality in the Communication of Faith?

A sixth question in communicating faith is one that has surfaced in a new way with the diversity of peoples who are living now within the island of Ireland. Large numbers of migrants and other newcomers, as already noted, have come to Ireland over a short period of time. The presence of new people, after some initial skepticism, has been generally welcomed: "Great credit is due to those people, organizations, and parishes that have come forward to acknowledge the dignity of the refugees and asylum-seekers in their midst, accept their history and appreciate the cultures and peoples from which they come."[37] The many gifts of these and other newcomers are being recognized. Communication of faith in Ireland is, as a result, a new reality. Ethnic, cultural, and religious difference brings with it new perspectives, new ways of seeing the truth, new ways of understanding the world: indeed, "each new era has been blessed by God with charisms which lift up the Gospel in a new and vibrant manner."[38] Irish society has awakened to the need for a radical inclusiveness that questions deeply the cozy worlds that have sometimes been constructed without those who have special needs, without the socially deprived, without the elderly, without newcomers.

Dialogue in faith demands not only tolerance, but respect. It must reverence the beliefs and traditions of the individual's own faith community and that of others. It should reach out to embrace all within the community and all beyond that community who are happy to engage. It should reach out further again to invite all people to search together in love and to open up the possibility of a renewed sense in society of God's gracious presence in all of life. It should reach out, too, beyond life itself, and embrace death, prompted by the Christian hope of everlasting life in God's love: "Jesus Christ shows us how the truth of love can transform even the dark mystery of death into the radiant light of the resurrection."[39] The realization that we are all poor, isolated, and disabled in one way or another, unable to explain fully our thoughts, our feelings, and our actions, allows us to reach out, to each other and to God, as we really are:

37. Irish Catholic Bishops' Conference, *Prosperity with a Purpose: Christian Faith and Values in a Time of Rapid Economic Growth* (Dublin: Veritas, 1999), 96.
38. Breandán Leahy, "Revelation and Faith," in *Evangelising for the Third Millennium*, ed. Maurice Hogan and Thomas J. Norris, 82 (Dublin:Veritas, 1997).
39. *Sacramentum caritatis*, 35.

The person who understands his or her inner vulnerability is conscious of inner fragility, has experienced failure and defeat, will be the one who will find it easiest to understand and accept the other.[40]

Making Communication in Faith Possible?

A final question that must be engaged with, if there is to be any meaningful attempt to communicate faith, is the provision of the necessary resources to move forward and put the best of what has been discovered into practice. This means finding the necessary financial resources, resources of personnel, and structural resources, as well as textbooks and other material resources; it is so easy to put off decisions, to wait for the right moment, to think it essential to have everything in place before anything can be achieved.

By addressing the need for renewed effort and realistic structures, at all the levels discussed in this article, the Christian community in Ireland can demonstrate its concern that good planning takes place, recognizing that all members of the church have responsibility together for its evangelizing mission. Parish communities, clusters of parishes, and deaneries can be renewed as agents of evangelization, catechesis, and ongoing faith development. In order for this to be achieved, dioceses will need to provide support at the local level, establishing, sometimes in conjunction with other dioceses, a faith development service that encourages local initiatives by providing expertise and reassurance. At a national level there should be a clear sense of coherence and cooperation, such that good ideas are made available to all and structures are interlinked to produce effective results. Faith development in Catholic schools should be given renewed attention and support, and teacher training for religious education and formation strengthened. The preparation of those called to faith development ministries in parishes as well as in schools should be carefully attended to so that all are able to understand each others' roles and are trained to collaborate well together. Materials and resources developed to bring the good news of the life, ministry, death, and resurrection of Jesus to all should continue to be given priority. Initiatives in support of communicating Christian faith should take careful

40. John Hull, in conversation with Andrew. G. McGrady, "Beholding the Stranger in Our Midst," in *Welcoming the Stranger: Practising Hospitality in Contemporary Ireland*, ed. Andrew G. McGrady, 107 (Dublin: Veritas, 2006).

note of the requirements of learners, of teachers of all kinds, including parents, and of the Christian community.

A Closing Thought

Only when there is an awareness of the significant questions posed for faith today can there be a new beginning in the communicating of that faith. Attentiveness and willingness to engage are essential. The Eucharistic community, gathered around Jesus and moved by the Spirit of Life, must recognize, respect, and engage with the people and the questions of our day. In this way, the church will continue to challenge itself and the world to build the kingdom of God's love here and now. Within the Christian year, as Timothy Radcliffe observes, and in the Christian life, "we inhabit a story that gives us hope."[41]

41. Timothy Radcliffe, *What Is the Point of Being a Christian?* (London: Burns and Oates, 2005), 140.

18 Communicating the Catholic Faith in the United States

Merylann J. Schuttloffel

When I read John Sullivan's summary of his personal and professional faith experiences (see Chapter 22), I find that they mirror my own as an educator of faith, in the home (as a parent), in schools (as a teacher and principal), at the university (as a professor), in the church community (as a parishioner in various religious education roles), and through my work as presenter or facilitator of in-service training and formation for Catholic educational leaders. These life experiences influence my views on the practice of communication as it relates to religious education. In this text, religious education is considered from numerous perspectives. To add my own particular focus to the topic, I will consider communication and religious education through the prism of the contemplative principle.[1] The contemplative principle is a concept that integrates the Catholic faith with leadership practice for the purpose of thoughtful, coherent decision making. The role of communication within this process is essential.

1. Merylann J. Schuttloffel, *Character and the Contemplative Principal* (Washington, D.C.: National Catholic Educational Association, 1999).

First, this chapter examines Catholic identity within the context of the American Catholic Church today. I suggest that contemporary views of Catholic identity impact religious education. Next, the contemplative principle is introduced as a decision-making process that emphasizes communication as a core leadership quality.[2] The communication-leadership dynamic is integral to the creation of a catechetical community imbued with faith internship experiences. Then, three models of religious education are described. Each model of religious education encourages educational leadership to create a catechetical community, though within a different educational context. The chapter concludes with some contemplative recommendations for American religious education.

Catholic Identity within the Catholic Church in the U.S. Today

The American Catholic Church has undergone significant sociological change during the past half century. Economic prosperity, employment opportunities, and higher education expanded and facilitated the integration of Catholics into American society. A contemporary American identity represented a historical shift from the immigrant identity defined by ethnic culture (e.g. Italian-Catholic, German-Catholic, Irish-Catholic).[3]

Vatican II reinforced by societal events (e.g., the Civil Rights movement) called forth the American laity to play a significant role within the church and nation. This evolution to the current reality can be underscored by the presence of five sitting Catholic Supreme Court justices, a Catholic Speaker of the House of Representatives, numerous Catholic members in the Congress, and several Catholic candidates for the 2008 presidential nomination. Catholics have successfully moved from being defined as "a Catholic who is American" to "an American who is Catholic." In an American culture where immigrant assimilation was a long-time goal, Catholics have achieved the status of the founding white Protestants.[4]

2. Schuttloffel, *Contemplative Leadership that Creates a Culture for Continuous Improvement* (Washington, D.C.: National Catholic Educational Association, 2008).

3. Timothy Meagher, "Ethnic, Catholic White: Changes in the Identity of European American Catholics," in *The Catholic Character of Catholic Schools*, ed. James Youniss, John J. Convey, and Jeffrey A. McLennan, 190–218 (Notre Dame, Ind.: University of Notre Dame Press, 2000).

4. William V. D'Antonio, James D. Davidson, Dean R. Hoge, and Juan L. Gonzales Jr., *Young Adult Catholics: Religion in the Culture of Choice* (Notre Dame, Ind.: University of Notre Dame Press, 2001).

This new reality has been well documented in recent research on the Catholic Church.[5] One result of Catholic assimilation is an increasing number of nominal Catholics, predominately through immigration and their attendant rising birthrate, and native Catholics, who increasingly see less distinction between themselves and other Christian denominations.[6] Today's Catholics have less involvement with their parish church and base their attachment to the church on what Hoge calls "ethnic and family factors."[7] He suggests, "In that respect Catholics are similar to American Jews, whose Jewish identity does not depend crucially on religious beliefs. Catholics remain Catholic, even if they are unhappy or unconvinced of Catholic teachings."[8]

However, there is evidence that Catholics do have a sense of what they consider essential or core (ranked "very important") to their identity as Catholics. Ranking high on the survey list are these items: helping the poor (84 percent), the resurrection of Jesus (84 percent), sacraments, particularly the Eucharist (76 percent), and teachings about Mary (74 percent). Other items follow in diminishing importance, ending with a celibate male priesthood (29 percent). A description of the American Catholic identity from this research reflects what most Catholics already suspect about their church: that is, Catholics have a sense that some beliefs are central, but there are differences of opinion on what those essential beliefs are.[9] This situation creates what are often called "cafeteria Catholics," those who remain ostensible Catholics, but are selective about the practices and beliefs they espouse.

American Catholics have moved from a defensive posture in the larger American culture to a proactive stature with the potential for transformational influences. Within this environment two agendas coexist for religious education: first, to transmit Catholic theology and church teachings, and second, to sufficiently catechize Catholics to become change agents within the larger culture. Before continuing this chapter, there are two features of the American educational scene that require some definition, or at least clarification, for the benefit of an international audience.

5. William V. D'Antonio, James D. Davidson, Dean R. Hoge, and Mary L.Gautier, *American Catholics Today: New Realities of Their Faith and Their Church* (Lanham, Md.: Rowman and Littlefield, 2007).

6. Ibid.

7. Dean R. Hoge, "A Demographic Framework for Understanding Catholicism in America," *Seminary Journal* 2, no. 1 (2006): 61–68.

8. Ibid., 63.

9. Ibid., 64.

First, religious education within the United States implies faith education that takes place within the family, the parish or religious institution of worship, or parochial schools. Religious education does not exist within the government schools, even as an accessory to regular education. And in government schools religious education seldom exists even for informational purposes. Two important traits about American education provide some explanation for this situation.[10]

There is an important distinction between the environments for religious education within the United States and the United Kingdom. Historically, the United States has maintained what is referred to as "a wall of separation" between church and state. From the earliest colonial settlements that were created for religious freedom, in Colonial times and after the Revolutionary War, the common school in America was fundamentally a Protestant school. Initially religious sects maintained their own schools, but eventually the common school was created and supported by local community tax dollars. After an increase in the number of immigrants in the mid-1800s, particularly Catholic immigrants, efforts were initiated to remove anti-Catholic bias from the government (what in the U.S. are referred to as public) schools. Over the decades, as ethnic plurality increased, the government's response to debates about religion in schools typically was to remove more and more religion from government schools. This situation remains today. The only study of religion students might have within a government school typically falls under the course caption of "the study of world religions" from a literature or historical perspective.

Another important distinction between American education and education in many other countries is that in the United States, education has always been considered a local enterprise. Historically, "local" meant that individual villages, townships, counties, and cities had their own school districts. Within those school districts there was considerable individuality, latitude, and authority. Recently, individual states more powerfully play the local unit of school governance. Even today nearly ninety percent of education funds are raised locally (in state and local districts). When federal intrusion into education does occur, it usually surrounds issues of equality and equity. This historical tradition of local school control has prevented

10. John D. Pulliam and James J. Van Patten, History of Education in America (Upper Saddle River, N.J.: Prentice Hall, 2007).

the kind of conformity in American schools that is routine in other governance systems. Local control has also allowed communities to restrict student exposure to an education about religions and social norms that were perceived as unacceptable to the local norms. In recent times, as local populations become more mobile and diverse, the courts have strengthened the wall between church and state in order to preserve civil liberties.[11]

Current administrative theories emphasize the importance of communication skills for effective leadership.[12] Contemplative practice also recognizes communication as an integral element of leadership practice. Next I set the stage for a discussion of three religious education models that emphasize the role of leadership.

The Significance of Communication for Leadership

In my monograph *Character and the Contemplative Principal*, I argue for decision making that challenges Catholic school principals to integrate Gospel values into their daily lives through the decisions they make.[13] Contemplative practice relies on more than contemporary management theory for Catholic school leaders. The contemplative principle is a process model for reflective practice that focuses on school leader decision making rooted in a Gospel vision that transforms the school community to a catechetical community where students [and adults] learn to live their faith.

Sergiovanni's leadership schema[14] and Van Manen's reflective framework[15] provide the theoretical underpinnings of the contemplative principle. But it is Catholic theology and Catholic teaching that provide the critical foundational beliefs. These beliefs then tint the leader's interpretive lens for reflection on the dilemmas that challenge all educational leaders. One dilemma facing religious educators is how to communicate the faith, both as a theology to be learned and as a lifestyle to be lived. The contemplative principle brings together the cognitive processes of meta-cognition (thinking about

11. Ibid.

12. Ronald A. Heifetz and Marty Linsky, *Leadership on the Line: Staying Alive through the Dangers of Leading* (Boston: Harvard Business School Press, 2002).

13. Schuttloffel, *Character and the Contemplative Principal*.

14. Thomas J. Sergiovanni, *Moral Leadership: Getting to the Heart of School Improvement* (San Francisco: Jossey-Bass, 1992).

15. Max Van Manen, "Linking Ways of Knowing with Ways of Being Practical," *Curriculum and Inquiry* 6, no. 3 (1977) 205–28.

one's own thinking) and leadership decision making (the resulting actions of one's thinking) within Catholic educational contexts.[16] The intended consequence of contemplative practice is that a catechetical community is created where faith-witnessing experiences serve as a faith internship.

Contemplative leaders recognize that virtually everything they say or do sends messages that influence the school's culture.[17] This continuous stream of communication has the potential to reinforce or diminish the faith experiences of members within the school community. A school community that reinforces faith experiences is a catechetical community. "The believer has received their faith from others and should hand it on to others" characterizes the distinctiveness of a catechetical community.[18] Religious education requires the knowledge and environment that will not only encourage the acquisition of faith knowledge, but model lifelong learning, leading to a mature faith practice. The goal of religious education becomes catechetical, then, when "it aims to achieve a more integral formation of the person rather than merely to communicate information."[19]

The next section presents three models of religious education. The emphasis within each model is on the potential for students to learn the theological underpinnings of their faith, but to also experience how to live their faith. A contemplative analysis of each model is considered.

Three Religious Education Models from the United States

American Catholic schools, the first model, provide a powerful opportunity to create a faith learning community. As restated in the American bishops' recent statement,[20] Catholic schooling was recognized as an exemplary model for catechesis. A contemplative school leader plays an integral role in fashioning the Catholic school into a catechetical community by shaping the school's culture,[21] engaging the theological and cardinal characteristics

16. Schuttloffel, *Character and the Contemplative Principal*, 1999.
17. Ibid.
18. United States Conference of Catholic Bishops, *Catechism of the Catholic Church*, English translation (New York: William H. Sadlier, 1994), 46, par. 166.
19. United States Conference of Catholic Bishops, *National Director for Catechesis* (Washington, D.C.: United States Conference of Catholic Bishops, 2005), 10.
20. United States Conference of Catholic Bishops, *Renewing our Commitment to Catholic Elementary and Secondary Schools in the Third Millenium* (Washington, D.C.: United States Conference of Catholic Bishops, 2005).
21. Timothy J. Cook, *Architects of Catholic Culture: Designing and Building Catholic Culture in Catholic Schools* (Washington, D.C.: National Catholic Educational Association, 2001).

of Catholicity,[22] and providing opportunities to develop spiritual leadership in students and adults.[23] Religion coursework, service learning opportunities, psychosocial development, academic coursework, and reciprocal support arrangements with families integrate to create a faith internship experience within a catechetical community.

Within the faith internship experience, as the *National Directory of Catechesis* argues, "[the Catholic school] is not simply an institution which offers academic instruction of high quality, but, even more important, is an effective vehicle of total Christian formation."[24] From a contemplative stance this means that the principal, teachers, staff, parents, and parishioners witness the faith through actions that provide witness of the Catholic lifestyle that students may learn to embrace. A faith internship is the faith learner's lived experience within a school-based catechetical community.

There are some practical challenges to the faith internship experience within a parish school. The relationship between the school and the parish, the catechetical formation of teachers and staff, the priorities of parents for the school are only a few examples of how the role of a Catholic school as a catechetical community might be thwarted. Some supporters of Catholic schooling suggest that current declining enrollment trends signal a weakening of the relationship between the catechetical role of the Catholic school and the faith life of the typical American Catholic. This analysis is consistent with Hoge's argument that Catholic schools may be an artifact of a bygone era.[25] At the same time, many Catholic school supporters recognize that a faith internship experience that more aggressively links schooling and catechesis provides the only rationale for a Catholic school's existence.

Principal preparation is an integral element in the process to create a catechetical community that supports a faith internship model. Without a principal (e.g., school head) who has a sufficient theological understanding to build the rationale for this model and continue its effective use through creation of the supportive conditions for teachers, students, and parents to

22. Thomas H. Groome, "What Makes a School Catholic?" in *The Contemporary Catholic School: Context, Identity and Diversity*, ed. Terence H. McLaughlin, Joseph O'Keefe, and Bernadette O'Keeffe (London: Falmer Press, 1996).

23. Richard M. Jacobs, *Building Spiritual Leadership Density in Catholic Schools* (Washington, D.C.: National Catholic Educational Association, 2005).

24. United States Conference of Catholic Bishops, *National Director for Catechesis* (Washington, D.C.: United States Conference of Catholic Bishops, 2005), 230.

25. Dean R. Hoge, William Dinges, Mary Johnson, and Juan L. Gonzales Jr., *Young Adult Catholics: Religion in the Culture of Choice* (Notre Dame, Ind.: University of Notre Dame Press, 2001).

witness their faith, a faith internship is unlikely. Within various dioceses special programs exist to prepare and assist principals in acquiring the appropriate knowledge and skills for contemplative practice to initiate a catechetical community.

A contemplative analysis of the parish school model considers numerous technical questions that challenge principals as they manage a Catholic school: Who should attend Catholic schools (inclusion/exclusion)? Who should pay for and support Catholic schools (real cost/stewardship)? Have Catholic schools become too disengaged from parish life (academic performance/catechesis)?

At the interpretive level of reflection school principals must grasp the meaning created by a faith internship experience. Often parents and teachers portray any focus on catechesis and evangelization as a diminishment of academic excellence. This is a dangerous assumption that must be addressed through an understanding of Catholic identity based in sound theology. Instruction in the underpinning beliefs that shape Catholic identity may help to mitigate this argument.[26] Further instruction in Catholic teaching as described through the Catechism of the Catholic Church[27] also provides a depth of understanding on the compatibility of faith and reason in the Catholic scholastic world.[28] Other Catholic Church documents specifically directed toward the Catholic school provide important starting points to give understanding to the messages a principal tries to communicate.[29] Discussions with parents, parishioners, teachers, staff, and students help to give meaning to the concept of a faith internship within each unique school catechetical community. Questions related by interpretive reflection typically revolve around these topics: What to do about mixed messages (parent practice of the faith/school practice of the faith)? Who creates catechetical meaning within the school community (pastor/principal)? The interpretation of meaning and messages within a school culture must be grounded in

26. Groome, *What Makes Us Catholic* (San Francisco: HarperOne, 2003).

27. *Catechism of the Catholic Church.*

28. The Sacred Congregation for Catholic Education, *The Catholic School* (Ottawa: Publications Service Canadian Conference of Catholic Bishops, 1977).

29. Jane E. Regan, *Toward an Adult Church: A Vision of Faith Formation* (Chicago: Loyola Press, 2002); Edwin J. McDermott, *Distinctive Qualities of the Catholic School* (Washington, D.C.: National Catholic Educational Association, 1997); Congregation for Catholic Education, *The Religious Dimension of Education in a Catholic School* (Washington, D.C.: United States Catholic Conference, 1988); National Conference of Catholic Bishops, *To Teach as Jesus Did: A Pastoral Message on Catholic Education* (Washington, D.C.: United States Catholic Conference Publications Office, 1972).

Gospel values and Catholic teaching. Without a commitment to these foundational elements, critical reflection will not find any substantial rationale for the decisions made by school leadership or other members of the catechetical community.

This model raises significant questions at the critical level of reflection: Who should determine the purpose of a Catholic school? What is the practical role of the school in catechesis and evangelization? How do we balance family and school educational roles?

At the schoolhouse unit, the faith internship experience attempts to maintain the focus of Catholic schooling on the preparation of the whole person, including spiritual formation. The concept of an internship implies that students will learn the Catholic lifestyle from the witnesses they experience in their daily lives. The contemplative principle reminds those in leadership that their responsibility rests with making decisions that shape a school into a catechetical community that exemplifies values based in the Gospel of Jesus Christ. Communication is an essential skill for a catechetical community to be authentic and successfully acculturate the faith.

A second model that offers the possibility of promoting a unity of purpose for parish catechesis is the implementation of a total Catholic education board that guides all parish catechetical efforts. Catholic schools have transitioned their governance to advisory boards over the last thirty years. These advisory boards provided pastors the counsel of lay expertise, particularly in the areas of finance, facilities, development, and marketing. A parallel trend has been the creation of religious education boards that served the same advisory role to pastors concerning the best practices for the implementation of school-age and adult religious education programs. But as can be easily imagined, pastors are then caught directly in the tension between the needs of these two competing advisory bodies.

Recently, individual pastors and numerous bishops have recognized the futility of this situation. The creation of a total religious education board responds to this dilemma by refocusing parish religious education into a holistic catechetical mission. The entire parish becomes a catechetical community that supports faith learning across a lifetime. Key to the successful implementation of a total religious education board is a pastor that has the ability to collaborate and problem-solve with lay leadership. Also crucial to the process are lay leaders who have the requisite formation and theological education to place their experiences within the larger historical Catholic

Church context, who understand the theological basis for appropriate decision making, and then have the ability to integrate that knowledge base into contemplative solutions. In other words, advisory boards also require a contemplative stance. Without the requisite knowledge, skills, and character attributes, often only administrative solutions are generated, rather than those resolutions coherent with a catechetical community.

Any promising vision for the future rests on leadership education and formation that enhance theological knowledge, personal qualities, and relational skills. Pastors as well as lay catechists must have the personal qualities and relational skills to meet the challenges inherent in catechesis for a complex twenty-first-century parish. Catholic Church documents and leadership literature are replete with rationales and specific skills about what catechesis is needed and how leadership needs to implement these parish-wide religious education programs.[30]

Total parish catechesis is one possibility that invites school leaders, lay parish ministers, and pastors to become collaborators, unified in their catechetical mission. The concept of faith internship is consistent with Groome's "three great expansive horizons,"[31] as expressed by the *General Directory for Catechesis*.[32] First is a holistic Christian faith that emphasizes not only the requisite knowledge, but the way of life socialized by a Catholic culture. The second horizon is inclusiveness of participants in catechesis. Each member of the parish catechetical community is both teacher and learner of the faith. Third is a comprehensive pedagogy that connects lived experience to scripture and tradition. A parish-wide catechetical community model exemplifies the three horizons. A catechetical community would provide all members with faith internship experiences that allow their faith to develop to maturity. A catechetical community is supported by contemplative practice that connects beliefs and decision making.

Collaboration is a key skill necessary to create a parish catechetical com-

---

30. Ronald A. Heifetz, Ronald Linsky, and Marty Linsky, *Leadership on the Line: Staying Alive Through the Dangers of Leading* (Boston: Harvard Business School Press, 2002); Joseph P. Sinwell, ed., *The Baptismal Catechumenate: An Inspiration for All Catechesis* (Washington, D.C.: National Catholic Educational Association, 2002); Robert I. Colbert and Janice A. Kraus, eds., *Perspectives on Leadership and Catechesis* (Washington, D.C.: National Catholic Educational Association, 2001); and Groome, "Claiming and Breaking Ground: The General Directory for Catechesis," in *Empowering Catechetical Leaders*, ed. Groome and Michael J. Corso (Washington, D.C.: National Catholic Educational Association, 1999).

31. Groome, "Claiming and Breaking Ground," 238–40.

32. Congregation for the Clergy, *General Directory for Catechesis* (Washington, D.C.: United States Catholic Conference, 1997).

munity filled with faith internship experiences.[33] Effective collaboration requires communication skills that emphasize active listening, a key element in successful communication.[34] And a contemplative stance regards genuine two-way communication as essential to sending messages that create a climate that supports a catechetical community.

A contemplative analysis of the total parish education model considers at a technical level of reflection the challenge to find ways that mutually support dioceses and parishes in their efforts to recruit, educate, and form the most competent leadership for the development and expansion of a parish catechetical community.[35] What knowledge, skills, and dispositions must be conveyed through education and formation to prepare catechetical leaders for every parish educational ministry? How can this be done? What resources are needed? Who is going to implement this leadership formation plan? What structures must be created? How might a total catechetical board assist this process?

Why is a parish catechetical community vital to the future Catholic Church? This is the critical level of reflection, because it analyzes the substantive rationale for this model. What are the values and beliefs about leadership conveyed through a catechetical formational process? What tensions in beliefs might exist among various ministries or members of a parish community? How might the Gospel values and Catholic tradition become more integrated as the substance of decisions about leadership formation and, ultimately, about leadership practice in religious education?

And at the interpretive level of reflection, what messages are currently being sent to the parish by the divisive, often combative relationship between the parish school community and the parish religious education community? What message is sent to parishes when leadership education and formation is haphazard, informal, or nonexistent? What meaning is attached to religious education when the leadership of various ministries operates in a competitive mode? What new meaning is created by a total catechetical governance board? What new messages might be sent by a total catechetical governance board?

33. Loughlan Sofield and Carroll Juliano, *Collaboration: Uniting Our Gifts in Ministry* (Notre Dame, Ind.: Ave Maria Press, 2000); and Sofield and Donald H. Kuhn, *The Collaborative Leader: Listening to the Wisdom of God's People* (Notre Dame, Ind.: Ave Maria Press, 1995).
34. Schuttloffel, *Contemplative Leadership.*
35. David DeLambo, *Lay Parish Ministers: A Study of Emerging Leadership* (New York: National Pastoral Life Center, 2005); Schuttloffel, *Contemplative Leadership.*

These challenging leadership questions might be addressed through the creation of a parish catechetical community that supports the acquisition of theological knowledge and the appropriation of Catholic lifestyle behaviors. A total catechetical governance board would be the structural vehicle to strategize, implement, and evaluate a parish catechetical community. The underpinning values and beliefs that support this model are implicit in the role of the church to pass on the Gospel of Jesus Christ and church teaching through religious education.

A strong argument is made that Catholic higher education has a responsibility to provide the kind of education that integrates the intellectual challenges of university study with character development that seeks to resolve the moral dilemmas confronting leadership.[36] Catholic higher education is a venue for future leaders to seek not only knowledge in relation to moral questions, but a contemplative stance that integrates Gospel values and Catholic Church teaching with decision making. Since many Catholic social justice documents have shaped Catholic secondary school curricula and religious education programs, in all probability, incoming students to Catholic higher education have been influenced by their previous service experiences.[37] One might speculate that many students choose Catholic higher education because they seek to continue their commitment to social justice issues through volunteerism and charity. Service learning, situated within Catholic higher education, exemplifies a third model for religious education directed at young adults.

Long before service learning existed as a methodological choice in higher education, volunteerism and charity were prevalent activities at Catholic colleges and universities. Campus ministry and its numerous service opportunities attracted some students, while other students sought secular activities through local civic organizations. Students tended to regard charity as the beginning of their involvement in social justice activism.

Student charity is not characterized by insignificant activities, but rather experiences more consistent with an introductory step into a phased development of service learning participation.[38] Service learning as a methodolo-

36. Patrick A. Duignan, "Formation of Authentic Educational Leaders for Catholic Schools," in *Leadership in Catholic Education*, ed. Deirdre J. Duncan and Dan. Riley, 172–83 (Sydney: HarperCollins, 2002).

37. Carol Cimino, Regina M. Haney, and Joseph M. O'Keefe, *Integrating the Social Teaching of the Church into Catholic Schools: Conversations in Excellence 2000* (Washington, D.C.: National Catholic Educational Association, 2001).

38. Dwight E. Giles and Janet Eyler, "The Impact of a College Community Service Lab-

gy provides the knowledge base necessary to transform charitable acts into a confrontation with political, institutional, financial, and sociological structures of social injustice. Students that choose to make a developmental leap in purpose transition to *social change* activity.[39] The induction and preparation of future Catholic Church leadership could be a result of this process. Service learning, with the appropriate supportive conditions, assists the university to become a catechetical community providing faith internship experiences to young adult students who choose to become engaged in social change.

Within the Catholic faith tradition, and hopefully within the culture of a Catholic college or university, the opportunity exists to assist students to reflect on service experiences in view of their conscience formation and their future contribution to the transformation of society by Gospel values. American bishops state in their pastoral letter, "Individuals whose conscience has been tutored by the Gospel understand that their task is not only to resist evil but to help transform the world."[40] Catholic scholars could argue that academic service-learning provides a unique opportunity to shape students' consciences.[41]

On a Catholic college or university campus, three values overlap among the goals of campus ministry, the goals of the faculty, and the goals of academic service-learning: (1) educating for justice, (2) facilitating student personal development, and (3) developing church and civic leadership. Students readily grasp the contribution of the two worldviews: academic and religious. Students reconcile these two worldviews into an integrated whole in academic service-learning experiences that resonate with life in a catechetical community.

Using the reflective language of contemplative practice, at a technical level, the challenge is to find ways that mutually support university faculty and campus ministry staff in their efforts to educate and form the most competent leadership for the current and future Catholic Church. What knowledge and skill does Catholic university leadership require to shape a catechetical community? How does a Catholic university provide students with a faith in-

---

oratory on Students' Personal, Social and Cognitive Outcomes," *Journal of Adolescence*, no. 17 (1994): 327–39.

39. Keith Morton, "The Irony of Service: Charity, Project and Social Change in Service-Learning," *Michigan Journal of Community Service Learning* (Fall 1995): 19–32.

40. National Conference of Catholic Bishops, *Empowered by the Spirit: Campus Ministry Faces the Future* (Washington, D.C.: United States Catholic Conference of Bishops, 1985).

41. Julie Mahoney, "Hope, Holiness and Wholeness: The Mission of Catholic Campus Ministry to Higher Education," *Religious Education*, no. 59 (3-S) (1974): 28–36.

ternship experience? What knowledge, skills, and dispositions must be conveyed through education and formation to prepare church and civic leadership?

At the critical level of reflection, why is this educational and formational process important to the future Catholic Church? What are the values and beliefs about leadership conveyed through academic service-learning experiences? What tensions in beliefs about preparing future leadership might exist among the various constituencies on campus? How might the Gospel values and Catholic Church tradition become more integrated as the substance of decisions about leadership formation and, ultimately, about leadership practice and religious education through service?

And at the interpretive level of reflection, what messages are currently being sent to the university's students because of the lack of integration between the academic and religious aims of the university? What message is sent to students when the education and formation of Catholic Church leadership education are not viewed as appropriate roles for Catholic higher education? What meaning is attached to a lived faith and lived leadership when there is a lack of integration within Catholic higher education?

Often students at a faith-based institution lack the maturity of understanding in their faith tradition to recognize its connection to the social justice issues they experience in their service-learning activities. From this perspective, two questions remain: (1) How can academic service-learning assist in the student's personal transformation? (2) How can academic service-learning assist students to learn to transform society? Many faculty and administrators find these confounding questions at a Catholic college or university. The response to these questions is critical if Catholic colleges and universities are to offer an education that is more than vocational preparation. Creating a catechetical community for young adults potentially provides a faith learning opportunity for the challenges of the Gospel in the larger world.

Reflections, Reservations, and Recommendations for the Future

This chapter has examined three models of religious education that require specialized leadership skills, with an emphasis on communication. The contemplative principle provided the leadership framework for the creation of a catechetical community. I suggested that Catholic schools, parishes, and Catholic higher education create catechetical communities that support faith internship experiences within each unique context. A catechetical community requires attention to leadership knowledge and skills, particularly communication. Most significant is how the catechetical community itself personifies communicating the faith.

There are noteworthy challenges with the three models for religious education presented. At the core of each model is the creation of a catechetical community that is pervasive in its Catholic culture. Some Americans might view this type of community as a return to the Catholic ghetto of the past. Surely that is not my intention. I believe that children, students, and young adults who will become the future Catholic Church must have an opportunity to know their faith well enough to recognize its distinctive features and its challenges. There cannot be rote memorization of guidelines and passive acceptance, but a deeply rooted understanding of the intentions for Catholic Church teaching. Questions must be encouraged so that the wisdom of the church's response might be explored. To create a catechetical community, the contemplative principle and a comprehensive contemplative pedagogy are essential. A catechetical community requires authenticity, as learners will appropriate the lessons they are given.

The lack of value placed on their Catholic faith by parents is the root impediment to the school or the parish religious education program becoming a catechetical community. Parents as the primary educators of their children must take up their responsibility and recognize their need to become more theologically educated. Many parents' lack of theological understanding is a by-product of the softened post–Vatican II religious education programs. The increase in mixed-faith marriages also diminished attachment to devotional practices. Mass attendance as an indicator of commitment to the Catholic Church gives a dismal view of the future church.[42]

If a potential transformation for the current reality exists, it is through the concept of a catechetical community, but with an additional emphasis on adult faith formation.[43] Reaching out to Catholics who are uninformed or unformed about the connection between their faith and their daily life is of immediate and paramount importance. Continuing faith growth and

42. D'Antonio, et al., *American Catholics Today.*

43. Jane E. Regan, *Toward an Adult Church: A Vision of Faith Formation* (Chicago: Loyola Press, 2002).

development must become a Catholic norm in order to challenge childlike faith with a mature understanding.

Objections to Catholic higher education as a catechetical community might resonate with some faculty as an attack on academic freedom. The reality could not be further from the truth. Young adults should have broad exposure to the challenging questions of modernity and the secular responses. *But there should also be the expectation that at Catholic colleges and universities there would be exposure to the Catholic Church's teaching in response to these same questions.* This should not be a debate that is avoided or feared by a catechetical community with confidence in its theological underpinnings. I recognize that this argument is difficult for many academics, who squirm at the intersection of faith and reason. My position is that examining this juncture is an appropriate role for Catholic higher education. Government and private institutions already provide options for debate, but without the theological expertise or the underlying consideration of the Catholic Church's teaching principles. Young Catholics are learning the theology of the Internet, or satellite radio and television. Catholic higher education must invest in the intellectual preparation of future Catholic leadership for the Catholic Church and civic institutions; else who will absorb that responsibility? I believe strongly that young Catholic adults who are exposed to the richness of Catholic scholarship will readily transform the college or university into a catechetical community for themselves without mandate or indoctrination.

Communication of the faith cannot be as an isolated event. A lived faith must be learned as a living faith. Contemplative leadership practice supports the creation of a catechetical community where the Catholic faith becomes a witnessing lifestyle. A faith internship imparts those lifestyle experiences within the Catholic school, parish, or higher educational institution. Of paramount importance is the preparation of leadership with the knowledge, skills, and dispositions to collaborate for a vision that creates a catechetical community. Contemplative leadership is aware that communicating the faith cannot be an isolated occasion, but must be an integrated way of life.

19 Communicating Faith in Contemporary Europe

Dealing with Language Problems In and Outside the Church

Lieven Boeve

Communicating the faith seems to have become more difficult than ever in Europe. From an age-old overall Christian continent, Europe recently seems to have entered a post-Christian era. Discussion about the Christian roots and character of Europe at least reveals that the role of Christianity on the old continent is no longer taken for granted. This has even led the present supreme pontiff, Benedict XVI, profiling himself as a pope-for-Europe, to strongly advocate for the intrinsic link between Christianity and Europe, against what he describes as the reigning secularist and relativist Enlightenment culture.[1] The ideological discussions on the Christian heritage of Eu-

1. Cf., e.g., Joseph Ratzinger, *Values in a Time of Upheaval*, with Marcella Pella (2004; New York: Crossroad, 2006); Ratzinger, *Without Roots: The West, Relativism, Christianity, Islam* (2004; New York: Basic Books, 2006). For a historical-systematic presentation of Joseph Ratzinger's/Benedict XVI's views and some comments, see Lieven Boeve, "Europe in Crisis: A Question of Belief or Unbelief? Perspectives from the Vatican," *Modern Theology* 23, no. 2 (2007): 205–27.

rope, however, should not obfuscate the fact that, on the sociocultural level, Europe is going through processes that have profoundly changed its religious situation. It is my contention that it is these processes that determine the climate in which church leaders, theologians, and other Christians are communicating the Christian faith, and it is these processes that also continue to challenge the way in which they perform this task. Moreover, it appears that the difficulty of communicating the faith is felt not only in the public forum, but also in the churches themselves. Communication of the faith with both non-Christians and Christians alike seems to go wrong. To a growing degree, pastors and theologians seem not to be able to speak the right language to express the Christian faith in an authentic, plausible, and relevant way.

In this essay I will first shed some light on these sociocultural processes changing Europe's religious situation, distinguishing these developments from their ideological evaluations. Afterward I will reflect on the consequences for communicating the Christian faith, both inside and outside church communities. As will become clear, in both cases we are confronted with language problems—to be distinguished and dealt with, however, in their own right. In the last part, we will discuss the problems that often occur in this regard.[2]

Although these ideas have been developed in conversation with and in response to the contemporary situation of Christianity in Europe, I am quite confident that the reflections presented here may also serve an American audience. Inasmuch as, first, the sociocultural processes changing the European religious landscape are linked to the worldwide process of globalization, and, second, religious plurality is a feature that has been prominent much more outside than inside Europe, the theological answer to both elaborated upon in this contribution may most likely inspire theologians from outside the European borders. This holds definitely true for the linguistic distinction we signal in the last section, referring to the outer and inner direction of our theological and ecclesial communication, including the problems that occur when this distinction is not respected.

---

2. The present contribution rehearses and elaborates on some of the ideas developed in Boeve, "Religion after Detraditionalization: Christian Faith in a Post-Secular Europe," *Irish Theological Quarterly* 70, no. 2 (2005): 99–122, and developed more extensively in Boeve, *God Interrupts History: Theology in a Time of Upheaval* (New York: Continuum, 2007), chaps. 1 and 3.

Religion in Europe

I would like to briefly mention three important features regarding the sociocultural developments that are changing the religious situation of Europe: first, the detraditionalization and individualization of individual and collective identities, and second, the pluralization of the European religious scene. Additionally, inasmuch as these processes influence Christian identity construction, a more reflexive Christian self-consciousness is needed.

The Detraditionalization and Individualization of Identity Formation

The term *detraditionalization* not only alludes to Europe's declining institutional Christian horizon (often referred to as *secularization*), but also hints at the more generally observed sociocultural interruption of traditions (religious as well as class and gender), which are no longer able to pass themselves on effortlessly from one generation to the next. Identity formation can no longer be perceived as quasi-automatically being educated into pregiven horizons, views, and practices that condition one's perspectives on meaning and social existence. It is from such a broader perspective of detraditionalization that the hampering of the transmission process of the Christian tradition should be observed. Christianity is no longer a given and unquestioned horizon of individual and social identity.

The titles given to the three subsequent books containing the Belgian results of the European Values Study are particularly telling. In 1984, the research group in charge of this study published "The Silent Turn," showing that Belgium was turning away from a more traditional Roman Catholic profile. In 1992, the same group published "The Accelerated Turn," claiming that the process of change was evolving faster than ever. The title of the third book, "Lost Certainty," published in 2000, indicates that the processes of detraditionalization are reaching their end. In little less than a few decades, Belgium has evolved from a society broadly perceived as traditionally Catholic into a detraditionalized society.[3]

At this point a caveat should be introduced: detraditionalization should

3. See, respectively, Jan Kerkhofs and Rudolf Rezsohazy, eds., *De stille ommekeer: Oude en nieuwe waarden in het België van de jaren tachtig* (Tielt: Lannoo, 1984); Jan Kerkhofs, Karel Dobbelaere, and Lilianne Voyé, eds., *De versnelde ommekeer: De waarden van Vlamingen, Walen en Brusselaars in de jaren negentig* (Tielt: Lannoo, 1992); Karel Dobbelaere, Mark Elchardus, Jan Kerkhofs, Lilianne Voyé, and Bernadette Bawin-Legros, *Verloren zekerheid: De Belgen en hun waarden, overtuigingen en houdingen* (Tielt: Lannoo, 2000).

be understood as a descriptive category, referring to a structural development wherein traditions are no longer self-evidently taken for granted and
passed on to the new generations. In this regard, it is to be distinguished
from an ideological aversion of tradition, or nihilism or relativism. The latter should be analyzed as strategies to cope with the changed situation, having become possible because of the structural changes, but not necessarily
the (only) response to them. Moreover, detraditionalization is not only a feature of a post-Christian reality, but also affects other religious and ideological affiliations. Therefore, all of them—Christian and non-Christian—have
to come to terms with this changed sociocultural reality.[4]

The flip side of detraditionalization is *individualization*. In a detraditionalized society, every individual is charged with the task of constructing his
or her personal identity. Traditions no longer automatically steer this construction process. Rather they have become available options. They appear
together with other and new options among the possibilities from which
an individual must choose. In other words, to a growing degree, personal
identity has become (structurally) reflexive. This is due to the fact that every choice made is in principle challenged by the alternative possible choices. Once having chosen, one can in principle be urged to answer for one's
choice (at least to oneself). Furthermore, this also holds true for those who
still opt for classical or traditional identities, because under the influence
of detraditionalization and individualization, their relationship to tradition
has changed, having become more reflexive. To one degree or another, people are aware that their choices—at least in principle—could have been very
different, and that contingency, opportunity, and context play an important
part in their making. In short: both Christian and non-Christian identity
formation have changed through these processes, and—inasmuch as tradition is important for these identities—have to come to terms with them.

It should be clear that individualization is a descriptive category as well,
and cannot be confused with individualism. Again, the latter is to be considered as a strategy to cope with the new situation of identity construction, resulting from the structural processes mentioned. Individualism, then, holds
that the needs, values, and views of the individual (and only the individual) should be the norm in the process of identity construction. The socio-

4. In Belgium, for example, the well-organized atheist-humanist movements also have
difficulties in the transmission of their ideological heritage to the new generations.

cultural process of individualization, on the contrary, refers to the changed structural conditions of the formation of identity and the increase in (potential) reflexivity that is brought about thereby. The question of whether people consciously take on the possibility to make their choices more reflexively (or let them be overtaken, e.g., by the market) has nothing to do with the process as such or with its structural character.

In our introduction, however, we hinted already to the fact that the distinction between individualization (the necessity of identity construction resulting from detraditionalization) and individualism (absolute self-determination) tends to be forgotten in many, primarily pessimistic, analyses of contemporary culture. Such analyses persistently fail to distinguish between structural processes and strategies to deal with the resulting situation. The current European context is then too easily and indiscriminately identified with nihilism and relativism, with loss and decay. Consequently, the relation of Christianity to that context is considered all too often as being foremost oppositional, perceived even as a "clash of cultures." What is overlooked then, is that whatever the questionable ideological responses to the sociocultural developments are, the underlying processes also affect Christian identity formation today. Structurally speaking, Christian identities have also become more reflexive. They are no longer plainly self-evident, but engaged in processes of appropriation and challenge, of choice and answerability. The younger generations in Europe especially are all too aware of the fact that being a Christian today implies an explicit option, which is culturally not (always) supported.

The Pluralization of Religion in Europe

Our focus on the interpretation of the European Values Study data, however, might cause us to forget another important feature of the European religious situation: the pluralization of religion. Indeed, one of the important shortcomings of the EVS is its underrepresentation of other (world) religions, including Islam.[5] Religious pluralization, however, does not limit itself to the rise of Islam and the immigration of foreign religions. Together

5. Furthermore, information on other religions from the EVS focuses mainly on the way in which Christians and "post-Christians" perceive them. In this regard, the framework of the EVS is still too dependent on secularisation theories, and operates from a linear continuum between firmly churched Christians on the one hand and secularist atheists on the other. From such a framework, it is difficult to keep track of the so-called religious renewal and dynamic pluralisation of religion (both in and outside Christianity).

with detraditionalization, it has become a feature of the European population as a whole. The religious landscape of Europe therefore is much more complex than being roughly a distinction between Christians and non-Christians (i.e., "no-longer-Christians" and secularist atheists). It progressively presents us rather with a broad spectrum of religious and other fundamental life options alongside an increasing awareness of this plurality. In addition to Christians (subdivided into various different denominations), there are atheists, agnostics, Muslims, Jews, Buddhists, lapsed Christians, post-Christians,[6] the religiously indifferent, adherents of new religious movements (such as New Age), people we might describe, for want of a better word, as syncretists. In addition, each group can be further specified by a multiplicity of tendencies and lifestyles, some institutionally recognizable and some not. Even in largely classical European settings, the reality of migration, tourism, and the communication media have raised the consciousness of religious plurality and confronted one's (religious) identity construction, regardless of its nature, with religious diversity.

At this juncture, it is again important to make the distinction between pluralization as a descriptive category and pluralism and relativism as strategies of relating to pluralization. Similarly, when the Christian faith rejects the latter, it is challenged nonetheless, on account of pluralization, to reconsider its own position in the current context. More than has hitherto been the case, the encounter with a diversity of religious others makes Christians aware of the particularity of their own tradition. As a result, in the same way as with individualization, pluralization invites Christian identity formation to integrate a larger degree of reflexivity and a recognition of the specificity of being Christian in relation to those religiously other, including atheists and agnostics, "something-ists" and the indifferent, Muslims, Buddhists, and members of new religious movements.

---

6. The category "post-Christian" refers to the large group of people who are only partially initiated and enjoy nothing more than a fragmentary involvement with faith and faith communities, although they are for the most part baptized and may well have been educated in confessional schools. This becomes manifest, for instance, in their occasional and declining participation in Christian rites of passage and their poor, non-integrated knowledge of the Christian tradition—often in spite of many years of catechesis and religious education in schools.

In Need of a More Reflexive Christian Identity

Of course the distinction between processes and (ideological) strategies does not do away with the often questionable ways—from a Christian perspective—of dealing with identity construction prevalent in our societies, such as, on the one hand, individualism, relativism, nihilism, aestheticism, but also, on the other hand, racism, nationalism, traditionalism, and fundamentalism. Indeed, both series of strategies seem to be insidious ways to deal with the challenges for personal and collective identity construction brought about by detraditionalization and pluralization. In the former, the loss of pre-given patterns leads to lifestyles in which no meaning, value, or truth is taken to be normative, unless the preferences of the individual. For the latter reactions, the threefold insecurity resulting from detraditionalization, the never-ending task to construct one's own identity, and the challenges of otherness for one's identity are averted by withdrawing into a self-securing identity, offered by one's ethnicity, nation, tradition, religion.[7]

Moreover, the distinction between processes and strategies also allows us to properly analyze the domination of our life-world by the economy and the market. Of all the (cultural) actors and influences that endeavor to steer identity construction at the individual and social level (religions being examples hereof as well), the media and the market appear to be the most significant in this respect.[8] Indeed, there is a risk that both the church and individual believers consciously or unconsciously adopt the patterns of consumer culture, with the church functioning as a supplier of spiritual goods and believers as consumers of what the church, but also other religious providers, have to offer. Especially with regard to the plurality of religious traditions or groups, competition could press the church into adopting market-

7. For a more elaborate analysis and comment on these strategies, see Boeve, *Interrupting Tradition: An Essay on Christian Faith in a Post-Modern Context* (Grand Rapids, Mich.: Eerdmans, 2003), chaps. 3 and 4.

8. The latter, in particular, is omnipresent. Economization determines both the way in which culture manifests itself to us and the way in which we have access to it and can relate to it: (a) Cultural objects are separated from their original associations and narratives, and made available for exchange on the market. (b) At the same time, we are trained in the discipline of consumption and learn to see culture from a consumer perspective and to make use of it as such. Such economization also deeply influences the way in which we relate to religion and tradition; see, for example, the important study by Vincent Miller, *Consuming Religion: Religious Belief and Practice in a Consumer Culture* (New York: Continuum, 2004), and European reactions thereto in Boeve and Kristien Justaert, *Consuming Religion in Europe*, a special edition of *Bulletin ET* 17, no. 1 (2006).

ing strategies in order to present itself as providing immediately available solutions to the religious needs of people, instant answers to human questions. At the same time religious consumers, often influenced by advertisements and marketing, are trained to choose out of the multiple offerings of religions, traditions, and spiritualities what would seem to best fit their religious needs.

The challenge for the church, pastors, and theologians at this point is how they can contribute to a Christian formation of identity that enables believers to act in a world that is marked both by detraditionalization, pluralization, and individualization and by many (sometimes religiously deficient) ways of dealing with these manifestations, including the insidiously streamlining powers of the market. This will at least include raising the self-reflexivity of Christians, making them able to cope—both culturally and theologically—with the no-longer self-evident nature of their tradition and the structural need of identity construction. At the same time, in relation to religious others, Christians have to become more aware of the particularity of their own tradition (and the specific choice that belonging to it implies) and learn to relate their faith productively to the challenging otherness of (religious) others. Due to the fact that in our current context the Christian tradition is no longer self-evident and appears to be only one among many traditions, it requires from Christians the reflexive competence to identify with this, their faith tradition, and to account for this identification, both within the church and in the public forum. Because of the changes in context, Christian faith is in need of a recontextualization: a reconsideration of the way in which faith and context are related to each other.[9]

It is from within such a framework that our considerations on communicating the Christian faith in Europe will be presented in the following paragraphs.

Communicating the Christian Faith in Europe: Distinguishing between an Inner and an Outer Perspective

As we have observed, Christian faith is no longer situated in a context that is to be analyzed in the foremost as being secular, but rather as detradi-

9. In *Interrupting Tradition* and *God Interrupts History*, I have proposed a theology of interruption to deal with these challenges and this response from a cultural-theological and methodological perspective.

tionalized and (religiously) pluralized. These contextual developments have major influences on the way in which Christians enter into dialogue with the current culture and society while being part of this culture and society. This new situation indeed calls for an adjustment in the analysis and strategic approach of communicating the faith. I suggest, therefore, that we make a methodological distinction between an *outer* and an *inner* perspective with regard to the Christian's engagement, dialogue, or communication with the current context.

—On the one hand, there is the growing consciousness, *ad extra*, of the narrative particularity of one's own Christian identity, positioning the Christian faith in the midst of a complex, dynamic, and plural, but also ambiguous, public forum. How are we to bear witness to the good news within this postsecular and post-Christian forum?

—On the other hand, *ad intra*, the progressively detraditionalized and pluralized context challenges the way in which this particular tradition, for Christians themselves, is handed down today. Thus, in relation to the contextual particularization of the Christian tradition and the confrontation with the religious other, we might ask: how can Christians attain to a renewed, recontextualized self-understanding (which is both contextually plausible and theologically legitimate)? How can they make sense of their own faith and adequately express this understanding—with themselves being part of the current context?

The distinction between *ad extra* and *ad intra* entails a methodological consideration, because Christians, including their pastors and theologians, are always already involved in the culture within which they live, being a constitutive part of it. Moreover, the distinction we are making is in no way to be considered absolute: in practice both dimensions continually intersect.

Communicating the Faith in the Public Forum

The *ad extra* dimension of the communication of Christian faith with regard to our detraditionalized and pluralized culture deals with the question of how to present the faith to a public forum that is no longer as such (even implicitly) permeated by a Christian horizon of meaning, thus to persons and groups who are not (or are no longer) Christian. This is not only an interpersonal but also an intrapersonal task, insofar as our "fragmented selves" make up the parts of different worlds. Communicating in the public forum what the Christian faith stands for has become more difficult and even quite problematic, due to the decrease of common presuppositions and of a shared language within which to perform this communication. Termed more technically, the question posed here is that of the *communicability* of the particularity of the Christian narrative. The Christian experience of reality can only be adequately communicated to those who have a minimal *familiarity* with the particularities of the Christian narrative, or are at least prepared to become acquainted with it.

The main problem pointed at here is—so to speak—a "language problem." To somebody, for instance, who does not possess any concept or narrative pointing at God, it is very difficult to explain what a Christian experience of God might mean. Within a plural context, religious experience cannot simply be identified with the experience of God, nor is such identification even necessary for it to be termed a religious experience. Speaking of the Christian message about "life after death" is not self-evident when, on the level of culture, concepts of reincarnation and resurrection get confused. Furthermore, and also from within an interreligious perspective, religions appear to be very different, and their distinct "languages" constitute real barriers for (inter)religious communication. The very elements that seem to bind the three so-called "prophetic religions"—also referred to as "religions of the book" or "religions of revelation"—make them at the same time very different from each other. Islam, Christianity, and Judaism differ considerably in their perception of the "prophet": Mohammed, Jesus, or Moses respectively; in the role their sacred scriptures (Qur'an, Bible, and Torah) play within the respective religious tradition; and the way in which the revelation of God in history is understood.

Paying greater attention to the irreducible particularity of the Christian narrative is one of the lessons taught to Christians (but also non-Christians) by the current context. The Christian narrative constitutes its own (dynamic)[10] symbolic space, that is, its own hermeneutical horizon. Becoming acquainted with Christianity is thus something akin to learning a language, a complex event that presumes grammar, vocabulary, formation of habits, and competence as much as it does empathy. It entails, at its minimum, becoming acquainted with the "narrative thickness" of what it is to be a Christian.

This insight is critical as regards two common claims made frequently

10. In this regard, see our reflections on the inner perspective.

among pastors and theologians. First, some claim that there is still a sufficiently substantial, and (often) implicit, overlap between the Christian tradition and European culture. This may be true for certain regions and groups, but is, as we have observed, definitely not the case for the European religious scene as a whole. A great number of formally baptized Christians indeed are hardly familiarized with Christian narratives and practices, and as a matter of fact have become "post-Christian."[11] Moreover, an often-heard complaint is that, in culture in general, basic knowledge about Christianity, for instance, in the public media, is lacking and even misinformed, often limited to the old clichés, and because of this, barely able to present developments in church and faith in all fairness. At this point, the effects of detraditionalization within the public forum become obvious.

Second, some suggest that the communication of faith could be better facilitated if one starts from the frequent structural analogies and kinship relations between the Christian faith and other (religious) positions—forming a kind of common ground. After all, each of them maintain some kind of spirituality, advocate an ethics, hold ideas on the meaning of personal and social life, express their convictions in narratives and rituals. Upon such a general or universal human substratum, then, Christianity (but also the other religions) are constructed, and, on the basis of this, it could be understood and explained in the public forum. No doubt the knowledge of such parallel structures can contribute to the understanding of Christian faith. However, it can never replace the need to familiarize oneself with the "narrative thickness" of Christianity. As already mentioned, in what religions seem to have in common often reside their main differences. Such an awareness of difference results from the growing consciousness of pluralization.

Considering the *ad extra* dimension of communicating the faith therefore points us toward the need to respect the specific "language," or the particular "narrative thickness," of the Christian tradition when presenting it in the public forum. This implies as well that if one wants to know something of Christianity, one will have to familiarize oneself to a certain degree with its narratives, vocabulary, practices, and views—regardless of whether one is sharing (or is willing to share) them or not.

11. See note 6.

Faith Communication in the Church

We can also consider the relation with context from an inner perspective. The contextual changes put pressure on the Christian tradition as it has been given shape in the previous decades and centuries and is handed down to us. After all, the Christian narrative tradition is, because of its incarnational drive, profoundly contextual and therefore recontextualizes itself time and again when changes occur in the context in which it is preached and lived. One can read the history of church and theology as one long illustration hereof: both on a large scale (e.g., the Germanic recontextualization after the demise of the Roman Empire, Thomas Aquinas' renewal of theology with the help of Aristotelianism, the *aggiornamento* of Vatican II) and in small, concrete cases and biographies (at the occasion of, for instance, the birth of a child, suffering a misfortune, the reading of a inspirational book, an intriguing encounter with a religious other). Repeatedly, Christian tradition has been immersed in, and is placed under pressure by, contextual newness, and often thereby challenged to a critical-creative recontextualization, sometimes even to such an extent that it thereby thoroughly changed itself. It is on this level that the renewal of tradition takes shape. In the process of handing down the tradition to different times and places, tradition develops. Tradition is indeed an active process. It becomes different, so to speak, to remain the same: a contextually appropriate, living witness to the saving God of Jesus Christ.[12]

The *ad intra* perspective thus focuses on the way in which the Gospel is appropriately expressed today. A recent example of this is the preference of inclusive language in theological God-talk, which is an expression of the contextually Christian consciousness that God's being cannot be limited in terms of gender, and, furthermore, that our relationship to God should no longer be conceived and evoked in purely patriarchal terms. Another illustration is offered by the rediscovery of the specific Jewish-Christian features of dogmatic concepts such as the resurrection and its distinction from the thinking patterns of Greek immortality to a far greater degree (and thereby helping theology to move toward a post-metaphysical, hermeneutical

---

12. For an elaboration on the concept of recontextualization, and the conditions to which recontextualization today has to give answer in order to be both contextually plausible and theological legitimate, see my *Interrupting Tradition* (chaps. 1 and 6) and *God Interrupts History* (chaps. 1–3).

approach). As a last example, consider the rise of the modern sciences, especially cosmology and evolutionary biology, which has forced Christians to conceive differently of creation, and God as Creator—an effort that is threatened today with the rise in certain circles of creationism and intelligent design.

From the *ad intra* perspective as well, faith communication in times of contextual change is to be considered a "language problem": the old language no longer adequately evokes the new, contextually anchored experiences of faith. With recontextualization, the language game of Christian faith itself (or, as stated above, its own symbolic space, hermeneutical horizon or circle), begins to shift—not just to give in to the context, but to remain faithful to its own message. For, ultimately, the criterion for recontextualization is of course not the context, but revelation.

Confusing Language Problems: Cause of Hampering Faith Communication

The main problem of a lot of pastoral and theological analyses and strategies regarding the communication of faith today is that they conflate these two methodologically distinct outer and inner perspectives. This mistake arises from the fact, first, that this methodological distinction cannot always be made as sharply in practice,[13] and, second, that in both cases, as indicated, problems of language are detected. In each case, however, the problem at hand is different. Disrespecting this difference results in wrong solutions for legitimate questions. This is the case when an *ad intra* solution is presented for an *ad extra* problem, and the reverse.

The Renewal of Faith Language ad Intra as a Solution for the Communicability of Christian Faith in the Public Forum

The *ad intra* problem of searching for a new language is often wrongly seen as the solution for the communication problems *ad extra*. The fact that the Christian faith can no longer make itself understood in the public forum is then attributed foremost to the deficiency of faith language. Only when the Christian faith (its teaching and practices) will be expressed in contex-

---

13. An encounter with someone of another religion or worldview can result in a heightened consciousness of the limits of the communicability *ad extra* because of the Christian narrative particularity, while at the same time urging an *ad intra* recontextualization of this narrative (which in its turn will become again the basis for the communication *ad extra*).

tual categories in which all people, Christians and non-Christians alike, understand, Christian faith will become attractive again—or so runs the argument.

An example hereof is the difficulty involved in communicating the unique place of Jesus Christ in the interpretation of the Christian relationship with God. The same difficulty occurs with the credibility and relevance of the Christian sacramental praxis. Pleading for a revision of the Christian God image on the basis that our contemporaries, having problems believing in a God who reveals Godself in history, favor rather vague, nonpersonal, immanent, and holistic views, constitutes another example.[14] Changing the language (Christ is a symbol [the incarnation a myth], sacraments are rites, God is "something more"), then, often does away with what is really constitutive for Christianity.

The presumptions behind this proposed solution are often, first, that the Christian faith has alienated itself from culture—frequently on account of its traditionalistic and institutional rigidity—and must (and thus also can) make a return move by adapting itself to the context. Underlying this presumption is apparently also the idea that this alienation is the reason behind the massive exodus from the church in recent decades and that a change in language is the solution to invert this problem. Another presumption holds that our contemporaries are open in principle toward a Christian interpretation of life, if only its message were presented well enough. Both presumptions still work from a secularization perspective, and do not see the very different features of a detraditionalized and pluralized, post-Christian and postsecular context.[15]

It is of course true that tradition, when it refuses recontextualization in times of contextual shifts, severely jeopardizes its survival, and risks ending up as traditionalism and a mere opposition to culture and society. The *ad extra* language problem, however, is of a different nature and has less to do with the innovation of faith language than an initial familiarity with the "language" and "narrative thickness" of Christianity. It is therefore a misconception to think that an *ad intra* recontextualization will solve the problem of the communicability of Christian faith in a detraditionalized and plu-

14. Cf., for example, Boeve, *God Interrupts History*, chap. 7: "I believe that there is Something more."

15. Cf. what was said about these presumptions in the section "Communicating the Faith in the Public Forum" in this chapter.

ralized public forum, let alone that it would (once more) convince non-and ex-Christians of the validity of the Christian narrative and motivate their (re) turn to the church.

Precluding ad Intra Discussions with ad Extra Arguments

However, presenting an *ad extra* solution to solve *ad intra* questions and discussions is equally harmful for the integrity and vigor of the Christian tradition. Questions pressing for recontextualization, for instance, regarding church organization, priesthood, church and world issues, family ethics (but also with respect to the examples given earlier: the uniqueness of Christ, the sacramental praxis, God images) are not infrequently replied to by referring to the specificity of the language of the tradition. The argument runs then that only those who have truly mastered this language can really comprehend, and also accept, that matters are as they are, and thus cannot be changed. The often difficult but necessary recontextualization is thereby prematurely short-circuited. Those asking legitimate questions for renewal are then reproached with a lack of familiarity with the tradition they want to renew. In other words, the particularity of tradition is played off against its contextuality, or more specifically, against new contextual experiences of being Christian that seek expression in the tradition (to be) handed down. The desire to protect the Christian tradition against a context that is primarily considered inimical results in its closure, in traditionalism and opposition.

Another form of an *ad extra* solution applied to the *ad intra* problematic relates to the reduction of that which is Christian to what is structurally universally human. In varying discussions, such human substratum then functions as a meta-discourse behind/under/above the Christian narrativity. The Christian sacraments, for example, then draw their meaningfulness (and legitimization) exclusively from the fact that sacraments are rituals, and that ritualization constitutes a primordial human need. Such a strategy may be employed equally by those supporting a status quo and by those desiring changes on the level of the *ad intra* problematic. In both cases, anthropological rather than theological arguments are used: for the former, sacraments cannot be changed because rituals precede and constitute subjectivity; for the latter, rituals can be adapted because they are particular instantiations of the need of the *homo religiosus* to ritualize its existence. In both cases the theological dynamic of God's revelation in human language and history is not given its proper due, and a real theological hermeneutics gets obstruct-ed.[16]

The Border between Inner and Outer

To conclude this discussion, let us inquire further: where should we place the border between an inner and an outer perspective on the dialogue of Christian faith with the context in which it is to be situated? Where, from a Christian perspective, does religious otherness start? What should be considered as "internal Christian plurality," and what as "external religious diversity"? Those who draw a very wide frontier, something not completely unusual in a time of accelerated detraditionalization, are de facto conflating ad intra and extra. The ambiguity of a lot of post-Christian religiosity is lost sight of by too quickly recuperating it as a motor of recontextualization (ad intra). Recontextualization then too easily turns into accommodation and assimilation. It is striking that people who analyze contemporary culture and society in terms of secularization rather than pluralization fall into this trap. Secularity and experiences of human wholeness generally then form the points of contact for their theologizing. Far be it from me to minimalize the importance of these experiences for theology, but from within a perspective of pluralization and individualization, they do appear in a different light. Not everything that is recognized as human and/or valuable needs to be immediately accommodated, let alone recuperated, by Christians. However, it is no less true that those who draw the frontier too narrowly lose access to valuable new impulses for recontextualization. They risk closing themselves off from new experiences of being a Christian today and ultimately draw back in the closed particularity of their own tradition, losing the ability to critically and productively engage the context and its challenges.

The latter is, and has always been, precisely the task of Christian faith: bearing witness to the saving activity of a loving God involved in human histories and calling people forth to engage in the coming of God's reign. In this regard, the current post-Christian and postsecular context, whatever its ambiguities, definitely offers new opportunities to contemporary Christians, asking them to play their part in this endeavor.

16. Cf. Boeve, God Interrupts History, chap. 5: "The Sacramental Interruption of the Rites of Passage."

Aspects of Communication

Part 5 ended with Boeve showing the challenges posed to faith communicators by features of contemporary culture. Part 6, while not forgetting these challenges, looks favorably on the promising opportunities opened up by close engagement with aspects of culture, with particular reference to art, literature, and film and the rapidly developing scene of online learning. However, despite the need for positive engagement with culture, in the final two essays Sullivan emphasizes the inescapable and principal medium of communication of faith, whether *ad extra*, in the public domain, or *ad intra*, within the church—that is, the person of the communicator of faith. Ultimately it will be because of his or her personhood that others will be ready to trust, to open up, to be vulnerable to, to receive, and to respond to an act of communication—or, conversely, to resist, resent, refuse, and reject what is offered. The personhood of faith communicators will be instrumental in facilitating or inhibiting the promotion of right relationships between themselves and learners in all contexts, and thus simultaneously will facilitate or inhibit right relationships with the teaching, practices, and way of life being conveyed.

Thus, in this section, virtuous communication receives attention in three ways. First, in Torevell's chapter, the kinds of attentiveness and sensitivity required if one is to engage with aesthetic modes of communication are revealed. The power and the limits of artistic endeavor are exposed, as both of these contributors show, with reference to examples from history and more recent times, how insights into the human condition (as the theatre of God's grace) emerge from aesthetic promptings for us to see and to feel. They also show how the capacity to see is intimately linked to the capacity to feel. As with liturgy, engagement with the aesthetic dimension—here film, art, sculpture, poetry, and the novel—can help us to blend the embodied and the imaginative, the affective and the spiritual, in ways that open us to epiphanies of the divine, that allow us to "see" beyond the literal and further than the limited light of "normal" rationality, and that give us an experience of being moved by what is other, beyond where we are now.

Second, Stuart-Buttle explores the potential of new learning technologies for faith communication among adults. The church has always found herself responding to and deploying new media for communication, although it is often difficult to see clearly the challenges posed by a new mode of communication at the moment when it is adopted, especially if one thinks of its operation as constituting merely a modification of earlier forms. Stuart-Buttle's chapter offers a fine example of the discerning reading of culture frequently called for in earlier chapters of this book. She is strongly rooted in tradition, realistic in assessing the nature of new technological developments, deeply perceptive about their implications for communication and education in matters of faith, and helpful in pointing out the dangers and the opportunities that virtual learning presents for formation. Issues about authority and community, as these arise in new pedagogical contexts, are given careful consideration in her judicious evaluation of online technologies as "fresh wineskins."

Third, in the final two essays, Sullivan returns to the heart of any pedagogy—personal encounter and relationship. The connections between a religious faith and the activity of education have often been close, though sometimes harmonious and sometimes laden with tension. While no effort to educate can be free of prior governing assumptions and beliefs about the nature of the world, the development and destiny of human beings, a picture of how society should "work" and expectations about what constitutes a fulfilled life, this prior "script" can be written too tightly, leaving too little room for maneuver for learners other than passive acceptance of what is offered. However, in reaction against this overprescription, prior "scripts" or worldviews can be kept so much at bay that the educational endeavor is conducted in a piecemeal and fragmented fashion, with no connecting story or guidelines for coherence. Pedagogues—of all kinds—need to guard against the distortions of power that might be imported incognito alongside the proper exercise of authority. If allowing faith considerations to dominate in educational settings is inappropriate, so too is an attempt to divorce faith from education. In "Education and Religious Faith as a Dance," Sullivan mines the metaphor of dance in order to bring out more clearly important features of the moves and relationships inherent in and integral to teaching and learning in general, and to teaching and learning in matters of faith in particular.

Communicating faith is a form of pastoral activity. It is carried out on behalf of the people of God. It aims to empower them for discipleship. It builds bridges between the living tradition of the church and particular people and the contexts in which they find themselves. It must come across with integrity, so that the message resonates with the life of the communicator. Without this, it is bogus and artificial. It must be true to the community it represents. Without this it could slip into being idiosyncratic and misleading about what is being conveyed. It must be empowering of learners (and disciples) so that they can be centers of initiative themselves, take responsibility for their own lives, and possess sufficient freedom to accept willingly, with the grace of God, how to give themselves away. Without such empowerment of learners, educators and communicators invite passivity, timidity, conformity, and rigidity. In "Communicating Faith and Relating in Love," the centrality of loving relationships is underlined as being the real foundation for communicating faith. Loving relationships require constancy in intention but flexibility of expression. Right speech depends on deep listening to God and to God's people. The universal message of God's love is mediated by human love and takes into account the particularities of each person and context.

20   "The Attempt Was All"

The Endeavor of Aesthetics in the Communication of Faith

David Torevell

In this chapter I outline how the novel *Atonement*, by Ian McEwan, and its film adaptation offer important ideas about the expression and communication of faith through aesthetic means.[1] I take "faith" here to mean the ongoing desire and disposition to live according to Christian values, especially those expressed through the life and ministry of Christ. The word "atonement," chosen here as the single word title of the book and film, can be traced back to 1526, when the biblical scholar William Tyndale sought to translate the Latin term *reconciliatio* into English. Originally the noun "atonement," or at-one-ment, implied being reconciled or being at one with others and with God. The verb "to atone" was a later addition and took on the sense of expiation for sin, whereby an *act* of atonement required that something be *done* for an offense committed, invariably including some kind of suffering.[2]

---

    1. Ian McEwan, *Atonement* (London: Jonathan Cape, 2001), screen adaptation by Joe Wright, director, 2007.

    2. See Patrick Sherry, *Images of Redemption: Art, Literature and Salvation* (London: T. and T. Clark, 2003), 31–37.

McEwan's use of this archaic word carries an important contemporary resonance, and his choice of the word is a deliberate device to imply a theological significance to the novel as a whole. The historicity and gravity of the word "atonement" gives a religious undercurrent to the central concern of the work and prompts us into asking: is it possible to speak about "atonement" at the present time, and how might such atoning reconciliation be brought about in and through art?

Not unlike the visual dynamic setup in Rembrandt's classic painting The Return of the Prodigal Son, the recurrent echoing of the phrase "Come back . . . come back" and its reworking at different narrative levels in the book and film present the reader and viewer with a constant reminder of the challenging human need to return to a place of reconciliation after a period of estrangement. The story concerns a terrible miscarriage of justice. In 1935, at the age of thirteen, the precocious central character, Briony Tallis, accuses her family housekeeper's son, Robbie, of a sexual act he did not commit. As a consequence, he is imprisoned and estranged from the person he loves, Cecilia, the sister of Briony. After imprisonment, Robbie finds himself fighting in the Second World War, and he eventually dies at Dunkirk. The story traces the lifelong struggle of Briony to seek forgiveness for her childhood sin. For example, when Briony returns to the flat where Robbie and Cecilia have themselves been reunited after his imprisonment and war experience, she confesses her deep sorrow for the hurt she has caused:

"I'm very very sorry. I have caused you such terrible distress." They continued to stare at her, and she repeated herself. "I'm very sorry."

It sounded so foolish and inadequate, as though she had knocked over a favorite houseplant, or forgotten a birthday

Robbie said softly, "Just do all the things we've asked."

It was almost conciliatory, that "just" but not quite, not yet.[3]

One of the central themes of the book is, how far can the artist achieve atonement through her work? At the end of the novel and film, Briony, now an author, finally expresses her dilemma with this question: "The problem these fifty-five years has been this; how can a novelist achieve atonement when, with her absolute power of deciding outcomes, she is also God? There is no one, no entity or higher power that she can appeal to, to be reconciled

3. McEwan, Atonement, 348.

with, or that can forgive her. There is nothing outside her. In her imagination she has set the limits and the terms. No atonement for God, or novelists, even if they are atheists. It was always an impossible task, and that was
precisely the point. The attempt was all."[4] The *power* and *limits* of the artistic
endeavor are exposed here. The artist is never God. Imagination is possible,
but the *dangers* of the imagination are also evoked (it must be remembered
that Briony's vivid imagination was responsible for seeing things that were
not there and for telling untruths, as well as for her precocious creative writing). And yet, what can take place is an "attempt" to bring about atonement,
realizing at the same time that there is no higher power who might forgive
Briony. So, in the human but courageous artistic attempt, art *can* bring about
something important—*the attempt is all.*

Throughout the narrative of *Atonement*, McEwan invites us to question
how far art, despite its construction of falsity, might bring about reconciliation. The repeated "attempts" at completing the novel are recounted: "There
was a crime . . . it was only in the last version that my lovers end well. . . . All
the preceding drafts were pitiless"[5]—they lacked compassion. The novelist here confesses her earlier cowardice. Briony was "unable to confront her
bereaved sister." But she pointedly adds that if she had later told the truth
and narrated the way it actually was, "Who would want to believe that, except in the service of the bleakest realism?"[6] Those who request what really
happened are given an answer: "The answer is simple: the lovers survive and
flourish."[7] The healing and overriding power of art is recalled at this point:
"As long as there is a single copy, a solitary typescript of my final draft, then
my spontaneous, fortuitous sister and her medical prince survive to love."[8]

Such representations of "invented truth" are not necessarily acts of be-
trayal, but rather spring from a motivation of compassion. Art here becomes
the bulwark against the despair and torment of the world, finding a way forward out of the grim reality of the world. It is an act of virtuous charity, not
cowardly evasion: "I like to think that it isn't weakness or evasion, but a final act of kindness, a stand against oblivion and despair, to let my lovers
live and to unite them at the end."[9] At first she admits she was not tempted to overreach this "stand" by including her own forgiveness by the central characters: "I gave them happiness, but I was not so self-serving as to let

---

4. Ibid., 371.
6. Ibid., 371.
8. Ibid.
5. Ibid., 370.
7. Ibid.
9. Ibid., 371–72.

them forgive me," she writes.[10] But then she questions her earlier decision and adds, "Not quite, not yet. If I had the power to conjure them at my birthday celebration. . . . Robbie and Cecilia, still alive, still in love, sitting side by side in the library, smiling at *The Trials of Arabella*. It's not impossible."[11] Indeed, one might muse, what is possible in the hands of the artist? If the novelist were to set forth a final scene of reconciliation, then she herself would undergo the atonement Robbie and Cecilia had already experienced and art would become an agent of redemption again. The artist here creates the possibility of ceaseless acts of atoning forgiveness.

Atonement navigates delicately these waters of artistic creation, its possibilities and pitfalls, its unlimited horizons of hope as well as its unyielding boundaries. But in company with McEwan's story, I now focus on its transformative potential and suggest that as long as art survives, it has a power to bring about not only a description of those things that matter most to us as human beings, but the thing itself. This redemptive nature of artistic endeavor is explored well by McEwan and director Joe Wright (with assistance from Christopher Hampton's adaptation) and is the concern of this chapter. Anthony Minghella's appearance as interviewer at the close of the film also suggests that the film director, just as much as the novelist, has the potential to be an agency of redemption and reconciliation.

The Artist as "Redeemer"

In the light of the above comments, in this section I examine how art's "attempts" to express those things that matter most to us as human beings have the potential to bring about remarkable changes in the way we view and experience the world. "Historical Reflections" offers some brief historical contextualization in relation to my argument about the expressive power of art. "Transcendence and Revelation" points to the potential of art to encourage feelings of transcendence and revelatory insight into "religious" understandings of the world and the self; finally, in "Embodiment and the Incarnation," I emphasize the embodied dimension of artistic expression in relation to a theology of the incarnation.

If artistic endeavor has a unique power to transfigure ourselves and the world, then it engages in a distinctly "religious" enterprise. Burch Brown's

---

10. Ibid., 372.
11. Ibid.

work on the interface between art and theology is instructive here. He suggests that art is able "to transfigure the world or some hypothetical counterpart," and addresses the human need "to discover, imagine, and come to grips with a world that can be thought and felt to matter, both in its goodness and beauty and in its evil and horror."[12] He goes on: "Because the worlds of art represent things felt to matter (even while distanced from immediate concerns) and amounting to more than what is strictly logical, quantifiable, and measurable, the mind that thinks through the alternative worlds of works of art reconsiders even this present world in terms of qualities and values and purposes."[13] For example, although these "alternative worlds" are self-consciously exposed in *Atonement*, their force is never undermined. *Atonement* confronts us with both the reality of sin or wrongdoing *and* its related imperative to seek atonement; in the process, we are enticed to consider the impact that art itself might have on the world. Although the theological contextualization might be somewhat awkward or jarring for some in the twenty-first century, the human challenge is the same—to *feel* and think through the human predicament of the characters, to measure their responses against ours, and finally to reflect on how this vision of a redeemed world is represented by art. Like McEwan, therefore, I highlight here the redemptive significance of art in its capacity to represent the world as it is, how it might be changed, and to offer glimpses into what it might be like in the future—in other words, to demonstrate art's atoning and religious vision of the world.

But how does art do this? Primarily, I think, by its prophetic appeal to feeling. By this I mean that in offering an emotional as well as intellectual challenge to see how the world really is and then *how it might be*, art is able to call forth a moral sensitivity from its audience. Burch Brown comments that due to art's distinctive mode of communication, "the *heart* itself benefits."[14] But "Where the worlds of art and actuality converge, and yet in converging do not conform to the heart's desire, there it becomes the heart's will to transform or be transformed. Art then can become prophetic in mode, showing what is unjust or senseless, and possibly what is required in response. . . . Mimesis in art is always in some degree metamorphosis."[15]

12. Frank Burch Brown, quoted by Gesa Thiessen, *Theological Aestethics: A Reader* (London: SCM, 2004), 266.

13. Ibid., 267.   14. Ibid.

15. Ibid., 267–68.

What is required in response to a broken or sinful world is what the artist is best at showing. The reaction of Briony to her "original sin" was to last over a lifetime. There was no one act of atonement, but rather a relentless working through of her own guilt over time. Even at the very end of the novel/film the atoning process continues.

Art, then, has the means to become an *effective agency* as well as descriptor of redemption. From theology's side, it could be claimed that abstract doctrinal formulations of faith are made real, vibrant, and personal through art. In his discussion of images of redemption Sherry puts it like this: "There are fundamental responses like grief, guilt, repentance, expiation, and forgiveness, which are part of the texture of ordinary life. Such responses underlie both doctrine and theology. . . . Putting the point another way, one might say that experiences and behavior underlie soteriologies."[16] I am not suggesting this is *why* art expresses such human emotions (i.e., to illuminate religious doctrines), but I am arguing that many theological doctrines themselves are rooted in human feelings and experience and that art has a capacity to engage with such human concerns effectively.

Rahner's work on aesthetics is helpful in examining art's capacity to engage with human concerns and therefore to be a *locus theologicus*. He claims the arts ought to be seen as a natural companion of theology, since they invariably express humanity's existential concerns: "If and insofar as theology is man's reflexive self-expression about himself in the light of divine revelation, we could propose the thesis that theology cannot be complete until it appropriates these arts as an integral moment of itself and its own life, until the arts become an intrinsic moment of theology itself."[17] It is incumbent upon the church, therefore, to recognize the role the arts must play. They have the potential to appeal to the personal concerns, hopes, and fears of all humanity by their exploration of the depths of the human existence, offering revelatory insights into humanity, and therefore into the divine. The medium itself expresses this revelation; as Rahner asks in relation to music: "why should a person not think that when he hears a Bach oratorio, he comes into contact in a very unique way with God's revelation about the human not only by the words it employs, but by the music itself?"[18] Art puts a person "in touch with those depths of human experience wherein reli-

16. Sherry, *Images of Redemption*, 6.
17. Karl Rahner, quoted by Thiessen, *Theological Aesthetics*, 218.
18. Ibid., 219.

gious experience takes place";[19] sadly, he contends, we lack a "poetic theology" that can do precisely this. However, art need not be explicitly "religious" in content to achieve this. Rahner writes, "it could be that a painting of Rembrandt, even not religious . . . confronts a person in his total self in such a way as to awaken in him the whole question of existence. Then it is a religious painting in the strict sense."[20] For example, when certain works of Rembrandt make divine forgiveness and grace "visible," they become, as Sherry reminds us, far more than theological illustrations, and consequently their expressions of human redemption cannot be easily translated into neat theological discourse.

I believe this is what the contemporary British sculptor Antony Gormley is suggesting when he comments on his own work: "When we are touched what part of us is moved? Is it our minds, our spirits or our souls? And what is the difference? I'm afraid I don't have much interest in the eternal soul—at least it's not much use just now—but the spirit: that part of us that is quickened when something really gets to us I have great respect for. An adventure in proving the existence of the spirit in the postmodern deconstructive age was what "Field" turned out to be."[21] Gormley has commented that he wants to create "an image that is open enough to be interpreted widely, that has multiple and generative potential for meaning but is strong enough to be a focus."[22] This hope, I think, is realized in his works *Angel of the North* and *Another Place*, which invite a range of responses, both theological and secular. The *Angel of the North* is situated near the AI road in Gateshead, England, and stands twenty meters high with a wingspan of fifty-four meters protecting the surrounding landscape. Made from two hundred tons of steel, it has attracted worldwide attention since its positioning in February 1998. *Another Place* is a composition of one hundred iron human figures looking out toward the horizon of Crosby Beach, Merseyside, England, and stretching one kilometer into the Irish Sea. I have used this work myself to offer reflection on the liturgical challenges facing the Christian church today, but it can quite easily be interpreted in more secular terms as an expression of the ceaseless human search for happiness and fulfillment.[23]

19. Ibid.   20. Ibid., 221.

21. Antony Gormley, quoted by Graham Howes, *The Art of the Sacred: An Introduction to the Aesthetics of Art and Belief* (London : I. B. Tauris, 2007), 141.

22. Ibid., 141.

23. See David Torevell, *Liturgy and the Beauty of the Unknown: Another Place* (Aldershot, UK: Ashgate, 2007).

Conversely, explicitly religious representations always have the potential to connect with what might be called the *spiritual dimension of human existence*. The success of the Seeing Salvation exhibition at the National Gallery, London, in 2000 is instructive here. The exhibition brought together a collection of paintings from different historical periods that represented moments in Christ's life, from his birth through to his death and resurrection. It attracted thousands of visitors from around the world. Why, we might ask, in an increasingly secular culture, were paintings of the life of Christ so popular? Was it because the artists' work in the exhibition somehow presented the events of Christ's life as holding *human significance* and their ability to express universal meaning? It was not the historical details of the episodes in Christ's life that seemed to matter, but the capacity to engage onlookers emotionally with images reflective of their own humanity. As MacGregor comments, "Theological concepts must be given human dimensions . . . paintings are uniquely able to address universal questions through the intelligence of the heart. In the hands of great artists, the different moments and aspects of Christ's life become archetypes of all human experience. These are pictures that explore truths not just for Christians, but for everyone."[24] For example, one visitor to the exhibition recorded how, on seeing an early fifteenth-century miniature crib with a motionless Christ, she immediately thought of one of her children's crib death. Another wrote in gratefulness to the curator: "I found the exhibition intensely moving and as a mother who had just lost her son . . . unforgettable in its imagery and emotion. Thank you."[25]

Some might contend that the artist is in danger of becoming a semidivine figure, since she has in her possession (to borrow McEwan's phrase), an "absolute power of deciding outcomes."[26] Clearly, the artist does have mastery over a range of materials and devices to decide outcomes. Coupled with the creative force of the imagination, this constitutes a formidable power. Indeed, the history of artistic endeavor reveals how numerous artists have seen themselves as co-creators with the divine and have rejoiced in their influence on the world. In believing this, they take McEwan's notion much further by suggesting that not only are their "attempts" potentially re-

24. Neil MacGregor, "Introduction," in Gabriele Finaldi, *The Image of Christ: The Catalogue of the Exhibition Seeing Salvation*, 7 (London: National Gallery, 2000).

25. Howes, *The Art of the Sacred*, 52.

26. McEwan, *Atonement*, 371.

storative, but are effectively so, since they actually share in God's redemptive life. No higher vocation of the artist is possible. The artistic endeavor here is literally God-given. It is the approach that Pope John Paul II celebrates in his *Letter to Artists* (1999).

Historical Reflections

It is helpful to review briefly key moments in the history of art to appreciate more clearly its significance in the theological endeavor. It was during the scholastic period of the thirteenth century and beyond that theology itself underwent a radical transformation as it moved out of the monastery and cathedral into the university setting. What characterized scholastic theology was the substitution of an affective understanding of faith by an abstract and argumentative one. I think Seasoltz is right to suggest that faith transmuted into more of an intellectual assent to propositions rather than an incorporation into the mystical and indeed social body of the church, often released through a embodied and affective experience of the divine. He comments, "This resulted in a subtle shift in Christian priorities as proofs marginalized affections, as analysis displaced poetry, as mind took precedence over heart, and as religious language changed from communication charged with affective and aesthetic overtones to one dominated by critical analysis and rigorous argument."[27] Consequently, the emotional dimension of Christianity became less important, and with it, those aesthetic vehicles of the divine, including art and architecture, decreased in significance. The faith experience of Christians in the West was being transmuted from a largely holistic absorption into the Christian mysteries through aesthetic means into a predominantly mentalist approach. This was to be exacerbated by the Protestant Reformation's wariness about the aesthetic and the bodily.[28] The development of empirical and scientific investigation further developed this split between religious and intellectual life, placing science at the pinnacle and as the most reliable means of knowing the truth. With the invention of the printing press came an encouragement to more individual means of accessing knowledge, with the result that corporate and social

27. R. Kevin Seasoltz, *A Sense of the Sacred: Theological Foundations of Christian Art and Architecture* (London: Continuum, 2005), 22.

28. See Philip Mellor and Chris Shilling, *Re-forming the Body: Religion, Community and Modernity* (London: Sage, 1998).

life became attenuated. As the bonds that had tied communities together through aesthetic experience of the divine within ecclesial contexts began to decline, a new understanding of the importance of the arts emerged.

The word "aesthetic" was given much of its contemporary significance after A. G. Baumgarten, the German disciple of Leibniz, published his tract *Aesthetica* in 1736. From this time on, aesthetics became largely divorced from religion. Before the eighteenth century, the majority of artistic creations had retained an unbroken association with the divine, seeing their role as co-creators, as persons who had received special gifts from the Creator enabling them to produce works of beauty and truth, some of which would give glory and praise to God. During modernity, however, a radical reappraisal of the arts took place as they gradually came to substitute religion as the primary agent in nurturing the "soul," the "spiritual," and the inner life, whatever modern men and women reconceived such vocabulary to mean. Meaning and purpose in artistic endeavor became separated from religious activity. Inevitably, this had enormous consequences for the way education itself was conceived. Art, not religion, was the guiding force. As Scruton notes, "The aesthetic began to replace the religious as the central strand in education. Art and literature ceased to be recreations and became studies."[29]

By coining the word "aesthetics," Baumgarten referred to those areas of philosophical reflection that were primarily governed by feeling and intuition and that could not be definitely analyzed and conceptualized. As a consequence, science became a separate area of investigation to theology. Prior to this time artists were primarily craftsmen, skilled workers who knew how to design and construct buildings. Beauty was not a distinct quality for which one worked but rather a natural consequence of applying oneself to the task in hand: "What we currently call art was the natural beauty and truthfulness that resulted from humanly made things well executed."[30]

The Enlightenment, therefore, produced an understanding of art separated from religion, and thereafter much art replaced religion in its attempts to express the most profound questions confronting humanity, even if artists have found themselves expressing the absurdity or apparent meaninglessness of human life rather than its deeper significance.

---

29. Roger Scruton, *An Intelligent Person's Guide to Culture* (London: Duckworth, 1998), 28.
30. Seasoltz, *A Sense of the Sacred*, 25.

Transcendence and Revelation

The eighteenth-century philosopher Immanuel Kant assisted in reversing the hierarchy of religion and aesthetics, but in a very different manner. He did not replace God with art, but by arguing that aesthetic judgment was a means of experiencing *through feeling* intimations of the divine, he gave the arts pride of place. Now religious experience was set alongside aesthetic experience. For Kant rational argument could not prove God's existence, but through experiencing beauty and the sublime, it was possible to have hints of a divine presence. Feeling and the imagination became paramount. In *Critique of Judgment* he suggests that aesthetic experience triggers ineffable feelings of transcendence that at times overwhelm us. The artist is able to "exhibit aesthetic ideas; and by an aesthetic idea I mean a presentation of the imagination which prompts much thought, but to which no determinate thought, i.e., no (determinate) *concept* can be adequate, so that no language can express it completely and allow us to grasp it."[31]

The artist, according to Kant (and McEwan would surely agree), has an enormous power given to her through the imaginative faculty to express profound human feelings and experiences. She is able to use her imaginative creativity to express those things that are invisible. He writes that the "imagination (in its role) as a productive cognitive power is very mighty when it creates, as it were, another nature out of the material that actual nature gives it. Such presentations of the imagination we may call *ideas* . . . they are inner intuitions to which no concept can completely be adequate."[32] It is the poet, suggests Kant, who besides giving "sensible expression to rational ideas of invisible things, the realm of the blessed, the realm of hell, eternity, creation and so on" also represents those things "exemplified in experience, such as death, envy, and all the other vices, as well as love, fame, and so on; . . . he ventures to give these sensible expression in a way that goes beyond the limits of experience, namely with a completeness for which no example can be found in nature."[33]

Kant's notion of the power of art is advanced further by those who designate a "presence" or "mystery of being" to its various manifestations. The

---

31. Immanuel Kant, quoted by Clive Cazeaux, *The Continental Aesthetics Reader* (London: Routledge, 2000), 25.

32. Ibid.

33. Ibid.

Orthodox theologian Sergei Bulgakov suggests in *The Lamb of God* (*Agnets Bo-zhi*) that the incarnation is the divine means of transfiguring the world into an advanced form of beauty. From the beginning, the Word puts God at the service of the world and in this act of obedience prefigures the obedient act of atonement in the passion; the son is, as the Book of the Apocalypse confirms, "the Lamb slain since the beginning of the world" (13:8). However, the incarnation is worthless unless there is in humanity an innate capacity to be united with God in spite of the presence of sin.[34] Consequently, Bulgakov presents us with an *ontology of the image* in relation to humanity's ability to see, make, reflect, and receive images, suggesting that images of Christ depend on a prototype or original image that are reality's ideal reproductions. Nichols comments about Bulgakov's theology of art: "The artist tries to point to the authentic being of things by giving them a more fully iconic expression than they enjoy in nature."[35] Art has the capacity to understand form and is able to grasp and communicate "the beauty of the primal ideal image of things."[36] Bulgakov writes that the "creative act of art, by iconizing a thing, consists first of all in perceiving by means of its prototype; then in expressing that prototype in appropriate media. . . . The icon is the expression of the true primal image which, by way of the thing represented, has a real being in the world."[37] This "real being in the world" gives to artistic expression an immense significance, for it is through art that we begin to see the true nature of things and their mystery of being. Art is given an immense status here, since the "attempt" is itself an expression of truth.

Others, like Nichols, point less ambitiously to *analogies* between works of art and religious revelation. He suggests that art carries an inexhaustible plenitude that entices us to experience a transcendent meaning beyond the expression itself, without ever rendering the material it uses superfluous. The affective world the artist creates confronts us with an address that is morally and spiritually challenging. Art also has the capacity to create a bond of sympathy with the world expressed that encourages a diminution of the ego. Nichols puts it like this: "The revelatory event breaks in . . . as the aesthetic experience arises in a moment of communion from the art object

---

34. Aidan Nichols, *Redeeming Beauty: Soundings in Sacral Aesthetics* (Aldershot, UK: Ashgate, 2007), 78.
35. Ibid., 79.
36. Ibid., 79.
37. Sergei Bulgakov, quoted by Nichols, *Redeeming Beauty*, 79–80.

in a gallery or church, and he finds himself reorganizing his own world of meaning, what counts for him as 'the real' in its light."[38] Divine revelation, like art, never imposes its claims on us, but offers an invitation to a form of life, encouraging us to realign our own existence in relation to the vision on offer.

Aesthetics has a particular advantage over natural theology here, since it is able to use and point to concrete form as the creative vehicle toward mystery beyond form. In this, it echoes the cataphatic and apophatic nature of all religious knowledge by using what is known to lead us to the unknown. If we refer back to Kant, we might acknowledge that the transcendence that art invites us to "experience" is always ironically "beyond experience." We might say that art has the power to express the mystery of being through and beyond sensory experience. Nichols describes it thus: "What the artwork mediates to us is a particular reality in its depth. It sheds light on that reality exactly in the mystery of its being. . . . The artist's form, concrete, particular, given, cataphatic, yields up to us a meaning which is inexhaustible, mysterious and apophatic."[39]

Embodiment and the Incarnation

Here I develop further Kant's understanding of artistic creation as bringing about "another nature" through nature itself, with reference to the incarnation in Christianity. The eighth-century iconoclastic debate surrounding the embodied expression of Christianity pushed the church (due to its fear of the sin of idolatry) into coming to terms with the legitimacy of using the material (in this case, visible images) to express the divine. If we extend this notion of the expression of the story of Christianity more generally, we are alerted to some important strands in the communication of faith. Such communication is often best served by means of a synaesthetic matrix located within embodied representation.[40] When the expression of faith is able to blend simultaneously two or more senses to produce a heightened perception of its content, then its communication becomes potentially enthralling. For example, *Atonement* not only uses a sound score of repetitious typewrit-

---

38. Nichols, *The Art of God Incarnate: Theology and Image in Christian Tradition* (London: DLT, 1980), 113.

39. Nichols, *The Art of God Incarnate*, 116.

40. See Don Saliers, *Music and Theology* (Nashville: Abingdon Press, 2007).

ing to emphasize the constructed mode of the film from an existing written form, but presents to the viewers' eyes the tortuous but redemptive working out of *Atonement* on screen. We literally see and hear (and therefore correspondingly feel) how atonement might be practiced in actual human terms and (depending on our personal acquaintance with the Christian narrative) how this might be related to divine atonement. This is not a cerebral act of propositional assent, but a holistic incorporation into an aesthetic representation.

Hart is right to suggest that the church must be wary of *abstracting* the meaning of the Christian story from the concrete details of Christ's ministry as set down in scripture. He writes, "That God has graciously placed himself in our midst for touching, hearing and seeing means that this same 'physical' and historical manifestation must always be the place where we put ourselves in our repeated efforts to know him again and ever more fully."[41] In the epiphanies that are presented to us through the arts we always come to know more than the material. Our imagination and reception might fail us when we do not see or hear more than is presented to us through artistic modes, but as Hart cleverly puts it in his appraisal of the necessity of the material: "these same eyes and ears do not see and hear *less* than what is presented physically, and what they see and hear is bound up inextricably with the 'more' that is there to be discerned."[42]

The notion of seeing "more" than the seen is important and has implications for the social significance of art. All art attempts to communicate something more than the eye can see, the ear can hear, or the body can touch. The German sociologist Georg Simmel, although often regarded as offering a pessimistic prognosis on modern culture, believed in the enduring human need for transcendence. His advocacy of aesthetic value in *The Philosophy of Money* is based on its dissociation with utility value. But in order for things to have value there must be a distance between consciousness and the object. Aesthetic experience has a double-edged nature, since it both draws observers into the object and at the same time remains distanced from their subjectivity.[43] Appreciation of beauty contrasts with a utilitarian handling of things, and the tragedy of culture is that it has fostered a com-

41. Trevor Hart, "Through the Arts": Hearing, Seeing and Touching the Truth," in *Beholding the Glory: Incarnation through the Arts*, ed. Jeremy Begbie, 24 (London: DLT, 2000).

42. Hart, "Through the Arts," 23.

43. See Cazeaux, *The Continental Aesthetics Reader*, 299.

modified and calculated form of social relations, erasing the more elusive and "unseen" manifestations of reality. Money and religion are opposed, since the latter offers a gaze at what lies beyond calculation and utility. Flanagan comments that Simmel's approach to religion "is directed to its social manifestations in ways that direct attention towards refraction of the unseen. These are expressed in terms of color, the vivid property of light of religion, properties that bind form into a theological content";[44] he adds that Simmel's "distinctive contribution to understanding the link between visual culture and piety lies in his emphasis on how the unseen acts through acts of the creative imagination."[45] For example, in one of Simmel's essays on Christianity and art (1997), he addresses the linkage between this world and the next, as he points to art's empowerment "to the soul to supplement one world with the other and thereby to experience itself at the point of union."[46]

Conclusion

The high acclaim given to the film *Atonement* is a testimony to its enduring and timeless themes of repentance and reconciliation and to its evocative reflection on the nature and purpose of art. Surely the huge level of international recognition enjoyed by the film reflects the power of that medium to communicate those values that matter most to human beings and, in so doing, to offer a vision of the possibility of a redeemed world. Although McEwan as artist suggests that there is no higher power to which he can appeal—"no atonement for God or novelists"—I have tried to demonstrate that art's "religious" nature can be defended and sustained. And, by referring to McEwan's *Atonement*, I have argued that art itself can operate as a redemptive offering to an imperfect and disjointed world, largely through its representation of *what is and what might be*. This is part of its importance and why artists' courageous and ongoing "attempts" are so much in need: indeed, the attempt is all.

---

44. Kieran Flanagan, *Seen and Unseen: Visual Culture, Sociology and Theology* (London: Palgrave, Macmillan, 2004), 160.
45. Flanagan, *Seen and Unseen*, 171.
46. Georg Simmel, quoted by Flanagan, *Seen and Unseen*, 174.

21   Communicating Faith and
Online Learning

Ros Stuart-Buttle

This chapter focuses on communicating faith through online learning. It reflects my experience as both a practitioner and researcher of online adult religious education across varied programs, including undergraduate theology and religious studies, adult faith formation in the community, and initial and ongoing formation for lay, diaconal, and priestly ministries. My experience lies mainly within the Roman Catholic sector, but it is hoped that the wider Christian educative community will also find something of interest and value.

The chapter hopes to add voice to an emerging discussion about online learning technologies and lifelong education in Christian faith. It is not possible here to explore the nature of contemporary digital society, the rise of learning technologies or their claims for transforming education, nor the vast arena of religion online. Nor is it possible to present an account of my own journey into web-based Christian education or my work within online learning and adult faith formation. However, this chapter does aim to say something about online communication and online learning, as well as highlight opportunities and pitfalls relating to the implications for adult education in faith. Two particular areas of focus emerge, relating to online community and online authority.

Starting Points

Two key presuppositions are made at the start of this chapter. The first concerns the fundamental principles that underpin a Roman Catholic understanding of religious education and faith formation. At the core is recognition of a positive anthropology of the human person created *imago dei* with human dignity, goodness, and freedom. There is a belief in the sacramentality of the created world and human living, graced and transformed by the presence of God at work in the ordinary and everyday. An emphasis on relationship and community shows us who we are as beings in relation to God and one another and directs us toward a common, shared Eucharistic life. The commitment to a 2,000-year-old living tradition of scripture, experience, and teaching by generations who have gone before invites us to be a pilgrim people for today, called to work for social justice, Gospel values, and the common good of God's kingdom on earth with a spirituality of openness, hospitality, and inclusion. A holistic understanding and vision of Catholic education considers the "whole" person and aims not only to form and inform, but ultimately to transform both the individual person and human society.[1]

The second presupposition is that today we live and learn in an online world. Before the early 1990s the Internet was still little known, yet it is now viewed as the fastest-growing and most sophisticated communications system in human civilization; it has been described as "a resource of unparalleled possibilities."[2] Brief statistics help illustrate this point. Internet World Statistics indicates that there were 40,362,842 Internet users in the United Kingdom (representing 66.4 percent of the population) in December 2007, an increase of over 162 percent compared to the year 2000.[3] The average Internet user in the UK spends around 23 hours a week online, amounting to over 50 days a year.[4] Data from the Pew Internet and American Life Project

1. Thomas H. Groome, *What Makes Us Catholic* (San Francisco: HarperOne, 2003).
2. Alan Jolliffe, Jonathan Ritter, and David Stevens, eds., *The Online Learning Handbook: Developing and Using Web-based Learning* (London: Routledge, 2001), 1.
3. "Usage and Population Statistics," *Internet World Stats*, http://www.internetworldstats.com/ (accessed July 2, 2008).
4. *YouGov*, http://www.yougov.com/uk/ (accessed July 1, 2008).

indicates a similar increase in the U.S. Internet population and online activity. A study from 2006 shows 73 percent of respondents (about 147 million American adults) to be regular Internet users, up from 66 percent (about 133 million adults) from January 2005.[5] The rise of Web 2.0 technologies for online collaboration and social networking also show rising trends, especially among younger generations. It has been estimated that more than 250 million people globally use an online networking site regularly, while MySpace, launched in 2003, has attracted more than 116 million registered members, cementing online social networks as a global cultural phenomenon.[6] While statistics are open to interpretation and can only offer a snapshot at best, nevertheless it does seem safe to claim that Internet technologies are now a routine feature of contemporary living for increasing numbers of people.[7]

Internet and Education

The influence and impact of Internet technologies for education and training can be seen across education sectors from K–16 schools to tertiary education and both formal and informal lifelong learning. The Internet, used initially to augment distance learning, now belongs to mainstream educational theory and practice. Online platforms or virtual environments that build innovative networks of communication and shared interaction demonstrate the increasing adoption of diverse e-learning applications including email, synchronous chat, asynchronous discussion forums, weblogs, wikis, and e-portfolios as key tools in a new pedagogy for collaborative networking.[8] Increasingly it seems that opportunities for learning now exist in a myriad of ways. Schools, colleges, seminaries, and universities frequently offer a multiplicity of sites (home, work, college, local center), a va-

5. "Internet, Broadband, and Cell Phone Statistics," *Pew Internet*, http://www.pewinternet.org/ (accessed January 16, 2009).

6. Financial Times Online, "*The High Priestess of Internet Friendship*," available online at http://www.ft.com/cms/s/59ab33da-64c4-11db-90fd-0000779e2340.html (accessed February 2, 2007).

7. Lorna Dawson and Douglas Cowan, eds., *Religion Online: Finding Faith on the Internet* (New York and London: Routledge, 2004).

8. Department for Children, Schools and Families, *Towards a Unified eLearning Strategy: Consultation Document* (Nottingham: DfES Publications, 2003); and Department for Children, Schools and Families, *Harnessing Technology: Transforming Learning and Children's Services* (Nottingham: DfES Publications, 2005); see also British Educational Communications and Technology Agency, *Learning Networks in Practice* (2007), available online at http://www.becta.org.uk/.

riety of modes (full- or part-time), a choice of times (day, evening, weekend, block) and with increasing options for technology to create a virtual campus for blended or fully online learning. From educational institutions around the world there has been steady growth in the number, type, and availability of degrees, study programs, and courses using online educational technologies and Internet delivery. The advertising and marketing of courses and qualifications, with the student as customer choosing which institution and which course is "best buy" and "best fit," is commonplace in today's educational climate. In a Western culture of increasing individualism, free choice, and self-determination, the reality is that online programs in Christian faith are likely to be chosen and conducted in one's own time, pace, and place and obtained from a provider who may no longer be a local educational or ecclesial institution, but a distant or virtual service offering specific learning for purchasers who are both clients and learners. The greater flexibility offered by online delivery, together with a growing modularization of courses and costs, an emphasis on certification and accreditation, within a language and culture of quality control and assurance, all add up to a changing educational scene for both the learner and the learning institution in contemporary digital society.[9]

The research literature field and the reflections of e-learning practitioners communicate the potential of the virtual environment for collaborative and creative learning. Widespread claims are made for the benefits that online learning can bring. A greater flexibility of access and widening participation in education sits alongside a new diversity of education provision. Innovative approaches to online teaching and learning pedagogy are linked to improved learner engagement and educational experience. Multimedia content and e-learning design can create participative and collaborative learning opportunities as well as foster personalized and self-directed learning. New feedback and assessment practices using learning technologies can bring educational advantages for both learner and institution. However, as the body of research literature and practitioner evidence builds, the "gains" can be balanced by increasingly discernable "losses." Technological concerns relating to learner accessibility, systems compatibility, and usability cannot be ignored, while social and educational aspects of online learning raise challenges and questions such as learner non-participation, the quality of online

9. Peter Jarvis, *Adult and Continuing Education* (London: Routledge, 1995).

communication and relationships within a learning network, the changing role of the teacher, clashes between traditional institutional approaches and virtual delivery, and indeed the very question of whether technology contributes to or hinders educational provision and effective learning.

Virtual Treasure or Trap?

Religious communication and activity are not excluded from this unfolding online culture. Evidence from online search engines suggests that millions of people use the Internet for religious purposes and that the number of religious websites has grown exponentially in recent years. A Pew Internet and American Life Project Religion Surfers survey in 2001 showed 28 percent of Americans using the Internet to engage in a range of religious activities.[10] A Cyberchurch Report predicted that during the course of the decade, up to 100 million Americans would rely on the Internet for some form of religious or spiritual activity.[11] A glance at the vast array of Roman Catholic websites, estimated to comprise over 70 percent of the total Christian presence online, indicates the importance of the Internet for communication, mission, education, and evangelization in a contemporary world. My own faith tradition has seen a recent explosion in use of the Internet and related online media for communicating faith and bringing the Gospel to a wider audience in a dialogical engagement of church with today's culture. Benedict XVI's message for the 43rd World Communications Day states:

The digital generation has come of age in the world of computers, mobile telephones, text and instant messaging, blogging, platforms for video content, internet chat rooms and on-line social networks. It would be a mistake, however, to see these changes as merely technological; they have also revolutionized the culture of communications. They have changed the ways people communicate, the ways they associate and form communities, the ways by which they learn about the world.[12]

---

10. *Pew Internet and American Life Project Religion Surfers Survey 2001*, in *Religion Online: Finding Faith on the Internet*, ed. Lorna Dawson and Douglas Cowan, 19 (New York and London: Routledge, 2004).

11. The Barna Group, *Cyberchurch Report*, 2001, in Heidi Campbell, "Embodied Church vs. Disembodied Congregation: Challenges Created by Online Religious Networks," *Journal of Media and Religion* 3, no.2 (2004): 81–99.

12. Benedict XVI, Message for 43rd World Communications Day, *New Technologies, New Relationships*, May 24, 2009, available online at http://www.zenit.org (accessed January 23, 2009).

The new media technologies have been explored in magisterial documents on social communications since the 1960s. A number of thinkers both inside and outside the church have also wrestled with the nature and impact of the Internet on society, especially in relation to human communication, identity, relationships, and ethics. Some see the advance of technology as a threat, while others seek to relate church and culture in a more positive engagement. The call to take up online technologies for education and lifelong learning in the church therefore raises a number of questions. Should Catholic educators move into online religious education and formation? How can the new communications technologies be employed wisely and appropriately? Do we risk a naïve assimilation and integration of technology into our practice of religious education and of absorbing the expectations and values of the culture in which technology is embedded? Do we make implicit or explicit assumptions that Internet-based communications technologies cannot be used within religious education and faith formation? If we do so, do we risk losing touch with where people are at today? So a key question that underpins this might ask if online communication technologies are a virtual treasure or trap for Christian education in faith.

Online Relationships and Community

Web 2.0 is changing our understanding of human communications, behavior, and relationships. New forms of communications are fostered by digital technology. But what is the quality of relationships in an Internet network? Do web-based communications create new links between people or replace existing ones? Who is my neighbor in cyberspace? Do Internet relationships and online communities bring genuine communication or merely a networked connection?[13] Such questions concern the Christian educator. If education in faith looks toward forming and transforming human persons in fullness of relationship to God and neighbor, then the value and dignity of the human person and the nature of online community and human relationships demand attention. The Pontifical Council for Social Communications document *Ethics in Communication* reminds us that Gospel communication must always be genuine, truthful, and serve au-

13. David Pullinger, *Information Technology and Cyberspace* (London: Darton, Longman, and Todd, 2001).

thentic community among persons. This serves as both measure and challenge for Christian online learning.[14]

Western society is claimed to be information-rich but wisdom-poor. Social fragmentation, the fracturing of family life, the increasing isolation of individuals, the anonymity of communicating online, and an illusion of superficial sociality are charges laid at the feet of information and communication technologies, specifically the Internet. Sociologists have challenged the concept of a digitalized network society as a source of meaning for personal and communal identity and relationship.[15] This is a serious concern for those who seek to use virtual technologies for educating others in theology and faith formation. If we hold that the Trinitarian *communio* lies at the core of understanding not only the personhood of God, but also ourselves as human persons called to share in both the divine relationship and in human community, then Christian online educators must work toward building genuine relationships in faith in the online network or virtual classroom. Given the nature of the digital medium, the diverse environment of a typical online user group and the transitory nature of an online student cohort, this might seem initially to be something of a paradox or even impossibility.

Rheingold's seminal work claimed that

Virtual communities are social aggregations that emerge from the Net when enough people carry on public discussions long enough, with sufficient human feeling, to form webs of personal relationships in cyberspace.[16]

Here we might distinguish local community from associative community. The former refers to people sharing a common interest in a specific geographical locality. The latter refers to a dispersed group with shared attributes, activity, or experience. Evidence suggests that online Christian networks based around local physical communities and churches tend to support and supplement rather than supplant local church offline activity and involvement.[17] But Christians also gather in associative communities

14. Pontifical Council for Social Communications, *Ethics in Communication* (2000), available online at http://www.vatican.va/roman_curia/pontifical_councils/pccs/documents/rc_pc_pccs_doc_20000530_ethics-communications_en.html.

15. David Lyon, *Jesus in Disneyland: Religion in Postmodern Times* (Cambridge: Polity Press/Blackwell, 2000).

16. Howard Rheingold, *The Virtual Community: Homesteading on the Electronic Frontier* (Cambridge, Mass.: MIT Press, 2000).

17. Heidi Campbell, *Exploring Religious Community Online* (New York: Peter Lang, 2005).

on the Web for religious and spiritual activity.[18] This offers new possibilities to counteract the radical individualism of a contemporary world.[19] Physical barriers of distance and isolation can be overcome for people separated or marginalized by distance, age, lifestyle, illness, or work circumstances, while personal, ecclesial, and spiritual relationships are enabled by sharing in virtual faith networks.[20]

The idea of virtual community is not without critics. Can computer-mediated networking offer genuine community, or is it a pseudo-community that, far from enabling meaningful contact, only represents impersonal and disembodied contact among virtual strangers? The argument runs that it is impossible to construct meaningful communities in the artificiality of digitized space, as there is no meaningful person-to-person interaction that occurs. Instead it is only a networked individualism.[21] But can genuine human relationships exist only by meeting in physical person? Certainly, online communications lack physical clues of voice, facial expression, gesture, body language, touch, emotions (although developing digital audio/visual technologies are changing this, and online netiquette has developed shorthand symbols or emoticons to express and share emotion and feelings online). But are physical human embodiment and presence necessary for genuine community and relationship to occur? Some say yes, that we understand ourselves as an embodied Christian community with an incarnational faith that is denied when physical presence is lacking. Others claim that when they gather online with their virtual learning group, together they can and do understand the promise of Jesus' presence and see themselves as part of the church's community of faith.

A further challenge arises over the understanding of human self and identity in the virtual world. Who am I online, and how do you know that I am who I say that I am? How does the religious educator "know" his/her student online? The communication of human identity and exchange is a highly complex process of interconnecting factors. In cyberspace, old patterns of identity and presence are changing. The Internet can be an information

18. Franz Foltz and Frederick Foltz, "Religion on the Internet: Community and Virtual Existence," *Bulletin of Science, Technology and Society* 23, no. 4 (2003): 321.

19. Gordon Graham, *The Internet: A Philosophical Inquiry* (London: Routledge, 1999).

20. Gwilym Beckerlegge, *From Sacred Text to Internet* (Aldershot, UK, and Hants/Burlington, VT: Ashgate, 2002).

21. Campbell, "Embodied Church vs. Disembodied Congregation: Challenges Created by Online Religious Networks," *Journal of Media and Religion* 3, no. 2 (2004): 81–99.

store, a social networking space, a means of transactions, a tool for education, and a place for entertainment and play.[22] If we view cyberspace primarily as a medium where different personas are adopted for fun, entertainment, or imaginary role-play, then I can be one person online and another person in physical life. I can have multiple personae in both real and virtual worlds. But what is acceptable in healthy online role-play is not acceptable if it involves concealment of identity for illegal or immoral purposes, or if it disconnects online personalities from the moral framework (and here I do not underestimate the dangers of cyberspace for encouraging addictive or destructive patterns of identity and behavior). So the question of "who am I online?" becomes significant for Catholic educators who seek to help persons to genuinely grow in knowledge and understanding of themselves, of one another, and of God.

Christian faith formation belongs to the community of faith. The "indispensable role and context of community" have been recognized throughout Roman Catholic documents on education since Vatican II. Christian faith grows and develops in familial and ecclesial community, not personal isolation. The mature Christian is "enabled by the community, within the community to contribute to the life of the community." The community is the "source, locus and means" of all catechesis and education gathered in the name of Christ.[23] This must apply to the virtual faith learning community, too. This may be a local, cohesive group who regularly meet together for blended or hybrid learning or a group of remote learners who come together only in a virtual campus. They will most likely represent diverse backgrounds of place, age, work, personal circumstances, and life experiences. They may represent different parishes, ministries, and levels of faith commitment, knowledge, and practice. They will have their own reasons for coming to online adult religious education and demonstrate different attitudes, skills, and needs. Many will participate in the sacramental and liturgical life of local churches, but others may be on the periphery of parish belonging or at odds with the teachings or practice of the tradition. They will most likely be a community of communities as disparate and diverse as any

22. Pullinger, Information Technology and Cyberspace.

23. Congregation for the Clergy, "General Directory for Catechesis" in An Anthology of Catholic Teaching on Education, edited by Leonard Franchi, 158 (London: Scepter, 1997); see also Catholic Bishops' Conference of England and Wales Committee for Catechesis and Adult Christian Education, The Priority of Adult Formation (London: Catholic Media Trust, 2000).

other adult group who comes together in college, seminary, or diocese for the purpose of adult faith education.

The virtual learning environment will be a key factor in encouraging and fostering the online learning community of faith. This must be open, welcoming, and accessible to members, yet safe and secure in terms of web filtering and offering a confidential space and supportive ethos. The communicative tools, whether email, asynchronous discussion conferencing, or synchronous live messaging, need to be user-friendly and not form barriers that prevent or stifle communication and interaction. A good deal of resource investment may be needed for an induction event for people to become comfortable and confident in using the learning system. The underlying pedagogy upon which online theological and faith-based courses and learning materials are designed and developed will need to ensure that community interaction and engagement are promoted and supported. Conversation, collaboration, and community can be listed as among the essential criteria for the application of new technologies in our religious learning environment.[24] Focusing on these at the heart of both the educative process and the way the technology is employed will enable the shared commitment and communication of an online learning group. This may help to counter arguments suggesting a dehumanization and overtechnologizing of education, but the challenge should not be viewed lightly.

Schulte suggests that one way for Christian educators to build online community is by

listening to the individuals who are their students, by being less technologists and more "wise caretakers" of the educational dimension of God's world, and by using learning technologies to model wisdom, truth, compassion, justice and peace in humility before the power of the Holy Spirit.[25]

Emphasis on such values may be a gift that the Christian community can bring to secular online education. They will be needed for a genuine faith experience to be expressed among a virtual learning group and for a sense of online *communio* to grow with relationships that deepen and mature over

24. Sr. Angela Zukowski, "Kaizening into the Future: Distance Education," in *Catholic School Leadership*, ed. Thomas C. Hunt, Thomas Oldenski, and Theodore Wallace, 174–88 (London and New York: Falmer, 2000).

25. Quentin Schultze, "Faith, Education and Communication Technology," *Journal of Education and Christian Belief* 8, no.1 (2004): 9–21.

time. Participation and collaboration among the online group, both faculty and student body, need to arrive at a mutual respect and valuing of each other, together with an inclusion and openness to academic and spiritual inquiry, that can foster a sincere sharing that enables individuals to grow and deepen in religious knowledge, understanding, and commitment. This would seem to be the experience of at least some of my recent adult students:

AF: The insights gained from other people's perspectives are challenging, inspiring and eye-opening and have enriched my faith greatly already. It's that feeling of "gosh, I'd never have thought of it that way" which can really open up new doors in one's mind. The word of God is alive and active and I guess it is so through all of us as we share our thoughts. It's great being part of this online learning community . . . both the course content and the wonderfully honest, generous way in which everyone has shared their insights and experiences have really made a difference to my faith. There's been a real sense of solidarity re the struggles and pain people have experienced, as well as the joy and faith. . . . This course, for me, has married up those two aspects—living relationships and an exploration of theological truth—in such a way that one casts light upon the other. . . . I hadn't realized that a computer discussion board could be so humanly powerful and make such real links between people.

PW: I am out of breath from the breadth and depth of the thoughts shared here . . . there has been change, there has been an encounter and there has been a renewal in our group.

My research and practical experience suggests that many people value the genuine relationships they find with their online peers, relationships that sometimes are lacking in their experience of local church, and that in their online learning network can bring blessings of honesty, openness, discussion, and dialogue. This does not deny the challenges posed by the virtual medium, but it does suggest that in working with adult Catholics who desire to grow in knowledge and understanding of their faith, it would be a missed opportunity to overlook or ignore the possibilities that new communications and learning technologies can offer.

Online Authority

A second issue for communicating faith and online learning concerns authority. The Internet brings open access, open thinking, and open dissemination of information. It often exists without social, political, academic, or religious control. How to balance this with the authority of religious tradition and the meta-narrative of revelation merits attention. The populism of cyberspace presents a new virtual world of knowledge, communication, creativity, and expression and ever-increasing opportunities to contribute directly to the formation of this world. But the quality of information and interaction can be open to misinformation, deception, or publicity of the trivial and the false. There are genuine opportunities for greater knowledge, engagement, and understanding in ways not previously imagined, but at the same time, communication and information exchange can become the preserve of the individual who is able control or use it as he wishes and for whatever purpose.[26] This poses another challenge for online Christian education. O'Donnell sees the new technologies as both promise and threat. On the one hand, they enable an open source or "circle of gifts" approach, whereby people can produce, contribute, and draw upon shared information with free exchange and distribution, which opens up access to information and resources for the nonspecialist. On the other hand, the mass of information in cyberspace, often unregulated and unrestricted, means that traditional and established leadership or opinion has shifted and may carry no particular authority.[27]

Questions of how to relate Christian teaching, rooted in the authority of divine revelation and the tradition of the church, with contemporary digital culture are both complex and challenging. The 2005 study On the Way to Life examined the landscape of today's culture as the context for Catholic religious education and catechesis and situated the rise of information and communications technology as one of the "problematic" features. The study hinted at the change, not only in the transmission of mass information with easy and immediate access to sources of authority beyond the traditions and institutions, but also at changing methodologies of learning and the subversion of traditional roles once deemed to be authoritative, such as the priest and the teacher.[28] Doctrines and teachings once centralized and controlled through official channels are now openly challenged, contradicted, or just ignored on the superhighway of media technology.

26. Gordon Graham, *The Internet: A Philosophical Inquiry* (London: Routledge, 1999).

27. James O'Donnell, *Avatars of the Word: From Papyrus to Cyberspace* (Cambridge, Mass.: Harvard University Press, 2000).

28. Heythrop Institute for Religion, Ethics and Public Life, *On the Way to Life: Contemporary Culture and Theological Development as a Framework for Catholic Education, Catechesis and Formation* (London: Catholic Education Service, 2005).

Into this changing landscape is also added the pedagogy of constructivism upon which much online learning theory and practice rests. This broad educational theory places the learner actively engaged in building her knowledge and meaning. In particular, social constructivism associated with the work of Vygotsky (1896–1934) focuses on the social-cultural context of learning and claims that we learn best by participating in activities and tasks that involve interaction with other learners and teachers. Constructivist approaches, therefore, use dialogue, collaboration, and engagement as fundamental aspects of the learning process and are contrasted with more formal, traditional, and didactic teaching methods. Online learning, in adopting broad constructivist approaches, engages learners in both independent activity and undertaking learning activities with peers. The virtual classroom integrates the cognitive and social environments and pays critical importance to both the social negotiation of meaning and the collaborative construction of knowledge. This offers an active process for exploring personal experience, knowledge, and understanding within an online community of reflection and practice. It enables personal learning through online peer exchange and group interaction.

The move away from content-driven or transmission models of adult Christian education in recent years to more process-orientated models may not be unfamiliar to many of us engaged as religious educators. The implications and significance of the constructivist approach as one example of the process model have been explored by others in the academy.[29] But it is relevant to this chapter to enquire about the specific challenges posed by the pedagogy and practice of social constructivist principles for Christian online learning. We can ask whether the nature of cyberspace together with social constructivist principles encourage online learners to rely more on their own judgments, experiences, and peer sharing in the virtual network as opposed to or in challenge of the authority of the magisterium, catechism, or religious textbook. In other words, do the new technologies encourage an experience of authority or the authority of experience? How Christian educators balance a "circle of gifts" approach in the online classroom with the creation and presentation of online study materials that maintain the orthodoxy and canonicity of the tradition becomes a key question for the school,

29. Michael Grimmitt, ed. *Pedagogies of Religious Education: Case Studies in the Research and Development of Good Pedagogic Practice in RE* (Essex: McCrimmons, 2000); see also Peta Goldburg, "Broadening Approaches to Religious Education through Constructivist Pedagogy," *Journal of Religious Education* 55, no. 2 (2007): 8–12.

university, or seminary that delivers web-based religious education. Online courses can open up the expression of religious content and activities in ways that are genuinely interactive, dialogical, and formative through tools such as discussion boards, live chat, shared weblogs, e-portfolios, and group wikipedias. Yet the danger of ending up with a syncretism of popular opinion or "religion à la carte" that leads to a trivialization of Christian truth becomes clear. Challenges may be lessened by online programs that operate as closed networks with secure user registration, clearly identified learning objectives, and tutor-moderated communications. The management of the virtual campus, along with the design of the online study materials and the wise and skilled leadership of the online tutor, may help ensure that the learning network keeps within a framework of Christian teaching and tradition. But the contrasting challenge of avoiding forced uniformity or orthodoxy in the learning network should also be noted. There is a creative tension for the educational provider or tutor whose task is to uphold the wisdom of scripture, teaching, and the tradition, yet at the same time encourage communal inquiry, shared learning, and peer communication according to the characters, needs, hopes, fears, experience, and lived reality of networked learning groups.

The horizontal nature of online interaction can be integrative and enriching.[30] Evaluations received from my adult learners suggest that the virtual classroom can offer a safe and reflective sacred space to talk about religious beliefs and practices, ask difficult questions, and share fears and concerns or honest disagreement with one another.

CM: There is a wonderful "freshness" about this kind of environment for religious and spiritual education.

FG: In our rapidly changing and often challenging climate, that current debate can be included and questions raised and discussed in a challenging but empathetic group of like minded Christian people is a blessing to many who rarely have this opportunity elsewhere in their lives. . . . As the weeks have gone on I have become more comfortable with the technology, more excited with the prospect of being part of the opportunity to bring further opportunities for reflection and learning to others as well as being enthused and stimulated by going on a faith journey with them myself.

---

30. Morten Hojsgaard and Margit Warburg, *Religion and Cyberspace* (London and New York: Routledge, 2005).

A further question arises over the role of traditional authority in terms of the specialist or teacher and the leveling of hierarchy associated with the virtual world. Online learning views the teacher less as expert and more as facilitator; it reflects a move away from the "sage on the stage" to "guide on the side."[31] This could represent a loss of authority for the religious expert who has been traditionally been the one in control of the curriculum. But if online religious education is viewed as a dialogical model of "invitational power" rather than a "controlling power," it brings an approach that is less driven by the expert or institution and more driven by the individual learner. It invites and welcomes choice, freedom, expression, and engagement rather than merely delivering a fixed set of content or religious information.[32] It suggests an approach to religious learning that has roots in personal encounter and communal relationships facilitated by a committed teacher or leader. It is a model of encounter that we find at the heart of the Gospel.

MH: The creativity of online learning flowing out from the set content of the unit and the wise guidance of the tutor but then taking life from the responses of the individuals involved has been an unexpected blessing.

A model of invitational power may be familiar to educators in adult education who understand their role as accompanying and facilitating the faith journey of others. But for those who view religious education more as a confessional transmission of the teachings of faith, then this model of online learning might seemingly expose a fluid doctrinal environment that promotes a dangerous relativistic and individualistic postmodern religious expression. Online religious education might appear as representative or symptomatic of a clash between the church's traditional authority and the open nature and individual autonomy of cyberspace. However, for others like myself, engaged in online religious teaching and learning, it can bring opportunities for collaborative learning that help nurture adult communities to grow in faith, ministry, and vocation for Christian living.

31. Gilly Salmon, E-Moderating: The Key to Teaching and Learning Online (London: Kogan Page, 2003).
32. Pullinger, Information Technology and Cyberspace.

Conclusion

In working alongside colleagues in schools, universities, dioceses, and seminary, I have encountered mixed views about Christian adult education and online learning. These sometimes reflect a lack of understanding or practical experience or questions rooted in genuine caution, suspicion, fear, or doubt. None should be dismissed or taken lightly. Communicating faith through online learning must present the opportunities as well as the challenges, and the allure of new learning technologies should not cloud our critical faculties.[33] For some, like myself, engaged in online teaching and learning, there is an excitement and vision for the online educational mission of the contemporary church, especially in the adult community and lifelong learning sectors. When new online technologies are employed with sound educational pedagogy and Gospel values in the wisdom of the Spirit, then they can indeed be good news for Christian education in today's world.

33. Neil Selwyn, Stephen Gorard, and John Furlong, eds., *Adult Learning in the Digital Age* (London and New York: Routledge, 2006).

22   Education and Religious Faith as a Dance

John Sullivan

How are we to understand the relationship between religious faith and education? What are the dynamics at work in the process of educating people in matters of faith? What are the key factors that ensure that this process is educational? In addressing these three questions I make certain assumptions.

First, I assume there is a multiplicity of legitimate ways that one might understand the relationship between religious faith and education. My contribution here can offer, at best, merely a modest proposal of *one* potentially fruitful way to envisage this relationship: namely, the metaphor of dance. I do not claim that the metaphor of dance as a way to understand the relationship between religious faith and education is the only, or even the best, way to envisage this relationship. I merely suggest that it offers some worthwhile insights into the nature of educating faith, insights that merit being captured and considered.

Second, I assume that the processes involved in educating people in matters of faith, as in all education, are not static or fixed; nor do they operate according to one specified right order. They escape strictly logical description, will transcend scientific analysis, and will often—even for those most experienced in this field—appear dramatic and unpredictable, perhaps even mysterious. Given this complexity, the best teachers, while being technically competent, hold only lightly onto the techniques, tools, and approaches recommended for them and perceive their task as an art that requires the "soft" skills and sensitivities of human relationships rather than the already formatted application of laid-down methods. My employment of the metaphor of dance seeks to bring out into the open the functioning of some of these "soft" skills and the delicacy of the educational endeavor.

Third, I assume that there is bound to be some tension between educational imperatives and imperatives that focus more on promoting religious fidelity, though I do not believe that this tension is doomed to be destructive, even if this has happened in some cases in the past. The conversion, commitment, participation, belonging, surrender, and dedication required by religious faith do not have to be embraced at the cost of neglecting the capacity for questioning, critique, detachment, testing, individual authenticity, and appropriation expected of the educated person. Again, my use of the metaphor of dance seeks to demonstrate the dialectic between these two polarities, so that they can be held within a creative tension.

In this chapter I will be considering the relationship between religious faith and education from a pedagogical perspective. That is, I will draw upon my personal and professional experience as an educator of faith for nearly forty years, in the home as a parent, in secondary schools as a teacher, at the university as a professor, in the church community, as a parishioner occasionally involved in adult religious education, and finally (but also very frequently) in working as a facilitator of in-service training and formation for teachers from diverse educational settings. This experience has been accumulated in educational settings where religious faith can be taken for granted, even privileged, as well as in settings where its articulation is so carefully constrained as to make it seem an unwelcome intruder. It has been enriched by ecumenical encounters with Christians of many different parts of the family of faith and by international conferences in the UK, Ireland, the Netherlands, the U.S., Canada, and Australia. I will reflect on the balancing acts required of those charged with educating others in faith, the qualities that seem called for from teachers in mediating between the needs of students and the nature of the faith they are being introduced to. I restrict my comments to Christian faith, though many of the key points made here about the processes involved in educating people in matters of faith have some application beyond Christianity.

There are two parts to the chapter. In the first part I compare two contrasting ways of relating education and religious faith, finding both of them unsatisfactory. The first of these, which I shall call the way of domination, takes two different forms: one allows educational considerations to dominate when religious faith is the focus of study; the other privileges faith considerations over educational ones. Domination in any relationship is to the detriment of each party or element. In this instance both education and faith suffer. The second way of relating education and religious faith, often developed in response to strife caused by one or the other form of domination, I will call the way of separation or divorce. If religious faith and education are divorced, in order to keep the peace between them, both, I contend, can be distorted and diminished.

In the second part I explore the metaphor of dance as a way of drawing out insights concerning a healthier way of relating education and religious faith than either of the ways of domination or divorce. In the process of advocating the dance metaphor, I also endeavor to expose the dynamics of interaction arising as education meets religious faith.

Neither Domination nor Divorce

Before the rise of the historical perspective, critical questioning, awareness of alternative worldviews (an essential aspect of pluralism), and the development of a hermeneutics of suspicion, it was natural that religious faith should be taught as if automatically true, as part of belonging to society and as authoritative over one's life. It was quite acceptable that such faith was reinforced by diverse agencies that jointly provided a comprehensive plausibility structure. In some quarters religious faith is still taught in this way, but much less frequently. In the traditional model, faith was taught unilaterally, from above to below, and was to be received without question or modification. Curriculum, pedagogy, modes of assessment, institutional and community ethos, together with shared and regular worship, provided an ecology in which what was taught, how it was taught, and the goals of such teaching would all be directed by the church. Only what fitted under the church's umbrella could be included. Where candidates for new knowledge that contradicted revelation, or what was accepted as orthodox teaching derived from revelation, surfaced, these were filtered out, ignored, or suppressed.

Whenever received religious orthodoxy is rigidly protected, not allowed to be interrogated, isolated from alternative perspectives, and only permitted to be interpreted in strictly prescribed ways, there is the danger that its assimilation will be shallow and that the faith of adherents will be precarious in the face of unforeseen difficulties. On the one hand, they will be anxious to avoid serious questioning. On the other, the faith community will be inflexible when it comes up against those who differ from them. Such faith might be inadequately appropriated. Its special features, through ignorance of alternatives, might be unappreciated. Its capacity to respond creatively, when called upon to apply itself to new frontiers of knowledge or experience, might be strangled at worst or at least stunted and inhibited. In this situation religious faith dominates the process of education to the detriment of both education and faith. This kind of domination is unhelpful, for individuals and for society, and it does not work for either. It certainly does not equip faith effectively, and it invites a damaging counterattack.

Instead of religious faith dominating—and undermining—education, in a self-defeating way, the opposite stance can be taken. Here educational considerations, according to some educational orthodoxies, filter out religious concerns, prevent religious ways of "reading" the world, downgrade religious knowledge as unworthy of study, and remove religious practice from educational environments. Faith must be kept on hold in a school or university context, retained for the private sphere of life, but has no currency in the public domain. Church and state, faith and the public life of society, are kept strictly separate. *Laïcité* is the term the French use for this state of affairs. The school becomes the milieu in which citizenship in a plural, secular society is prepared for, a milieu that is uncontaminated by religious prejudice and unsullied by any deference toward faith. There is a huge, constantly growing literature on *laïcité* as a concept and as a political and educational policy that remains highly influential and hotly contested.[1]

---

1. See, for example, Henri Pena-Ruiz, *Dieu et Marianne* [God and Marianne] (Paris: Presses Universitaires de France, 1999); Emile Poulat, *Notre laïcité publique* [Our public secularity] (Paris: Berg International, 2003); Jean Bauberot, *Laïcité 1905–2005: Entre Passion et Raison* [Secularity 1905–2007: Between passion and reason] (Paris: Éditions du Seuil, 2004); Jean Bauberot, *La Laïcité à l'éprouve* [Secularity on trial] (Paris: Universalis, 2004); Jean-Louis Debré, *La laïcité à l'école* [Secularity in school] (Paris: Odile Jacob, 2004); Bernard Stasi, *Laïcité et République* [Secularity and the Republic] (Paris: La Documentation Française, 2004); Guy Coq, *La laïcité principe universel* [Secularity as a universal principle] (Paris: le félin, 2005); Roger Trigg, *Religion in Public Life* (Oxford: Oxford University Press, 2007), 116–21; Paul Valadier, *Détresse du Politique, Force du Religieux* [Anguish of politics, vigour of religion] (Paris: Éditions du Seuil, 2007); Philippe Foray, *La laïcité scolaire* [Secularity in the school] (Bern: Peter Lang, 2008).

Even where *laïcité* is not operative, the climate in many publicly fund-
ed schools and universities can be highly suspicious of religious faith, re-
sistant to its claims to truth, desirous of avoiding the questions it poses,
and uncomfortable with the sentiments it seems to advocate. The fear is
that "once a child is placed in one religious tradition rather than a different one, or for that matter in a nonreligious tradition, perspectives are set,
horizons shaped, understanding circumscribed, boundaries constructed,
roles marked off, and a collective identity stamped."[2] There is some justification behind this fear. It is important in my deployment later of the metaphor of dance that the embrace of the pupil by the teacher is a light one, with
a looseness of hold rather than a tight grip. Teaching from and for conviction should always leave space so that people do not feel trapped by their upbringing and education.

Often the official stance is not hostility to religion, but neutrality as
among all worldviews. For religious believers of different persuasions, however, it can seem as if the so-called neutral referee functions really like a
player in disguise, forcing them to suppress important aspects of who they
are. Even religious education, through excessive fear of indoctrination, has
often to take place in such a way that it avoids religious perspectives, commitments, and practices. Such an approach restricts itself to historical and
sociological observations about the behavior of the religious "specimens"
under scrutiny, rather than preparing people to be sensitive to the divine reality believers are responding to. This kind of religious education has become "dismembered."[3] It is rather like studying the materials and techniques of a painter without ever considering the object of the painter's art.
When, in the process of education, the "rules of the game" prevent adequate
space for religious ways of living, seeing, thinking, and acting, another form
of damaging domination is at work, undermining religious faith but also diminishing education.

The liberal Jewish philosopher of education Walter Feinberg judicious-
ly points out: "Without a religious foundation children will likely become
the victims of the dominant cultural tendencies and will develop few filters

2. Walter Feinberg, *For Goodness Sake: Religious Schools and Education for Democratic Citizenry* (New York: Routledge, 2006), 18.

3. John Sullivan, "Dismembering and Remembering Religious Education," in *Inspiring Faith in Schools*, ed. Penny Thompson, David Torevell, and Marius Felderhof (Aldershot, UK: Ashgate, 2007).

to appraise the egocentric commercialism that bombards them every day."[4] The surrounding culture is not a vacuum, but is filled already with powerfully operating messages. It is only too easy to be unaware of the lenses out of which we view the world, so familiar have these perspectives become for us. The way of domination, whether of education by religion, or of religion by education, lacks sufficient critical reflection and offers too narrow a perspective. As Feinberg says, "to engage in critical reflection entails distancing oneself from certain practices and meanings, entertaining doubt about certain beliefs, and being willing to consider evidence and arguments that might counter these beliefs."[5] This applies to believers of all kinds—and we are all believers in something, and therefore we are also simultaneously skeptics about other things. Feinberg wisely observes that skeptics wish to push the questioning and critique as far as possible, to give it absolute value, while believers fear such critique as destructive and as "annihilating the very standards that any meaningful criticism must employ."[6]

I have described two kinds of domination—by religion, of the process of education—and of religion, by the principles and procedures governing education. As indicated above, sometimes this second type of domination is presented as a divorce between, or as a keeping apart of, religious and secular education. Either way, fundamental assumptions are unduly protected from critique, alternative perspectives are ignored or, even worse, distorted, and what is passed on is too tightly prescribed and too limiting in its scope and reach. Both education in general and educating people in religious faith in particular need a breadth of material to be examined in the course of study, a breadth of methods employed in the engagement with those materials, a breadth of viewpoints to be encountered, and a breadth of languages for communication to be tried out in investigations and explorations.

Dance

The interface between church and society at the level of the classroom is described by Marguerite Léna as "a line of fracture between young people and adults." She says that "the right place of an educator is to stand along this line of fracture as a worker for unity"; she must "stay on this line with

4. Feinberg, For Goodness Sake, 95.
5. Ibid., 103.
6. Ibid.

firmness and peace."[7] Léna urges us that "without either demonizing or canonizing our world, we have to know and love it enough to discern the roads
to life and the roads to death. . . . For educators, it is not a matter of tarnish-
ing the world but of humanizing it. For evangelizers it is a matter of sancti-
fying it."[8] I suggest that the metaphor of dance, as one way that educators in
matters of faith may understand their task, casts light on how standing on
Léna's line of fracture may be maintained. In fact it offers a more mobile and
flexible set of images than merely "standing" and indicates the kinds of balancing acts required.

If we consider the relationship between religious faith and education as
a kind of dance, what insights might this yield? I suggest it proposes to us
a set of polarities that, when combined, reveal some important features of
what is required in educating for faith. In a dance there is both structure and
spontaneity. Without the first, one would not know what moves to make.
Without the second, one's movements are merely predetermined, without
personal stamp being bestowed upon them.

There is a degree of stability, a predictable basic pattern or order, but this
can be open to variation or improvisation. There is repetition, which allows
us to learn the steps if we get them wrong the first time and to grow in confidence with practice. But there is also scope for creativity within the overall
schema of the dance, so that it becomes our own performance to a limited
extent, not simply a cloning of someone else's action.

There is a balance to be struck between solidity and space. Without solidity, there would be nothing definite to relate to, to lean on, to pass around,
to engage with. Without space between us, we would tumble into one another, step on one another's toes, and eventually bruise ourselves. Thus a
degree of "respectful hesitancy" is required, without which we might "blun-
der into the lives" of others "with our own agendas," thereby inhibiting their
personal growth.[9] In the dance that is educating faith teachers need to get
close, putting themselves on the same level as those they seek to reach, rath-

---

7. Marguerite Léna, "Défis éducatifs contemporains et vie consacrée," in *Pour l'éducation
et pour l'école: Des catholiques s'engagent* [For education and for the school: Catholics commit
themselves], ed. Claude Dagens (Paris: Odile Jacob, 2007), 109.

8. Léna, "Défis éducatifs," 114.

9. Ruth Givens, "Mending Walls: Recognizing the Influence of Boundary Issues in the
Teacher/Student Relationship," *Christian Scholars' Review* 36, no. 2 (Winter 2007): 127–40, at
138.

er than communicating to them from a distance or from above. On the other hand, there needs to be an element of mystery acknowledged in the other person, one we should not seek to penetrate or dissolve. If dancing entails holding on and letting go, then solidity gives us something to hold on to and space gives us somewhere we can let go. The teacher holds onto what she believes in, confident that she is already in touch with the source of truth, but remains open in the constant search for a better appreciation and appropriation of this truth, which always eludes our secure grasp or safe possession.

Such structure, stability, repetition, and solidity make possible the continuity that creates the conditions for formation in faith. They help us to have confidence that the faith encountered and responded to is not simply idiosyncratic, but also one that is shared with others around us and with previous believers. The parallel spontaneity, variation, creativity, and space ensure that in our encounter with faith, we are not diminished, our individuality is not suppressed, and that our involvement goes beyond passive acceptance to a more active receptivity and appropriation.

In a dance there is both movement and balance. In educating faith there are moments when we need to help people to be ready to move beyond where they are now, if they are to grow to the stature of mature discipleship. There are also moments when we offer milk, not meat, when we temper the demands, when we emphasize steadiness, when we counter some particular pressure as likely to confuse, upset, disturb, or disorient learners, rather than healthily challenge them. In order to establish and maintain this balance, the teacher must attend both to learners and to the object being studied. She requires a blend of confidence and assertiveness that enables her to take the initiative and intervene in the learning process. At the same time she must retain the necessary humility and spacemaking capacity to enable her to facilitate the initiative of learners, which might, on occasion, require from her some kind of withdrawal or backing off. Knowing when to stop intervening, when to refrain from explaining, and when one should leave well enough alone is vital for an educator.

In dancing, one needs a combination of self-awareness and awareness of the other. This includes one's immediate partner(s) and all those engaged in the dance around one. In fact one's self-awareness is not separated from one's awareness of these others; they are intimately linked. This applies too in the life of faith. One's faith is inspired by that of others. It models itself upon others. It can be hindered by others. It comes to self-consciousness by encounter with others, and it is open to development in response to the self-presentation of others.

I would describe the encounter between teacher and learner, not only in the task of educating others in matters of faith, but more generally, in the following way. Students surprise us by their singularity. They learn something different from what we teach them. They break through our expectations (positive and negative). We experience them as a foreign country. They make demands on us that force us to be more attentive to their otherness, rather than taking them for granted. Although we want them to be like us in some aspect of knowledge or skill, they cannot be a copy for they are—like us—originals, unique individuals. Our courses are intended for the general student, but we face real individuals. The material is new for them; through them, it becomes new for us. Their worlds are (at least slightly) changed in their encounter with us; our world is also changed when we respond to who they are.

Many centuries ago, St. Augustine expressed a very similar view when he said, "So potent is the feeling of sympathy, that when they are moved as we speak and we as they learn, we abide each with the other; and thus they, as it were, speak in us what they hear, while we, in a manner, learn in them what we teach."[10] This view was echoed, though in different terms, toward the end of the twentieth century by the inspirational Quaker educator Parker Palmer.

The teacher who knows the subject well must introduce it to students in the way one would introduce a friend. The students must know why the teacher values the subject, how the subject has transformed the teacher's life. By the same token, the teacher must value the students as potential friends, be vulnerable to the ways students may transform the teacher's relationship with the subject as well as be transformed. If I am invited into a valued friendship between two people, I will not enter in unless I feel that I am valued as well.[11]

The feelings described by Augustine and the kind of quality and influential relationship advocated by Palmer depend on real presence, spending time

10. St. Augustine, *On Catechizing the Uninstructed*, trans. E. Phillips Barker (London: Methuen, 1912), 31.

11. Parker Palmer, *To Know as We Are Known* (San Francisco: Harper and Row, 1983), 104.

with people, a willingness to be vulnerable to the exigencies and unforeseen turbulence of the exchanges and mutual trust being built up.

In the dance there is reciprocity and mutuality. There is a partner to relate to and in the best dances the partners depend on each other for the effectiveness of the dance; each has her or his part to play, without which I cannot play my part properly. In educating faith there should be a similar reciprocity. The teacher gives, but must always be ready to receive. Without being willing to listen and open to learn, the teacher loses the right to be heard and fails to model the behavior she wants others to adopt. Similarly, students, if they are to benefit from education, must be receptive and teachable. But their willingness to give themselves in this way is strengthened if they feel they have something to contribute as valued partners. Indeed they do in matters of faith, since each one is, in his or her inimitable manner, a unique expression of the image of God and each person's life gives access to a unique chapter in the history of salvation. The mutuality of dancing reminds us of the mutual self-giving required for the life of faith. We make our way to the kingdom of God hand in hand, deeply indebted to each other, rather than in isolation or by the strength of our own efforts.

The French philosopher of education Jean-Marie Labelle has devoted a whole book to educative reciprocity, building his argument by drawing heavily on the thought of the personalist thinker Maurice Nédoncelle. Labelle addresses similar themes to those I have explored above, touching upon various features of this reciprocity. These include movement, interaction, dialogue, trust, enriching exchange, giving and receiving, and mutual adaptation.[12] He does not confuse reciprocity with conviviality,[13] for the move toward reciprocity is not likely to be smooth, comfortable, or free from pain. "The greatest service students can render to their teacher is to make him put on hold his certitudes."[14] He points out that we cannot make ourselves fully available to others without the "capacity to put oneself in question."[15] If we are full of ourselves, we are less open to change—with willingness to change being integral to being willing to learn. If we are too sure of what we know, then we might be less willing to share authority, to "authorize" others to take the initiative, to make decisions and to exercise judgment—and thus

12. Jean-Marie Labelle, *La Réciprocité éducative* [Educative reciprocity] (Paris: PUF, 1996).
13. Ibid., 27.   14. Ibid., 28.
15. Ibid., 37.

take responsibility. Labelle goes so far as to say that "the teacher should be an expert on the relationship of reciprocity, always being put to the test."[16] This willingness, on the part of teachers, to be put to the test, rather than seeing the teaching-learning relationship as one where it is only the teacher who tests the student, requires them to take difference seriously. Indeed another French philosopher, Louis Lavelle, goes so far as to claim that "to recognize and appreciate differences is the essential function of the spirit."[17]

If Lavelle is right about the need to establish a right relationship with difference, then the dance that is the endeavor to educate others in faith depends on both discipline and lightness of touch and step. If one partner slips into a self-indulgent set of bodily movements, he risks losing connection with his partner; attentiveness and constraint are part of being together. So, too, in educating faith, there is a time for emphasizing discipline and a time to lighten up and let go. Too little discipline leads to a situation where learners cannot engage in depth with the object of study; too much can weary their spirits, become burdensome and imprisoning, rather than liberating good news. When discipline and lightness of touch and step are combined, we have the possibility of synchronization in the dance. This occurs when body, feelings, self, partner, other dancers, and the music all coalesce into one organic and flowing body. In educating faith it is worth aiming for a similar "flow."[18] With this kind of flow there will be for learners and teachers an experience of organic belonging and interaction. In such experiences, at their best, participants will feel that bodies are blessed, feelings are healed, and people are affirmed. As we respond to the "music" of the Gospel that invites us to celebrate, share, and respond to the graces and needs of creation, there will be mutual giving and receiving.

If there is any merit in exploring the metaphor of dance as offering insights into how one might relate religious faith and education, then perhaps it lies in the way it points to a two-way movement, or dialectic, between polarities. In learning we need a combination of trust or letting go of our reservations and self-protection, on the one hand, and, on the other hand, we need some degree of suspicion or holding back. Without the first, we cannot

16. Ibid., 101, quoting Ferry.

17. Louis Lavelle, quoted in ibid., 195.

18. Mihaly Csikszentmihalyi's work is referred to in *Wisdom: Its Nature, Origins and Development*, ed. Robert J. Sternberg (Cambridge: Cambridge University Press, 1990), and is described by Daniel Goleman, *Emotional Intelligence* (London: Bloomsbury, 1996), 90–93.

be reachable or teachable; without the second, we become simply gullible and open to abuse.

If they are to avoid suppressing the spirit of students, in the faltering emergence of their freedom, teachers should provide a safe space for play and experimentation. They also, however, have a duty to provide scaffolding, structure, and a cognitive framework, something substantial for their students to come up against and to grapple with.

Teachers need to bring into the classroom idealism and openness to transcendence in the life of the students and in their own activity. Far from being cynical about the possibilities for change in students, teachers should be alert to their potential. Guided by a strong belief in this potential, teachers should invite students to raise their horizons toward new possibilities. But at the same time the teacher cannot afford to fail to read accurately how things currently are, in terms of these students at this time and place. Lack of realism will be as powerful an impediment to promoting their growth as lack of idealism.

Another pair of qualities seems necessary here: on the one hand, confidence, while on the other hand, willingness to be vulnerable. Without confidence—in the worthwhileness of the endeavor, in the reliability of the object of study, in the authenticity of one's own calling, in the basic goodness of creation, in the divine image in one's pupils and the support of one's colleagues—one could not get started or make any progress. But without being willing to be vulnerable, one might be tempted to rely too much on one's own gifts, to treat pupils too automatically as the same, instead of as unique individuals, to try to maintain control, thereby suppressing opposition and thus crushing the fragile spirits of others. This would be to slip into unilateral transmission, rather than mutual dialogue and enrichment; it would suggest that the need for grace to bring our efforts to fruition has been forgotten.

From the insights derived from exploring the metaphor of dance I take it that educating faith is a delicate endeavor. Let me express this delicacy in four different ways. First, there is a need for restraint on the part of the teacher. The way we educate others in faith must be congruent with what we are educating them into: the methods used must match and adequately represent the message we seek to convey. If our dancing is not to tread on toes, we must be careful. Translated into educating faith, we must be humble. We do not know it all. We are not perfect. Our perspective is limited, incomplete, and distorted sometimes by selfish motives. Other people also have the image of God in them. They have something to offer us as well as something to receive from us. Their dignity should be respected. God is already at work in their lives. In bringing others to the light, the main agent is God's Holy Spirit, not us.

Second, an educator in faith, mindful of the polarities exposed in my exploration of the dance metaphor, must attend to two sets of questions: those posed by his or her students/audiences and those posed by the faith community and Gospel she or he represents. To ignore the first would be to come across as irrelevant to people's needs. To ignore the second would be to allow this audience or class to dictate all the terms, topics, and criteria for discussion and offer them nothing new, distinctive, or challenging. Thus an educator in faith should ask: who am I dealing with? What things matter to them? What perplexes them? What attracts them? How are they thinking? What is affecting their thinking? What are their priorities and values? What is being taken for granted? What is being ignored? What is not being mentioned at all? Which voices are surfacing and which are silent?

Third, the educator in faith has to combine an appreciation of the richness and potential of what he or she is steward of, on behalf of the believing community, with a capacity to resonate with gaps in the life of learners. This requires sensitivity to the hunger for the divine, the inner compass that points beyond the here and now, orienting us for something better and more desirable, the spirit of searching that resides somewhere in her or his audience. Educators in faith then need to seek ways to bring this hunger and this search to articulation, to hear it into speech and then to encourage it, support, it, reinforce it, and gently bring about an encounter with appropriate treasures from the living religious tradition. These treasures introduce people to new social practices, loyalties, networks, ways of thinking, concepts, and language.

Fourth, there is always a need for balance between the explicit and the implicit. To concentrate entirely on the explicit message but without attending to the life that underpins it and makes it credible is counterproductive and self-defeating. To focus only on the way of living but without making explicit the message and story that should be guiding, challenging, illuminating, and inspiring it would be to sell students short.

The notion of dance suggests a certain etiquette and courtesy: invitations can be refused, while coercion ruins the dance. The dance is open to abuse, so care must be taken to avoid such abuse. The care is in relation to how the teacher handles herself, how she handles the learners, how she handles the "text" or "tune" that she is responding to and inviting others to respond to, how she hands over herself to others, and how she receives others in return. The metaphor of dance is a powerful reminder that education is not a unilateral process.

It is only one metaphor, however, and it is not part of my claim that it suffices on its own to do justice to all the complexities involved in educating people in faith, or to imagine that it addresses all the multiple factors at work or that should be considered. I have left on one side here any attention to the erotic dimension in teaching and the caution that needs to accompany this dimension, to which George Steiner has recently alerted us.[19] Given the close connections, across many different cultures, between dance and the erotic, one might expect there to be aspects and implications of the metaphor that I have used, relating to the erotic, about which teachers should be aware.

The moral theologian Xavier Thévenot has also shrewdly exposed the surreptitious workings of sexuality in the teacher-student exchange.[20] We might well ask whether our bodily language confirms or contradicts our words, or as Thévenot refers to the match required here, does our analogical language reflect our digital language?[21] Digital language refers to the surface and logical meaning of our words, while analogical language relates to the impression our overall bearing, demeanor, behavior, and "tone" give off about a topic. Sometimes these two languages are in harmony, sometimes they conflict.

I also acknowledge that the metaphor of dance fails to do justice to the asymmetry of relationships, status, knowledge, maturity, duties, and expectations of each partner in the educational process. For the reciprocity at the heart of the dance metaphor does not mean an undifferentiated equality or sameness between the dancers. Some may find the dance metaphor, with its implicit "one-to-one" nature, slightly limiting, though there are, of course, many modes of dancing that are very much a group activity. The metaphor

19. George Steiner, *Lessons of the Masters* (Cambridge, Mass: Harvard University Press, 2003).

20. Xavier Thévenot and Jean Joncheray, eds., *Pour une éthique de la pratique éducative* [For an ethic of educative practice] (Paris: Desclée, 1991), 139–77.

21. Ibid., 176.

also fails to bring out adequately the nature and authority of the "score," "melody," "beat," or "rhythm" to which the dancers move.

The Dutch philosopher Adriaan Peperzak insightfully comments on the importance of particularity: "I . . . speak . . . as this limited guardian of a limited heritage, to a particular audience here and now . . . [and although] I still speak to the universally human in each individual or group, I must begin by accepting the limits of their and my particularity."[22] He refers to "this unique person with his or her uniquely personal properties, circumstances, stories, and style of life, who here and now speaks and listens to me, while I myself am likewise such a unique person, who is a 'you' for you."[23] In our concern for doing justice to the universality of the Gospel and the permanent and objective value of the church's teachings, perhaps we have been overconcerned about, and therefore unwilling to embrace, the risks of particularity in communicating the riches of tradition.

One risk is to step back before the particularity—of learners and of situations—so that we become silent or inaudible, invisible or absent, thereby failing to do justice to the tradition that has been entrusted to us. Another risk is that of being intrusive and invasive, dominating and bringing about dependence, thereby inhibiting genuine access to it and preventing authentic appropriation of it. In their detached engagement teachers of faith need to maintain vigilance over the type of influence they exercise.[24] The teacher has to mediate between the particularity of the tradition as he has so far received it and the concrete and complex particularity of the people whom he is inviting to engage with this tradition. Dance is one way—in my view a valuable way—of envisaging this endeavor.

22. Adriaan Peperzak, Thinking (New York: Fordham University Press, 2006), 102.
23. Ibid., 105.
24. Thévenot, Pour une éthique, 15.

23 Communicating Faith and Relating in Love

John Sullivan

Through communication people express emotions and needs, establish identity, build community, exchange goods, construct a range of social structures, embark on projects, and transmit values. Through communication they also seek meaning, interpret behavior, celebrate key moments, and reach out to others. These all entail some form of sharing and connection. Communication is not so much about information; more importantly it is about meaning and the exercise of our human capacities. Meaning requires an addressee—someone the meaning is intended *for*—as well as the one (or the community) who addresses, the source or "from-which" of meaning. We should see communication as a channel for relationship, as a medium in which there is both giving and receiving. All communication either explicitly or implicitly invites others into some form of relationship. The invitation can, of course, be refused as well as accepted; it can also be accepted on terms different from those intended. The response in turn gives something back to the "sender" and modifies the relationship.

The various modes and media for communication influence what we think, how we think, what we notice (and fail to notice); they affect how we see ourselves and others, how we relate to others, with political as well as philosophical and psychological dimensions developing from this "seeing." There is a huge and constantly growing literature on communication media, including oral, writing, printing, electric, computer-based, and digital technology communication.[1] There is one overriding lesson that comes through to me from these works: central to communication is relationship. Communication assumes, depends upon, and builds on relationship; it addresses and seeks to influence relationship; it does affect relationship, even though this often occurs in ways that were not intended. Relationships in turn inexorably influence communication: what is given, how it is conveyed, and what is received.

The sender might be said to be the subject or agent of communication. The sender envisages, with varying degrees of sensitivity and realism, a relationship with potential recipients. There is the target or object of communication, the receiver(s). They cannot fail to perceive a relationship implied in the act of communication, whether they welcome this or not. Communication has a topic or body of content. This will have implications for relationship, even if these implications are not explicit. The context has to be taken into account, with all its limitations and opportunities. Every context for communication carries the freight of concerns and questions, of hopes and anxieties. Relationship is integral to all these dimensions of the context. As we have seen, there are many media for communicating. Religious faith has been communicated via art, sculpture, and architecture, through poetry, dance, music, and drama, through law and politics, through literature and science, through philosophy and theology, and more recently via other media such as film, television, and the Internet. Each medium requires different kinds of engagement or relationship in terms of our energies, attention, priorities, responsiveness, and mode of being.

Successful communication occurs where there is some kind of match be-

---

1. For examples, see Gugliemo Cavallo and Roger Chartier, *A History of Reading in the West*, trans. Lydia Cochrane (Cambridge: Polity Press, 1999); Ronald J. Deibert, *Parchment, Printing, and Hypermedia* (New York: Columbia University Press, 1997); Robert S. Fortner, *Communication, Media, and Identity* (Lanham, Md.: Rowman and Littlefield, 2007); Marshall McLuhan, *Understanding Media* (London: Ark, 1987); Henri-Jean Martin, *The History and Power of Writing*, trans. Lydia Cochrane (Chicago: University of Chicago Press, 1994); James O'Donnell, *Avatars of the Word: From Papyrus to Cyberspace* (Cambridge, Mass: Harvard University Press, 2000); John Durham Peters, *Speaking into the Air* (Chicago: University of Chicago Press, 1999); Neil Postman, *Amusing Ourselves to Death* (London: Methuen, 1987); Alan Purves, *The Web of Text and the Web of God* (New York: Guilford Press, 1998).

tween sender and recipient and between purpose and method. I believe that, for all the technical difficulties there might be, the most important elements in miscommunication stem from failures in relationship. Despite all the gigantic leaps forward in our technological capacity to communicate, the effective communication of faith still depends on presence and relationship— being there with and for others really matters. It matters in terms of making a message understandable and accessible, by offering embodiment of what might otherwise come across as abstract. It matters in terms of making a message credible, through the power of personal example. It matters in terms of conveying conviction if and when there is harmony between our digital and our analogical language (see chapter 22).

In all this, inseparably intertwined, is our relationship with God, our relationship with ourselves, and our relationship with other people. The most central way that faith is communicated is in worship. Here we encounter God's enduring and constant invitation to new life; here we rehearse our tentative and faltering "yes" to this invitation. At its heart communicating faith is simply sharing God's love with all we meet in the multiple dimensions of our life, in most cases doing this implicitly via what is revealed of that love in the quality of our relationships. When we communicate faith explicitly we rely on the quality of our relationship with God to overflow into our relationships with others in order to bring people to a readiness to accept responsibility themselves, to enable them to hear and answer God's call and grace.

In considering the heart of communicating faith, let me begin by taking four leads from sacred scripture. First, on waking from sleep, Jacob says, "Truly, the Lord is in this place and I never knew it."[2] Communicating faith should begin with an acknowledgment that God is alive, active, and present throughout the world, long before we seek to get involved in his work. God is neither absent nor asleep before we step in. God's will is being expressed whether or not we take note of this, and God's purposes are being addressed even while we remain unaware of them. In this context, our task is to wake up and then help others to wake up to what God is communicating.

Second, we should not expect too much of our individual efforts, nor be too despondent when they fail, as they frequently do. The parable of the sower whose seed fell on different kinds of ground and thus met with differing degrees of fruitfulness[3] provides a warning. "Only a small fraction

2. Gen 28:16.   3. Luke 8:5–8.

of what we sow in communication is likely to result in understanding of our meaning or intent."[4] There are many slips possible in the act of communication, between what we mean to say and what we actually say, and between what people hear and how they interpret this. Even more is this true when what is communicated requires a radical change in the being of the hearer if it is truly to be received for what it is: the word of God calling us to new life. Bearing this in mind should prevent us from relying too much on our own efforts, even as we try, as we should, to share God's word.

Third, the great commandment in Matthew 22:37–39, to obey God, by loving him with all our heart, soul, mind, and strength and by loving our neighbor as ourselves, might be said to be even more important than the great commission (in Matthew 28:19–20a) to go out and spread the good news to all humankind. If we are not living the life we should be living, in harmony with the Gospel, then our willingness to communicate and our effectiveness in communicating the faith is distorted, obstructed, weakened, and contradicted when the noise of who we are drowns out the sound and sense of what we have to say. Thus the primary mode of communicating faith is to live it out in all dimensions of our existence, implicitly though this will usually be. Explicit attempts to communicate the word of faith are dependent for their effectiveness on the durability and fruitfulness of the ministry of witness. Can others discern how God is speaking to me and through my life in the many aspects of my existence? Is my life revelatory of God's design, illuminating the way for others? If we attend to the great commandment as our first priority and envisage any attempt to communicate our faith as an expression of the call to love along the lines shown us by God and as asked of us by God, then there is a chance that we will resist the temptations of domination that lie hidden (though sometimes they are only too blatant) in acts of communication.

Let me offer two renderings of how this task of love presents itself. In the first of these, a contemporary communications expert reminds us that "there is healing to accomplish, peace to encourage, injustice and abuse to be exposed, joy to be expressed, nobility and courage to be celebrated, faithful witness to be upheld."[5] In the second, Pope Benedict XVI, in his 2007 encyclical on hope (Spe Salvi, no. 29) quotes St. Augustine:

4. Fortner, Communication, Media, and Identity, 40.
5. Ibid., 254.

The turbulent have to be corrected, the faint-hearted cheered up, the weak supported; the Gospel's opponents need to be refuted, its insidious enemies guarded against; the unlearned need to be taught, the indolent stirred up, the argumentative checked; the proud must be put in their place, the desperate set on their feet, those engaged in quarrels reconciled; the needy have to be helped, the oppressed to be liberated, the good to be encouraged, the bad to be tolerated; all must be loved.

If sharing faith is integral to the life of a believer, then what and how we communicate must be reinforced, made credible and attractive by the loving quality of our life; if not, our communication becomes burdensome and a barrier to relationship.

Fourth, we should seek to focus our communication, not so much on what we have been given (in order to be passed on), but on those we are communicating with, as Paul reminds us in Second Corinthians. "You are a letter from Christ," he tells his addressees. "You are all the letter we need, a letter written on our heart. . . . [You are] a letter written not with ink but with the Spirit of the living God, written not on stone tablets but on the pages of the human heart."[6]

This capacity to see those we communicate with as being endowed with their own message from Christ, as his ambassadors, as the recipients of his grace, as the source of good news for us, turns communication in matters of faith into something that requires reciprocity and mutuality, not a process of unilateral transmission and a parallel one-sided acceptance. After all, the meaning carried in acts of communication comes from both sender and receiver. Whatever intentions a communicator might have in the message she gives, those on the receiving end filter this through their own concerns, give it their own "coloring" or "flavor," attribute some degree of value to the message (or discount it), and then decide whether to use it or to ignore it. The would-be communicator of faith needs to be open to the communication that flows from the lives of those he addresses. Thus John Stackhouse, bearing in mind one activity in the spectrum of endeavors that communicating faith includes, that of apologetics, draws our attention to the factors in a group of people that might influence how they receive a message. "Gender, age, race, education, physical and mental health, emotional state, prejudices, beliefs, appetites, preferences, and previous knowledge all affect the

6. 2 Cor. 3:2–3.

processes of human perception and interpretation."[7] Paying this kind of attention to those we seek to reach is part of what is entailed by sensitivity to particularity.

The diversity of contexts for communicating faith addressed in this book and the diversity of issues raised as key factors that facilitate such communication illustrate for me the constant balance to be struck between particularity and universality. On the one hand, each person and situation is unique; what "works" for this person or that situation is not guaranteed to "work" for another, in terms of effective communication. On the other hand, the love of God that is to be shared is universal: it is for all, without exception; it is constant, enduring, and never-failing; it is unconditional; it calls for a response, yet it leaves us free. We encounter the universal through the particular; we become open to the transcendent in our response to what is present to us in a particular here and now, through what is immanent. In the same way, we mediate or communicate the universal via the particular. If our communication is to do justice to God's way of reaching out to us— though the best we can manage here is merely a faint echo of this—then we have to find ways to match our message—better, God's invitation to new life and love—to particular people and concrete situations. This requires of us sensitive antennae, to pick up the bearing, interaction, and significance for people of the set of particularities they are experiencing at the moment of communication. It also requires of us that we display delicacy in our treatment of others as we respond to them. Stackhouse indicates some of the questions that should be asked about a group one wishes to reach out to.

Who am I dealing with? What are their questions, their cognitive style or styles, their concerns, and their criteria for deciding about religious matters? . . . I need to listen to all of what is being said; to how it is being said; to what is not being said; to what is really being said; and to why it is being said.[8]

This chimes with the advice given to university teachers by Ronald Barnett when he advocates the priority that they should give to supporting a student's will to learn; they should take note of "her feelings, attitudes, worries, anxieties, hopes, understandings, priorities, values, capabilities and felt certainties."[9] Too narrow a focus on communicating knowledge without

7. John Stackhouse, *Humble Apologetics* (New York: Oxford University Press, 2006), 26.
8. Ibid., 143.
9. Ronald Barnett, *A Will to Learn* (Maidenhead, UK: Open University Press, 2007), 28.

attention to the whole person is unlikely to lead to the "transformation of relationships, understandings, attitudes and actions"[10] required for Christian education and communication.

One cannot create the conditions for learning without serious and sustained listening. If we are aware of our own limitations and conscious of our neighbors' real dignity, then we will be motivated to listen. If we believe God is already at work in the lives of others, we will wish to listen to what is being said in these lives. As O'Brien puts this, "The key to preaching the Gospel is not first defined by how one *speaks* but how one *listens*."[11] We listen to learn from, not to win over or to conquer others. We listen so that they can share their experience, insights, and gifts and so that in turn we can share ours. If this happens then already we are now in a rich mode of communication as relationship rather than simply as message sending. Fortner sees relationship as absolutely central to a Christian understanding of communication. "Communication is the means to initiate, establish, maintain, or destroy relationship. . . . Through relationship we are to explore, legitimize, and care for what God entrusted to our care."[12] Such an understanding of communication as relationship fits well with Joseph Ratzinger's (now Pope Benedict XVI) analysis of listening:

To listen means to know and acknowledge another and to allow him to step into the realm of one's own "I." It is a readiness to assimilate his words, and therein his being, into one's own reality as well as to assimilate oneself to him in corresponding fashion. Thus, after the act of listening, I am another man, my own being is enriched and deepened because it is united with the being of the other and, through him, with the being of the world.[13]

In listening, we should attend, not only to concerns and constraints on people, but also to their aspirations and ideals. We can apply Jon Nixon's urging of university teachers to listen to the implicit questions posed by their students to our wider concern about communicating faith: "What kind of person do I want to be? What kind of life do I want to lead? What kinds of re-

10. Simon Oxley, *Creative Ecumenical Education* (Geneva: World Council of Churches Publications, 2002), 26.

11. George Dennis O'Brien, *Finding the Voice of the Church* (Notre Dame, Ind.: University of Notre Dame Press, 2007), 190.

12. Fortner, *Communication, Media, and Identity*, 70–71.

13. Joseph Ratzinger, in *The Nature and Mission of Theology*, quoted by O'Brien, in *Finding the Voice of the Church*, 196.

lationships do I want to form? What kinds of affiliation do I wish to foster? What sort of world do I want to inhabit?"[14]

One way of putting this is that we need to speak in the right voice. "If the actor speaks in the wrong voice as lover, villain, hero, or clown, the play is ruined. So with the Christian voice . . . spoken in the wrong voice—dictatorial, didactic, distant, or demeaning—the message fails."[15] The voice needs to match the character, to be in harmony with a role, to convey a message unambiguously and with conviction. A mismatch between voice and message confuses the hearer and becomes an obstacle; it functions as a stumbling block, and impedes receptivity. As O'Brien puts it, "speaking in the wrong voice obscures the Church."[16] The implication of O'Brien's labeling of wrong voices—dictatorial, didactic, distant, or demeaning—is that ecclesial communication should be invitational, willing to learn as well as to teach, intimate (and thus self-involving, making oneself vulnerable) and both respectful and up-building (or edifying).

"How can I put this, if I am to do justice to the truth I seek to convey and if I am to reach out adequately to the one I speak to?" This should be a constant question for the person engaged in communicating faith. There should be an almost sacred tentativeness, a desire for carefulness, in such communication, a sense of the unworthiness of our efforts, the failure of our words to represent what they seek to convey, yet at the same time, a real trust that God is present in both speaker and hearer at that moment, bringing more out of our inadequate attempt than either of us realizes. If our motives are open to purification and correction, through our life in the church, then our communication, even while being tentative, should also be confident, trusting in God as the source and goal of our communicative efforts, though never presumptive, overassured, or assuming we have a secure grasp of faith. By voice here I include the words chosen, the tone adopted, the body language that accompanies the words, and thereby, inescapably, the attitude conveyed. Even when there is a real harmony among all of these, there is no guarantee that the "sound" made will be heard in the way intended, since many factors can impede reception, some of these being in the circumstances and some in the character of the hearer.

14. Jon Nixon, "Forget the Form-filling, Just Listen and Learn," *Times Higher Education* (June 22, 2007).

15. O'Brien, *Finding the Voice of the Church*, xiv.

16. Ibid., 5.

"Why am I saying this?" "What are my motives?" These are also worth-while questions to pose to ourselves in our acts of communication. The political philosopher Robert Audi suggests that a crucial factor in how our voice comes across to others is our motivation.

> Our voice is determined more by motivation and manner than by semantics, more by why and how we say what we say than by its content. . . . Both in public and in private we tend to listen for voicing as well as content. We try to hear more than just what people say, and quite commonly accept—or reject—what others say because of how they voice it as well as because of what it is . . . we depend on voicing to help us get a sense not only of sincerity but also of credibility, cooperativeness, and other traits.[17]

Are we seeking to impose something, however valuable, on others? Are we hoping to maintain control over them? Do we see them as lacking, deficient, requiring some good from us? Or can we see them as source of grace and as an invitation to us to grow? The French philosopher Louis Lavelle (1883–1955) said that "the greatest good that we can do for others is not to communicate to them our richness but to reveal to them their own."[18] The richness residing in those we seek to communicate with will not be found if we are not open to it, willing to welcome it, understand it, and appreciate it. That means we should see them whole.

Each learner, each person we hope to reach out to, has his or her own outlook, presuppositions, aversions, allegiances, interests, questions, and problems. If the well-established principle of learning, *quidquid recipitur ad modum recipientis recipitur* (whatever is received, is received according to the mode of being of the receiver), still has merit, it means paying attention to all these features of learners I have just listed. Successful communication will touch these in some way, not suppress or bypass them. If these features of learners are engaged seriously, then much more so than when we rely on the logic of ideas or on authority, we are establishing the possibility of credibility. Reception of communication occurs when the conditions of credibility are created, when something offered or proposed becomes effective and not merely valid, when a response is awakened in those who receive; their

---

17. Robert Audi, *Religious Commitment and Secular Reason* (Cambridge: Cambridge University Press, 2000), 166.

18. Louis Lavelle, quoted in Xavier Dufour, *Enseigner: Une Oeuvre Spirituelle* [To teach: A spiritual work] (Paris: Parole et Silence, 2006), 63.

faith is activated and renewed, not inert. In contrast, nonreception happens when the receiver judges that what is being conveyed does not address his condition, fails to build him up, falls short of meeting his needs, or simply omits to answer his questions.

The would-be communicator of faith should be open to God's grace in her own life, vulnerable to its workings, docile, "get-at-able," receptive. She should be responsive to God's call in the myriad of ways this reaches us. This means being willing to act, displaying courage and engaging in risk-taking, letting go on occasion of familiar surroundings, or leaving behind the security of tried and tested methods. She participates in, shares with, and belongs to the church, "being-together," rather than working in isolation. She is also self-giving, in gratitude for what she has received, since, for her, sharing God's love and the gifts God has given to all, is at the heart of what communication is about.

Works Cited

Abraham, William. *Canon as Criterion in Christian Theology: From the Fathers to Feminism.* Oxford: Clarendon Press, 1998.

Abraham, William J., Jason E. Vickers, and Natalie Van Kirk, eds. *Canonical Theism: A Fresh Agenda for Theology and Church.* Grand Rapids, Mich.: Eerdmans, 2008.

Adams, Frank R. "Origins, Development and Implementation." In *Scottish Education Post-devolution,* edited by Tom G. K. Bryce and Walter M. Humes, 369–79. Edinburgh: Edinburgh University Press, 2003.

Alston, William P. *Perceiving God: The Epistemology of Religious Experience.* Ithaca, N.Y.: Cornell University Press, 1991.

Anderson, Robert. "The History of Scottish Education, pre-1980." In *Scottish Education Post-devolution,* edited by Tom G. K. Bryce and Walter M. Humes, 219–28. Edinburgh: Edinburgh University Press, 2003.

Appiananesi, Richard, and Chris Garratt. *Introducing Postmodernism.* Cambridge: Icon, 1999.

Aquinas, Thomas. *De veritate.* Question XI, Article 1. Vol. 2: *Truth,* trans. James V. McGlynn. Indianapolis: Hackett Publishing, 1994.

Aquino, Frederick D. *Communities of Informed Judgment: Newman's Illative Sense and Accounts of Rationality.* Washington, D.C.: Catholic University of America Press, 2004.

Arbuckle, Gerald A. *Earthing the Gospel: An Inculturation Handbook for Pastoral Workers.* London: Geoffrey Chapman, 1990.

Archbishops and Bishops of Scotland. *Catholic Directory for Scotland.* Glasgow: Burns Publications, 2007.

Archdiocese of Glasgow. *Adult Education, 2009.* Available online at http://www.rcag.org .uk/education_adultintro.htm (accessed January 19, 2009).

Archdiocese of Liverpool. *Syllabuses of Religious Instruction.* Liverpool: Rockliff Brothers, 1915.

———. *Syllabus of Religious Instruction for Schools*. Liverpool: Rockliff Brothers, 1943.

Arthur, James. *The Ebbing Tide: Policy and Principles of Catholic Education*. Leominster, UK: Gracewing, 1995.

———. *Faith and Secularisation in Religious Colleges and Universities*. London: Routledge, 2006.

Astley, Jeff. "The Place of Understanding in Christian Education and Education about Christianity." *British Journal of Religious Education* 16, no. 2 (1992): 90–101. Reprinted in *Critical Perspectives on Christian Education: A Reader on the Aims, Principles and Philosophy of Christian Education*, edited by Jeff Astley and Leslie J. Francis, 105–17. Leominster: UK: Gracewing Fowler Wright, 1994.

———. *The Philosophy of Christian Religious Education*. Birmingham, Ala.: Religious Education Press, 1994.

———. "Crossing the Divide." In *Inspiring Faith in Schools: Studies in Religious Education*, edited by Marius Felderhof, Penny Thompson, and David Torevell, 175–86. Aldershot, UK, and Burlington, Vermont: Ashgate, 2007.

Astley, Jeff, ed. *Learning in the Way: Research and Reflection on Adult Christian Education*. Leominster: Gracewing, 2000.

Astley, Jeff, and David Day, eds. *The Contours of Christian Education*. Great Wakering, UK: McCrimmons, 1992.

Astley, Jeff and Leslie J. Francis, eds. *Christian Perspectives on Faith Development: A Reader*. Leominster, UK: Gracewing Fowler Wright; Grand Rapids, Mich.: Eerdmans, 1992.

———. *Critical Perspectives on Christian Education: A Reader on the Aims, Principles and Philosophy of Christian Education*, Leominster, UK: Gracewing Fowler Wright, 1994.

Attfield, David. *Proclaiming the Gospel in a Secular Age*. Aldershot, UK: Ashgate, 2001.

Audi, Robert. *Religious Commitment and Secular Reason*. Cambridge: Cambridge University Press, 2000.

Augenstein, John, Christopher Kauffman, and Robert Wister, eds. *One Hundred Years of Catholic Education*. Washington, D.C.: National Catholic Educational Association, 2003.

Augustine, St. *On Catechising the Uninstructed*. Translated by E. Phillips Barker. London: Methuen, 1912.

———. *De Doctrina Christiana*. Translated by Roger P. H. Green. Oxford: University Press, 1997.

Australian Jesuit Education Office (AJEO). "Finding God in All Things." In *Ignatian Insights*. Sidney: AJEO, 2000.

Bales, Susan Ridgely. *When I Was a Child: Childrens' Perceptions of First Communion*. Chapel Hill: University of North Carolina Press, 2005.

Barnett, Ronald. *A Will to Learn*. Maidenhead, UK: Open University Press, 2007.

Barth, Karl. *Church Dogmatics*. Vol. I, Part 2, trans. G. T. Thomson and Harold Knight. Edinburgh: T. and T. Clark, 1956.

Barton, John. "The Bible and Its Authority and Interpretation." In *The Oxford Companion to Christian Thought*, edited by A. Hastings, A. Mason, and H. Pyper, 69–72. Oxford: Oxford University Press, 2000.

Bass, Dorothy. "Introduction." In *Practising Theology*, edited by Miroslav Volf and Dorothy Bass, 1–9, at 3. Grand Rapids, Mich.: Eerdmans, 2002.

Bauberot, Jean. *Laïcité 1905–2005: Entre Passion et Raison*. Paris: Éditions du Seuil, 2004.

———. *La Laïcité à l'éprouve*. Paris: Universalis, 2004.

Beckerlegge, Gwilym. *From Sacred Text to Internet*. Aldershot, UK, and Hants/Burlington, VT: Ashgate, 2002.

Benedict XVI. *Address to the Bishops of Kenya (2007)*. Available online at http://www .Catholic.org/featured/headline.php?ID=52448 page=1 (accessed November 2, 2007).

———. *Jesus of Nazareth: From the Baptism in the Jordan to the Transfiguration*. London, New York and Berlin: Bloomsbury, 2007.

———. *Sacramentum caritatis*, 2007. Available online at http://www.vatican.va/holy_ father/benedict_xvi/apost_exhortations/documents/hf_ben-xvi_exh_20070222_ sacramentum-caritatis_en.html.

———. *Spe Salvi*. London: Catholic Truth Society, 2007.

Bennett, John. "The Academy and Hospitality." *CrossCurrents* 50, nos. 1–2 (Spring/ Summer 2000): 26.

Bishops' Conference of Scotland. *Religion in Scotland's School: A Report to European Council of Episcopal Conferences (CCEE)*, 2006. Available online at http://www.chiesacattolica.it/ cci_new/PagineCCI/AllegatiArt/30/Scozia_ingl.doc.

Boeve, Lieven. *Interrupting Tradition: An Essay on Christian Faith in a Post-Modern Context*. Grand Rapids, Mich.: Eerdmans, 2003.

———. "Religion after Detraditionalization: Christian Faith in a Post-Secular Europe." *Irish Theological Quarterly* 70, no. 2 (2005): 99–122.

———. "Europe in Crisis: A Question of Belief or Unbelief? Perspectives from the Vatican." *Modern Theology* 23, no. 2 (2007): 205–27.

———. *God Interrupts History: Theology in a Time of Upheaval*. New York: Continuum, 2007.

Boeve, Lieven, and Kristien Justaert. *Consuming Religion in Europe*. A Special Issue of *Bulletin ET* 17, no. 1 (2006).

Bourg, Florence Caffrey. *Where Two or Three Are Gathered: Christian Families as Domestic Churches*. Notre Dame, Ind.: University of Notre Dame Press, 2004.

Bradford, John. *Caring for the Whole Child: A Holistic Approach to Spirituality*. London: Catholic Children's Society, 1995.

British Educational Communications and Technology Agency. *Learning Networks in Practice*, 2007. Available online at http://www.becta.org.uk/.

Brother Kenneth. *Catholic Schools in Scotland 1872–1972*. Glasgow: John S. Burns and Sons, 1972.

Brown, Callum G. *Religion and Society in Scotland since 1707*. Edinburgh: Edinburgh University Press, 1997.

———. *The Death of Christian Britain: Understanding Secularisation 1800–2000*. London: Routledge, 2001.

Brown, Frank Burch. Quoted by Gesa Thiessen, *Theological Aesthetics: A Reader*, 266–68. London: SCM, 2004).

Bruffee, Kenneth. Quoted by Sheryl Burkhalter, in "Four Modes of Discourse." In *Beyond the Classics? Essays in Religious Studies and Liberal Education*, edited by Frank Reynolds and Sheryl Burkhalter, 160. Atlanta: Scholars Press, 1990.

Brusselmans, Christiane, and Brian Haggerty. *We Celebrate the Eucharist*. Morristown, N.J.: Silver Burdett, 1986.

Bryk, Anthony S., Valerie E. Lee, and Peter B. Holland, eds. *Catholic Schools and the Common Good*. Cambridge, Mass., and London: Harvard University Press, 1993.

Buber, Martin. *Between Man and Man*. London: Fontana, 1974.

Bulgakov, Sergei. Quoted by Aidan Nichols, *Redeeming Beauty: Soundings in Sacral Aesthetics*. Aldershot, UK: Ashgate, 2007, 79–80.

Burkhalter, Sheryl. "Four Modes of Discourse." In *Beyond the Classics? Essays in Religious Studies and Liberal Education*, edited by Frank Reynolds and Sheryl Burkhalter, 160. Atlanta: Scholars Press, 1990.

Byrne, Anne, and Chris Malone. *Here I Am: A Religious Education Programme for Primary Schools*. London: HarperCollins, 1992, 2000.

Byrne, Gareth. "Children's Religious Education: Challenge and Gift." In *Nurturing Children's Religious Imagination: The Challenge of Primary Religious Education Today*, edited by Raymond Topley and Gareth Byrne, 243–44. Dublin: Veritas, 2004.

————. *Religious Education Renewed: An Overview of Developments in Post-Primary Religious Education*. Dublin: Veritas, 2005.

————. "Lifelong Faith Development in Home, Parish and Other Educational Environments." In *Exploring Religious Education*, edited by Anne Hession and Patricia Kieran. Dublin: Veritas, 2008.

Byrnes, James Thomas. *John Paul II and Educating for Life: Moving toward a Renewal of Catholic Educational Philosophy*. New York: Peter Lang, 2002.

Campbell, Heidi. "Embodied Church vs. Disembodied Congregation: Challenges Created by Online Religious Networks." *Journal of Media and Religion* 3, no. 2 (2004): 81–99.

————. *Exploring Religious Community Online*. New York: Peter Lang, 2005.

Carr, David. *Making Sense of Education*. London: Routledge Falmer, 2003.

Cary, Phillip. "Study as Love." In *Augustine and Liberal Education*, edited by Kim Paffenroth and Kevin Hughes, 65. Aldershot, UK: Ashgate Publishing, 2000.

Cassidy, Eoin G. "Modernity and Religion in Ireland: 1980–2000." In *Measuring Ireland: Discerning Values and Beliefs*, edited by Eoin G. Cassidy, 17–45. Dublin: Veritas, 2002.

Catechism of the Catholic Church. London: Geoffrey Chapman, 1994.

Catholic Bishops' Conference of England and Wales. *The Sign We Give: A Report of the Working Party on Collaborative Ministry*, 1995. Available online at http://www .catholic-ew.org.uk (accessed June 9, 2007).

————. Committee for Catechesis and Adult Christian Education. *The Priority of Adult Formation*. London: Catholic Media Trust, 2000.

Catholic Education Commission Scotland. *A Framework for S5/6 Religious Education*. Glasgow: Catholic Education Commission Scotland, 1998).

Catholic Education Service. *Spiritual and Moral Development Across the Curriculum*. London: Bishops' Conference of England and Wales, 1995.

Catholic Primary School Management Association. *Management Board Members' Handbook*, Dublin: Catholic Primary School Management Association, 2004.

Catholic Truth Society. *General Directory for Catechesis*. London: Catholic Truth Society, 1997.

Cavallo, Gugliemo, and Roger Chartier. *A History of Reading in the West*. Trans. Lydia Cochrane. Cambridge: Polity Press, 1999.

Cazeaux, Clive. *The Continental Aesthetics Reader*. London: Routledge, 2000.

Congregation for Catholic Education. *The Catholic School*. Rome: Sacred Congregation for Education, 1977.

————. *Lay Catholics in Schools.* Rome: Sacred Congregation for Education, 1982.

————. *The Religious Dimension of Education in a Catholic School.* Washington, D.C.: United States Catholic Conference, 1988.

Church Schools Review Group. *The Way Ahead: Church of England Schools in the New Millennium.* London: Church House Publishing, 2001.

Cimino, Carol, Regina M. Haney, and Joseph M. O'Keefe. *Integrating the Social Teaching of the Church into Catholic Schools: Conversations in Excellence 2000.* Washington, D.C.: National Catholic Educational Association, 2001.

Ciriello, Maria J. *The Principal as Spiritual Leader.* Washington, D.C.: United States Catholic Conference, 1994.

Coakley, Sarah. "Deepening Practices: Perspectives from Ascetical and Mystical Theology." In *Practising Theology,* edited by Miroslav Volf and Dorothy Bass, 78–93, at 79. Grand Rapids, Mich.: Eerdmans, 2002.

Colbert, Robert I., and Janice A. Kraus, eds. *Perspectives on Leadership and Catechesis.* Washington, D.C.: National Catholic Educational Association, 2001.

Congregation for Catholic Education. *The Religious Dimension of Education in a Catholic School.* Rome: Vatican Polyglot Press, 1988.

————. *Educating Together in Catholic Schools: A Shared Mission between Consecrated Persons and the Lay Faithful.* Rome: Sacred Congregation for Catholic Education, 2007.

Congregation for the Clergy. *General Directory for Catechesis.* 1997; Dublin: Veritas, 1998.

————. "General Directory for Catechesis." In *An Anthology of Catholic Teaching on Education,* edited by L. Franchi. London: Scepter, 1997.

Conway, Eamonn, Bairbre de Búrca, Denis O'Callaghan, Oliver Maloney, and John Littleton. "The Value of Theology." *The Furrow: A Journal for the Contemporary Church* 53, no. 6 (2002): 323–39.

Cook, Timothy J. *Architects of Catholic Culture: Designing and Building Catholic Culture in Catholic Schools.* Washington, D.C.: National Catholic Educational Association, 2001.

Coq, Guy. *La laïcité principe universel.* Paris: le félin, 2005.

Cotter, Christopher. "Integrating Tradition and Experience." *Journal of Religious Education* 48, no. 2 (2000): 9.

Cottingham, John. *The Spiritual Dimension: Religion, Philosophy and Human Value.* Cambridge: Cambridge University Press, 2005.

Conroy, James, ed. *Catholic Education: Inside Out/Outside In.* Dublin: Veritas, 1999.

Crowe, Frederick E. *Lonergan.* London: Chapman, 1992.

Cunningham, David S. *These Three Are One: The Practice of Trinitarian Theology.* Malden, Mass.: Blackwell Publishers, 1998).

Cupitt, Don. *Life Lines.* London: SCM Press, 1986.

Csikszentmihalyi, Mihaly. "The Psychology of Wisdom: An Evolutionary Interpretation." In *Wisdom: Its Nature, Origins and Development,* edited by Robert J. Sternberg, 25–51. Cambridge: Cambridge University Press, 1990.

Dagens, Claude, ed. *Pour l'éducation et pour l'école: Des catholiques s'engagent.* Paris: Odile Jacob, 2007.

D'Antonio, William V., James D. Davidson, Dean R. Hoge, and Mary L. Gautier. *American Catholics Today: New Realities of Their Faith and Their Church.* Lanham, Md.: Rowman and Littlefield, 2007.

D'Antonio, William V., James D. Davidson, Dean R. Hoge, and Juan L. Gonzales Jr.

Young Adult Catholics: Religion in the Culture of Choice. Notre Dame, Ind.: University of Notre Dame Press, 2001.

Daly, Tom. "Learning Levels." In *Australian Lonergan Workshop*, edited by William Danagher, 233–48. New York: University Press of America, 1993.

Davis, Caroline Franks. *The Evidential Force of Religious Experience*. Oxford: Clarendon Press, 1989.

Dawkins, Richard. *The God Delusion*. Boston: Houghton Mifflin Company, 2006.

Dawson, Lorna, and Douglas Cowan, eds. *Religion Online: Finding Faith on the Internet*. New York and London: Routledge, 2004.

Day, David, SJ. "Ignatian Education: From Foundational Insights to Contemporary Praxis." In *Briefing Papers: Occasional Readings on Topics That May Be of Particular Interest to Ignatian Education*. Australian Jesuit Education Office, no. 1 (December 1994).

D'Costa, Gavin. *The Meeting of the Religions and the Trinity*. Edinburgh: T. and T. Clark, 2000.

———. *Theology in the Public Square: Church, Academy and Nation*. Oxford: Blackwell, 2005.

———. *Christianity and World Religions: Disputed Questions in the Theology of Religions*. Oxford: Blackwell, 2009.

DeLambo, David. *Lay Parish Ministers: A Study of Emerging Leadership*. New York: National Pastoral Life Center, 2005.

Debré, Jean-Louis. *La laïcité à l'école*. Paris: Odile Jacob, 2004.

Deibert, Ronald J. *Parchment, Printing, and Hypermedia*. New York: Columbia University Press, 1997.

Department for Children, Schools and Families. *Towards a Unified eLearning Strategy: Consultation Document*. Nottingham: DfES Publications, 2003.

———. *Harnessing Technology: Transforming Learning and Children's Services*. Nottingham: DfES Publications, 2005.

Department of Education. *Revised Core Syllabus for Religious Education*. Dublin: Stationery Office, 2007. Available online at http://www.deni.gov.uk/index/80-curriculum-and-assessment/80-curriculum_and_assessment-religiouseducationcoresyllabus_pg.htm.

Department of Education and Science. *The Primary Curriculum: Introduction*. Dublin: Stationery Office, 1999.

———. *Junior Certificate Religious Education Syllabus*. Dublin: Stationery Office, 2000.

———. *Religious Education: Junior Certificate Guidelines for Teachers*. Dublin: Stationery Office, 2001.

———. *Leaving Certificate Religious Education Syllabus*. Dublin: Stationery Office, 2003.

———. "Planning for Religious Education: A Curriculum Framework for Senior Cycle." In *Religious Education: Leaving Certificate Guidelines for Teachers*, 201–23. Dublin: Stationery Office, 2005.

———. *Religious Education: Leaving Certificate Guidelines for Teachers*. Dublin: Stationery Office, 2005.

DePaul, Michael, and Linda Zagzebski, eds. *Intellectual Virtue: Perspectives from Ethics and Epistemology*. Oxford: Oxford University Press, 2003.

Devine, Thomas M. *The Scottish Nation*. London: Penguin Press, 2006.

Dickinson, R. "Teens and the Church." *Baptist Times* (September 20, 2007).

Dobbelaere, Karel, Mark Elchardus, J. Kerkhofs, L. Voyé, and B. Bawin-Legros. *Verloren zekerheid: De Belgen en hun waarden, overtuigingen en houdingen.* Tielt: Lannoo, 2000.

Dominian, Jack. *Living Love: Restoring Hope in the Church.* London: Darton, Longman, and Todd, 2004.

Downey, Michael. *Understanding Christian Spirituality.* New York: Paulist Press, 1997.

Dufour, Xavier, ed. *Enseigner: Une Oeuvre Spirituelle.* Paris: Parole et Silence, 2006.

Duignan, Patrick A. "Formation of Authentic Educational Leaders for Catholic Schools." In *Leadership in Catholic Education,* edited by Deirdre J. Duncan and Dan Riley, 172–83. Sydney: HarperCollins, 2002.

Dulles, Avery. *Models of the Church.* New York: Doubleday, 1987.

———. "The Systematic Theology of Faith: A Catholic Perspective." In *Handbook of Faith,* edited by James Michael Lee, chap. 7. Birmingham, Ala.: Religious Education Press, 1990.

Duminuco, Vincent J., SJ. *The Jesuit Ratio Studiorum: 400th Anniversary Perspectives.* New York: Fordham University Press, 2000.

Dykstra, Craig. *Growing in the Life of Faith.* Louisville, Ky.: Geneva Press, 1999.

Dysinger, Luke. "*Accepting the Embrace of God: The Ancient Art of Lectio Divina,*" 2005. Available online at http://www.valyermo.com/ld-art.html (accessed January 19, 2009).

Earl, Patricia. "Challenges to Faith Formation in Contemporary Schooling in the USA: Problem and Response." In *International Handbook of Education,* edited by Gerald Grace and Joseph O'Keefe. Dordrecht: Springer, 2007.

Elias, John L. *A History of Christian Education: Protestant, Catholic and Orthodox Perspectives.* Malabar, Florida: Krieger, 2002.

Episcopal Conferences of Africa and Madagascar (SECAM). *Message from the Symposium on the Situation of Zimbabwe,* 2007. Available online at http://www.sceam-sceam.org/newsInfo.php?id=58 (accessed on November 25, 2007).

Everist, Norma Cook, ed. *Christian Education as Evangelism.* Minneapolis: Fortress Press, 2007.

Fahey, Tony. "Is Atheism Increasing? Ireland and Europe Compared." In *Measuring Ireland: Discerning Values and Beliefs,* edited by Eoin G. Cassidy, 46–66. Dublin: Veritas, 2002.

Feheney, Matthew, ed. *From Ideal to Action: The Inner Nature of a Catholic School Today.* Dublin: Veritas, 1998.

Feinberg, Walter. *For Goodness Sake: Religious Schools and Education for Democratic Citizenry.* New York and London: Routledge, 2006.

Ferré, Frederick. *Basic Modern Philosophy of Religion.* London: Allen and Unwin; New York: Charles Scribner's Sons, 1967.

Finaldi, Gabriele. *The Image of Christ: The Catalogue of the Exhibition Seeing Salvation.* London: National Gallery Company, 2000.

Financial Times Online. "*The High Priestess of Internet Friendship.*" Available online at http://www.ft.com/cms/s/59ab33da-64c4-11db-90fd-0000779e2340.html (accessed February 2, 2007).

Fitzgerald, Timothy. *The Ideology of Religious Studies.* Oxford: Oxford University Press, 2000.

Fitzpatrick, Thomas A. *Catholic Secondary Education in South West Scotland before 1972.* Aberdeen: Aberdeen University Press, 1986.

———. "Catholic Education." In *Scottish Life and Society: A Compendium of Scottish Ethnology Volume 11*, edited by Heather Holmes, 435–55. East Linton, UK: Tuckwell Press, 2000.

———. "Catholic Education in Scotland." In *Scottish Education Post-devolution*, edited by Tom G. K. Bryce and Walter M. Humes, 272–81. Edinburgh: Edinburgh University Press, 2003.

Flanagan, Kieran. *Seen and Unseen: Visual Culture, Sociology and Theology*. London: Palgrave Macmillan, 2004.

Flannery, Austin, ed. *Vatican Council II: The Conciliar and Post Conciliar Documents*. Leominster, UK: Fowler Wright Books, 1981

———, ed. *Vatican Council II: More Postconciliar Documents*. Leominster: Fowler Wright Books, 1983.

Foltz, Franz, and Frederick Foltz. "Religion on the Internet: Community and Virtual Existence." *Bulletin of Science, Technology and Society* 23, no. 4 (2003): 321–30.

Foray, Phillipe. *La laïcité scolaire*. Bern: Peter Lang, 2008.

Fortner, Robert. *Communication, Media, and Identity*. Lanham, Md.: Rowman and Littlefield, 2007.

Foster, Robert F. *Modern Ireland 1600–1972*. London: Penguin Press, 1988.

Fowler, James W. *Stages of Faith: The Psychology of Human Development and the Quest for Meaning*. San Francisco: Harper and Row, 1981.

———. *Faithful Change: The Personal and Public Challenges of Postmodern Life*. Nashville, Tenn.: Abingdon, 1996.

Fowler, James W., and Sam Keen. *Life Maps: Conversations on the Journey of Faith*. Waco, Tex.: Word Books, 1978.

Fuller, Louise. *Irish Catholicism since 1950: The Undoing of a Culture*. Dublin: Gill and Macmillan, 2004.

Gadamer, Hans Georg. *Truth and Method*, trans. Joel Weinsheimer and Donald G. Marshall. London: Sheed and Ward; New York: Crossroad, 1993.

Gallagher, James, and Bishops' Conference of England and Wales. *Living and Sharing Our Faith: A National Project of Catechesis and Religious Education—Guidelines*. London: Harper Collins, 1986.

Gallagher, Tom. *Glasgow—The Uneasy Peace: Religious Tension in Modern Scotland*. Manchester: Manchester University Press, 1987.

Gardner, Howard. *The Unschooled Mind*. London: Fontana, 1993.

Giles, Dwight E., and Janet Eyler. "The Impact of a College Community Service Laboratory on Students' Personal, Social and Cognitive Outcomes." *Journal of Adolescence*, no. 17 (1994): 327–39.

Giussani, Luigi. *The Risk of Education*. New York: Crossroad, 2001.

Givens, Ruth. "Mending Walls: Recognizing the Influence of Boundary Issues in the Teacher/Student Relationship." *Christian Scholars' Review* 36, no. 2 (Winter 2007): 127–40.

Glover, Jonathan. *Humanity: A Moral History of the Twentieth Century*. New Haven: Yale University Press, 1999.

Goldburg, Peta. "Broadening Approaches to Religious Education through Constructivist Pedagogy." *Journal of Religious Education* 55, no. 2 (2007): 8-12.

Goldman, Alvin I. *Knowledge in a Social World*. Oxford: Clarendon Press, 1999.

Goleman, Daniel. *Emotional Intelligence*. London: Bloomsbury, 1996.

Gower, Ralph. *Conversations with Children*. Bootle, UK: Sefton Education Authority, 2003.

———. *The Effect of Postmodernism upon Children and Their Religious Education*. Bootle, UK: Sefton Education Authority, 2005.

———. "How to Stop Churches Becoming Old Peoples' Clubs." 2007, unpublished.

Grace, Gerald. *Catholic Schools: Mission, Markets and Morality*. London: Routledge Falmer, 2002.

Grace, Gerald, and Joseph O'Keefe, eds. *International Handbook of Catholic Education*. Dordrecht: Springer, 2007.

Grace, Gerald, and Nick Weeks. *Theological Literacy and Catholic Schools*. London: Centre for Research and Development in Catholic Education, Institute of Education, University of London, 2007.

Graham, Gordon. *The Internet: A Philosophical Inquiry*. London: Routledge, 1999.

Gray, Howard. "The Experience of Ignatius Loyola: Background to Jesuit Education." In *The Jesuit Ratio Studiorum: 400th Anniversary Perspectives*, edited by Vincent J. Duminuco, SJ, 1–21. New York: Fordham University Press, 2000.

Greco, John, and Ernest Sosa. *The Blackwell Guide to Epistemology*. Oxford: Blackwell Publishers, 1999.

Greeley, Andrew M., and Conor Ward. "How Secularised Is the Ireland We Live In?" *Doctrine and Life* (December 2000): 591–92.

Gimmitt, Michael. *Religious Education and Human Development*. Great Wakering, UK: McCrimmons, 1987.

Grimmitt, Michael, ed. *Pedagogies of Religious Education: Case Studies in the Research and Development of Good Pedagogic Practice in RE*. Essex, UK: McCrimmons, 2000.

Groome, Thomas H. *Christian Religious Education: Sharing Our Story and Vision*. London: Harper and Row, 1980.

———. "What Makes a School Catholic?" In *The Contemporary Catholic School: Context, Identity and Diversity*, edited by Terence H. McLaughlin, Joseph O'Keefe, and Bernadette O'Keeffe, 107–25. London: Falmer Press, 1996.

———. *Educating for Life: A Spiritual Vision for Every Teacher and Parent*. Allen, Tex.: Thomas More Press, 1998.

———. Claiming and Breaking Ground: The General Directory for Catechesis. In *Empowering Catechetical Leaders*, edited by Thomas H. Groome and Michael J. Corso. Washington, D.C.: National Catholic Educational Association, 1999.

———. *What Makes Us Catholic*. San Francisco: HarperOne, 2003.

Giusti, Simone S. *In Parrocchia Ho Incontrato Cristo*. Rome: Edizione Paoline, 2004.

Hagen, J. G. "Science and the Church." In *Catholic Encyclopaedia*, 1912. Available online at http://www.newadvent.org/cathen/13598b.htm (accessed July 2007).

Handley, James E. *The Irish in Scotland 1798–1845*. Cork: Cork University Press, 1943.

Hart, Trevor. "'Through the Arts': Hearing, Seeing and Touching the Truth." In *Beholding the Glory: Incarnation through the Arts*, edited by Jeremy Begbie, 1–26. London: DLT, 2000.

Hastings, Adrian. *Church and Mission in Africa*. London: Burns and Oates, 1997.

Hederman, Mark Patrick. *Anchoring the Altar: Christianity and the Work of Art*. Dublin: Veritas, 2002.

Heifetz, Ronald A., Ronald Linsky, and Marty Linsky. *Leadership on the Line: Staying Alive through the Dangers of Leading*. Boston: Harvard Business School Press, 2002.

Hesburg, Theodore M., ed. *The Challenge and Promise of a Catholic University*. Notre Dame, Ind.: University of Notre Dame Press, 1994.

Hession, Anne, and Patricia Kieran. *Exploring Religious Education*. Dublin: Veritas, 2008.

Hetherington, Stephen. "How to Know (That Knowledge-That Is Knowledge-How)." In *Epistemology Futures*, edited by Stephen Hetherington, 71–94. Oxford: Clarendon Press, 2006.

Hetherington, Stephen, ed. *Epistemology Futures*. Oxford: Clarendon Press, 2006.

Heythrop Institute for Religion, Ethics and Public Life. *On the Way to Life: Contemporary Culture and Theological Development as a Framework for Catholic Education, Catechesis and Formation*. London: Catholic Education Service, 2005.

Hick, John. *Faith and Knowledge*. Glasgow: Collins, 1974.

———. *The Second Christianity*. London: SCM Press, 1983.

———. *Who or What Is God?* London: SCM Press, 2008.

Hirst, Paul H. "Education, Knowledge and Practices." In *Beyond Liberal Education*, edited by Robin Barrow and Patricia White, chap. 9. London: Routledge, 1993.

Hirst, Paul H., and Richard S. Peters. *The Logic of Education*. London: Routledge and Kegan Paul, 1971.

Hitchens, Christopher. *God Is Not Great: How Religion Poisons Everything*. New York: Twelve Books/Warner Books, 2007.

Hobson, Peter R., and John S. Edwards. *Religious Education in a Pluralist Society*. London: Woburn Press, 1999.

Hofinger, Johannes. *The Art of Teaching Christian Doctrine: The Good News and Its Proclamation*. London: Sands, 1961.

Hoge, Dean R. "A Demographic Framework for Understanding Catholicism in America." *Seminary Journal* 1, no. 2 (2006): 61–68.

Hoge, Dean R., William Dinges, Mary Johnson, and Juan L. Gonzales, Jr.. *Young Adult Catholics: Religion in the Culture of Choice*. Notre Dame, Ind.: University of Notre Dame Press, 2001.

Hojsgaard, Morten, and Margit Warburg. *Religion and Cyberspace*. London and New York: Routledge, 2005.

Holman, Michael, SJ. "The Christian Ministry of Teaching." In *Contemporary Catholic Education*, edited by Michael Hayes and Liam Gearon, 70. Leominster: Gracewing, 2002.

Honore, Carl. *In Praise of Slow: How a Worldwide Movement Is Challenging the Cult of Speed*. London: Orion Books, 2005.

Howard, Thomas Albert. *Protestant Theology and the Making of the Modern German University*. Oxford: Oxford University Press, 2006.

Howes, Graham. *The Art of the Sacred: An Introduction to the Aesthetics of Art and Belief*. London: I.B. Tauris, 2007.

Hughes, Richard. *How Christian Faith Can Sustain the Life of the Mind*. Grand Rapids, Mich.: Eerdmans, 2001.

Hull, John M. *Studies in Religion and Education*. Lewes, UK: Falmer, 1984.

Hünermann, Peter. *Ekklesiologie im Präsens, Perspektiven* [Ecclesiology in the present, prospects]. Münster: Aschendorff, 1995.

Hunt, Thomas C., Thomas Oldenski, and Theodore Wallace, eds. *Catholic School Leadership*. London: Falmer, 2000.

Hunter, Archibald M. *Interpreting the Parables*. London: SCM, 1964.

Immink, F. Gerrit. *Faith: A Practical Theological Reconstruction.* Grand Rapids, Mich.: Eerdmans, 2005.

International Commission on the Apostolate of Jesuit Education (ICAJE). "Ignatian Pedagogy: A Practical Approach." In *Foundations,* edited by Carl E. Meirose, SJ, 237–71. Washington, D.C.: Jesuit Secondary Education Association, 1993.

Irish Catholic Bishops' Conference. *Guidelines for the Faith Formation and Development of Catholic Students: Junior Certificate Syllabus.* Dublin: Veritas, 1999.

———. *Prosperity with a Purpose: Christian Faith and Values in a Time of Rapid Economic Growth.* Dublin: Veritas, 1999.

———. *Towards a Policy for RE in Post-Primary Schools.* Dublin: Veritas, 2003.

———. Conference of Religious in Ireland, Irish Missionary Union. *Our Children, Our Church: Child Protection Policies and Procedures for the Catholic Church in Ireland.* Dublin: Veritas, 2005.

———. *Guidelines for the Faith Formation and Development of Catholic Students: Senior Cycle.* Dublin: Veritas, 2006.

———. *Nurturing Our Children's Faith.* Dublin: Veritas, 2006. Available online at http://www.catechetics.ie.

———. *Catholic Primary Schools: A Policy for Provision into the Future.* Dublin: Veritas, 2007.

———. *National Directory for Catechesis.* Forthcoming.

Irish National Teachers' Organisation. *Teaching Religion in the Primary School.* Dublin: INTO Publications, 2003.

Jackson, Robert. *Religious Education: An Interpretive Approach.* London: Hodder and Stoughton, 1997.

Jacobs, Jonathan. "Theism, Blame and Perfection." *Heythrop Journal* 41, no. 2 (April 2000): 142.

Jacobs, Richard M. *The Vocation of the Catholic Educator.* Washington, D.C.: National Catholic Educational Association, 1996.

———. *Building Spiritual Leadership Density in Catholic Schools.* Washington, D.C.: National Catholic Educational Association, 2005.

Jameson, Frederic. *Postmodernism, or, the Cultural Logic of Late Capitalism.* London: Verso, 1990.

Jamieson, Christopher. *Finding Sanctuary: Monastic Steps for Everyday Life.* London: Phoenix, 2006.

Janssen, Jacques. "Youth Culture and Spirituality in Europe." *Networking* 3, no. 3 (2002): 3.

Jarvis, Peter. *Adult and Continuing Education.* London: Routledge, 1995.

John Paul II. "Catechesi Tradendae," 1979. In *An Anthology of Catholic Teaching on Education,* edited by Leonard Franchi. London: Scepter, 2007.

———. *Familiaris Consortio,* 1981. Available online at http://www.vatican.va/holy_father/john_paul_ii/apost_exhortations/documents/hf_jp-ii_exh_19811122_familiaris-consortio_en.html.

———. *On Catholic Universities,* 1990. Available online at http://www.vatican.va/holy_father/john_paul_ii/apost_constitutions/documents/hf_jp-ii_apc_15081990_ex-corde-ecclesiae_en.html.

———. *Redemptoris Missio: Encyclical Letter of the Supreme Pontiff John Paul II on the Permanent Validity of the Church's Missionary Mandate.* London: Catholic Truth Society, 1991.

Available online at http://www.vatican.va/holy_father/john_paul_ii/encyclicals/
documents/hf_jp-ii_enc_07121990_redemptoris-missio_en.html.

———. *Veritatis splendor*, 1993. Available online at http://www.vatican.va/holy_father/
john_paul_ii/encyclicals/documents/hf_jp-ii_enc_06081993_veritatis-splendor_
en.html.

———. *Ecclesia in Africa*, 1995. Available online at http://www.vatican.va.holy_father/
john_paul_ii/apost_exhortations/documents/hf_jp-i (accessed November 4, 2007).

———. *On the Relationship between Faith and Reason*, 1998. Available online at http://www
.vatican.va/holy_father/john_paul_ii/encyclicals/documents/hf_jp-ii_enc_15101998_
fides-et-ratio_en.html.

———. *Ecclesia in America*, 1999. Available online at http://www.vatican.va/holy_father/
john_paul_ii/apost_exhortations/documents/hf_jp-ii_exh_22011999_ecclesia-in-
america_en.html.

———. *Ecclesia in Asia*, 1999. Available online at http://www.vatican.va/holy_father/
john_paul_ii/apost_exhortations/documents/hf_jp-ii_exh_06111999_ecclesia-in-
asia_en.html.

———. *Novo millennio ineunte*, 2000. Available online at http://www.vatican.va/holy_
father/john_paul_ii/apost_letters/documents/hf_jp-ii_apl_20010106_novo-
millennio-ineunte_en.html.

Jolliffe, Alan, Jonathan Ritter, and David Stevens, eds. *The Online Learning Handbook:
Developing and Using Web-based Learning*. London: Routledge, 2001.

Jones, Gregory. "Beliefs, Desires, Practices, and the Ends of Theological Education."
In *Practising Theology*, edited by Miroslav Volf and Dorothy Bass, 185–205. Grand
Rapids, Mich.: Eerdmans, 2002.

Jones, Gregory, and Stephanie Paulsell. *The Scope of Our Art: The Vocation of the Theological
Educator*. Grand Rapids, Mich.: Eerdmans, 2001.

Kehl, Medard. *Die Kirche: Eine Katholische Ekklesiologie* [The Church, a Catholic ecclesiol-
ogy]. Würzburg: Echter Verlag, 1993.

Kerkhofs, Jan, Karel Dobbelaere, and Lilianne Voyé. *De versnelde ommekeer: De warden van
vlamingen, walen en Brusselaars in de jaren negentig*. Tielt: Lannoo, 1992.

Kerkhofs, Jan, and Rudolf Rezsohazy, eds. *De stille ommekeer: Oude en nieuwe waarden in het
België van de jaren tachtig*. Tielt: Lannoo, 1984.

Kinast, Robert. *What Are They Saying about Theological Reflection?* New York: Paulist Press,
2000.

Knights, Philip, and Andrea Murray. *Evangelisation in England and Wales: A Report to the
Catholic Bishops*. London: Catholic Bishops' Conference of England and Wales, 2002.

Kowal, Susan. "After the First Elation." *The Tablet* (July 21, 2007).

Krumplemann, Frances. "Reading the Bible." In *The Modern Catholic Encyclopedia*, edited
by Michael Glazier and Monika K. Hellwig, 717–18. Dublin: Gill and MacMillan,
1994.

Krych, Margaret. "What Are the Theological Foundations of Education and Evangelism?" In *Christian Education as Evangelism*, edited by N. C. Everist, 30. Minneapolis:
Fortress Press, 2007.

Küng, Hans. *On Being a Christian*, trans. Edward Quinn. Glasgow: Collins, 1977.

Kvanvig, Jonathan. *The Value of Knowledge and the Pursuit of Understanding*. New York:
Cambridge University Press, 2003.

Labelle, Jean-Marie. *La Réciprocité éducative*. Paris: PUF, 1996.

Lambert, Lake. "Active Learning for the Kingdom of God." *Teaching Theology and Religion* 3, no. 2 (2000): 78.

Lambert, Pierrot, Charlotte Tansy, and Cathleen Going. *Caring about Meaning: Patterns in the Life of Bernard Lonergan*. Montreal: Thomas More Institute, 1982.

Lane, Dermot A. "Challenges Facing Catholic Education in Ireland." In *From Present to Future: Catholic Education in Ireland for the New Century*, edited by Eithne Woulfe and James Cassin, 131. Dublin: Veritas, 2006.

Lavelle, Louis. Quoted by Jean-Marie Labelle, *La Réciprocité éducative*. Paris: PUF, 1996, 195.

Leahy, Brendan. "Revelation and Faith." In Evangelising for the Third Millennium, edited by Maurice Hogan and Thomas J. Norris, 82. Dublin: Veritas, 1997.

Learning and Teaching Scotland (LTS). *Curriculum for Excellence*. 2009. Available at http://www.ltscotland.org.uk/curriculumforexcellence/ (accessed January 19, 2009).

Lee, James Michael, ed. *Handbook of Faith*. Birmingham, Ala.: Religious Education Press, 1990.

Lee, Moira. "Experiencing Shared Inquiry through the Process of Collaborative Learning." *Teaching Theology and Religion* 3, no. 2 (2000): 111.

Leichner, Jeannine Timko. *Called to His Supper: A Preparation for First Holy Communion*. Huntington, Ind.: Our Sunday Visitor, 1992.

Léna, Marguerite. "Défis éducatifs contemporains et vie consacrée." In *Pour l'éducation et pour l'école: Des catholiques s'engagent*, edited by Claude Dagens, 109. Paris: Odile Jacob, 2007.

Lodge, Anne. "First Communion in Carnduffy: A Religious and Secular Rite of Passage." *Irish Educational Studies* 18 (Spring 1999): 210–20.

Lonergan, Bernard. "The Place of Understanding in Christian Education and Education about Christianity." *British Journal of Religious Education* 16, no. 2 (1992): 90–101. Reprinted in *Critical Perspectives on Christian Education: A Reader on the Aims, Principles and Philosophy of Christian Education*, edited by Jeff Astley and Leslie J. Francis, 105–17. Leominster, UK: Gracewing Fowler Wright, 1994.

———. *Insight*. London: Longmans, Green, 1958.

———. "Method." In *Method in Theology*, chap. 1. London: Darton, Longman, and Todd, 1972.

———. *Method in Theology*. 1972; Toronto: University of Toronto Press, 2003.

———. "Cognitional Structure." In *Collected Works of Bernard Lonergan*. Vol. 4, *Collection: Papers by Bernard Lonergan*, edited by Frederick E. Crowe and Robert M. Doran, 205–21. Toronto: University of Toronto Press, 1988.

———. *Insight: A Study in Human Understanding*. Vol. 3, *The Collected Works of Bernard Lonergan*, edited by Frederick E. Crowe and Robert M. Doran, 1957; Toronto: University of Toronto Press, 1992.

Lovat, Terence. "The Support Text and the Public Syllabus: A Case for Integrity." *Journal of Religious Education* 48, no. 2 (2000): 35.

Loyola University. *Loyola Institute for Ministry Extension Program*, 2009. Available online at http://lim.loyno.edu/extension/prospectus.html (accessed January 19, 2009).

Lyon, David. *Jesus in Disneyland: Religion in Postmodern Times*. Cambridge: Polity Press/Blackwell, 2000.

Lytch, Carol E. *Choosing Church: What Makes a Difference for Teens*. Louisville, Ky., and London: Westminster John Knox Press, 2004.

Maan, Bashir. *The New Scots*. Edinburgh: John Donald Publishers, 1992.

MacGregor, Neil. "Introduction," 6–7. In *The Image of Christ: The Catalogue of the Exhibition Seeing Salvation*, by Gabriele Finaldi. London: National Gallery, 2000.

Macquarrie, John. *Paths in Spirituality*. London: Harper and Row, 1972.

Mahoney, Julie. "Hope, Holiness and Wholeness: The Mission of Catholic Campus Ministry to Higher Education." *Religious Education* 59 (3-S) (1974): 28–36.

Martin, Henri-Jean. *The History and Power of Writing*. Trans. Lydia Cochrane. Chicago: University of Chicago Press, 1994.

Martin, Thomas. "Aristotle's *Confessions* as Pedagogy: Exercises in Transformation." In *Augustine and Liberal Education*, edited by Kim Paffenroth and Kevin Hughes, 43. Aldershot, UK: Ashgate Publishing, 2000.

Mauzawa, Tomoko. *The Invention of World Religions, Or, How European Universalism Was Preserved in the Language of Pluralism*. Chicago: Chicago University Press, 2005.

Maximus the Confessor, St. "Capita de caritate."In *The Philokalia: The Complete Text Compiled by St. Nikodimos of the Holy Mountain and St. Makarios of Corinth*. Vol. 2, edited by G. E. H. Palmer, Philip Sherrard, and Kallistos Ware. London: Faber and Faber, 1981.

McCallion, Michael J., David R. Maines, and Steven W. Wolfel. "Policy as Practice: First Holy Communion in a Contested Situation." *Journal of Contemporary Ethnography* 25, no 3 (1963): 300–26.

McCann, Joseph. "Improving Our Aim: Catholic School Ethos Today." In *Reimagining the Catholic School*, edited by Noel Prendergast and Luke Monahan, 160–61. Dublin: Veritas, 2003.

McCarthy, Daniel. "Maturing towards God." *The Tablet*, October 18, 2008.

McCarthy, David Matzko. *Sex and Love in the Home*. London: SCM Press, 2004.

McClelland, Vincent Alan. *Cardinal Manning*. Oxford: Oxford University Press, 1962.

McDermott, Edwin J. *Distinctive Qualities of the Catholic School*. Washington, D.C.: National Catholic Educational Association, 1997.

McEwan, Ian. *Atonement*. London: Vintage Books, 2007.

McGinn, Bernard. *The Doctors of the Church: Thirty-three Men and Women Who Shaped Christianity*. New York: Crossroad, 1999.

McGrady, Andrew G. "Beholding the Stranger in Our Midst." *Welcoming the Stranger: Practising Hospitality in Contemporary Ireland*, edited by Andrew G. McGrady, 107. Dublin: Veritas, 2006.

———. "The Religious Dimension of Education in Irish Schools at the Start of the Third Millennium." In *From Present to Future: Catholic Education in Ireland for the New Century*, edited by Eithne Woulfe and James Cassin, 182. Dublin: Veritas, 2006.

McGrail, Peter. *First Communion: Ritual, Church and Popular Religious Identity*. Aldershot, UK: Ashgate, 2007.

McGrane, Bernard. *Beyond Anthropology: Society and the Other*. New York: Columbia University Press, 1989.

McKinney, Stephen J. "The Faith School Debate: Catholic Schooling in Scotland." *Pastoral Review* 3, no. 4 (2007): 28–34.

———. "Immigrants and Religious Conflict: Insider Accounts of Italian, Lithuanian and Polish Catholics in Scotland." In *Global Citizenship Education: Philosophy, Theory and Pedagogy*, edited by Michael A. Peters, Harry Blee, and Alan Britton. Rotterdam: Sense Publishers, 2007.

———. "Symbol or Stigma? The Place of Catholic Schools in Scotland. *The Catalyst* 7 (2007): 12–14.

———. "Catholic Education in Scotland." In *Scottish Education*, edited by Tom G. K. Bryce and Walter M. Humes. 3rd ed. Edinburgh: Edinburgh University Press, 2008.

McLaughlin, Terence H. "A Catholic Perspective on Education." *Journal of Education and Christian Belief* 6, no. 2 (2002): 122.

McLaughlin, Terence H., Joseph O'Keefe, and Bernadette O'Keeffe, eds. *The Contemporary Catholic School*. London: Falmer, 1996.

McLuhan, Marshall. *Understanding Media*. London: Ark, 1987.

Meagher, Timothy. "Ethnic, Catholic White: Changes in the Identity of European American Catholics." In *The Catholic Character of Catholic Schools*, edited by James Youniss, John J. Convey, and Jeffrey A. McLennan, 190–218. Notre Dame, Ind.: University of Notre Dame Press, 2000.

Mellor, Philip, and Chris Shilling. *Re-forming the Body: Religion, Community and Modernity*. London: Sage, 1998.

Meynell, Hugo. "On the Aims of Education." In *Proceedings of the Philosophy of Education Society of Great Britain*, 10 (July 1976): 79–97.

Miller, Vincent. *Consuming Religion: Religious Belief and Practice in a Consumer Culture*. New York: Continuum, 2004.

Miller-McLemore, Bonnie. "Contemplation in the Midst of Chaos: Contesting the Maceration of the Theological Teacher." In *The Scope of Our Art*, edited by Gregory Jones and Stephanie Paulsell, 48–74, at 66. Grand Rapids, Mich.: Eerdmans, 2001.

Mitchell, Basil. *The Justification of Religious Belief*. London: Macmillan, 1973.

———. *Faith and Criticism*. Oxford: Clarendon Press, 1994.

Mitchell, Martin J. *The Irish in the West of Scotland 1797–1848*. Edinburgh: John Donald Publishers, 1998.

Monaghan, Eilis. *Faith and Disadvantaged Youth: A Sign for the Future*. Master's thesis, Mater Dei Institute of Education, Dublin City University, 2002.

Toal, Vincent. "St. Dominic's Scripture Study Group." *Flourish* (October 2006).

Moore, Louise. "Staff Development in the Catholic School." In *Catholic School Leadership*, edited by Thomas C. Hunt, Thomas Oldenski, and Theodore J. Wallace, 96. London: Routledge, 2000.

Moran, Gabriel. *Religious Education as a Second Language*. Birmingham, Ala.: Religious Education Press, 1989.

———. *Showing How: The Act of Teaching*. Valley Forge, Pa.: Trinity Press International, 1997.

Morey, Melanie, and John Piderit. *Catholic Higher Education*. Oxford: Oxford University Press, 2006.

Morton, Keith. "The Irony of Service: Charity, Project and Social Change in Service-Learning." *Michigan Journal of Community Service Learning* (Fall 1995): 19–32.

Mulligan, James. *Catholic Education: Ensuring a Future*. Ottowa: St. Paul University/Novalis, 2005.

Nagel, Thomas. *The View from Nowhere*. Oxford: Oxford University Press, 1989.

National Conference of Catholic Bishops. *Empowered by the Spirit: Campus Ministry Faces the Future*. Washington, D.C.: United States Catholic Conference of Bishops, 1985.

———. *Equality and Impartiality*. New York: Oxford University Press, 1991.

Neidhart, Helga. "Leadership Spirituality in the Context of Catholic Education." In *Leadership in Catholic Education 2000 and Beyond*, edited by Patrick Duignan and Tony D'Arbon. Strathfield NSW: Australian Catholic University, 1998.

Network of Sacred Heart Schools. *We Hold in Trust 2006–2007*, 2007. Available online at http://www.sofie.org/ftm/introduction/.

Newman, John Henry Cardinal. *The Via Media of the Anglican Church I*. 1877. In *A Newman Synthesis*, edited by Erich Przywara, 164–65. London: Sheed and Ward, 1930.

———. *The Idea of a University*. London: Longmans, Green, 1931.

———. *A Grammar of Assent*. Notre Dame, Ind.: University of Notre Dame Press, 1979.

———. *An Essay in Aid of a Grammar of Assent*, edited by Ian T. Ker. Oxford: Clarendon, 1985.

Nichols, Aidan. *The Art of God Incarnate: Theology and Image in Christian Tradition*. London: DLT, 1980.

———. *Redeeming Beauty: Soundings in Sacral Aesthetics*. Aldershot, UK: Ashgate, 2007.

Nixon, Jon. "Forget the Form-filling, Just Listen and Learn." *Times Higher Education Supplement* (June 22, 2007).

Notre Dame Task Force on Catholic Education. *Making God Known, Loved, and Served: The Future of Catholic Primary and Secondary Schools in America*. Notre Dame, Ind.: Notre Dame Task Force on Catholic Education, 2006.

O'Brien, George Dennis. *Finding the Voice of the Church*. Notre Dame, Ind.: University of Notre Dame Press, 2007.

O'Carroll, Ciarán. *Church History*. 2 vols. Theology for Today Series. Dublin: Priory Institute, 2007.

O'Connell, Timothy. *Making Disciples*. New York: Crossroad, 1997.

O'Donnell, James. *Avatars of the Word: From Papyrus to Cyberspace*. Cambridge, Mass.: Harvard University Press, 2000.

O'Donovan, Oliver. *Begotten or Made?* Oxford: Clarendon Press, 1984.

O'Hagan, Francis J. *The Contribution of the Religious Orders to Education in Glasgow during the Period 1847–1918*. Lampeter, UK: Edwin Mellen Press, 2006.

O'Malley, John W. "How the First Jesuits Became Involved in Education." In *The Jesuit Ratio Studiorum: 400th Anniversary Perspectives*, edited by Vincent J. Duminuco, SJ. New York: Fordham University Press, 2000.

Osmer, Richard R., and Friedrich Schweitzer. *Religious Education between Modernization and Globalization: New Perspectives on the United States and Germany*. Grand Rapids, Mich.: Eerdmans, 2003.

Ottenhoff, Donald. "Seeking Christian Interiority: An Interview with Louis Dupré." *The Christian Century* (July 1997): 16–23. Available online at http://www.religion-online.org/showarticle.asp?title=214 (accessed August 25, 2007).

Oxley, Simon. *Creative Ecumenical Education*. Geneva: World Council of Churches Publications, 2002.

Paffenroth, Kim and Hughes, Kevin, eds. *Augustine and Liberal Education*. Aldershot, UK: Ashgate Publishing, 2000.

Palmer, Parker. *To Know as We Are Known*. San Francisco: Harper and Row, 1983.

Pannenberg, Wolfhart. "Theological Questions to Scientists." In *The Sciences and Theology in the Twentieth Century*, edited by Arthur R. Peacocke, 3–16, 4. London: Oriel Press, 1981.

Paterson, Lindsay. *Scottish Education in the Twentieth Century*. Edinburgh: Edinburgh University Press, 2003.

Paterson, Lindsay, and Cristina Iannelli. "Religion, Social Mobility and Education in Scotland." In *British Journal of Sociology* 57, no. 3 (2006): 353–77.

Paul VI. *Evangelisation in the Modern World (Apostolic Exhortation Evangelii Nuntiandi of his Holiness Pope Paul VI)*. London: Catholic Truth Society, 1975. Available online at http://www.vatican.va/holy_father/paul_vi/apost_exhortations/documents/hf_p-vi_ ex (accessed November 13, 2007).

Pauw, Amy Plantinga. "Attending to the Gaps between Beliefs and Practices." In *Practicing Theology*, edited by Miroslav Volf and Dorothy Bass, 41. Grand Rapids, Mich.: Eerdmans, 2002.

Pena-Ruiz, Henri. *Dieu et Marianne*. Paris: Presses Universitaires de France, 1999.

Peperzak, Adriaan. *Thinking*. New York: Fordham University Press, 2006.

Peters, John Durham. *Speaking Into the Air*. Chicago: University of Chicago Press, 1999.

Peterson, Michael L. *With All Your Mind: A Christian Philosophy of Education*. Notre Dame, Ind.: University of Notre Dame Press, 2001.

Pew Internet. "Internet, Broadband, and Cell Phone Statistics." Available online at http://www.pewinternet.org/ (accessed January 16, 2009).

Pew Internet and American Life Project Religion Surfers Survey 2001. In *Religion Online: Finding Faith on the Internet*, edited by Lorna Dawson and Douglas Cowan, 19. New York and London: Routledge, 2004.

Plantinga, Alvin. "On Christian Scholarship." In *The Challenge and Promise of a Catholic University*, edited by Theodore M. Hesburg, 267–96. Notre Dame, Ind.: University of Notre Dame Press, 1994.

Plantinga, Alvin, and Nicholas Wolterstorff, eds. *Faith and Rationality: Reason and Belief in God*. Notre Dame, Ind.: University of Notre Dame Press, 1983.

Pohl, Christine. "A Community's Practice of Hospitality: The Interdependence of Practices and of Communities." In *Practicing Theology*, edited by Miroslav Volf and Dorothy Bass, 121–36, at 132–33. Grand Rapids, Mich.: Eerdmans, 2002.

Pojman, Louis P. *Religious Belief and the Will*. London: Routledge and Kegan Paul, 1986.

Pontifical Council for Justice and Peace. *Compendium of the Social Doctrine of the Church*. Rome: Città del Vaticano: Libreria Editrice Vaticana, 2004.

Pontifical Council for Social Communications. *Ethics in Communication, 2000*. Available online at http://www.vatican.va/roman_curia/pontifical_councils/pccs/documents/ rc_pc_pccs_doc_20000530_ethics-communications_en.html.

Postman, Neil. *Amusing Ourselves to Death*. London: Methuen, 1987.

Poulat, Émile. *Notre laïcité publique*. Paris: Berg International, 2003.

Prendergast, Noel, and Luke Monahan, eds. *Reimagining the Catholic School*. Dublin: Veritas, 2003.

Price, James L. "The Biblical View of Faith: A Protestant Perspective." In *Handbook of Faith*, ed. James Michael Lee, chap. 6. Birmingham, Ala.: Religious Education Press, 1990.

Pulliam, John D., and James J. Van Patten. *History of Education in America*. Upper Saddle River, N.J.: Prentice Hall, 2007.

Pullinger, David. *Information Technology and Cyberspace*. London: Darton, Longman, and Todd, 2001.

Purnell, A. Patrick. *Our Faith Story: Its Telling and Its Sharing*. London: Collins, 1985.

Purves, Alan. *The Web of Text and the Web of God*. New York: Guilford Press, 1998.

Radcliffe, Timothy. *What Is the Point of Being a Christian?* London: Burns and Oates, 2005.

Rahner, Karl. "Peaceful Reflections on the Parochial Principle." In *Theological Investigations*. Vol. 2, *Man in the Church*. London: Darton, Longman and Todd, 1963.

———. *The Christian of the Future*. London: Burns and Oates, 1969.

———. *Belief Today*. New York: Sheed and Ward, 1976.

———. *Foundations of Christian Faith*. New York: Crossroad, 1978.

———. *The Practice of Faith: A Handbook of Contemporary Spirituality*. New York: Crossroad, 1983.

———. Quoted by Gesa Thiessen, *Theological Aesthetics: A Reader*, 218, 219, 221. (London: SCM, 2004).

Rahner, Karl, and Herbert Vorgrimler. *Concise Theological Dictionary*. London: Burns and Oates, 1983.

Ratzinger, Joseph. *The Nature and Mission of Theology*. San Francisco: Ignatius Press, 1995.

———. *Called to Communion*. San Francisco: Ignatius Press, 1996.

———. *Values in a Time of Upheaval*. With M. Pella. 2004; New York: Crossroad, 2006.

———. *Without Roots: The West, Relativism, Christianity, Islam*. 2004; New York: Basic Books, 2006.

Raz, Joseph. *Engaging Reason: On the Theory of Value and Action*. Oxford: Oxford University Press, 1999.

———. *Value, Respect, and Attachment*. Cambridge: Cambridge University Press, 2001.

Regan, Jane E. *Toward an Adult Church: A Vision of Faith Formation*. Chicago: Loyola Press, 2002.

Reichberg, Gregory. "Studiositas, the Virtue of Attention." In *The Common Things: Essays on Thomism and Education*, edited by Daniel McInerny. Washington, D.C.: American Maritain Association, 1999.

Reiser, William. *Love of Learning, Desire for Justice*. Scranton: University of Scranton Press, 1995.

Reynolds, Frank, and Sheryl Burkhalter, eds. *Beyond the Classics? Essays in Religious Studies and Liberal Education*. Atlanta: Scholars Press, 1990.

Rheingold, Howard. *The Virtual Community: Homesteading on the Electronic Frontier*. Cambridge, Mass.: MIT Press, 2000.

Riggs, Wayne D. "Understanding 'Virtue' and the Virtue of Understanding." In *Intellectual Virtue: Perspectives from Ethics and Epistemology*, edited by Michael DePaul and Linda Zagzebski, 203–26. Oxford: Oxford University Press.

Roberts, Robert C., and W. Jay Wood. *Intellectual Virtues: An Essay in Regulative Epistemology*. Oxford: Clarendon Press, 2007.

Rodger, Alex. "Religious Education." In *Scottish Education Post-devolution*, edited by Tom G. K. Bryce and Walter M. Humes, 600–5. Edinburgh: Edinburgh University Press, 2003.

Rodger, Alex. "Human Spirituality: Towards an Educational Rationale." In *Education, Spirituality and the Whole Child*, edited by Ron Best, 45. London: Cassell, 1996.

Roebben, Bert, and Michael Warren, eds. *Religious Education as Practical Theology*. Leuven: Peeters, 2001.

Rogus, Joseph F., and Colleen A. Wildenhaus. "Ongoing Staff Development in Schools." In *Catholic School Leadership*, edited by Thomas C. Hunt, Thomas Oldenski, and Theodore Wallace, 167. London: Falmer, 2000.

Romano, Antonio. *The Charism of the Founders*. Slough: St. Pauls, 1994.

Rylands, Paddy. *Sharing the Gift: Preparing to Celebrate the Sacraments with Families in the Parish*. London: Collins, 1989.

Sacred Congregation for Catholic Education. *The Catholic School*. Rome: Libreria Editrice Vaticana; Ottawa: Publications Service Canadian Conference of Catholic Bishops, 1977.

———. *Consecrated Persons and Their Mission in Schools*. Rome: Libreria Editrice Vaticana, 2002.

———. *Lay Catholics in Schools: Witnesses to Faith*. 1982. Available online at http://www.vatican.va/roman_curia/congregations/ccatheduc/documents/rc_con_ccatheduc_doc_19821015_lay-catholics_en.html (accessed January 19, 2009).

Sacred Congregation for the Clergy. "General Catechetical Directory" (1971). In *Vatican Council II: More Postconciliar Documents*, edited by Austin Flannery, OP. Leominster: Fowler Wright Books, 1983.

Sacks, Jonathan. *To Heal a Fractured World: The Ethics of Responsibility*. London and New York: Continuum, 2005.

Saliers, Don. *Music and Theology*. Nashville: Abingdon Press, 2007.

Salmon, Gilly. *E-Moderating: The Key to Teaching and Learning Online*. London: Kogan Page, 2003.

Saris, Wim. *Together We Communicate*. London: Collins, 1982.

Scharer, Matthias, and Bernd Jochen Hilberath. *The Practice of Communicative Theology: An Introduction to a New Theological Culture*. New York: Crossroad, 2008.

Schindler, David L. *Heart of the World, Center of the Church*. Edinburgh: T. and T. Clark, 1996.

Schmitt, Frederick F., ed. *Socializing Epistemology: The Social Dimensions of Knowledge*. Lanham, Md.: Rowman and Littlefield, 1994.

———. "Social Epistemology." In *The Blackwell Guide to Epistemology*, edited by John Greco and Ernest Sosa, 354. Oxford: Blackwell Publishers, 1999.

Schneiders, Sandra M. "The Charism of Religious Life." In *Loving the World as God Loves*, 7–15. Twelfth U.S. Religious Formation Conference, 2001. Available online at http://www.smnz.org.nz/maristlibrary/religiouslife.pdf.

Schultze, Quentin. "Faith, Education and Communication Technology." *Journal of Education and Christian Belief* 8, no. 1 (2004): 9–21.

Schuttloffel, Merylann J. *Character and the Contemplative Principal*. Washington, D.C.: National Catholic Educational Association, 1999.

———. "Contemporary Challenges to Recruitment, Formation and Retention of Catholic School Leadership in the USA." In *International Handbook of Education*, edited by Gerald Grace and Joseph O'Keefe, 85–102. Dordrecht: Springer, 2007.

———. *Contemplative Leadership that Creates a Culture of Continuous Improvement*. Washington, D.C.: National Catholic Educational Association, 2008.

Schwehn, Mark. *Exiles from Eden*. New York: Oxford University Press, 1993.

Scott, Kieran. "To Teach Religion or Not to Teach Religion: Is That the Dilemma?" In *Religious Education as Practical Theology*, edited by Bert Roebben and Michael Warren, 145–73. Leuven: Peeters, 2001.

Scottish Bible Society and the Contextual Bible Study Group. *Conversations: The Companion*. Edinburgh: Scottish Bible Society, 2006.

Scottish Catholic Bishops. *The Approach to Religious Education in the Catholic Secondary School*. Edinburgh: SCB, 1974.

Scottish Catholic Education Service (SCES). Available online at http://www.sces.uk.com (accessed January 19, 2009).

Scottish Central Committee on Religious Education (SCCORE). *Bulletin 1: A Curricular Approach to Religious Education*. Edinburgh: HMSO, 1978.

———. *Bulletin 2: Curriculum Guidelines on Religious Education*. Glasgow: Consultative Committee on the Curriculum, 1981.

Scottish Education Department (SED). *Moral and Religious Education in Scottish Schools* (The Millar Report). Edinburgh: HMSO, 1972.

Scottish Office Education Department (SOED). *Religious and Moral Education*. Edinburgh: Scottish Office Education Department, 1992. Available online at http://www .ltscotland.org.uk/5to14/htmlunrevisedguidelines/Pages/RE/Main/recontents.htm (accessed January 19, 2009).

Scottish Office Education Department/Catholic Education Commission (SOED/CEC). 1994. *5–14 Religious Education (Roman Catholic Schools)*. Available online at http://www. ltscotland.org.uk/5to14/htmlunrevisedguidelines/Pages/re_rc/main/rerccontents. htm (accessed January 19, 2009).

Scruton, Roger. *An Intelligent Person's Guide to Culture*. London: Duckworth, 1928.

Seasoltz, R. Kevin. *A Sense of the Sacred: Theological Foundations of Christian Art and Architecture*. London: Continuum, 2005.

Second Vatican Council. *Sacrosanctum Concilium*, 1963. Available online at http:// www.vatican.va/archive/hist_councils/ii_vatican_council/documents/vat-ii_ const_19631204_sacrosanctum-concilium_en.html.

———. *Lumen Gentium*, 1964. In *Vatican Council II: The Conciliar and Post Conciliar Documents*, edited by Austin Flannery. Leominster, UK: Fowler Wright Books, 1981. Available online at http://www.vatican.va/archive/hist_councils/ii_vatican_council/ documents/vat-ii_const_19641121_lumen-gentium_en.html.

———. *Ad Gentes*, 1965. Available at http://www.vatican.va/archive/hist_councils/ii_ vatican_council/documents/vat-ii_decree_19651207_ad-gentes_en.html

———. *Apostolicam Actuositatem*, 1965. In *Vatican Council II: The Conciliar and Post Conciliar Documents*, edited by Austin Flannery. Leominster, UK: Fowler Wright Books, 1981. Available online at http://www.vatican.va/archive/hist_councils/ii_vatican_council/ documents/vat-ii_decree_19651118_apostolicam-actuositatem_en.html.

———. *Dei Verbum*, 1965. In *Vatican Council II: The Conciliar and Post Conciliar Documents*, edited by Austin Flannery. Leominster, UK: Fowler Wright Books, 1981. Available online at http://www.vatican.va/archive/hist_councils/ii_vatican_council/docu-ments/vat-ii_const_19651118_dei-verbum_en.html.

———. *Gaudium et spes*, 1965. Available online at http://www.vatican.va/archive/hist_ councils/ii_vatican_council/documents/vat-ii_cons_19651207_gaudium-et-spes_ en.html.

Selwyn, Neil, Stephen Gorard, and John Furlong, eds. *Adult Learning in the Digital Age.* London and New York: Routledge, 2006.

Sergiovanni, Thomas J. *Moral Leadership: Getting to the Heart of School Improvement.* San Francisco: Jossey-Bass, 1992.

Seymour, Jack L., ed. *Mapping Christian Education: Approaches to Congregational Learning.* Nashville, Tenn.: Abingdon, 1997.

Seymour, Jack L., and Donald E. Miller, eds. *Contemporary Approaches to Christian Education.* Nashville, Tenn.: Abingdon, 1982.

———. *Theological Approaches to Christian Education.* Nashville, Tenn.: Abingdon, 1990.

Sherry, Patrick. *Images of Redemption: Art, Literature and Salvation.* London: T. and T. Clark, 2003.

Shorter, Aylward. *Evangelisation and Culture.* London: Geoffrey Chapman, 1994.

Sinwell, Joseph P., ed. *The Baptismal Catechumenate: An Inspiration for All Catechesis.* Washington, D.C.: National Catholic Educational Association, 2002.

Skinnider, Martha. *Catholic Elementary Education in Glasgow, 1818–1918.* In *Studies in the History of Scottish Education 1872-1939*, edited by T. R. Bone, 13–70. London: University of London Press, 1967.

Smart, Ninian. *Dimensions of the Sacred: An Anatomy of the World's Beliefs.* London: HarperCollins, 1966.

———. *The Phenomenon of Religion.* London: Macmillan, 1973.

———. "What Is Religion?" In *New Movements in Religious Education*, edited by Ninian Smart and Donald Horder, 13–22. London: Temple Smith, 1975.

———. *The Phenomenon of Christianity.* London: Collins, 1979.

———. "Religious Studies in the United Kingdom." *Religion* 18 (1998): 8.

Smith, Paige, and Ronald Nuzzi. "Beyond Religious Congregations: Responding to New Challenges in Catholic Education." In *International Handbook of Catholic Education*, edited by Gerald Grace and Joseph O'Keefe, 103–24. Dordrecht: Springer, 2007.

Society of Jesus. *Characteristics of Jesuit Education.* London: Irish and British Provinces of the Society of Jesus, 1987.

Sofield, Loughlan, and Carroll Juliano. *Collaboration: Uniting Our Gifts in Ministry.* Notre Dame, Ind.: Ave Maria Press, 2000.

Sofield, Loughlan, and Donald H. Kuhn. *The Collaborative Leader: Listening to the Wisdom of God's People.* Notre Dame, Ind.: Ave Maria Press, 1995.

Stackhouse, John. *Humble Apologetics.* New York: Oxford University Press, 2006.

Starkey, Paul. "Handing Over the Baton: From Religious to Lay Administration." *Catholic School Studies* 70, no. 2 (1997): 62.

Stasi, Bernard. *Laïcité et République.* Paris: La Documentation Française, 2004.

Staud, John, ed. *Carnegie Conversation on Catholic Education.* Notre Dame, Ind.: Alliance for Catholic Education Press at University of Notre Dame, 2008.

Steiner, George. *Lessons of the Masters.* Cambridge, Mass.: Harvard University Press, 2003.

Sternberg, Robert J., ed. *Wisdom: Its Nature, Origins and Development.* Cambridge: Cambridge University Press, 1990.

Stout, Jeffrey. *The Flight from Authority: Religion, Morality, and the Quest for Autonomy.* Notre Dame, Ind.: University of Notre Dame Press, 1981.

Sullivan, John. *Catholic Schools in Contention: Competing Metaphors and Leadership Implications.* Dublin: Veritas, 2000.

———. "Wrestling with Managerialism." In *Commitment to Diversity*, edited by Mary Eaton, Jane Longmore, and Arthur Naylor. London: Cassell, 2000.

———. *Catholic Education: Distinctive and Inclusive.* Dordrecht: Kluwer, 2001.

———. "From Formation to the Frontiers." *Journal of Education and Christian Belief* 7, no. 1 (2003): 7–21.

———. "Addressing Difference as Well as Commonality in Leadership Preparation for Faith Schools." *Journal of Education and Christian Belief* 10, no. 1 (Spring 2006): 75–88.

———. "Dismembering and Remembering Religious Education." In *Inspiring Faith in Schools*, edited by Penny Thompson, David Torevell, and Marius Felderhof. Aldershot, UK: Ashgate, 2007.

Sullivan, Patricia, and Timothy Brown. *Setting Hearts on Fire: A Spirituality for Leaders.* New York: St. Paul's, 1997.

Swinburne, Richard. *The Existence of God.* Oxford: Clarendon Press, 2004.

———. *Faith and Reason.* Oxford: Clarendon Press, 2005.

Sykes, Stephen. *The Identity of Christianity: Theologians and the Essence of Christianity from Schleiermacher to Barth.* London: SPCK, 1984.

Symposium of Episcopal Conferences of Africa and Madagascar. *A Message from the Symposium of Episcopal Conferences of Africa and Madagascar (SECAM) on the State*, 2007. Available online at http://www.sceam-secam.org/newsInfo.php?id=58 (accessed on November 25, 2007).

Teeven, Donna. "Philosophical Hermeneutics and Theological Education." *Teaching Theology and Religion* 3, no. 2 (June 2005): 85.

Tekippe, Terry. *Theology: Love's Question.* London: University of America, 1991.

Thatcher, Adrian. "Spirituality as an Academic Discipline." In *Spirituality and the Curriculum*, edited by Adrian Thatcher, 57. London: Cassell, 1999.

———., ed. *Spirituality and the Curriculum.* London: Cassell, 1999.

Thévenot, Xavier, and Jean Joncheray, eds. *Pour une éthique de la pratique educative.* Paris: Desclée, 1991.

Thiessen, Elmer J. *Teaching for Commitment: Liberal Education, Indoctrination, and Christian Nurture.* Leominster, UK: Gracewing, 1993.

Thiessen, Gesa. *Theological Aesthetics: A Reader.* London: SCM, 2004.

Thirty Years a' Praying. TV Program. RTE One Television, episode 2 (April 16, 2007).

Topley, Raymond. "Bernard Lonergan's Levels of Consciousness Applied to Christian Religious Education." Ph.D. diss., Graduate Theological Foundation, Indiana, 2004. Copies housed at St. Patrick's College, Drumcondra; The Lonergan Centre, Milltown Institute; The Lonergan Institute, Boston College; and The Lonergan Research Institute, Regis College, Toronto.

Torevell, David. *Liturgy and the Beauty of the Unknown: Another Place.* Aldershot, UK: Ashgate, 2007.

Tozzi, Carlos Alberto. *Parent and Family Religious Education: A Case Study Based on an Ecological Theory of Human Development.* PhD diss., Fordham University, 1994.

Trigg, Roger. *Religion in Public Life.* Oxford: Oxford University Press, 2007.

United States Conference of Catholic Bishops. *To Teach as Jesus Did: A Pastoral Message on*

Catholic Education. Washington, D.C.: United States Conference of Catholic Bishops, 1972.

———. *Catechism of the Catholic Church. English translation.* New York: William H. Sadlier, 1994.

———. *Co-workers in the Vineyard of the Lord.* Washington, D.C.: United States Conference of Catholic Bishops, 2005.

———. *National Directory for Catechesis.* Washington, D.C.: United States Conference of Catholic Bishops, 2005.

———. *Renewing our Commitment to Catholic Elementary and Secondary Schools in the Third Millennium.* Washington, D.C.: United States Conference of Catholic Bishops, 2005.

———. "*Mission Statement: Objectives.*" http://www.usccb.org/education/whoweare .shtml, accessed January 2009.

Valadier, Paul. *Détresse du Politique, Force du Religieux.* Paris: Éditions du Seuil, 2007.

Van Manen, Max. "Linking Ways of Knowing with Ways of Being Practical." *Curriculum and Inquiry* 6, no. 3 (1977): 205–28.

Veling, Terry. *Living in the Margins.* New York: Crossroad, 1996.

Veverka, Fayette Breaux. "Boundaries and Border Crossings: Educating for Religious Particularity and Pluralism." Paper presented at the Education and Ethos Network Symposium on "Identity: A Contested Concept." Nijmegen, The Netherlands, February 2001.

Volf, Miroslav. "Theology for a Way of Life." In *Practicing Theology,* edited by Miroslav Volf and Dorothy Bass, 245–263, at 257. Grand Rapids, Mich.: Eerdmans, 2002.

Volf, Miroslav, and Dorothy Bass, eds. *Practicing Theology.* Grand Rapids, Mich. Eerdmans, 2002.

Von Hügel, Friedrich. *Essay and Addresses on the Philosophy of Religion.* 2nd series. London: Dent, 1926.

Walker, Lynn. *All Is Gift: Guidelines for Parish Catechists—Working with Children.* London: Collins, 1987.

Walzer, Michael. *Thick and Thin: Moral Argument at Home and Abroad.* Notre Dame, Ind.: University of Notre Dame Press, 1994.

Watkins, Clare. *Living Baptism: Called Out of the Ordinary.* London: Darton, Longman, and Todd, 2006.

———. "Traditio: The Ordinary Handling of Holy Things—Reflections de Doctrina Christiana from an Ecclesiology Ordered to Baptism." *New Blackfriars* 87 (March 2006).

Watts, John. *A Canticle of Love: The Story of the Franciscan Sisters of the Immaculate Conception.* Edinburgh: Birlinn, 2006.

Webb, Stephen. "Teaching as Confessing." *Teaching Theology and Religion* 2, no. 3 (October 1999):150.

Westerhoff, John. "Christian Education as a Theological Discipline." *Saint Luke's Journal of Theology* 21, no. 4 (1978): 287.

White, Gerry. "Education and the Constitution." In *Religion, Education and the Constitution,* edited by Dermot A. Lane, 84–117. Dublin: Columba Press, 1992.

Williams, Kevin. *Faith and the Nation: Religion, Culture and Schooling in Ireland.* Dublin: Dominican Publications, 2005.

Williamson, Catherine E. "Passing on the Faith: The Importance of Parish-Based Catechesis." PhD diss., University of Brighton, England, 1999.

Wolterstorff, Nicholas P. *Educating for Life: Reflections on Christian Teaching and Learning.*
Grand Rapids, Mich.: Baker Book House, 2002.

Wood, W. Jay. *Epistemology.* Leicester: Apollos, 1998.

Woulfe, Eithne, and James Cassin, eds. *From Present to Future: Catholic Education in Ireland
for the New Century.* Dublin: Veritas, 2006.

Wragg, Edward C., and George A. Brown, eds. *Questioning in the Primary School.* New revised edition. London: Routledge Falmer, 2001.

Ziebertz, Hans-Georg. *Religious Education in a Plural Western Society: Problems and Challenges.* Munster, Hamburg, and London: Lit Verlag, 2003.

Zukowski, Sr. Angela. "Kaizening into the Future: Distance Education." In *Catholic
School Leadership,* edited by Thomas C. Hunt, Thomas Oldenski, and Theodore Wallace, 174–88. London and New York: Falmer Press, 2000.

Zulehner, Paul. *Aufbrechen oder Untergehen: So Geht Kirchenentwicklung* [To take off or go under: How the Church evolves]. Ostfilderns: Schwabenverlag, 2003.

Contributors

Frederick D. Aquino is associate professor of theology and philosophy in the Graduate School of Theology at Abilene Christian University.

Jeff Astley is professor and director of the ecumenical North of England Institute for Christian Education, based at the University of Durham.

Lieven Boeve is professor of fundamental theology at the Catholic University of Leuven and for several years was president of the European Society of Catholic Theology.

Gareth Byrne is head of the School of Education at Mater Dei Institute of Education, a College of Dublin City University.

Gavin D'Costa is professor of Catholic theology at the University of Bristol.

Michael Edwards, who died in June 2010, was director of education for the British Province of the Society of Jesus.

Ralph Gower, now retired, has served the church as a Baptist minister for more than fifty years, taught religious education in schools and colleges, and worked in local education authority administration at senior levels.

Atli Jónsson, a priest of the Diocese of Reykjavik, Iceland, is currently working as parish priest in Southport, Archdiocese of Liverpool, UK.

Victorine Mansanga, SND, a Notre-Dame de Namur Sister, was a research student at Liverpool Hope University; she has taught and exercised leadership in schools and colleges and in her order.

Peter McGrail, a priest of the Roman Catholic Archdiocese of Liverpool, is associate professor in Catholic studies at Liverpool Hope University.

Stephen J. McKinney is a senior lecturer and head of the Department of Religious Education at the University of Glasgow.

Frances Orchard, CJ, is vicar general of the Congregatio Jesu, a Roman Catholic religious congregation founded by Mary Ward; now based in Rome, she travels worldwide on behalf of her congregation and its schools.

Merylann "Mimi" J. Schuttloffel is professor of educational administration and policy studies at the Catholic University of America.

Ros Stuart-Buttle was for several years the director of educational outreach at Ushaw College, Durham, UK. She is a doctoral student at Liverpool Hope University.

John Sullivan is professor of Christian education at Liverpool Hope University.

Raymond Topley, who died in September 2009, was head of the Department of Religious Studies and Religious Education at St. Patrick's College, Drumcondra, Dublin.

David Torevell is associate professor in the Department of Theology and Religious Studies/Philosophy and Ethics at Liverpool Hope University.

Clare Watkins is a Catholic theologian, teacher, writer, and consultant, based in Cambridge.

Index

active receptivity, 195, 351
ad extra, xxiv, 1, 231, 301, 303, 305–7, 309
ad intra, xxiv, 1, 231, 301, 304–9
adult: faith development, 269; faith education, xxv, 337; faith formation, xix, xx, 81–84, 86, 96, 291, 328; religious education, xviii, 285, 328, 336, 345
aesthetic: communication, xxiv; experience, 322–24, 326
Africa, xxii, 241, 249, 250, 252–60; Africans, 251–53, 257, 259; culture, 250, 252, 254, 256; languages, 251, 255
America, North, 41, 254, 261; Americans, 291, 294, 330, 332; bishops, 282, 289; Catholics, 279, 283; Catholic schools, 279, 283; children, 67; Church, 230, 278; context, xxii, 67, 80; culture, 278, 279; education, 279, 280, 281; identity, 278; Jews, 279; laity, 278; religious education, 278; resource for parish catechesis, 75; society, 278
Angel of the North (Gormley), 319
Another Place (Gormley), 319
apophatic, 325
appropriation, 8, 14, 47, 194, 288, 297, 345, 351, 358

Aquinas, Thomas, 20, 46, 47, 71, 168, 304
art: expressive power, 316; history of, 320–21
arts, the, xvi, 111, 318, 322, 323, 326
atonement, 313–18, 324, 326, 327
Atonement (McEwan), xxiv, 313, 315–17, 325–27
Attfield, David, xiv, xv
attitude test, 122, 126, 127
audience, xiv, xv, 213, 279, 294, 317, 332, 356, 358
Augustine, St., 46, 168, 352, 362
authority, xxi, xxv, 43, 47, 75, 89, 104, 106, 107, 112, 118, 121, 127, 167, 182, 190, 191, 193, 200–207, 214–16, 252, 264, 280, 310, 311, 339–40, 342, 353, 358, 367; crisis of, xxi, 199–203, 213; online, 329, 338–39
autonomy, xxi, 5, 105, 118, 182, 200, 204, 205, 207, 211, 212, 222, 342

baptism, 19, 20, 37–39, 48, 55, 62, 104, 129
Barnett, Ronald, 364
Barth, Karl, 19, 22
Bass, Dorothy, 7

Communicating Faith was designed and typeset in Quadraat by Kachergis Book Design of Pittsboro, North Carolina. It was printed on 50-pound Natural and bound by Versa Press of East Peoria, Illinois.